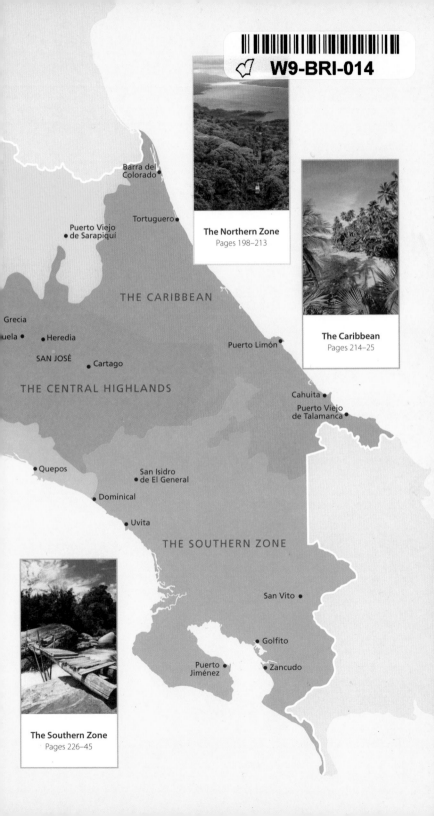

W9-BRI-014

Barra del
Colorado

Puerto Viejo
de Sarapiquí

Tortuguero

The Northern Zone
Pages 198–213

THE CARIBBEAN

The Caribbean
Pages 214–25

Grecia

uela

Heredia

SAN JOSÉ

Cartago

Puerto Limón

THE CENTRAL HIGHLANDS

Cahuita
Puerto Viejo
de Talamanca

Quepos

San Isidro
de El General

Dominical

Uvita

THE SOUTHERN ZONE

San Vito

Golfito

Puerto
Jiménez

Zancudo

The Southern Zone
Pages 226–45

EYEWITNESS TRAVEL

COSTA RICA

EYEWITNESS TRAVEL

COSTA RICA

Main Contributor **Christopher P. Baker**

DK

LONDON, NEW YORK,
MELBOURNE, MUNICH AND DELHI
www.dk.com

Managing Editor Aruna Ghose
Art Editor Benu Joshi
Senior Editor Rimli Borooah
Senior Designer Priyanka Thakur
Editor Ankita Awasthi
Designer Shruti Singhi
Senior Cartographer Uma Bhattacharya
Cartographer Kunal Kumar Singh
Picture Researcher Taiyaba Khatoon
DTP Coordinator Shailesh Sharma
DTP Designer Vinod Harish

Main Contributor
Christopher P. Baker

Photographers
Jon Spaull, Linda Whitwam

Illustrators
P. Arun, Ashok Sukumaran, T. Gautam Trivedi, Mark Warner

Printed and bound by L. Rex Printing Co. Ltd, China

First American Edition 2005

Published in the United States by DK Publishing,
345 Hudson Street, New York, New York 10014

14 15 16 17 10 9 8 7 6 5 4 3 2 1

Reprinted with revisions 2008, 2010, 2012, 2014

Copyright © 2005, 2014 Dorling Kindersley Limited, London
A Penguin Random House Company

All rights reserved. Without limiting the rights under copyright
reserved above, no part of this publication may be reproduced, stored
in or introduced into a retrieval system, or transmitted, in any form, or by any
means (electronic, mechanical, photocopying, recording, or otherwise)
without the prior written permission of both the copyright owner and
the above publisher of this book.

A catalog record for this book is available from the
Library of Congress.
ISSN 1542 1554
ISBN 978-1-46541-215-7

Floors are referred to throughout in accordance with American usage;
ie the "first floor" is at ground level.

MIX
Paper from
responsible sources
FSC
www.fsc.org   FSC™ C018179

**The information in this
DK Eyewitness Travel Guide is checked regularly.**
Every effort has been made to ensure that this book is as up-to-date as possible at
the time of going to press. Some details, however, such as telephone numbers,
opening hours, prices, gallery hanging arrangements and travel information are
liable to change. The publishers cannot accept responsibility for any consequences
arising from the use of this book, nor for any material on third party websites, and
cannot guarantee that any website address in this book will be a suitable source of
travel information. We value the views and suggestions of our readers very highly.
Please write to: Publisher, DK Eyewitness Travel Guides, Dorling Kindersley, 80 Strand,
London WC2R 0RL, UK, or email: travelguides@dk.com.

Front cover main image: Waterfall at the Río Celeste, Parque Nacional Volcán Tenorio

◀ Costa Rican jungle landscape with Volcán Arenal in the background

Contents

Introducing
Costa Rica

A performance of traditional
dance near Cartago

Wild Costa Rica

Exquisite orchid

Playa Chiquita, the Caribbean

Traditional carved and painted Bribri gourd

Fresh produce at the Santa Cruz market, Guanacaste

Teatro Nacional
(see pp114–15)

HOW TO USE THIS GUIDE

This guide helps you to get the most from a visit to Costa Rica, providing expert recommendations and detailed practical information. *Introducing Costa Rica* maps the country and sets it in its historical and cultural context. *Wild Costa Rica* is a detailed guide to wildlife viewing. The six regional sections, plus *San José*, describe important sights, using photographs, maps, and illustrations. Restaurant and hotel recommendations can be found in *Travelers' Needs*. The *Survival Guide* contains practical tips on everything from transport to personal safety.

San José

All the sights included in the capital city are numbered and plotted on an *Area Map*. Information on the sights is easy to locate as it follows the numerical order used on the map.

Sights at a Glance lists the chapter's sights by category: Museums and Theaters, Historic Buildings, Parks and Theme Parks, Markets and Neighborhoods, etc.

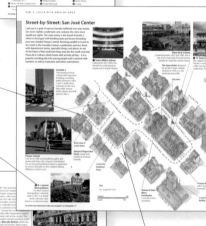

All pages relating to San José have orange thumb tabs.

1 Area Map
For easy reference, sights are numbered and located on a map. City center sights are also marked on the San José Street Finder maps *(see pp130–33)*.

2 Street-by-Street Map
This gives a bird's-eye view of the key areas in each sightseeing area.

Stars indicate the sights that no visitor should miss.

A suggested route for a walk covers the more interesting streets in the area.

3 Detailed Information
All the sights in San José are described individually. Addresses, telephone numbers, and other practical information are also provided for each entry. The key to the symbols used in the information block is shown on the back flap.

THE CENTRAL HIGHLANDS

Simmering volcanoes dominate the landscape of the Central Highlands as they tower over the country's central plateau – a broad valley at an altitude of around 3,300 ft (1,000 m). With steep slopes lushly covered by verdant forests and coffee bushes, the region offers glorious scenery. The climate is invigorating – one reason why two-thirds of the country's population live here today.

1 Introduction
A general account of the landscape, history and character of each region is given here, explaining both how the area has developed over the centuries and what attractions it has to offer visitors today.

Costa Rica Area by Area

Apart from San José, the rest of the country has been divided into six regions, each of which has a separate chapter. The most interesting towns and sights to visit are numbered on a *Regional Map* at the beginning of each chapter.

Each area of Costa Rica can be easily identified by its color coding, shown on the inside front cover.

2 Regional Map
This shows the main road network and gives an illustrated overview of the whole region. All interesting places to visit are numbered and there are also useful tips on getting to, and around, the region.

Story boxes explore specific subjects further.

3 Detailed Information
All the important towns and other places to visit are described individually. They are listed in order, following the numbering on the Regional Map. Within each entry, there is further detailed information on major buildings and other sights.

For all the top sights, a Visitors' Checklist provides the practical information you will need to plan your visit.

4 Costa Rica's Top Sights
These are given two or more full pages. Historic buildings are dissected to reveal their interiors. National parks have maps showing facilities and trails.

INTRODUCING COSTA RICA

DISCOVERING COSTA RICA

Despite its small size, Costa Rica has an amazing variety of environments, from lowland rainforest to high-mountain páramo. The country is mostly mountainous and exploring it by car can be challenging and time consuming, although you are rewarded with incredible scenery. The following itineraries focus on the most popular sites and regions. Some long-distance journeys are inevitable, but we have endeavored to keep travel distances realistic. There is a two-day tour of San José; a four-day tour of the best of the Central Highlands; and a 14-day tour that takes in the highlights of Costa Rica, from the Poás and Arenal volcanoes to Manuel Antonio National Park and the wetlands of Tortuguero. Choose and combine itineraries to suit the time you have available.

Monumento Nacional Guayabo
Costa Rica's most important pre-Columbian site features mounds, petroglyphs, and walled aqueducts.

Best of the Central Highlands

- Enjoy a close-up look at wildlife you may not see in the wild at **Zoo Ave**.
- Hike amid the mists at **El Silencio Cloud Forest Reserve**.
- Marvel at traditional ox-carts being hand made at **Fábrica de Carreteras Eloy Alfaro** in **Sarchí**.
- Visit the **Doka Estate** to learn about coffee production and processing.
- Stare into the active crater at **Parque Nacional Volcán Poás**.
- Spend half a day at **La Paz Waterfall Garden** and enjoy its many nature exhibits.
- Visit **Monumento Nacional Guayabo** to see Costa Rica's most important indigenous site.

Parque Nacional
Rincón de la Vieja

Liberia

Laguna
de Arenal

Tabacón
Hot Springs
Resort
and Spa

La
Fo

Río Corobicí

Tilarán

Arenal
Hanging
Bridges

Parque
Nacior
Volcár
Arena

Tamarindo

Monteverde

GUANACASTE

Río Arapiuez

Río Nosara

*Golfo
de Nicoya*

Tárcoles

Key

— Best of the Central Highlands

— 14-Day Tour of Costa Rica

Jacó

PACIFIC OCEAN

Doka Estate, Sabanilla de Alajuela
Visitors to this National Historic Landmark with splendid views across the valley can learn all about the stages involved in coffee production and processing, and enjoy a delicious tasting session.

Detail of a ceramic mural in Barrio Amón, San José
The arty Barrio Amón neighborhood in San José is full of
interesting architecture, from Victorian edifices to Art Deco
mansions, some with ceramic murals showing traditional scenes.

14-Day Tour of Costa Rica

- Marvel at the pre-Columbian gold artifacts in **San José's** subterranean Museo del Oro Precolumbino.

- Learn about coffee production from the bean to the cup at the **Doka Estate** near Volcán Poás.

- Zipline across the rainforest canopy at **Parque Nacional Volcán Arenal**; soak in mineral pools at **Tabacón Hot Springs Resort and Spa**.

- Hike in the famous **Monteverde Cloud Forest Biological Reserve** and spot quetzals.

- Snorkel at **Parque Nacional Manuel Antonio**, then hike the trails in search of wildlife.

- Explore **Parque Nacional Tortuguero**, looking for crocodiles and river otters.

0 kilometers 25

0 miles 25

Tabacón Hot Springs
The landscaped mineral pools,
cascades, and lush gardens at
this resort and spa make an
ideal setting in which to relax.

Two Days in San José

Costa Rica's compact capital city concentrates its sites of interest downtown, including its spectacular pre-Columbian gold and jade museums.

- **Arriving** Juan Santamaría International Airport is located at Alajuela, about 12 miles (20 km) west of San José.

- **Transport** Taxis operate between the airport and downtown, and tour companies offer shuttle services. Hire a car for exploring further afield.

Day 1

Morning Begin your walking tour downtown in **Parque Central** (p110) to view the ornate Neo-classical **Teatro Mélico Salazar** (p112), built in 1928 with a triple-tiered horseshoe-shaped auditorium, and **Catedral Metropolitana** (p112), the city's preeminent church; don't miss the Capilla del Santísimo, entered by a gallery with a Christ figure draped in the Costa Rican flag. Now walk one block east to Plaza de la Cultura to admire the ornate interior of the Neo-Classical **Teatro Nacional** (pp114–15); the guided tour is not to be missed, not least for the mural of a coffee harvest on the intermezzo. Next head to the east side of the plaza to tour the sensational pre-Columbian gold displays on three levels in the **Museo del Oro Precolumbino** (pp116–17). Highlights include sections on gold craftsmanship, plus El Guerrero – a life-size figure of a *cacique* (chieftain) adorned in gold.

Afternoon Head to the **Museo Nacional** (p124) in the former Bellavista fortress: you'll enter through a butterfly garden to view displays dedicated to the nation's history from pre-Columbian to contemporary times. Now step north one block to view the **Asamblea Legislativa** (p124), the seat of government, open for pre-arranged tours, including to witness debates. End your day admiring the monuments in **Parque Nacional** (p124–5).

Day 2

Morning Admire the all-steel **Edificio Metálico** – now a school – on **Parque España** (p120) as you head for the **Museo de Jade Tristán Castro** (p121) to be awed by the astonishing pre-Columbian jade collection, which is the largest in the Americas. Next stroll **Barrio Amón** (p121), the city's most historical quarter, with several excellent cafés; focus your attention along Avenida 9 between Calles 3 and 7, with fine eclectic buildings and

Display at the Museo del Oro Precolumbino

exquisite ceramic murals depicting traditional Costa Rican scenes.

Afternoon Take a taxi to the **Museo de Arte Costarricense** (p128) and view the nation's most important artworks; don't miss the brass-and-stucco bas-relief mural in the Salón Dorado, and the contemporary sculpture garden to the rear. Now visit **Parque Sabana** (p128); stroll its green expanse, skirting the large lake, to reach the **Museo de Ciencias Naturales** (p128–9), where dioramas profile the nation's vast wealth of fauna.

> **To extend your trip...**
> Spend a day exploring the three villages of **Escazú** (p129), about 3 miles (5 km) west of downtown.

Colorful sculptures alongside the lake on the south side of San José's Parque Sabana

For practical information on traveling around Costa Rica, *see pp304–9*

Best of the Central Highlands

The highlands of Costa Rica teem with fascinating sites, from aerial tram rides to volcanic craters and zoos.

- **Duration** Four days – but extends to five days with the trip to Turrialba.
- **Arriving** Juan Santamaría International Airport, at Alajuela, is perfectly located in the heart of the Central Highlands.
- **Transport** Taxis can be hired at the airport, and a tour shuttle service is available. However, a 4WD hire-car is the best option for following this itinerary.
- **Booking ahead** Reserve your accommodations in advance.

The peaceful Parque Nacional in downtown San José

Day 1: Wildlife and Fauna Viewing

For a sampling of fauna to be seen in Costa Rica, visit **Zoo Ave Wildlife Conservation Park** *(p138)*, a private zoo with a vast array of tropical birds and most major mammals, including jaguar, tapir, and all four native monkey species. Nearby, admire exquisite flowers at the **Botanical Orchid Garden** *(p138)*, which displays scores of endemic and exotic orchid species. Next, head to the **El Silencio de Los Angeles Cloud Forest Reserve** *(p140–41)*, a great place to hike the trails in mist-shrouded forest atop the continental divide; stay overnight here, at Villablanca Cloud Forest Hotel *(p254)*, a former colonial hacienda.

Days 2 and 3: Zarcero–Sarchí–Poás

Head east via a rugged unpaved road offering spectacular scenery to the quiet mountain town of **Zarcero** *(p141)*, where a charming topiary park fronts the village church. Continue to the woodworking center of **Sarchí** *(p140)* to visit Fábrica de Carreteras Eloy Alfaro and watch traditional ox-carts being

hand crafted. At **Doka Estate** *(p144)*, mid-way up the slopes of Volcán Poás, take a guided tour to learn about coffee production in time-honored tradition at the nation's oldest operational *beneficio* (mill), dating from 1893. The Poás region has several excellent hotels. The following day take the snaking road up the mountain via Poasito to arrive early at **Parque Nacional Volcán Poás** *(p144)* to beat the clouds and view the still-active crater; make sure to hike to Botos Lake also, passing through elfin forest arching overhead. **La Paz Waterfall Gardens** *(p145)*, nearby, enthralls visitors with its waterfall hikes and nature exhibits, including snakes, frogs, birds, butterflies, and hummingbirds; an excellent buffet lunch is served. Allow half a day at both Parque Nacional Volcán Poás and La Paz Waterfall Gardens.

Day 4: Barva–Cartago–Orosi

Descend the flanks of Poás to **Barva** *(p146)*, a quaint town with colonial homes, a lovely main square, and a colonial church. Passing through **Heredia** *(p146)*, stop briefly to admire the cathedral and the circular fortress tower of El Fortín, on the main plaza. Then skirt San José and head east to **Cartago** *(p147)* to admire its **Basílica de Nuestra Señora de los Angeles** *(pp148–9)*, which is dedicated to the nation's patron saint; the Byzantine exterior is matched

by a magnificent interior made entirely of hardwoods painted in floral motifs. If you are fascinated by flora, stop at **Jardín Botánico Lankester** *(p147)* before descending to the **Orosi Valley** *(pp152–4)*, a coffee-growing and activity center with colonial-era churches. Stop en route at **Mirador de Orosi** *(p152)* to admire the view, and don't miss the lovely **Iglesia de San José** *(p154)*, in Orosi, and the remains of the church at **Ujarrás** – the oldest colonial ruins in the country *(p154)*. To exit the valley, circle Lago de Cachí, stopping at **Casa el Soñador** *(p154)* to view rustic carvings.

> **To extend your trip…**
> Continue east to the **Monumento Nacional Guayabo** *(pp158–9)*, 12 miles (19 km) north of **Turrialba** *(p155)*, 27 miles (44 km) east of Cartago.

The attractive 19th-century Iglesia de San Bartolomé de Barva

14-Day Tour of Costa Rica

This itinerary combines several of Costa Rica's ecosystems and takes you from San José and the Central Highlands to some of its most popular national parks.

- **Duration** 14 days, with suggestions for extending it to 19 days.

- **Arriving** San José's Juan Santamaría Airport is located in the center of the country.

- **Transport** This tour is most easily done by car – a 4WD vehicle is essential.

Day 1: San José
Pick a day from the city itinerary on page 12.

Day 2: Volcán Poás
Drive up the slopes of Volcán Poás to visit the **Doka Estate** *(p144)* for an immersion in coffee culture, from planting to the roasting room, at the nation's oldest coffee *beneficio* (mill), still operating by water-wheel. Next continue uphill to **Parque Nacional Volcán Poás** *(p144)* to peer into an active volcano from a viewpoint above the mile-wide (1.6-km) *caldera*; then hike the trail through eerie elfin forest to jade-colored Laguna Botos. Continue the short distance to **La Paz Waterfall Gardens** *(p145)* to hike in cloud forest to waterfalls and to view snakes, poison-dart frogs, and hummingbirds;

Abundant vegetation in Monteverde Cloud Forest Biological Reserve

another highlight here are the wildcats, which include jaguars. The park's restaurant has wonderful views. The Poás region has several hotels.

Days 3 and 4: La Fortuna and Volcán Arenal
Continue down the northern slopes of Volcán Barva to visit the **Museo de Cultural Indígena**, dedicated to honoring contemporary indigenous culture, at **Centro Neotrópico SarapiquíS** *(p209)*, the setting for Parque Arqeológico Alma Alta – a pre-Columbian archeological site. Now head west, with a stop at **La Marina Zoológica** *(p209)*, which displays many large mammal species, including tapirs bred here. Arrive at the day's end at **La Fortuna** *(p202)*, gateway to the **Parque Nacional Volcán Arenal** *(p203)*, which protects the environment surrounding one of the world's most active volcanoes. Spend day four hiking the park, which teems

with wildlife, and enjoying other local activities, such as soaking al fresco at **Tabacón Hot Springs Resort and Spa** *(p202)*, with pools and cascades fed by thermal waters; and ziplining at **Arenal Theme Park** *(p203)*, where an aerial tram transports you to a viewpoint with spectacular views over **Volcán Arenal** and **Laguna de Arenal** *(pp204–6)*.

Days 5 and 6: Laguna de Arenal–Tilarán–Monteverde
Admire the scenery as you drive around **Laguna de Arenal** *(pp204–6)*, perhaps stopping at **Arenal Hanging Bridges** *(p205)* to explore the rainforest. Continue via the pleasant town of **Tilarán** *(p184)* – stop to admire the interior of its arch-roofed church – to reach **Monteverde** *(pp178–82)*. This pastoral mountain community is packed with nature sites, art galleries, and adventure activities. Don't leave before hiking in **Monteverde Cloud Forest Biological Reserve** *(p181)*, ziplining at **Sky Walk/ Sky Trek** *(p182)*, watching bats flit along a flyway at **Bat Jungle** *(p180)*, and admiring the Jewels of the Rainforest Bio-Art Exhibition, the world's largest private insect collection, at **Selvatura Park** *(p182)*.

> **To extend your trip...**
> Drive north via **Liberia** *(p185)* to spend two days at either **Parque Nacional Rincón de la Vieja** *(p186)* or **Tamarindo** *(p190)*.

Days 7 and 8: Jacó– Quepos–Manuel Antonio Parque Nacional
Descend to the Pacific coast, where you can view crocodiles on a river safari at **Tárcoles** *(p168)*; book ahead for a river safari. Chic hilltop Hotel Villa Caletas *(p168)* favors sophisticates, but is a great place to stop for a meal and great view across the Golfo Nicoya while en route to the beach resort of **Jacó** *(p168)*. Here, thrill-seekers might try

Turquoise-blue waters of a crater lake at Parque Nacional Volcán Poás

For practical information on traveling around Costa Rica, *see pp304–9*

A guided boat tour through Parque Nacional Tortuguero

a leap of faith at **Pacific Bungee** (p168), or ascend into the rainforest aboard a gondola at **Pacific Rainforest Aerial Tram** (p168). Continue to the **Quepos** (p170) area for two nights: the region has dozens of hotels. Spend day 8 exploring **Parque Nacional Manuel Antonio** (pp172–3) – a jewel of Costa Rica's park system, with beaches, a coral reef for snorkeling, plus forest trails that guarantee a wealth of wildlife viewing.

Day 9: Valle del Río Savegre–Dominical

Drive south along the Pacific shore and head inland up the **Valle del Río Savegre** (p170) to experience the exhilaration of whitewater rafting at Rafiki Safari Lodge (see p256). In the afternoon, continue south to the laid-back backpackers' and surfers' paradise of **Dominical** (p234), a perfect place to take a surfing lesson or simply relax by the beach. Nature lovers might wish to view venomous snakes close up at **Parque Reptilandia** (p234). Stay overnight at **Dominical** or **Escaleras** (p234).

> **To extend your trip...**
> Spend a day south of Dominical at the **Parque Nacional Marino Ballena** (p234) with activities such as whale-watching, and horseback riding at Refugio Nacional de Vida Silvestre Rancho Merced.

Day 10: Cerro de la Muerte–San Gerardo de Dota

Begin with a horseback ride and hike to **Don Lulo's Nauyaca Waterfalls** (p234) in the mountains inland of Dominical. Passing through the market center of **San Isidro** (p230), follow the snaking mountain road that ascends **Cerro de la Muerte** (p230) to reach **San Gerardo de Dota** (p150), a remote mountain village set in the Shangri-La vale. Birders might divert from San Isidro to **Los Cusingos Neotropical Bird Sanctuary** (p230) for a guided hike. San Gerardo de Dota has many lodges.

Day 11: San Gerardo de Dota–San José

Spotting Resplendent quetzals is easy around San Gerardo de Dota. After a morning of guided

Spectacular sunset at Dominical, a surfers' paradise

birding or horseback riding, drive down the mountain for an overnight stay in **San José**.

Days 12 and 13: Tortuguero

Fly to the landlocked Caribbean village of **Tortuguero** (p221) for two days exploring the **Parque Nacional Tortuguero** (p221); the many nature lodges there offer guided wildlife tours by boat, or take a canoe trip into the heart of the wetland mosaic. In turtle nesting season (June–November), don't miss a night-time guided turtle-viewing tour on the beach. It is essential to book a lodge and guided boat trip ahead. Nature lodges line Tortuguero Lagoon, and the village has budget accommodations (see p259).

Day 14: Rainforest Aerial Tram–San José

Transfer along the Tortuguero Canal by boat to Marina for a shuttle connection to San José. Time permitting, stop at **Rainforest Aerial Tram** (p213) to explore the forest canopy aboard an open-air teleférico (aerial tram). Early morning and late afternoon are the best times to spot wildlife along the way. Either fly home or stay overnight in San José.

> **To extend your trip...**
> Fly to **Puerto Jiménez** (p242) to spend two days exploring the **Peninsula de Osa** (pp240–43).

Putting Costa Rica on the Map

Washed by the waters of the Caribbean Sea and Pacific
Ocean, the republic of Costa Rica lies wholly within the
tropics, between 8 and 11 degrees north of the Equator.
Bordered by Nicaragua to the north and tapering
gradually southward to Panama, it covers
19,650 sq miles (50,900 sq km). Much of this
extremely mountainous country is uninhabited
and overlaid with several types of tropical
forest; almost one-third of the land area is
protected within reserves. Administratively,
the country is divided into seven provinces
and 81 *cantones* (counties). It has a
population of 4.5 million, heavily
concentrated in the Central Highlands,
with some 350,000 people living in
the capital, San José.

Lago de
Nicaragua

Isla
Mancarrón

La Cruz
Isla
Bolaños

Aguas
Claras

Islas
Murciélagos

Golfo de
Papagayo

Liberia

Panamá

El Coco

Río Tempisque

Río Corobicí

Cañas

Tila

GUANACASTE

Tamarindo

Santa Cruz

Guaitíl

Nicoya

Isla Chira
Golfo
de Nicoya

Las
Jun

Ostional
Río Nosara

Nosara

Carmona

Puntarena

Sámara

0 kilometers 50
0 miles 50

PUNTARE

Malpaís

Montezu

Isla Cabo
Blanco

Pacific Ocean

Isla del Coco

Isla Manuelita
Isla Pajara
Bahía Chatham
Bahía Weston
Punta Paceco
Isla Cascara
Isla Conico
Bahía Wafer
Cabo Barreto
Cabo
Punta
Atrevida
María
Parque Nacional
Isla del Coco
Cabo Lionel
Isla Montagne
Isla Dos
Amigos
Isla Juan Bautista
Bahía Yglesias
Punta Turrialba
Isla Muela
Cabo
Dampier
0 kilometers 3
0 miles 3

Isla del Coco
(310 miles)

Nueva Guinea

NICARAGUA

Punta Gorda

Chiles

Río San Juan

ALAJUELA

Río San Carlos

Río San Juan

Barra del
Colorado

HEREDIA

Río Toro

Río Chirripó

Puerto Viejo
de Sarapiquí

Tortuguero

a Fortuna

Ciudad Quesada
(San Carlos)

Zarcero

LIMÓN

Guápiles

mar   Sarchí

Sacramento

Siquirres

Alajuela

Heredia
SAN JOSÉ

Río Reventazón

Puerto Limón

Juan
Santamaría

Cartago

Turrialba

Río Banano

SAN
JOSÉ

Orosi

Tapanti

CARTAGO

LIMÓN

Cahuita

Puerto Viejo de
Talamanca

Tárcoles

Bribri

Manzanillo

Jacó

COSTA
RICA

San Gerardo
de Dota

Río Uren

Quepos

San Isidro de
El General

Río Teribe

Dominical

Buenos
Aires

PANAMA

Río General

Palmar
Norte

Río Colon

Isla
Boca Brava

San
Vito

Isla Violín

Boquete

Bahía Drake

Río Sierpe

PUNTARENAS

Isla del
Caño

Rincón

Golfito

Ciudad Neily

Coto 47

Dolega

Zancudo

Puerto
Jiménez

Golfo
Dulce

La Cuesta

David

Bahía de
Charco Azul

Inset map:

UNITED STATES
OF AMERICA

Atlantic
Ocean

MEXICO

Gulf
of
Mexico

CUBA

DOMINICAN
REPUBLIC

HAITI

BELIZE

CARIBBEAN ISLANDS

HONDURAS

GUATEMALA
EL SALVADOR

Caribbean
Sea

NICARAGUA

GUYANA

SURINAM

FRENCH
GUIANA

COSTA RICA

VENEZUELA

PANAMA

COLOMBIA

Caribbean Sea

Key

▬▬ Pan-American Highway

▬▬ Major road

▬▬ International border

▬▬ Provincial border

- - - Ferry route

For additional map symbols see back flap

A PORTRAIT OF COSTA RICA

Dominated by mountain ranges and verdant forests, gouged by fertile valleys, and flanked by lovely beaches and the ocean, Costa Rica is undoubtedly one of the most beautiful places on earth. Vivid colors of nature, a virtually unmatched range of outdoor activities, friendly, hospitable people, and the subtle charm of an essentially rustic lifestyle – all combine to make the country one of the world's favorite tropical holiday destinations.

Straddling the Meso-American isthmus at the juncture of North and South America, this diminutive nation is barely 300 miles (480 km) north to south and 175 miles (280 km) at its widest point, near the Nicaraguan border. Occupying one of the world's most geologically unstable areas, the country is subjected to powerful tectonic forces that trigger earthquakes and punctuate the landscape with smoldering volcanoes. With scores of micro-climates, the emerald landscape is a quiltwork of 12 different life zones, from coastal wetlands to subalpine grassland.

Costa Rica is characterized by a homogeneity of culture unique among Central American nations, with the Spanish influence being all-encompassing and indigenous culture having little impact. However, non-Spanish cultures exist in a few pockets, such as the Jamaican ethos of the Caribbean coast. Another distinctive feature is the nation's conservation ethic, as evidenced by its nationwide network of wildlife parks and refuges, which embraces about 30 percent of its area, more than any other nation on earth.

Conserving Nature's Wonders

The greatest appeal of Costa Rica is its astonishing wealth of flora and fauna, protected within more than 190 biological reserves, national parks, wildlife refuges, and similar entities. The Reserva Natural Absoluta Cabo Blanco was created as the first protected reserve in the country in 1963. Since then, more parks and reserves have been set up every year.

However, destruction of the natural habitat continues, even in some protected regions. The park service is understaffed and lacks the funds to compensate owners for expropriated land. Thus, the wetlands of Refugio Nacional de Vida

A farmhouse on the flanks of Volcán Arenal, in the Northern Zone

◄ Painted mural showing a traditional Costa Rican scene of coffee picking

The guanacaste tree, Costa Rica's national tree

The Government

A democratic republic, Costa Rica has a government headed by an elected president, who is assisted by two vice-presidents and a cabinet of 17 members. The Asamblea Legislativa (Legislative Assembly) is a single chamber of 57 popularly elected *diputados* (deputies), limited to two terms. The president appoints regional governors, who preside over the seven provinces of San José, Alajuela, Cartago, Guanacaste, Heredia, Limón, and Puntarenas.

Silvestre Caño Negro are imperiled by landowners reclaiming precious marshlands for farming. Animal populations are declining in Parque Nacional Manuel Antonio due to loss of habitat. Illegal hunting menaces the populations of jaguars, tapirs, and wild pigs in Parque Nacional Corcovado. Logging, however, has been tamed and forests, which diminished by two-thirds since Columbus stepped ashore in 1491, are increasing in the area once again.

Fortunately, there are several conservation organizations that are unstinting in their efforts to save flora and fauna. Also, the government's focus on integrating protected regions by grouping them into 11 distinct regional units within a Sistema Nacional de Areas de Conservación (National System of Regional Conservation Areas) is a giant step in the right direction.

Two parties dominate the political scene and have traditionally alternated in power with each election. The social-democratic Partido de Liberación Nacional (National Liberation Party) champions welfare programs, while the conservative Partido de Unidad Social Cristiana (Social Christian Unity Party) is pro-business. All citizens between 18 and 70 years of age are mandated to vote. A Special Electoral Tribunal appointed by the Supreme Court oversees the integrity of elections.

Costa Rica declared neutrality in 1949 and has no official army, navy, or air force, although branches of the police force have a military capability. Citizens proudly proclaim that since the late 19th century, only two brief periods of violence have marred the nation's democratic development, and the

The famed Reserva Biológica Bosque Nuboso Monteverde (Monteverde Cloud Forest Biological Reserve)

country has avoided the bloodshed that has afflicted neighboring countries. However, it has not been aloof from Latin American issues: in 1987, President Oscar Arias won the Nobel Peace Prize for brokering peace on the isthmus.

The Economy

Costa Rica's thriving economy is today powered mainly by tourism. With its stupendous landscape of mountains, beaches, and forests full of exotic flora and fauna, the country offers opportunities for outdoor life and active adventures. The focus is on ecotourism, promoted by the Instituto Costarricense de Turismo (Costa Rica Tourism Institute) under the advertising slogan of "Costa Rica – No Artificial Ingredients." Another factor aiding tourism is the country's reputation for stability in an area rent by political upheavals. Well-planned specialized lodges, large hotels, and beach resorts serve the spectrum from budget to deluxe markets.

Papayas being sorted for sale in a town market

San José is one of Central America's major financial centers with a burgeoning high-technology industrial sector. Beyond the capital, the country is still largely agricultural. Land ownership is widespread, except in Guanacaste, where large-scale cattle *fincas* (farms) prevail. Coffee, pineapples, and bananas are Costa Rica's three main crops.

Costa Rican traditional costume

The People

Costa Ricans are known as Ticos because of their habitual use of this term as a diminutive – for instance, "*momentico*" for "just a moment," instead of the usual "*momentito*." The majority are descendants of early Spanish settlers. Indigenous peoples account for a fraction of the population, and live tucked away in remote reserves. Concentrated on the Caribbean coast, Afro-Caribbeans are mainly descended from Jamaicans who came as contract labor in the 19th century, and form a large community. A sizeable Chinese population also exists, mainly in the Caribbean province of Limón. Tens of thousands of North Americans and people of other nationalities have also settled in Costa Rica, drawn partly by its fabulous climate.

About eight out of ten Costa Ricans are nominally Catholic, and a significant portion of the population are regular practitioners of the faith. The most venerated figure is La Negrita, the country's patron saint, who is believed to grant miracles. Although proselytizing is illegal, the influence of evangelical Christians is growing, especially in poorer areas and among the indigenous communities.

The bustling capital city, San José

Traditional oxcart used for farming in the Costa Rican countryside

The country has the highest rate of literacy and life expectancy in Latin America. Internet access is relatively widespread, and cell-phone use is the highest in Central America. Roads and electricity extend into even the most remote backwaters, and today few communities are entirely isolated from the modern world. In fact, Josefinos (residents of San José) lead a typically modern urban lifestyle, and the capital has a well-developed and entrepreneurial middle-class. However, old traditions survive in the countryside, where a peasant lifestyle still prevails, the horse is the main form of transport, and oxen are used as day-to-day beasts of burden.

Life revolves around the family – usually headed by a matriarch – and an immediate circle of *compadres* (friends and fellow workers). Individuals tend to guard their personal lives closely and are more inclined to invite acquaintances to dine at restaurants than to welcome them into their homes. However, Ticos are a warm-hearted people and always treat strangers with great civility.

Costa Ricans are proud of their country's neutrality and stable democracy. Although a recent influx of immigrants with "Indian" features from neighboring countries has caused much resentment, Ticos are generally a liberal, tolerant people with a concern for societal harmony and welfare.

Effigies carried along a street as part of Good Friday celebrations

The Arts and Sports

Crafts dominate the artistic scene, mainly because of the tremendous creativity displayed by artisans. Woodcarvers such as Barry Biesanz produce hardwood bowls of immense delicacy. The indigenous influence lives on in the creation of gold jewelry, which adopts the pre-Columbian motif of animist figurines. Other native crafts include the pottery created by the community of Guaitíl in the style of their Chorotega ancestors.

In the 20th century, the arts scene was dominated by the nation's *campesino* (peasant) heritage, which found its most influential expression with the Group of New Sensibility in the 1920s. Headed by Teodorico Quirós Alvarado (1897–1977), the movement evolved a stylized art form depicting idyllic rural landscapes, with cobbled streets, adobe dwellings, and peasants with oxcarts against volcanic backgrounds. Their influence remains to this day, notably in miniature paintings that are a staple in many homes and souvenir stores.

Exceptions to the insipid art of the mid-20th century were the powerful depictions of peasant life by the internationally renowned sculptor Francisco Zúñiga (1912–98). Contemporary artists such as Rodolfo Stanley and Jiménez Deredia have invigorated the scene with compelling avant-garde works.

Carlos Luis Fallas's novel *Mamita Yunai* (1941), about the plight of banana workers, is the sole literary work of international note. Costa Ricans are great theatergoers, however, and theater venues are scattered all over San José and some other cities. Josefinos dress up to hear the National Symphony Orchestra perform in the Teatro Nacional and at the less formal annual International Festival of Music, while the young dress down to dance to fast-paced Latin *merengue* in clubs and bars. Virtually every town has a bandstand where people enjoy folk music featuring the *marimba*, a form of xylophone. The guitar is the main accompaniment to the *punto guanacasteco*, the national folk

A traditional dance performance near Cartago

dance performed by men and women in traditional costume.

Played on weekends by local teams throughout the country, soccer is the national obsession for men. Rodeos and *topes* (horse parades) are a focus of general festivities, while *corridas de toros* (non-fatal bull-running) are popular with men eager to prove their *machismo*. Most Costa Ricans are passionate about activities performed in the open air such as running and cycling, which is only to be expected in this land of nature and the outdoors.

A local soccer match in progress in Heredia

Landscapes of Costa Rica

Few countries on earth can rival Costa Rica for diversity of flora and fauna. Despite its tiny size, the nation is home to almost 5 percent of the world's identified living species, including more types of butterflies than the whole of Africa. This astonishing wealth of wildlife is due to the country's great variety in relief and climate, from lowland wetlands to cloud-draped mountaintops. As a result, Costa Rica boasts 12 distinct "life zones," each with a unique combination of climate, terrain, flora, and fauna.

Perfectly conical Arenal, Costa Rica's most active volcano

Lowland Rainforest

Rainforests *(see pp26–7)* cloak many of the plains and lower mountain slopes of the Caribbean lowlands and Pacific southwest. These complex ecosystems harbor much of the country's wildlife. Tapirs and jaguars inhabit the understory, while birds and monkeys cavort in the treetops.

Montane Cloud Forest

More than half of Costa Rica is over 3,300 ft (1,000 m) above sea level. Much of the higher elevation terrain is swathed in cloud forest *(see p183)*, where mists sift through the treetops and branches are festooned with bromeliads and dripping mosses. Bird and animal life is profuse.

Ceiba trees are giants of the rainforest, often towering 230 ft (70 m) tall. Their thick trunk is covered with conical thorns.

Poor man's umbrella is a common name for *Gunnera insignis* due to its leaves' huge size.

Labios ardientes, or "hot lips", is named for this flower's resemblance to pouting lips.

Heliconia flowers grow from long, erect, brightly colored bracts that in many species resemble lobster claws.

Aguacate, or wild avocado, is a favorite food of the resplendent quetzal.

Tank epiphytes are bromeliads whose waxy whorled leaves hold water, like a cistern.

Coasts

The total length of Costa Rica's coastline is over 800 miles (1,290 km). On the Pacific, promontories and scalloped bays are common, while the Caribbean coast is almost ruler-straight. Small patches of coral reef fringe the coast off the Central Pacific and southern Caribbean shores. Many beaches provide nesting grounds for various species of marine turtles.

Beaches in Costa Rica come in every color, from white and gold to chocolate and black. Most are backed by forest.

Mangroves, which thrive in alluvial silts deposited by rivers, form a vital nursery along the coastline for marine creatures, such as the olive ridley turtle, and avian fauna, such as the frigate bird.

Dry Forest

Once covering most of Guanacaste and Nicoya, dry forests *(see p187)* today cover only about 200 sq miles (520 sq km) of Costa Rica. The mostly deciduous flora sheds its leaves during the seasonal drought, making wildlife easier to spot. Conservationists are trying to revive dry forest ecosystems.

Wetland

Wetlands range from coastal mangroves *(see p237)* such as the Terraba-Sierpe delta in the Pacific southwest, to inland lagoons such as Caño Negro in the north. Many habitats are seasonal, flooding in the wet season from May to November; wildlife gathers by waterholes in the December–April dry season.

The poró, or cotton tree, blazes brilliant yellow in January and February. Its blooms resemble buttercups.

Corteza amarilla trees typically burst into bloom the same day toward the end of the dry season.

Raffia palms are associated with swamplands and grow leaves up to 25 ft (7.5 m) long.

Water hyacinths choke lagoons and canals and are a favored food source for manatees.

Gumbo limbo is often called "naked tourist tree" for the way its bark peels, like sunburned skin.

Water lilies are found in shallow lakes and can clog slow-moving waterways.

The Rainforest Ecosystem

The lowlands of Costa Rica are enveloped in tropical rainforest, its canopies forming an uninterrupted sea of greenery. Hardwood trees, such as mahogany and kapok, may tower 200 ft (61 m) or more, and rely on wide-spreading roots to support their weight. The forests comprise distinct layers, from ground to treetop canopy. Each layer has its own distinct microclimate as well as flora and fauna, with the vast majority of species concentrated at higher levels. Animals such as kinkajous, sloths, and arboreal snakes are adapted for life in the branches, which are weighed down by vines, epiphytes, and other vascular plants.

Major Rainforest Reserves

- PN Carara *see p168*
- PN Corcovado *see p243*
- PN Tapantí-Macizo la Muerte *see p155*
- PN Tortuguero *see p221*
- RNVS Gandoca- Manzanillo *see p224*

Bromeliads adorn the branches. These epiphytes ("air plants") have nested leaves that meet at the base to form cisterns. Leaf litter falling into these tanks provides nourishment for the plants.

Creeping vines of many varieties grow on the tree trunks, and use grappling hooks and other devices to reach sunlight.

Buttress roots have evolved to hold towering trees steady. These thin flanges radiate out in all directions from the base of the trunk, like the fins of a rocket. The largest can be 10 ft (3 m) high and extend 16 ft (5 m) from the base.

Heliconias grow abundantly on the forest floor, and draw hummingbirds, insects, and other pollinators to their flaming red, orange, and yellow bracts.

Walking palms literally migrate across the forest floor over decades atop stilt roots only loosely attached to the ground.

The soil of rainforests is thin since leaf litter decomposes rapidly and nutrients are swiftly recycled. Heavy rainfall further leaches the soil.

Emergent trees rise above the forest canopy where their crowns are often buffeted by high winds. Many species bloom flamboyantly in season.

The upper canopy forms an unbroken stretch of foliage. About 80 percent of rainforest vegetation is concentrated here, as is most wildlife.

Orchids

Understory species, adapted for varying amounts of sunlight, may grow to 80 ft (24 m) tall. Many are genetically coded to grow rapidly whenever a large tree falls, which opens a space for new growth.

The forest floor is sparsely vegetated. Rain on the canopy can take up to an hour to reach the ground.

Fauna

Rainforests shelter many of the largest and most endangered mammal species, such as tapirs, peccaries, and jaguars. Most animal and bird species are well camouflaged and difficult to spot in the shadows of the dark, dappled forest.

Squirrel monkeys, or *titis*, are the smallest as well as the most endangered of Costa Rica's monkeys, and are found only in Pacific southwest rainforests. They live in large bands and are omnivorous.

The jaguar, known locally as *tigre*, requires a large territory for hunting. It is endangered, mainly because of illicit hunting and loss of rainforest habitat.

Pit vipers are well camouflaged and perfectly adapted for stealthy hunting in the understory, where they feed on small birds and rodents.

Toucans are easily recognized by their distinctive calls and colorful beaks. These predominantly fruit-eating birds are found in all of Costa Rica's rainforests.

The harpy eagle, the largest member of the eagle family, clings to existence in the rainforests of Corcovado and Gandoca-Manzanillo.

Canopy Tours

Costa Rica is the world leader in "canopy tours," which allow active travelers to explore the forest canopy more than 100 ft (30 m) above the jungle floor. Facilities such as suspended walkways and rappels by horizontal zipline cable, which usually link a series of treetop platforms, offer a monkey's-eye view. "Aerial trams" (modified ski lifts) are a more sedentary option. Such experiences can be a fascinating way to learn about treetop ecology and compare various forest environments, from rainforest to montane cloud forest. Zipline tours are more for the thrill – it is unlikely that wildlife will be spotted while whizzing between trees at high speed. The one drawback of canopy tours is that they often disturb the local ecology, scaring away many creatures.

Treetop platforms are usually built around the trunks below the treetop canopy, and are supported by branches. Some tours offer the option of overnighting on the platform.

Aerial trams operate like ski lifts, using similar technology. Naturalist guides accompany visitors on the Rainforest Aerial Trams (near Jacó and Parque Nacional Braulio Carrillo) and Arenal Rainforest Tram to educate visitors about forest ecology.

All forest types in Costa Rica, from dry forest to montane cloud forest, host canopy tours. By going on several tours, visitors can experience diverse habitats.

Trails with interpretive signs, found at most canopy tour sites, provide insights into life at ground level. Combined with the tours, they provide a broad understanding of the interrelationships between ecology at different levels. Most trails are slippery – sturdy footwear with good grip is recommended.

Zipline tours follow "trails," comprising a series of steel cables that run between trees or span canyons, and can exceed 1 mile (2 km). Sped by gravity, the visitor "flies" between the spans, securely attached in a harness.

Towers and cables made of reinforced concrete and steel are built to the highest standards according to government regulations.

Suspended walkways held aloft by steel cables permit the best wildlife viewing. Visitors can follow their own pace and stop at will to watch a creature. Many sites have "trails" formed from a series of walkways.

Visitors' centers are located at some sites, and often feature restaurants, exhibits, and gift stores.

Bridges, built for utilitarian purposes before the canopy tour concept took hold, have been incorporated into some tours. Some of the more ramshackle ones can be slightly unnerving.

The Beginnings

The American scientist Dr. Donald Perry pioneered the concept of the "canopy biologist" in the 1970s, when he developed a system of ropes, pulleys, and a radio-controlled cage to move through the treetops at his research site near Rara Avis. Perry's successful "automated web" led him to eventually build an aerial tram that would permit the public the same privileged access for educational purposes.

Dr. Donald Perry exploring the forest canopy at Rara Avis

Beaches of Costa Rica

Most of Costa Rica's shoreline, which extends for 800 miles (1,290 km), is lined with beaches in a range of colors, from sugar white to varying shades of gray and brown. On the straight Caribbean coast, beaches stretch for miles, while the ones on the serrated Pacific coast are separated by rocky headlands. In most places, thick forest edges right up to the shore, lending a dramatic beauty to even the dullest brown sands. The coastal waters are relatively murky due to silt washed down by numerous rivers and there are few coral reefs. Beaches run the gamut from developed areas, with resorts and various amenities, to isolated, virtually undiscovered stretches of sand. Dozens of beaches offer great swimming and surfing *(see p191).*

Playa Naranjo, hemmed by tropical dry forest, is difficult to access, but offers tremendous wildlife viewing, including sightings of leatherback turtles. Mangroves nearby harbor caimans and crocodiles *(see p191).*

Playa Conchal, or "Shell Beach," is acclaimed for its snow-white beach, comprised of billions of minute seashells. The turquoise waters are unusually clear *(see p190).*

Playas del Coco
(see p190)

Playa Flamingo
(see p190)

Los Chiles

THE NORTHERN Z

Liberia

La Fortuna

GUANACASTE AND
NORTHERN NICOYA

Ciud
Quesa
(San Carlo

Nicoya

Puntarenas

THE CENTRAL PACIF
AND SOUTHERN NICO

Jacó

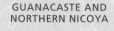

Playa Ostional is one of about 12 beaches worldwide where endangered Pacific ridley turtles crawl ashore en masse to nest *(see p194).*

Playa Grande is Costa Rica's most important nesting site for leatherback turtles. This long, scalloped beach of coral-gray sands is also a famed surfing destination, attracting hundreds of surfers every year *(see p190).*

Playa Jacó, popular with surfers and lined with hotels, is a lively beach resort *(see p168).*

Playa Montezuma is a beautiful, coconut-fringed, cream-colored beach. Its rough waters are unsafe for swimming *(see p166).*

Playa Guiones is several miles long and extremely deep at low tide *(see p194).* It has tidepools, and it has been identified as a site of *arribadas (see p195)* of Pacific ridley turtles.

Playa Carrillo is virtually undeveloped, despite the hotels dotting the nearby hills. Fishing boats gather in a cove at the southern end of this palm-shaded beach, which is backed by an airstrip.

Tortuguero's beach is an unbroken, 23-mile (37-km) long stretch of gray sand backed by forest. It is a prime nesting site for green turtles, who emerge glistening from the surf to lay eggs in the sand *(see p221)*.

Cahuita's beaches – Playa Negra with its black sands and the golden Playa Blanca – are edged by rainforest. The forest and the coral reef bordering Playa Blanca are protected within Parque Nacional Cahuita *(see p222)*.

Playa Cocles is a popular surfing center. Splendidly scenic, it is perfect for sunbathing, although swimmers should beware the riptides.

Tortuguero

erto Viejo
Sarapiquí

THE
CARIBBEAN

JOSÉ

Cartago

Puerto Limón

ENTRAL HIGHLANDS

uepos

San Isidro
de El General

THE SOUTHERN ZONE

Golfito

Puerto
Jiménez

Playa Manuel
Antonio
(see p172)

0 km   25

0 miles   25

Playa Zancudo has miles of gray sand and excellent surf *(see p244)*.

Gandoca-Manzanillo, a remote reserve with gray-black beaches, also contains swamps and mangroves inhabited by crocodiles, manatees, and varieties of birds. Four species of marine turtles nest in the beach sands *(see p224)*.

Bahía Ballena is an unspoilt bay fringed with a mile (1.6-km) long gray sand beach. Dolphins and whales congregate offshore, where a coral reef offers fine snorkeling.

The Story of Costa Rican Coffee

Costa Rica is famed for its flavorful coffee. *Coffea arabica* – a bush native to Ethiopia – was introduced to the country in 1779. For more than a century, beginning in the 1830s, the *grano de oro* (golden grain) was Costa Rica's foremost export, funding the construction of fine buildings. The nation's mountains provide ideal conditions for the coffee plant, which prefers consistently warm temperatures, distinct wet and dry seasons, and fertile, well-drained slopes. More than 425 sq miles (1,100 sq km), concentrated in the Central Highlands, are dedicated to coffee production.

Guided tours of plantations and *beneficios* (processing factories) give visitors a chance to see beans being processed, as well as offering demonstrations of "cupping" (tasting).

Coffee Plantations

After being raised in nurseries, 8 to 12 month-old coffee seedlings are planted beneath shade trees in long rows perpendicular to the slope to help avoid soil erosion. They require precise amounts of sunlight, water, and fertilizer.

Coffee seedlings ready to be planted

Worker weeding in a coffee plantation

Shade trees allow the proper amount of sunlight to filter through.

Elevations between 2,650 and 4,900 ft (800–1,500 m) are ideal for coffee estates.

The volcanic soil contains the nutrients that coffee bushes require.

The Early Days

Before the construction of the railroads in the late 19th century, coffee beans were packed in gunny sacks and transported to the port of Puntarenas in *carretas* (oxcarts). Trains of oxcarts loaded with coffee traveled down the mountains of Costa Rica in convoys. From Puntarenas, the beans were shipped to Europe, a journey that took three months.

Carreta (oxcart) transporting sacks of coffee

Berries to Beans

Typically it takes four years for the shiny-leafed coffee bush to mature and fruit. With the arrival of the rains in early May, small white blossoms appear, giving off a jasmine-like scent. The fleshy green berries containing the beans gradually turn red as they ripen. Each berry contains two hemispherical seeds, or beans. Well-tended bushes produce *cerezas* (cherries) for about 40 years.

White coffee blossoms

Green and red berries

The harvest normally begins in November. Traditionally, entire families would head into the fields to help with harvesting. Although children can still be seen picking coffee, today Nicaraguans and indigenous peoples form the majority of the labor pool.

The red berries are hand-picked by workers.

Handwoven wicker baskets are usually used to hold the berries.

Coffee workers wait in line to measure baskets of freshly harvested coffee. The berries are shipped to a *beneficio* for processing.

At the beneficio, the berries are cleaned. The fleshy outer pulp is then stripped off and returned to the slopes as fertilizer.

The moist beans are dried, either in the traditional manner by being laid out in the sun, or in hot-air ovens.

The dried beans have their leathery skins removed before being roasted.

Packaging

The roasted beans are sorted by quality, size, and shape. Export-quality beans are vacuum-sealed in foil bags and typically come in light roast, dark roast, espresso, decaffeinated, and organic varieties. Lower grade beans for the domestic market are sold loose at local markets as *café puro* (unadulterated) or *café tradicional* (containing 10 percent sugar).

Coffee packed for export

Roasted coffee beans

Different varieties of coffee

Ground coffee

Coffee bags

Coffee liqueur

The Indigenous Groups

Sparsely inhabited at the time of Columbus's arrival, the country today has 40,000 indigenous inhabitants, who account for less than 1 percent of the total population. They belong to seven main tribes – Chorotega, Boruca, Bribri, Cabécar, Guaymí, Guatuso/Maleku, and Huetar. Living relatively marginalized from mainstream society in 22 remote reserves, the tribes sustain themselves by hunting and farming; and some continue to create traditional handicrafts. The aboriginal way of life is under constant threat by missionary activity and by the government's habitual espousal of logging and mining interests over those of indigenous peoples. Few tribes speak their native language, and even fewer have been able to keep their religious traditions free from outside influences.

The Guatuso/Maleku retain their language and customs. They are known for bark cloth (mastate) painted with the fingertips.

The Bribri today comprise 10,000 individuals, who cling to their collective faith in Sibú, the creator of the universe. They welcome visits to the Reserva Indígena KeköLdi (see p225), where some Bribri continue to live in traditional huts.

Carved and painted gourds, called jícara by the Bribri, are used as vessels and objects of decoration by most indigenous groups. Pictured here is a Bribri jícara.

Motifs depict natural elements. To preserve tribal identity, names of the elements are carved in traditional languages as well as in Spanish.

Huts are thatched to the ground.

A traditional Bribri hut – a windowless, conical structure

Indigenous Artifacts

Many of the traditional crafts of Costa Rica's indigenous peoples emphasize their relationship with the rainforest. Age-old techniques continue to be used in contemporary works. Crafts, clothing, and musical instruments of several tribes, as well as shamanic totems, are displayed in the Museo de Cultura Indígena (see p209).

Where Indigenous Peoples Live

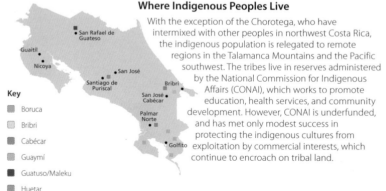

With the exception of the Chorotega, who have intermixed with other peoples in northwest Costa Rica, the indigenous population is relegated to remote regions in the Talamanca Mountains and the Pacific southwest. The tribes live in reserves administered by the National Commission for Indigenous Affairs (CONAI), which works to promote education, health services, and community development. However, CONAI is underfunded, and has met only modest success in protecting the indigenous cultures from exploitation by commercial interests, which continue to encroach on tribal land.

San Rafael de Guateso

Guaitil

Nicoya

San José

Santiago de Puriscal

Bribri

San José

Cabécar

Palmar Norte

Golfito

Key

- Boruca
- Bribri
- Cabécar
- Guaymí
- Guatuso/Maleku
- Huetar

The Chorotega of Guanacaste and Northern Nicoya were the largest tribe in the pre-Columbian era. Today, about 1,000 true-blood Chorotegas live in matriarchal families, and take pride in their distinctive pottery.

The Boruca inhabit ancestral lands in the hills west of the Terraba valley. They are famed for their balsa-wood masks *(mascaras)* of animals representing supernatural beings, used in the Fiesta de los Diablitos *(see p236)*.

Chorotega pottery, with its characteristic earth-tones, continues to be produced in Guaitíl *(see p197)*.

Designs are created by pecking tender green gourds with a needle. The residual skin surrounding the design is then scraped away. As the gourd dries, the skin turns dark brown.

The Huetar of the Puriscal region still practice the ancient Festival of the Corn but in many other aspects have been integrated into mainstream society.

Ulú (healing cane) used by shamans

The Cabécar live in the Talamanca-Cabécar Reserve *(see p225)* and today consist of about 5,000 individuals. Shamanic rituals remain an integral part of Cabécar culture.

The Guaymí of southwest Costa Rica retain a strong cultural identity, including the Guaymí language. Uniquely, women still wear the traditional garment with decorative triangular patterns, as well as *collares* (necklaces) of colorful beads.

Guaymí Painters experiment freely with scenes of daily life, images of natural forms, and spiritual symbols.

Traditional Guaymí dress

COSTA RICA THROUGH THE YEAR

A major factor in planning a visit to Costa Rica is the weather. The dry season (December–April) offers the best climate and draws the most visitors. Christmas and New Year, as well as Easter, when Costa Rica celebrates its most colorful festivals, are the peak periods: schools and offices close, and the nation goes on holiday. Late April and May are relatively less crowded. Promoted by the tourism department as the "green" season, the wet months (May–November) see fewer visitors and lower prices: for those willing to brave the rains, this is a good time to visit. Religious ceremonies and folk festivities are held year-round, though the celebrations usually lack the color and vitality of Mexico and Guatemala. *Topes* (horse shows) and rodeos are the staples of provincial events. Note that while many rodeos include bull-baiting, visitors can choose not to view the events. The Caribbean moves to its own beat, and a strong Afro-Caribbean heritage influences its festivities.

Floats depicting Costa Rican fauna, Fiesta de la Luz, San José

Dry Season

The cooler, drier months are ideal for beach holidays, especially in Guanacaste and Northern Nicoya, where it hardly rains. Town squares are ablaze with jacaranda and flame-of-the-forest. With coastal waters in the south at their clearest, scuba diving is excellent. Wildlife viewing is also at its best, with deciduous trees dropping their leaves. Dirt roads with river fordings are more easily passed, although off-road driving can kick up billowing clouds of dust. However, this is peak season throughout the nation, with high prices and fully booked hotels and car rentals.

December

Fiesta de los Negritos
(Dec 8), Boruca. The indigenous Boruca peoples celebrate their traditions with costumed dancing and drum and flute music.

Fiesta de la Yegüita *(Dec 12)*, Nicoya. The Festival of the Little Mare recalls a Chorotega legend and blends Indian and Catholic rituals. Villagers carry an image of La Virgen de Guadalupe in procession, and there are *corridas de toros* (bull runs), as well as fireworks and concerts *(see p196)*.

Los Posadas *(Dec 15)*. Before Christmas, carolers go house to house by night and are rewarded with food and refreshments.

Tope Nacional de Caballos *(Dec 26)*, San José. During the nation's most famous *tope*, the country's finest horsemen show off their skills in a parade of more than 3,000 horses along Paseo Colón.

Fiesta de la Luz *(Dec 26)*, San José. The nocturnal Festival of Light features floats decorated with colorful Christmas lights. The "Parade of Lights" passes from Parque Sabana to downtown via Paseo Colón. Fireworks light up the night sky.

Carnaval Nacional *(Dec 27)*, San José. Locals don costumes and dance in the streets to live music. A competition of brightly decorated floats is the highlight of the procession.

Fiesta de Zapote *(late Dec)*, Zapote. Citizens flock to this suburb of San José for the fairground, fireworks, *topes* and rodeos.

Fiesta de los Diablitos *(Dec 31–Jan 2)*, Buenos Aires and Boruca. Men dressed as devils rush through the two villages in the Boruca Indian community's reenactment of battles between their forebears and the Spanish *(see p236)*.

People dressed as devils at the Fiesta de los Diablitos

Carretas (oxcarts) gather for the Día del Boyero celebrations, Escazú

January
Fiesta de Palmares *(first two weeks of Jan)*, Palmares (near Alajuela). Concerts, rodeos, fireworks, and music highlight this festival, which also features fairgrounds and sporting events.

Fiesta Patronal de Santo Cristo *(mid-Jan)*, Santa Cruz. Rodeos, folk dancing, street festivities, and a parade of *carretas* (oxcarts) mark this two-day celebration honoring Santo Cristo de Esquipulas.

Festival de las Mulas *(late Jan)*, Playas Esterillos (near Jacó). Popular festival with mule races on the beach, as well as a crafts fair, *corridas de toros*, and music and dance.

February
Expo Perez Zeledón *(early Feb)*, San Isidro de El General. Cattle fair and orchid show, also featuring *topes*, rodeo, beauty contests, carousels, and displays of agricultural machinery. Local beers are sold at pop-up bars.

Good Neighbors Jazz Festival *(mid-Feb)*, Manuel Antonio. Jazz ensembles perform at hotels and other venues through the area.

Carnaval de Puntarenas *(last week of Feb)*. Parade floats, street fairs, music, and dancing enliven this coastal city for a week.

March
Día del Boyero *(2nd Sun)*, San Antonio de Escazú. A parade of colorfully decorated traditional oxcarts honors the *boyero* (oxcart driver). The streets come alive with music and dance.

International Festival of the Arts *(2nd week)*, San José. Theaters and other venues across the city bustle with live theater, dance performances, music concerts, visual art exhibits, and conferences.

Semana Santa *(Mar or Apr)*. Easter Week is the most important holiday celebration of the year, with processions nationwide, notably in Cartago and San Joaquín de Flores near Heredia. Costumed citizens reenact Christ's crucifixion in passion plays.

April
Día de Juan Santamaría *(Apr 11)*, Alajuela. Marching bands, a beauty pageant, and *topes* are part of the celebrations honoring the young national hero who was killed fighting against William Walker in the War of 1856 *(see p47)*.

Feria del Ganado *(mid-Apr)*, Ciudad Quesada. The nation's largest cattle fair also features a horse parade, *corridas de toros*, and various street festivities.

Feria de Orquídeas *(late Apr)*, San José. Hosted in the Museo Nacional, this orchid festival exhibits prize specimens, including some for sale.

Romería Virgen de la Candelaria *(3rd Sun)*, Ujarrás. A pilgrimage from Paraíso to Ujarrás terminates with games and celebrations to honor the supposed miracle attributed to the Holy Virgin that saved the town of Ujarrás from a pirate invasion lead by Henry Morgan in 1666 *(see p154)*.

Semana Universidad *(last week)*, San José. The campus of the University of Costa Rica is the setting for week-long free activities, including open-air art shows, concerts, and the crowning of the university queen.

The San José Symphony performing at a music festival

Wet Season

The onset of the rains marks the beginning of the off-season. Mountainous parts are prone to landslides, and many roads are washed out. Nonetheless, mornings are typically sunny, while afternoon rains help cool off sometimes-stifling days. This is the best time for surfing in the Pacific, and olive ridley turtles begin their *arribadas (see p195)*. Sportfishing is also at a premium, especially in northern Pacific waters. Toward the end of the wet season, Costa Rica is at its lushest, and swollen rivers provide plenty of white-water thrills. The Pacific southwest is subject to severe thunderstorms in October and November.

May

Día de los Trabajadores *(May 1)*. Trade unions organize marches in major cities to honor workers on Labor Day.

Fiesta Cívica *(early May)*, Cañas. Cowboy traditions are displayed at *corridas de toros* and *topes*. Street fairs feature folkloric music, dance, and traditional food.

Día de San Isidro Labrador *(May 15)*, San Isidro de El General. A celebration of the patron saint of farmers, with

Pilgrims at Cartago's Basílica de Nuestra Señora de los Angeles

an oxcart parade and an agricultural fair.

Corpus Christi *(May 29)*, Pacayas and Cartago. The two towns hold religious parades and church services.

June

Día de San Pedro y San Pablo *(Jun 29)*, San José. St. Peter and St. Paul are honored in religious celebrations around the city.

Compañía de Lírica Nacional *(mid-Jun–mid-Aug)*, San José. The National Lyric Opera Company presents a two-month long opera festival in San José's sumptuously decorated Teatro Mélico Salazar *(see p112)*.

July

Festival de la Virgen del Mar *(mid-Jul)*, Puntarenas. The "Sea Festival" honors Carmen, Virgin of the Sea, with religious processions, a carnival, fireworks, and a boating regatta.

Día de la Anexión de Guanacaste *(Jul 25)*. The annexation of Guanacaste by Costa Rica in 1824 is celebrated nationwide with music and folkloric dancing. Rodeos and bullfights are held at Liberia and Santa Cruz.

Chorotega Tourist Fair *(late Jul)*, Nicoya. This celebration of traditional Chorotega culture features artisan displays, indigenous foods, and several educational activities.

Festival de Música Credomatic *(Jul–Aug)*. International musicians perform predominantly classical music at venues around the nation.

August

Día de Nuestra Señora de la Virgen de los Angeles *(Aug 2)*, Cartago. Costa Rica's most important religious procession to honor its patron saint, La Negrita, draws the faithful from around the nation. The devout carry crosses or crawl on their knees to Cartago's famous basilica *(see p148)*.

Liberia Blanca Culture Week *(early Aug)*, Liberia.

Recorrido de toros (bullfight) at a fiesta in Parque Nacional Santa Rosa

A San José parade celebrating Día de la Independencia

Public Holidays

Año Nuevo (New Year's Day; Jan 1)

Jueves Santo (Easter Thursday)

Viernes Santo (Good Friday)

Día de Juan Santamaría (Apr 11)

Día de los Trabajadores (Labor Day; May 1)

Día de la Anexión de Guanacaste (Jul 25)

Día de Nuestra Señora de la Virgen de los Ángeles (Aug 2)

Día de las Madres (Mother's Day; Aug 15)

Día de la Independencia (Sep 15)

Día de las Culturas (Columbus Day; Oct 12)

Navidad (Christmas Day)

Cowboys come to town, and citizens don traditional attire to honor local traditions with music, dancing, and food.

Día de las Madres *(Aug 15)*. On Mother's Day, everyone honors their mother, who is usually taken out to lunch or dinner and serenaded by hired mariachis.

National Adventure Tourism Festival *(late Aug)*, Turrialba. Mountain biking, whitewater rafting, and kayaking are among the activities highlighted.

Día de San Ramón *(Aug 31)*, San Ramón (near Alajuela). The local patron saint is carried in procession. Tico culture is celebrated with marimba music, *topes*, processions, and regional dishes.

Semana Afro-Costarricense *(Aug or Sep)*, Puerto Limón and San José. This week-long festival celebrates Afro-Costa Rican culture. Activities range from art shows and lectures to musical performances and beauty pageants.

September

Correo de la Candela de Independencia *(Sep 14)*. Runners carrying a Freedom Torch from Guatemala travel from town to town, arriving in Cartago at 6pm, when the entire nation sings the national anthem. At night, children carry home-made lanterns in procession throughout the whole country.

Día de la Independencia *(Sep 15)*. Costa Rica's independence from Spain in 1821 is celebrated nationwide with street festivities, *topes*, and school marching bands.

Orosi Colonial Tourist Fair *(mid-Sep)*. Cultural events and exhibits celebrate the region's colonial heritage.

October

Carnaval *(2nd week)*, Puerto Limón. Ticos flock to the coast for a Caribbean-style Mardi Gras with parade floats, street fairs, live reggae and calypso music, and beauty pageants *(see p219)*.

Día de las Culturas *(Oct 12)*. Columbus's discovery of America is celebrated with cultural events throughout the nation, notably in Puerto Limón; the city's Carnaval culminates on this day.

A band at Puerto Limón's famous Caribbean-style Carnaval

Fiesta del Maíz *(mid-Oct)*, Upala (near Caño Negro). Locals craft clothes out of corn husks and make corn-based foods in a traditional celebration of *maíz* (corn).

Día del Sabanero *(Oct 18)*. *Topes* and celebrations mark Cowboy's Day. Liberia and Parque Nacional Santa Rosa have the most lively festivities.

November

Días de Todos Santos *(Nov 2)*. All Souls' Day is celebrated nationwide with church processions. Families visit cemeteries to remember loved ones and lay marigolds and other flowers on graves.

La Ruta de los Conquistadores *(mid-Nov)*. This week-long, coast-to-coast mountain bike championship, which aims to retrace the route of the Spanish conquerors across Costa Rica, is considered one of the world's most challenging.

Feria Agroecoturística *(mid-Nov)*, Atenas (near Alajuela). Log-felling contests, tractor tours, horseback rides, and an orchid show celebrate agricultural traditions at the Escuela de Ganadería reserve.

Fiesta de las Carretas *(late Nov)*, San José. Oxcarts are paraded from Parque Sabana and along Paseo Colón.

The Climate of Costa Rica

Most of Costa Rica experiences distinct dry (December–April) and wet (May–November) seasons, which Ticos call *verano* (summer) and *invierno* (winter). There are dozens of regional microclimates: San José and the *meseta central* (central plateau) are delightfully warm year-round; the eastern lowlands are swept by rain-laden Caribbean breezes; the southern Pacific coast has high precipitation; and in the dry season temperatures regularly rise above 35° C (94° F) in the parched northwest. Temperatures are affected by the varying altitudes, and can drop to below 0° C (32° F) on mountain summits. However, the sun is strong at all times of the year across Costa Rica, with sunrise at about 6am and sunset at 6pm.

LA FORTUNA

°C/F			
31/87	30/85	30/85	28/83
21/70	22/71	21/70	20/68
5 hrs	3 hrs	3 hrs	5 hrs
3.7 in	19.9 in	17 in	7.5 in
month **Apr**	**Jul**	**Oct**	**Jan**

High winds strike Guanacaste and Northern Nicoya in the wet season.

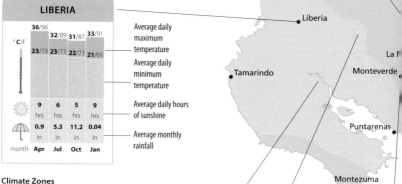

LIBERIA

°C/F			
36/96	32/89	31/87	33/91
23/73	23/73	22/71	21/69
9 hrs	6 hrs	5 hrs	9 hrs
0.9 in	5.3 in	11.2 in	0.04 in
month **Apr**	**Jul**	**Oct**	**Jan**

Average daily maximum temperature

Average daily minimum temperature

Average daily hours of sunshine

Average monthly rainfall

Liberia

Tamarindo

Monteverde

La F

Puntarenas

Montezuma

Climate Zones

- Warm dry: Rainfall in summer. Drought in places.
- Warm humid: Year-round rainfall, often torrential.
- Mild: High-elevation terrain. Springlike conditions year-round.
- Cool humid: East-facing mountain slopes with heavy rain.
- Cool dry: West-facing mountain slopes in rain shadow.
- Hot humid: Extreme rainfall. Frequent thunderstorms.

The Río Tempisque basin is the driest part of Costa Rica, with an average of only 18 inches (45 cm) of rain annually.

The western *cordilleras* bask in year-round sunshine.

PACIFIC OCEAN

Isla del Coco

Bahia Chatham

Bahia Wafer

Bahia Yglesias

0 km		3
0 miles		3

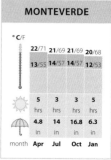

MONTEVERDE

°C/F			
22/71	21/69	21/69	20/68
13/55	14/57	14/57	12/53
5 hrs	3 hrs	3 hrs	5 hrs
4.8 in	14 in	16.8 in	6.3 in
month **Apr**	**Jul**	**Oct**	**Jan**

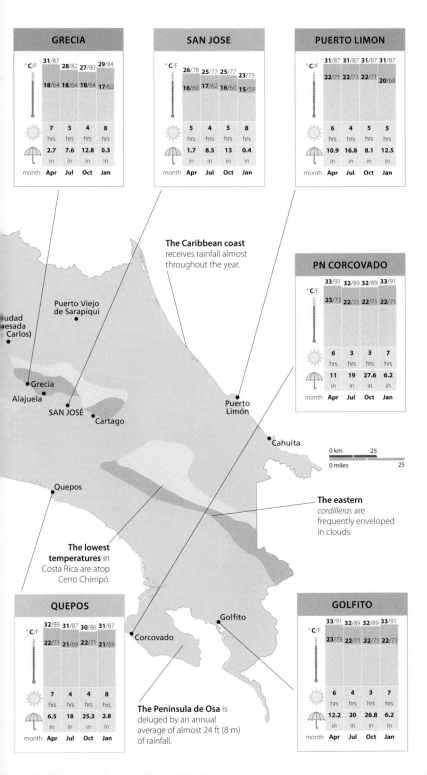

GRECIA

°C/F			
31/87	**28**/82	**27**/80	**29**/84
18/64	**18**/64	**18**/64	**17**/62
7 hrs	5 hrs	4 hrs	8 hrs
2.7 in	7.6 in	12.8 in	0.3 in
month **Apr**	**Jul**	**Oct**	**Jan**

SAN JOSE

°C/F			
26/78	**25**/77	**25**/77	**23**/73
16/60	**17**/62	**16**/60	**15**/59
5 hrs	4 hrs	5 hrs	8 hrs
1.7 in	8.5 in	13 in	0.4 in
month **Apr**	**Jul**	**Oct**	**Jan**

PUERTO LIMON

°C/F			
31/87	**31**/87	**31**/87	**31**/87
22/71	**22**/71	**22**/71	**20**/68
6 hrs	4 hrs	5 hrs	5 hrs
10.9 in	16.8 in	8.1 in	12.5 in
month **Apr**	**Jul**	**Oct**	**Jan**

The Caribbean coast receives rainfall almost throughout the year.

PN CORCOVADO

°C/F			
33/91	**32**/89	**32**/89	**33**/91
23/73	**22**/71	**22**/71	**22**/71
6 hrs	3 hrs	3 hrs	7 hrs
11 in	19 in	27.6 in	6.2 in
month **Apr**	**Jul**	**Oct**	**Jan**

Puerto Viejo de Sarapiquí

iudad esada Carlos)

Grecia

Alajuela

SAN JOSÉ

Cartago

Puerto Limón

Cahuita

0 km 25
0 miles 25

The eastern *cordilleras* are frequently enveloped in clouds.

Quepos

The lowest temperatures in Costa Rica are atop Cerro Chirripó.

QUEPOS

°C/F			
32/89	**31**/87	**30**/86	**31**/87
22/71	**21**/69	**22**/71	**21**/69
7 hrs	4 hrs	4 hrs	8 hrs
6.5 in	18 in	25.3 in	2.8 in
month **Apr**	**Jul**	**Oct**	**Jan**

Golfito

Corcovado

The Peninsula de Osa is deluged by an annual average of almost 24 ft (8 m) of rainfall.

GOLFITO

°C/F			
33/91	**32**/89	**32**/89	**33**/91
23/73	**22**/71	**22**/71	**22**/71
6 hrs	4 hrs	3 hrs	7 hrs
12.2 in	20 in	26.8 in	6.2 in
month **Apr**	**Jul**	**Oct**	**Jan**

THE HISTORY OF COSTA RICA

Contemporary Costa Rica has been shaped by a relatively benign history devoid of the great clash between pre-Columbian and Spanish cultures that characterized the formative period of neighboring nations. Following the colonial era, Costa Rica evolved stable democratic institutions that permitted sustained economic development. The nation's declaration of neutrality in 1948 continues to help forge its identity today.

When Christopher Columbus landed off the coast of Central America in 1502, the region had a history that went back 10 millennia. The indigenous peoples who inhabited the thickly forested and rugged terrain were relatively isolated from the more advanced and densely populated imperial cultures of Meso-America to the north and the Andes to the south. They were divided into several distinct ethnic groups and further subdivided into competing tribes ruled by caciques (chiefs). These peoples left no written record.

The semi-nomadic Chibchas and Diquís, who occupied the southern Pacific shores, were hunters and fishermen. They were expert goldsmiths as well, and also produced granite spheres of varying sizes for ceremonial purposes. The highland valleys were the domain of the Coribicí, subsistence agriculturalists skilled at using the "lost wax" technique to create gold ornaments. These groups had affinities with the Andean cultures, with whom they traded. The Votos of the northern lowlands were matriarchal and, like most other groups, used shamans to assist in the fertility rites that dominated religious belief. The agriculturalist Chorotega of the northwest lowlands were the most advanced. They traded with Meso-America, were famed for their elaborate jade ornamentation, and created a written language and calendar of Mayan origin. Most tribal names were ascribed by the Spanish and often indicated individual caciques.

Inter-clan warfare was common. Slaves from neighboring tribes were captured for labor and ceremonial sacrifice, while women were taken as concubines. Gold ornamentation indicated status. High-ranking individuals were interred with their wealth; their slaves were often killed and buried alongside to serve them in the afterlife. Each tribe lived communally in large thatched huts, and although modest urban settlements have been discovered, principally at Guayabo on the southern slopes of Volcán Turrialba, nowhere did elaborate temple structures result.

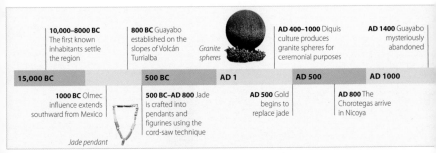

15,000 BC		500 BC	AD 1	AD 500	AD 1000

10,000–8000 BC The first known inhabitants settle the region

800 BC Guayabo established on the slopes of Volcán Turrialba
Granite spheres

AD 400–1000 Diquís culture produces granite spheres for ceremonial purposes

AD 1400 Guayabo mysteriously abandoned

1000 BC Olmec influence extends southward from Mexico

500 BC–AD 800 Jade is crafted into pendants and figurines using the cord-saw technique

Jade pendant

AD 500 Gold begins to replace jade

AD 800 The Chorotegas arrive in Nicoya

◀ A detail of a fresco by Diego Rivera (1886–1957) depicting the Spanish conquest in Central America

The Spanish Conquest

Columbus arrived in Bahía de Cariari, on the Caribbean coast, while on his fourth voyage to the New World. He spent 17 days in the land he called *veragua* (mildew), and his descriptions of the gold worn by the chiefs spelled doom for the indigenous population. Spanish conquistadors soon followed in his wake, driven by the quest for silver and gold. However, they failed to find any local source of the precious metals.

Colonization was initiated in 1506 when Ferdinand of Spain dispatched Diego de Nicuesa to settle and govern the region. Nicuesa's expedition north from Panama proved a disaster, as his troops were decimated by tropical diseases and guerrilla attacks. In 1522, a second expedition led by Gil González Davila explored the Pacific coast, converting the natives and seizing vast quantities of gold. Davila named the region *la costa rica* (rich coast). Many natives were enslaved under the *encomienda* system that granted Spaniards rights to native labor. Villa Bruselas, inland from today's Puntarenas, was Spain's first permanent settlement in Costa Rica, founded by Francisco Fernández de Córdoba in 1524. Davila's group and Córdoba's township, however, succumbed to tropical hardships and violent resistance by the natives. Despite this, by 1543, when the region was incorporated into the Captaincy-General of Guatemala, which extended from Yucatán to

Bust of Columbus and his son, Puerto Limón

Panama, most lowland areas had been charted and Spain's conquest was assured. Many natives were shipped to work the gold and silver mines of Peru and Mexico, while thousands died of smallpox, measles, influenza, and other European diseases that culminated in a 17th-century pandemic.

In 1559, Juan de Cavallón founded the settlement of Castillo de Garcimuñoz, with Spaniards, black slaves, and Indians brought from Guatemala and Nicaragua. Appointed governor in 1562, Juan Vásquez de Coronado penetrated the fertile Central Highlands and established El Guarco (today's Cartago) as capital of the region. For the next 250 years Costa Rica was a neglected colony of Spain, virtually forgotten by the governors of New Spain, based in Mexico.

Theodor de Bry's (1528–98) copperplate print depicting gold being seized by Spanish conquistadors

The Subsistence Era

By the 17th century, the relatively small supply of gold had been shipped to Spain, and the country had nothing to trade. Settlement was concentrated in the central valley of the interior highlands, where the absence of a large indigenous population and near total neglect by colonial authorities forced the Spanish settlers to work their own land. As a result, most of the land remained sparsely developed and agriculture existed at barely more than subsistence level. Moreover, the *mestizo* population (of mixed Spanish and Indian parentage) was small and the majority of inhabitants were predominantly Spanish. Thus, unlike the rigid feudal societies of its neighbors, Costa Rica evolved a fairly egalitarian social structure dominated by the independent farmer of meager means.

The northwestern regions of Nicoya and Guanacaste on the Pacific coast were exceptions. Spanish landowners established large cattle estates here, and exacted harsh tribute and labor from Indians and *mestizos* through the *encomienda* and *repartimiento* systems. The densely forested Caribbean coast, meanwhile, was part of the "Spanish Main," the domain of pirates and smugglers, who traded precious hardwoods, such as cocoa and

A 19th-century etching of Hacienda Santa Rosa, Guanacaste

Buccaneer, 17th century

mahogany, through the small port of Puerto Limón (it was closed by the Spanish in 1665 to combat smuggling). All through the 17th century, English buccaneers such as Henry Morgan and autonomous bands of Miskitos (a community of mixed-blood Indian and African slaves) regularly marauded inland settlements.

By the 18th century, exports of tobacco and hides to Europe began to boost national fortunes. Simple townships of adobe structures developed: Heredia (1706); San José (1737); and Alajuela (1782). Immigration from Europe gathered pace, and in the 1740s the increased demand for labor led to the forced resettlement of natives who had fled enslavement in the initial years of colonization and established communities in the Talamanca Mountains. On the whole, far-flung Costa Rica's parochial citizenry was spared the harsh taste of monopolistic, bureaucratic colonial rule; lacked an elite social class; and remained divorced from the bitter fight for independence from Spain that engulfed Central America at the end of the 18th century.

1723 Volcán Irazú erupts, destroying Cartago

1747 Talamanca Indians are forcibly resettled in the highlands

1808 Coffee introduced from Jamaica

1675   1700   1725   1750   1775   1800

1706 Heredia founded

1737 Villanueva de la Boca del Monte founded. Later renamed San José

1782 Alajuela founded

Coffee beans

The Formative Years of the Republic

The news that Spain had granted independence to the Central American nations on September 15, 1821, reached Costa Rica a month later. The country was torn between the four leading townships: the progressive citizens of San José and Alajuela favored total independence, while the conservative leaders of Cartago and Heredia preferred to join the newly formed Mexican empire. Although the four city councils met and drafted a constitution, the Pacto de Concordia, the discord erupted into a brief civil war in which the progressives triumphed. Costa Rica became a sovereign state of the short-lived Federation of Central America, formed by Guatemalan General Francisco Morazán. Under a law called the Ley de Ambulancia, the capital was to rotate between the four cities every four years.

Costa Rica's independence from Spain coincided with a boom in coffee production and the evolution of a monied middle-class dedicated to public education and a liberal democracy unique on the isthmus. Juan Mora Fernández was elected the first head of state in 1824. In 1835, Braulio Carrillo came to power. A liberal autocrat, he set up legal codes, as well as promoting a centralized administration in San José and large-scale coffee production. San José's growing prominence under Carrillo led to great resentment, which culminated in the War of Leagues (La

General Francisco Morazán

Guerra de la Liga) in September 1837, when the other three townships attacked San José but were defeated. In 1838, Carrillo declared Costa Rica's independence from the Federation, but was ousted by Morazán, on behalf of the emergent coffee oligarchy. Morazán was briefly named head of state in 1842, before being executed for attempting to conscript Costa Ricans to revive the Federation.

The Coffee Era

Costa Rica's smallholding farmers benefitted immensely from Europe's taste for coffee. Thousands of acres were planted, while income from the exports of *grano de oro* (golden grain) funded the construction of fine edifices in San José. This economic prosperity went hand in hand with a rare period of aggression, starting in 1856 when William Walker, a Tennessean adventurer, invaded Guanacaste. President Juan Rafael Mora raised a makeshift army that repulsed

Costa Rican workers picking ripe coffee berries, woodcut, 1880

1821 The Central American nations gain independence

1830s Coffee boom

1835–7 Ley de Ambulancia establishes rotating capitals

1837 San José becomes permanent capital

1856 William Walker invades Costa Rica

President Juan Rafael Mora (1814–60)

1824 Guanacaste secedes from Nicaragua to join Costa Rica

1838 Costa Rica withdraws from the Federation, declares independence

1849 *Cafetaleros* elevate Juan Rafael Mora to power, initiating political dominance of coffee barons

1869 General Tomás Guardia establishes compulsory, free education for all

1823 Federation of Central America proclaimed. Civil war

Walker but also created a group of ambitious, self-styled generals who from then on meddled in politics at the behest of their *cafetalero* (coffee baron) patrons. The most significant was General Tomás Guardia, who seized power in 1870. Guardia proved a progressive reformer, who promoted the construction of the Atlantic Railroad, which linked the highlands with Puerto Limón. The prodigious feat of hewing a railroad through the forested, rain-sodden, mountainous terrain was achieved by New York-born entrepreneur Minor Cooper Keith (1848–1929). Part of his terms for the project was a 3,100-sq-mile (8,050-sq-km) land lease in the Caribbean

Bas-relief in San José's Museo de Arte Costarricense

lowlands, on which he set up a banana plantation, and eventually established the influential United Fruit Company.

By the end of the 19th century, Costa Rica had evolved into a modern nation-state in which its citizens were active participants. When Bernardo Soto lost the presidential election in 1889 and refused to step down, street demonstrations forced his resignation. Similarly, students and women toppled war minister Federico Tinoco Granados, who staged a coup in 1917. However, the inter-war years were beset with labor unrest and social problems, which were exacerbated by a widening rift between the wealthy elite and impoverished underclass. Although the 1940–44 administration of President Rafael Angel Calderón established several bold social reforms, including a social security system, tensions rose as the country became increasingly polarized. The Calderón administration formed an anti-Nazi alliance with the Catholic Church and the Communist Party. This pitted itself against an equally unlikely anti-Calderonista alliance of intellectuals, labor activists, and the rural elite.

William Walker

In 1860, when he was executed, Walker was only 36. He was born in Nashville, and graduated as a doctor before starting to pursue a dream of extending slavery all over the Americas. In 1855, he rallied mercenaries and, with the blessing of President James Buchanan, invaded Nicaragua to establish a pro-US government. He went further, though, and proclaimed himself president. A year later he unsuccessfully attacked Costa Rica. Walker fled to New York, but returned to Central America in 1857, still filled with ambition. After a brief time in jail, he met his fate in front of a Honduran firing squad.

William Walker (1824–60)

1890 Atlantic Railroad completed | *Atlantic Railroad* | **1917** Federico Tinoco Granados seizes power | **1925** Sigatoka disease devastates banana fields | **1940–44** Calderón sponsors social reforms and founds the University of Costa Rica

| 1890 | 1900 | 1910 | 1920 | 1930 | 1940 |

1889 Liberal constitution drafted | **1897** A coffee tax finances construction of the Teatro Nacional in San José | **1930s** United Fruit Company expands its political and economic influence | **1934** Workers win the right to unionize | **1942** A German U-boat sinks a Costa Rican cargo vessel on July 2, leading to anti-German riots

The 1948 Civil War

In 1944, Teodoro Picado succeeded fellow party member Calderón after a violent and fraudulent election. Calderón ran for office four years later, but was defeated by a journalist, Otilio Ulate Blanco. Calderón objected, and the building housing the ballots was set ablaze by unknown arsonists. The Calderonista-dominated Congress annulled the election, and Ulate was arrested. This explosive situation paved the way for José "Don Pepe" Figueres, a radical utopian socialist. On March 11, 1948, Figueres declared the War of National Liberation to purify national politics. The badly trained and poorly equipped government forces were no match for Figueres' highly motivated guerrillas and, after 44 days of fierce fighting that claimed about 2,000 lives, the government was toppled.

Figueres entered San José in triumph on March 29, and established the "Second Republic." He nationalized the banking system and enacted enlightened social reforms. In 1949, Figueres forced congressional passage of a new constitution that disbanded the army, declared Costa Rica neutral, and extended universal suffrage to the Afro-Caribbean population. Still, key opponents and communists were executed in a bid to further consolidate his power. After 18 months as provisional president, Figueres handed the reins of government to Ulate.

Years of Prosperity and Terror

The 1950s, 60s, and 70s witnessed accelerating prosperity along with the

President José Figueres leading the parade of victorious civilian troops, San José, 1949

rapid expansion of the welfare state. Costa Rica's stability was severely threatened, however, by developments in Nicaragua, where on July 19, 1979, the Somoza regime was toppled by left-wing Sandinistas. Somoza's right-wing supporters, the Contras, set up clandestine bases in Costa Rica and were supported by the CIA in their attempts to overthrow the Sandinistas. These activities turned the northern border into a war zone. Meanwhile, Costa Rica's banana and coffee crops failed, while a transfer of capital out of the country led to an economic freefall. The Reagan administration pressured President Luis Alberto Monge to show support for the Nicaraguan right-wing paramilitary operations on Costa Rican soil in exchange for economic aid. Costa Rica's neutrality was dangerously compromised.

Revolutionary soldier

1949 New constitution adopted; Figueres later hands power to the winner of the 1948 election

1963 Volcán Irazú erupts during President John F. Kennedy's visit

1981 Costa Rica defaults on international loans

| 1950 | 1955 | 1960 | 1965 | 1970 | 1975 | 1 |

1948 Figueres launches War of National Liberation

1955 Nicaragua invades Costa Rica but is repulsed at Santa Rosa

1950s Pan-American Highway (Carretera Interamericana) connects Nicaragua and Panama

Social security symbol

1970s Expansion of social security system

1980s Cos Rica-base Contr destabilize th count

In 1986, Figueres' protegé Oscar Arias Sánchez became president of Costa Rica. The youthful leader protested against the activities of the US-backed Contras, and negotiated a peaceful resolution of regional conflicts. As a result, in August 1987, leaders of five Central American nations signed a treaty committing to free elections and a cessation of violence. Arias was awarded the Nobel Peace Prize for his role as mediator. He was succeeded in 1990 by Rafael Angel Calderón, son of the great reformer. The conservative Calderón administration introduced reforms to alleviate the country's international debt. Austerity measures helped, to some

Pedestrians crossing Avenida 2, San José

extent, to regenerate the economy. In a curious twist of fate, Calderón was replaced in 1994 by José María Figueres, son of Don Pepe, the elder Calderón's political nemesis.

The Environmental Era

The 1980s had seen the beginning of a huge tourism boom, which was fueled by Costa Rica's stewardship of its natural resources. The government committed itself to environmental protection, but economic scandals, anti-government demonstrations, and a series of natural disasters bedeviled the administrations of Figueres (1994–8), Miguel Angel Rodríguez (1998–2002), and Abel Pacheco de la Espriella (2002–6). In 2004, Rafael Angel Calderón and Miguel Angel Rodríguez were arrested on charges of corruption. (In October 2009 Calderón was sentenced to five years in prison.) Meanwhile, in 2004, José María Figueres was forced to resign as chairman of the World Economic Forum for receiving kickbacks. However, none of this has slowed the development of Costa Rica's ecotourism. Oscar Arias Sánchez successfully lobbied for a reversal of a law preventing former presidents from running for office again, and in 2006 he became the first ex-president to be elected to a second term. In 2010, his successor, Laura Chinchilla Miranda, became the first woman elected president in Costa Rica. Her term has been marked by tensions with neighboring Nicaragua.

Jose "Don Pepe" Figueres

"Don Pepe"
(1906–90)

Figueres, born on September 25, 1906, to Catalan immigrant parents, was largely self-educated. He studied in the USA in the 1920s, and returned to Costa Rica inspired by utopian ideals. After the 1942 anti-German riots, Don Pepe denounced the Calderón government in a radio address, during which he was arrested and subsequently exiled to Mexico. On his return in 1944, he set up a guerrilla training camp at La Lucha Sin Fin (The Endless Struggle), a farm high in the mountains south of San José, before launching the War of National Liberation. He founded the Partido de Liberación Nacional and was elected to two terms as president (1953–7 and 1970–74). He died on June 8, 1990.

Oscar Arias

35	1990	1995	2000	2005	2010	2015

1990s Costa Rica established as a world leader in ecotourism

1994 Banco Anglo Costarricense declares bankruptcy

2003 Supreme Court rules that former presidents may be re-elected

2009 Large earthquake devastates Poás region

2012 Largest earthquake in Costa Rica's history shakes the nation

1991 Earthquake in April causes great damage

1990s Large-scale immigration strains the social system. Drug trafficking accelerates

2000 Attempts to privatize electricity and telecommunications generate civil unrest

2007 Costa Rica joins the Central America Free Trade Area (CAFTA)

1987 Arias wins Nobel Peace Prize

WILD
COSTA RICA

THE WILDERNESS EXPERIENCE

Many come to Costa Rica to spot the resplendent quetzal; others for the thrill of close-up encounters with monkeys, sloths, and scarlet macaws. With so many diverse habitats, Costa Rica never disappoints nature lovers, largely because its wildlife is so abundant and easily seen. Visitors are captivated by a fascinating assortment of creatures that creep, crawl, prowl, and fly amid magnificent landscapes enshrined in national parks and reserves that cover almost one-third of this beautiful country.

Costa Rica prides itself on being one of the most biologically diverse countries on the planet. With a surface area of 19,730 square miles (51,100 sq km) and 801 miles (1,290 km) of coastline, this tiny tropical nation is barely as big as the state of West Virginia and only half the size of Iceland. However, Costa Rica boasts an estimated one million or more plant and animal species, including 10 percent of the world's butterfly species and an equal percentage of all known species of birds.

By the late 1960s, after decades of severe deforestation and dwindling animal populations, an appreciation that something precious was being lost began to develop. Today, multiple ecosystems – and the vast diversity of living creatures they support – are protected within a network of almost 200 national parks and reserves. Costa Rica has evolved from being a pioneer of ecotourism – promoting ecologically sensitive visits with the purpose of viewing wildlife in its natural habitat – into a world leader in this industry, with a dizzying array of tour companies specializing in birding and wildlife viewing, and an ever-growing number of Costa Ricans making a living as nature guides.

The wide range of options available permits visitors to stitch together a medley of distinct experiences and habitats. Whether it be viewing marine turtles laying eggs by night at Tortuguero National Park, or watching spider monkeys leaping through mist-shrouded trees at Santa Elena Cloud Forest Reserve, Costa Rica is sure to enthrall.

A diver photographing yellow tailed surgeon fish, Cocos Island National Park

◀ Walking along one of the many trails lining Monteverde Cloud Forest Biological Reserve

PRACTICAL INFORMATION

Tiny Costa Rica has such a rich diversity of parks and reserves – each with its own highlights – that it is easily possible to see a large percentage of its wildlife in as little as a week. Organizing and booking a visit is straightforward, since there are many reputable tour operators, both in-country and abroad, that can assist in planning a trip according to any budget and taste. The biggest difficulty may be deciding upon which regions and reserves to visit, and whether to opt for a DIY approach or go with an organized tour. Consider all available options before booking. The following pages will help you decide where to go, and serve as a guide to planning, packing, and preparation.

A skein of migrating ducks, Palo Verde National Park

Best Time to Go

Costa Rica is a year-round destination, but ideal conditions for wildlife viewing vary from region to region. Guanacaste is best visited in the dry season (Dec–Apr), when animals gather at water holes and many trees shed their leaves, providing better viewing of arboreal creatures. This is also the best time for birding: many migrants flock in from colder climates and waterbirds fill the wetlands. Because this is peak season, the most popular parks can be overrun with visitors.

Wet season (May–Nov) sees high rainfall throughout the country, and the landscape turns green and lush. Many trails become muddy, and accessibility to some areas may be restricted. Wetlands such as Caño Negro Wildlife Refuge flood, granting greater accessibility by boat. During prolonged rains it is possible to enjoy quiet time at eco-lodges, which often have scopes for close-up viewing.

Guided and Independent Tours

Independent travelers will no doubt chance upon many animals during their time in Costa Rica; however, in many habitats, the dense vegetation makes it hard to spot reclusive or well-camouflaged wildlife. Hiring a guide can make all the difference, as they are able to discern and point out creatures that you might otherwise miss, as well as impart information on local ecology. Guides can be hired through tour companies such as **Wildland Adventures**;

and most, like **Karla's Travel Experience**, have their own website.

Alternatively, you can let a tour company take care of all the planning by selecting a package deal.

Always choose a guide or tour company licensed by the **Costa Rica Tourism Board (ICT)**.

Planning your Trip

All national parks and many wildlife refuges are operated by the **National System of Conservation Areas (SINAC)**; other refuges and reserves are privately run. The relevant websites – and those of tour operators that specialize in wildlife viewing – are invaluable when planning your trip.

If you wish to visit several parks while in Costa Rica, invest in the **Amigos de los Parques Nacionales** (Friends of the National Parks) card, which allows entry to up to 12 national parks.

Most parks can be visited by car, although many can be reached only with a 4x4, and others are accessible only by

A group of youngsters on a guided tour of Monteverde

hiking or by boat, such as the Terraba-Sierpe International Humid Forest Reserve.

Bring wildlife identification books and charts and a pair of binoculars. Insect repellent, sunblock, sunglasses, and a flashlight are also essential.

What to Wear

Loose-fitting, lightweight, and quick-drying clothes made of breathable nylon or natural fabrics are ideal. Closed hiking shoes and long sleeves and pants help keep insects at bay; a hat will protect you from the sun. Natural colors let you blend into the background and avoid alerting wildlife. A warm fleece jacket and a windbreaker are essential for mountainous areas, while a lightweight poncho offers protection against the rain.

Choosing an Itinerary

Early morning and late afternoon are the best times to see wildlife. Come dusk, many animals such as monkeys bed down, and a different cast of creatures steps onto the stage, including bats, kinkajous, and frogs. Cats are also most active after dark, though seeing one is rare. The nighttime exploration of lagoons and wetlands by boat reveals crocodiles and nocturnal birds such as owls and the boat-billed heron.

National parks close before dusk, but several private reserves with lodgings offer night tours. Nocturnal hikes can also be booked via many tour operators and guides.

Children witnessing the slow progress of a leatherback turtle on a beach

Photographing Wildlife

An SLR camera is preferable to a point-and-shoot, and a lens with high magnification is essential for getting good-quality close-up images. A tripod or a lens with image stabilization will help reduce the risk of blurred images.

Be patient, still, and quiet. Creatures are often present but unseen, and they may show themselves after they get used to your presence. If you get too close, animals will flee, although at Manuel Antonio National Park, monkeys and raccoons are so used to humans they can often be photographed at close range.

Safety Tips and Health Issues

Always keep a safe distance from all animals, which can become aggressive if startled or if they feel threatened.

Crocodiles are present in lowland rivers, so do not swim there. Be aware of snakes – look down while walking; avoid feeling under rocks or in crevices; and never place your hand on a branch without looking, as many snakes are arboreal. If you're bitten, stay calm, move slowly, and seek medical assistance at once.

Never feed animals, as this makes them dependent on humans and creates the possibility of you being bitten.

Drink lots of water to prevent dehydration. Anti-malarial prophylactics are required only in the southern Caribbean region. Outbreaks of dengue also sometimes occur there.

Many eco-lodges provide access for disabled visitors and, often, specially adapted toilets and accommodations.

Taking Children

Although most children are thrilled at the sight of wildlife, they may quickly become tired and irritable after hiking in the heat of the tropics. Most wilderness lodges welcome children, and many offer special family programs, as do some tour companies, such as Wildland Adventures.

DIRECTORY

Guided and Independent Tours

Costa Rica Expeditions
Tel (506) 2257-0766.
w costaricaexpeditions.com

Costa Rica Tourism Board (ICT)
w visitcostarica.com

Journey Latin America (UK)
Tel (020) 3432-9175.
w journeylatin-america.co.uk

Karla's Travel Experience
Tel (506) 8915-2386.
w tortuguerovillage.com/karlastravelexperience

National Geographic Expeditions (USA)
Tel (888) 966-8687.
w national-geographicexpeditions.com

Wildland Adventures (USA)
Tel (206) 365-0686.
w wildland.com

Planning your Trip

Amigos de los Parques Nacionales
Tel (506) 2263-4162.
w amigosdelosparques.org

National System of Conservation Areas
Tel (506) 2248-2451.
w sinac.go.cr

Safaris, National Parks, and Wildlife Reserves

Costa Rica has almost 200 parks and reserves that, combined, protect every environmental habitat. The first-time visitor faces a daunting array of options, ranging from the dry deciduous forest of Santa Rosa National Park and riverine habitats of Palo Verde to the dense rainforest of the Osa Peninsula, in the southwest, and the high-mountain páramo of Chirripó National Park. This brief region-by-region overview of the country's top national parks and wildlife refuges, including private reserves, is provided to help narrow down the options.

THE NORTHERN ZONE

GUANACASTE AND NORTHERN NICOYA

THE CARIBBEAN

THE CENTRAL HIGHLANDS

THE CENTRAL PACIFIC AND SOUTHERN NICOYA

THE SOUTHERN ZONE

The Central Highlands

The nation's most visited park, **Poás Volcano National Park** lies 34 miles (54 km) northwest of San José. Most visitors drive up to the summit to view the active crater, but there are also four hiking trails offering a chance to spot the endemic Poás squirrel, sooty robins, and even the resplendent quetzal. Visit as early in the day as possible to avoid the clouds that typically set in by mid-morning.

The crater at **Irazú Volcano National Park** is also accessible by car. At 11,260 ft (3,432 m), it is at the limit of the tree line, and visitors can experience dwarf oak forest and páramo. The flora here has adapted to survive howling winds and bitter cold. The volcano junco, black-crowned antpitta, and yellow-eared toucanet are among the bird species most frequently seen. Both Poás and Irazú have trails accessible to disabled travelers.

A 4x4 is required to access **Turrialba Volcano National Park**, farther east. Trails lead around the crater rim and even into the caldera. The volcano began erupting in 2009 and has been periodically closed since. Since there is no ranger station, visitors are advised to stay at the only lodge in the area, the Volcán Turrialba Lodge, which offers guided hikes and horseback riding. Quetzals, jaguarundis, and red-tailed hawks are frequently seen here.

At the base of Turrialba, **Guayabo National Monument** protects the country's main archeological grounds. The 539-acre (218-ha) site is surrounded by moist montane forest and is a premier birding site, especially for toucanets and oropendolas. Trails lead past fascinating pre-Columbian petroglyphs; buy the booklet at the ranger station for a self-guided tour.

The altitude of **Braulio Carrillo National Park** ranges from 9,534 ft (2,906 m) at the summit of Volcán Barva to 118 ft (36 m) in the northern lowlands. Smothered in cloud forest at high elevations and dense rainforest below, it is often beset by clouds. Most of the nation's mammal species are here, plus more than 500 bird species. Rain gear is vital for exploring this park, as it is for **Tapantí-Macizo de la Muerte National Park**, on the northern slopes of the Talamanca massif and accessed via the Orosi Valley. Spanning 4,462 ft (1,360 m) in elevation range, it has trails for all abilities. February to April are the driest months here.

The Central Pacific and Southern Nicoya

Cabo Blanco Absolute Wildlife Reserve, at the southwest tip of Nicoya, was created in 1963 as the first protected area in Costa Rica. It takes its name ("White Cape") from the cliffs whitened by the guano of seabirds, including brown boobies. The public can access only one-third of this refuge,

The crater of Irazú volcano, in the Central Highlands

where the moist forest provides a home for large populations of monkeys, coatis, and carnivores.

Nearby, the private **Curú National Wildlife Refuge** is a major nesting ground for marine turtles, but its habitats also include mangrove and montane forest. Scarlet macaws and spider monkeys are bred here for release to the wild. Visitors can ride horses or take guided hikes.

In the Central Pacific, **Carara National Park** sits at the transition of the dry and moist zones. Despite its small size, it is rich in both Mesoamerican and South American flora and fauna. Trails are wide and level, offering excellent wildlife viewing. This is perhaps the best place in the country to see scarlet macaws, and crocodiles abound in the Tárcoles River.

Sightings of coatis, sloths, crab-eating raccoons, and white-faced monkeys are virtually guaranteed at **Manuel Antonio National Park**, and the steep Cathedral Point Trail is good for spotting agoutis. However, the park's proximity to dozens of hotels means it gets crowded; get there when the gates open. Licensed guides can be hired at the ranger station.

White-faced monkeys relaxing on a tree branch

centers, dormitory-style accommodations, and shops.

Hiking to the summit of the namesake volcano is a main reason many people visit **Rincón de la Vieja National Park**. Fumaroles and bubbling mud pools on the lower slopes are easily accessed by trails through scrub and dry forest that shelters coatis, monkeys, and some big cats.

Guanacaste National Park is one of Costa Rica's most rugged and remote parks, with only minimal facilities. Access requires a 4x4 vehicle and hiking. Attractions include pre-Columbian petroglyphs at the base of Volcán Cacao, which is topped by cloud forest.

In the extreme northwest, **Santa Rosa National Park** is centered on La Casona, the most hallowed historic site in Costa Rica. The dry forest and coastal wetlands support an unsurpassed list of animals.

Brown booby, often seen at Cabo Blanco

Surfers flock here to ride the waves. Santa Rosa has campsites, but in wet season access to the beaches is sometimes difficult; a 4x4 is obligatory.

Palo Verde National Park is one of the premier wetland habitats in Costa Rica, drawing huge flocks of migrant waterbirds. This is the nation's driest region, and the deciduous dry forests permit easy wildlife viewing. Animals to look out for here include roseate spoonbills, wood storks, and crocodiles.

To the west of Palo Verde, **Barra Honda National Park** centers on a limestone massif pitted with caves. Above ground, trails lead through scrub and dry forest. A local association offers guided hikes; a guide is obligatory for cave descents.

Leatherback Marine Turtle National Park is an important nesting site for the eponymous turtle. The nesting population has plummeted, but turtles can still be seen on the beaches between October and March.

Guanacaste and Northern Nicoya

The golden toad that inspired the creation of **Monteverde Cloud Forest Biological Reserve** is now extinct, and the park has become synonymous with the quetzal. Laced with trails, it is home to an astonishing variety of reptiles, mammals, and birds, including the three-wattled bellbird and emerald toucanet. At a higher elevation, **Santa Elena Cloud Forest Reserve** boasts some creatures, such as the spider monkey, not found at nearby Monteverde. Guides are available at both reserves, which also have visitors'

A canopy walk at Monteverde Cloud Forest Biological Reserve

The Northern Zone

Residents of **Caño Negro Wildlife Refuge** include neotropic cormorants, roseate spoonbills, and Nicaraguan grackle. The dry season brings millions of migratory waterfowl. Caiman abound in the wet season, when the area floods. Guided exploration is by boat from several eco-lodges.

The extraordinary **Arenal Volcano National Park** is one of the most popular parks. Centered on an active volcano, trails weave among the lava flows, and its forest is home to many creatures, from ocelots to opossums. There are many activities nearby.

Far less visited, **Tenorio Volcano National Park** is accessed from the village of Bijagua. The summit is off limits, but trails lead to teal-colored thermal pools, and tapirs are sometimes seen on the mid-elevation slopes.

La Selva Biological Station protects 3,707 acres (1,500 ha) of rainforest at the northern base of the Cordillera Central. Over 500 bird species and 120 mammal species have been recorded here. Reservations are required to visit and join its obligatory guided tours.

A sandy beach in Cahuita National Park, in the Caribbean region

The Caribbean

Requiring a 4x4 vehicle, the lush rainforest of **Barbilla National Park** extends up the slopes of the Talamanca Mountains. The ranger station has minimal facilities, and visitors will need to be self-sufficient. Poison-dart frogs are abundant and easily spotted, and the park is also home to a large number of snakes.

The watery realm of **Tortuguero National Park** can be accessed only by plane or boat. Cormorants, river otters, caiman, and monkeys exhibit themselves as if in a gallery to visitors exploring on guided boat trips from the many eco-lodges lining Tortuguero Lagoon. The beach here is the Caribbean's prime nesting site for green turtles, and nighttime

tours are a specialty. A true treat would be to see a manatee or a green macaw.

A canal connects to **Barra del Colorado Wildlife Refuge**, where crocodiles bask on mud banks, and the many broad rivers and lagoons boil with tarpon and snook. Most visitors base themselves at the sportfishing lodges.

Cahuita National Park adjoins Cahuita village – visitors can hop out of bed and enter the park within a few minutes' stroll. The park is blessed with beautiful white-sand beaches, a coral reef, and rainforest and wetland habitats.

Nearby, rugged **Hitoy-Cerere National Park** lies at the eastern foot of the Talamanca massif. Visitors must come with raingear, but on clear days the pristine rainforest abounds with frogs, reptiles, birds, and mammals.

One of the most important marine turtle nesting sites in the region, **Gandoca-Manzanillo Wildlife Refuge** encompasses swamps, mangroves, rainforest,

and a coral reef. Freshwater dolphins and manatees are often seen on guided boat trips. Parrots and toucans are also numerous. Many visitors volunteer for extended stays on work projects meant to save the turtle populations.

The Southern Zone

A bastion of tropical lowland rainforest, remote **Corcovado National Park** ranges from sea level to an elevation of 2,444 ft (745 m). Several lodges and tent camps lie at its doorstep, and camping is also allowed at the four ranger stations. Look out for squirrel monkeys, scarlet macaws, and red-eyed tree frogs. This is also the best place for a lucky encounter with jaguars, tapirs, and harpy eagles.

Piedras Blancas National Park, across the Golfo Dulce, is a smaller version of Corcovado, but with a less developed trail system. Lacking a ranger station, it is administered through the Esquinas Rainforest Lodge.

Cocos Island National Park lies about 310 miles (500 km) southwest of Costa Rica and is primarily a marine park visited by experienced scuba divers. The waters around Cocos offer a rare chance to swim with whale sharks, manta rays, and hammerhead sharks. Booby birds, frigatebirds, and several other bird species endemic to the island are other attractions. A permit is needed to go ashore.

In **Chirripó National Park**, hikers ascend through cloud forest to treeless páramo to

Arenal volcano, one of the most active in the world

summit Costa Rica's highest peak. Quetzals inhabit the forest, and cougars are often spotted on the high alpine plains. February and March are the driest months here.

Chirripó abuts the vast and mostly unexplored **International Friendship Park (La Amistad)**, spanning many ecosystems and extending into Panama. Visitors can access only a tiny fraction of this park, which is a haven for jaguars, tapirs, and other endangered mammals.

North of the town of Dominical, **Hacienda Barú National Wildlife Refuge** combines several habitats, including mangrove and rainforest.

Hawksbill and olive ridley turtles nest here, and trails offer a chance to spot anything from tamanduas to tayras. This private reserve has lodgings and offers the chance to go on dawn birding hikes, horseback rides, or to sleep on a treetop canopy.

Humpback whales are the main draw at the **Whale Marine National Park** (Dec–Mar and Jul–Oct). Dolphins can be seen year-round in the near-shore waters, where kayaking and snorkeling are popular activities.

The park merges south into **Terraba-Sierpe International Humid Forest Reserve**, a vast mangrove system that can be explored on guided boat trips.

A jaguar, one of the most elusive mammals in Costa Rica

DIRECTORY

The Central Highlands

Braulio Carrillo National Park
Tel 2233-4533 or 2266-1883.

Guayabo National Monument
Tel 2559-0117.

Irazú Volcano National Park
Tel 2200-5025.

Poás Volcano National Park
Tel 2482-1227 or 2482-2424.

Tapantí-Macizo de la Muerte National Park
Tel 2206-5615.

Turrialba Volcano National Park
Tel 2273-4335 (Volcán Turrialba Lodge) or 2248-2451 (SINAC, San José).

The Central Pacific and Southern Nicoya

Cabo Blanco Absolute Wildlife Reserve
Tel 2642-0093.

Carara National Park
Tel 2637-1080.

Curú National Wildlife Refuge
Tel 2641-0100.
W curu.org

Manuel Antonio National Park
Tel 2777-5185.

Guanacaste and Northern Nicoya

Barra Honda National Park
Tel 2659-1551.

Guanacaste National Park
Tel 2666-7718 or 2666-5051.

Leatherback Marine Turtle National Park
Tel 2653-0470.

Monteverde Cloud Forest Biological Reserve
Tel 2645-5122.
W cct.or.cr

Palo Verde National Park
Tel 2200-0125.

Rincón de la Vieja National Park
Tel 2200-0399.

Santa Elena Cloud Forest Reserve
Tel 2645-5390.
W reservasantaelena.org

Santa Rosa National Park
Tel 2666-5051.

The Northern Zone

Arenal Volcano National Park
Tel 2461-8499 or 8775-2943.

Caño Negro Wildlife Refuge
Tel 2471-1309.

La Selva Biological Station
Tel 2766-6565.
W ots.ac.cr

Tenorio Volcano National Park
Tel 2200-0135.

The Caribbean

Barbilla National Park
Tel 8396-7611 or 2768-8603.

Barra del Colorado Wildlife Refuge
Tel 2709-8086.

Cahuita National Park
Tel 2755-0461.

Gandoca-Manzanillo Wildlife Refuge
Tel 2759-9100.

Hitoy-Cerere National Park
Tel 2795-1446.

Tortuguero National Park
Tel 2709-8086.

The Southern Zone

Chirripó National Park
Tel 2742-5083.

Cocos Island National Park
Tel 2291-1215/16.

Corcovado National Park
Tel 2735-5036.

Hacienda Barú National Wildlife Refuge
Tel 2787-0003.
W haciendabaru.com

International Friendship Park (La Amistad)
Tel 2730-0846 or 2771-3155.

Piedras Blancas National Park
Tel 2741-8001 (Esquinas Rainforest Lodge).

Terraba-Sierpe International Humid Forest Reserve
Tel 2248-2451 (SINAC, San José).

Whale Marine National Park
Tel 2786-5392.

CONSERVATION

Costa Rica suffered severe deforestation and a rapid decline in the populations of many animal species in the 1900s. The disappearance of the *sapo dorado* (golden toad) and the plight of the great green macaw highlight the vulnerability of the country's wildlife. The rise of ecotourism and Costa Rica's efforts to protect its flora and fauna have led to the creation of a network of protected areas. Occupying about one-third of the country, this network includes 34 national parks, 56 wildlife refuges, 14 wetlands, and eight biological reserves. These conservation areas are administered by the National Conservation Areas System (SINAC) under the jurisdiction of the Ministry of the Environment and Energy (MINAE).

Deforestation is fueled by agricultural and real-estate development

Habitat Loss

The main environmental threat to Costa Rica comes from deforestation. Large swaths of the nation's lowlands have been cleared of rainforest rich in biodiversity to make room for large-scale cattle ranches and cash crops such as citrus, bananas, and pineapples. Peasant farmers also clear virgin mountain tracts for their own plots, and coastal forest has been felled at a quickening pace since the millennium as a result of a frenzied real-estate boom. More than 60 species of trees are now protected, and no tree may be felled without a government permit. However, compliance with the law is often tenuous.

Other threats to the local fauna and flora include pollution from fruit plantations, whose fertilizers and pesticides are blamed for killing off coral reefs at Cahuita; the trawl nets of shrimp boats, which result in the death of marine turtles; and the potentially lethal danger posed by uninsulated electricity cables, which unsuspecting monkeys, sloths, and other arboreal mammals use to cross between trees.

Hunting and Poaching

Hunting is legal in Costa Rica except in national parks and reserves. Nonetheless, illegal hunting continues even within protected zones such as Corcovado, where there are not enough rangers to ensure the protection of jaguars, peccaries, and tapirs, which are prized as trophy kills.

Culling tapirs and other large mammals threatens the jaguar population by removing its food source. Peasants consider wild cats and other large carnivores to be pests and often shoot them on sight.

Poaching for the illegal pet trade has contributed to the severe decline of parrot and monkey populations; and marine turtle nests continue to be poached for eggs, which are reputed by some to have aphrodisiac qualities when consumed raw.

CITES

The Convention on International Trade in Endangered Species of Wild Fauna and Flora (CITES) is an agreement that aims to regulate the trade in products of plant and animal species – from live monkeys to marine turtle-shell products – and ensure that such trade does not threaten the species' survival. Signed in 1963, CITES protects more than 33,000 species of flora and fauna worldwide. Costa Rican species listed as threatened or endangered include 16 bird, 13 mammal, eight reptile, and two amphibian species, plus dozens of plants. CITES requests that any trade in listed products be done only with a permit. Unfortunately, many species are trafficked illegally,

A leatherback turtle hatchling

Great green macaws at The Ara Project conservation center, Alajuela

including parrots and macaws, which are stolen from their nests as hatchlings and can fetch more than $1,500 on the international market. Many endemic orchid species are also at risk due to illegal poaching by collectors and smugglers – rare specimens may sell for $2,000 or more. As a result, the guaria morada orchid, the national flower, is extremely rare in the wild.

Endangered Species

Costa Rican law protects 166 animal species from hunting, capture, or sale, as well as all orchid species. One of the most critically endangered animal species is the leatherback turtle, which faces threats from fishing, egg poaching, pollution, and rampant development near its main nesting beach, Playa Grande. Other species in danger of local extinction include the three-wattled bellbird and the great green macaw. Efforts to save the macaw populations are now finally bearing fruit.

Ecotourism

The popularity of ecotourism has done wonders for conservation efforts in Costa Rica. Not only does it generate direct revenue from entrance fees to parks and reserves, but it also creates employment, serves as a deterrent to hunters and poachers, and fosters a strong conservation ethic within local communities. The economic incentive to protect, rather than cull, local wildlife is particularly evident at Tortuguero, a coastal community that previously lived by poaching turtle eggs. Today, former poachers earn their income as guides. Many private landholders have also been inspired to turn existing woodland into private reserves as a source of income, leading to an increase in the percentage of land under forest. Greater ecological sensitivity has also seen Costa Ricans successfully lobby against proposed gold-mining and offshore oil-drilling projects.

Macaw-Breeding Programs

With a large range throughout Central and South America, the scarlet macaw is considered a species of least concern. However, it has disappeared from many parts of Costa Rica, and the great green macaw is also listed as endangered. Several private initiatives have been set up to reverse the dramatic decline in population by breeding macaws for release into the wild as sustainable-size flocks, including in areas from which they have disappeared. The organizations leading these efforts include:
• The **Ara Project**, which breeds both green and scarlet macaws and is attempting to repopulate the southern Caribbean with green macaws;
• **Asoprolapa**, a program at Tambor that has freed more than 100 birds since 2007;
• **Zoo Ave**, which releases scarlet macaws into the wild, mainly from Piedras Blancas National Park.

DIRECTORY

SINAC/MINAE
Calle 25 & Avenidas 8/10, San José.
Tel 2248-2451.
W sinac.go.cr

Macaw-Breeding Programs

The Ara Project
Tel 8339-4329 or 8339-2407.
W thearaproject.org

ASOPROLAPA
Tel 8980-0594.
W delfines.com/costa-rica-photos/asoprolapa

Zoo Ave
Tel 2433-8989.
W zooavecostarica.org

A sign in Corcovado National Park asking visitors not to feed the wildlife

FIELD GUIDE

Costa Rica's national parks and other protected areas harbor an astounding diversity of wildlife, from large predators such as the jaguar to monkeys, sloths, and other arboreal creatures. Yet these mammals represent a mere fraction of what this country has to offer. Bird enthusiasts can look forward to sighting an enormous range of winged creatures, and there are also almost 400 species of amphibians and reptiles. No one knows the accurate number of insects.

The following pages are an introduction to some of the many wild creatures that inhabit Costa Rica. Some, such as the inquisitive coati and the gregarious white-faced monkey, can be seen daily in a wide range of habitats throughout the country. Others – including the wild cats, the furtive kinkajou, and similar nocturnal hunters – are more elusive and at best glimpsed only as fleeting shadows. Many creatures – such as marine turtles, humpback whales, and migrant birds – are seasonal visitors that arrive and depart at predictable times of year. The tiny Manuel Antonio National Park, in particular, is one of the nation's most visited destinations, and it is host to many popular favorites, including all four species of monkeys. While the main focus of this field guide is mammals, a more generic overview of

Costa Rica's varied cast of amphibians and reptiles is also provided, along with a few dozen of the more conspicuous and memorable bird species.

Despite the profligacy of wildlife in Costa Rica, much biodiversity has been lost during the centuries since the Spanish conquest, and many species are disappearing at an alarming rate. Jaguars, once numerous in many national parks nationwide, are now close to local extinction, and the spider monkey population in the wild today also hangs by a thread. Many endangered species can be seen at breeding facilities that work to save the most critically threatened creatures from a similar fate. Others are displayed at live exhibition centers and at rescue centers that work to rehabilitate injured and orphaned animals for return to the wild.

The stocky and powerful jaguar, found in protected areas of Costa Rican rainforest

◀ A colorful scarlet macaw in the luxuriant rainforest

Costa Rica's Wildlife Heritage

Until about three million years ago, North and South America were not connected. As the Central American isthmus rose from the sea, insects, reptiles, and rodents used the emerging islands as stepping stones between the continents. When the two land masses joined, North American mammals streamed south and South American marsupials moved north. Positioned at the juncture, Costa Rica became a hotspot of intermingling, leading to the evolution of new, distinctly tropical fauna. The country's diversity of climates, terrains, and habitats has fostered an astonishingly rich animal and plant life.

Key to Map

- Dry deciduous forest
- Lowland rainforest
- Mangrove swamp
- Wetland
- Montane forest
- Cloud forest
- Páramo
- Marine environment

Wetland
The spectacled caiman is abundant in Caño Negro Wildlife Refuge. It enjoys basking in the sun atop logs or mud banks.

La Cruz

Aguas Claras

Liberia

Cañas

La Fortuna

Santa Cruz

Las Juntas

Nicoya

Miramar

Carmona

Puntarenas

Sámara

Montezuma

Dry deciduous forest
Howler monkeys, the largest of Costa Rica's simians, are easy to spot in dry season, when trees shed their leaves.

Cloud forest
The Resplendent quetzal is the quintessential symbol of the cloud forest.

Mangrove swamp
White ibis roost communally in trees overhanging the nutrient-rich waters of mangrove forests.

The IUCN Red List

Established in 1963, the International Union for Conservation of Nature (IUCN) Red List of Threatened Species assesses the population status of more than 46,000 species of flora and fauna, highlighting those in most urgent need of conservation. Every species evaluated is assigned to one of the following categories:
- Extinct (EX) – No individuals known to survive;
- Extinct in the Wild (EW) – Survives only in captivity or as an introduced population outside its natural range;
- Threatened (three subcategories):
  - Critically Endangered (CR) – Extremely high risk of extinction in the wild;
  - Endangered (EN) – Very high risk of extinction;
  - Vulnerable (VU) – High risk of extinction;
- Near Threatened (NT) – Close to qualifying for Threatened status;
- Least Concern (LC) – No significant risk of extinction;
- Data Deficient (DD) – Insufficient information available for assessment;
- Not Evaluated (NE).

Montane forest
Glass frogs are most commonly associated with mid-elevation forests.

Páramo
The cougar, or mountain lion, stalks the treeless uplands of Chirripó National Park, where rabbits abound.

Lowland rainforest
The scarlet macaw is most numerous in Corcovado National Park, where it congregates at cliff-face salt licks.

Barra del Colorado
Tortuguero
Puerto Viejo de Sarapiquí
Guápiles
Siquirres
ajuela
SÉ
Cartago
Turrialba
Puerto Limón
Cahuita
Manzanillo
San Gerardo de Dota
Quepos
San Isidro de El General
ominical
Buenos Aires
Palmar Norte
San Vito
Rincón
Ciudad Neily
Golfito
Puerto Jiménez

Marine environment
Humpback whales arrive from northern and southern waters to mate and birth off Costa Rica's Pacific southwest coast.

Field Guide Key
- ◯ Diurnal
- ◉ Nocturnal
- 🌿 Dry deciduous forest
- 🌲 Lowland rainforest
- 🌴 Mangrove swamp
- 🌾 Wetland
- 🌳 Montane forest
- 🌫 Cloud forest
- 🌱 Páramo
- 〰 Marine

Cats

Elusive, solitary, and mainly nocturnal, cats belong to the Felidae family. Among the most difficult mammals to spot in the wild, these agile and stealthy killers are strictly carnivorous and feed on living creatures, from fish, rodents, and small birds to deer and tapirs. Each individual species varies in size and coloration, yet all cats are shaped like their domestic cousins, with round heads, keen eyes, and prominent canines; large paws with long, retractable claws; and sinuous bodies, plus long tails that aid balance. Most are well adapted to hunt both on the ground and in trees.

Family

Costa Rica's six felid species are split into three genera: Leopardus, with small to medium-sized spotted cats; Puma, with two species, both with uniform coloration; and Panthera, with the jaguar representing big cats whose larynx modification permits them to roar.

Ocelot

Species: **Leopardus Pardalis** • *Best Seen:* **Cahuita National Park, Santa Rosa National Park**

LC

The largest of Costa Rica's spotted felids, this graceful yet secretive cat is widely distributed throughout lowland and mid-elevation habitats, from the dry savannas of Guanacaste to the rainforests of Corcovado. Called manigordo by the locals, the ocelot has a stocky body; it can grow to 39 in (100 cm) in length, and weigh up to 22 lb (10 kg). Its short, sleek, and golden or cream-colored fur is spotted with orange rosettes ringed by black and arranged in irregular chains along its back. Like its cousins, the margay and the oncilla, the ocelot has a black stripe on each cheek and twin black stripes running up its forehead, plus a black-banded tail. Adults are solitary and will often defend their territories – which they mark with pungent urine and feces – to the death. Like all cats, the ocelot has superb night vision, which it puts to good use when prowling dense forests in search of prey. More omnivorous than most cats, the ocelot will even feed on amphibians, fish, and small reptiles, although its main diet consists of small mammals, such as rabbits and rodents. Females typically give birth to a single cub – but, occasionally, two or even three kittens – every two years. Once hunted extensively for its fur and for the illegal pet trade (these cats are relatively docile in captivity), the ocelot is now considered of least concern on the IUCN list of endangered species and can be found in a wide area ranging from northern Mexico to the Tropic of Capricorn.

Margay

Species: Leopardus Wiedii • Best Seen: Corcovado, Tapantí-Macizo la Muerte

NT

Less frequently seen than its larger cousin, the ocelot, to which it is superficially similar, the margay prefers a dense forest habitat, in which it is supremely adapted for life in the trees. This medium-sized cat has a longer tail and legs, and a smaller head with larger eyes, than the ocelot. An agile climber, it spends much of its time hunting birds and other creatures in the treetops, and it has evolved a special ankle structure that permits it to turn its feet 180 degrees. Capable of prodigious leaps, the margay can run headfirst down tree trunks and even hang from branches.

The margay, an agile climber adapted for life in the trees

Oncilla

Species: Leopardus Tigrinus • Best Seen: Braulio Carrillo, Monteverde

VU

Almost entirely nocturnal and therefore rarely seen, this ground-loving forest dweller prefers higher elevations than its cousins, the ocelot and the margay. While at a glance it resembles the margay, the oncilla – or tigrillo, as the locals call it – is much smaller, growing to only 23 in (59 cm) in length. It also has a short, narrow jaw and is unmistakable thanks to its huge eyes. Heavily hunted for its fur, the oncilla is listed as vulnerable.

The forest-dwelling oncilla, a small nocturnal predator

A cougar, second in size only to the jaguar

Cougar

Species: Puma Concolor • Best Seen: Chirripó, Sant Rosa

LC

Known locally as *león*, the cougar is the most adaptable of the New World felids – in Costa Rica it is found in every habitat. This master of ambush stalks large prey such as deer but also eats rodents, reptiles, and even insects. Adult males average 8 ft (2.4 m) nose to tail. The cougar has the longest hind legs relative to body size of any New World felid, good for big leaps and short sprints of up to 35 mph (56 km/h). The cougar's unicolored coat can range from silvery to tawny or chestnut, depending on its habitat.

Jaguarundi

Species: Puma Yagouaroundi • Best Seen: Barra Honda, Rincón de la Vieja

LC

Ranging from southern Texas to central Argentina, in Costa Rica this smaller relative of the puma is found in grassland, lowland scrub, and mid-elevation forest. It has a uniform coat, ranging from chestnut to dark chocolate, and an unusually long body with short legs, which have earned it the nickname "otter cat." Its ears are short and rounded, and its small face features piercing blue-green eyes. Although it purrs and hisses like a domestic cat, its vocalizations also include chirps and whistles. An agile hunter, the jaguarundi is diurnal, which makes it the most readily seen of Costa Rica's felids, often spotted darting across roads.

The jaguarundi, a versatile hunter

For Key to Field Guide icons *see p65*

Jaguar

The largest land predator and the only Panthera species in Central America, the elusive jaguar resembles the African leopard, but it is stockier and more powerful. Although this cat can climb trees, it mostly prowls the dense forest floor. Adult jaguars require a vast range for hunting. Habitat fragmentation and illegal hunting have caused a decline in numbers, and today the jaguar is confined to a few protected areas in Costa Rica, notably in Corcovado, where fewer than 50 individuals remain. The "Path of the Panther" project aims to establish a migratory corridor along the jaguar's entire range.

Although adults are mostly nocturnal and solitary, cubs spend much of their daylight hours playing and mock fighting with each other.

Family and Breeding

Like all New World cats, the jaguar is a loner. Each adult carves out a large territory for itself, marking it with scent trails. Females' home ranges (typically 8–15 sq miles/20–40 sq km) may overlap, though individuals avoid each other and chance meetings trigger an aggressive reaction. Males, whose territories cover 2–3 times the area of females, defend their turf against intrusions by other males, although actual fights between rivals are rare. Male and female adults generally meet only to mate, a brief and ill-tempered affair that can occur at any time of year. Pairs separate after mating, and females provide all the parenting. Cubs stay with their mother for up to two years before leaving to establish their own territory.

Females are fiercely protective of their cubs, not just against external predators, but also against male jaguars, which often kill existing cubs when taking over a rival's territory.

What you Might See

Sighting a jaguar in the wild is extremely rare. Chance encounters can occur, most notably on wide forest trails and on beaches when marine turtles are nesting, such as at Tortuguero and Corcovado National Parks. Exploring with an experienced guide may increase the odds of a sighting, but the movement of jaguars is highly unpredictable.

Good swimmers, jaguars stick close to water and like to cool off in lagoons and streams.

A tawny coat spotted with black rosettes offers excellent camouflage in the jungle.

IUCN status NT: Near Threatened

A jaguar's canines are strong enough to pierce even turtle shells

Feeding

Jaguars are solitary nocturnal hunters who rely on stealth, not speed, to ambush prey. They eat a wide variety of animals, from agoutis to caimans, but prefer large ungulates such as tapirs and brocket deer. Jaguars that inhabit coastal terrain are also known to hunt marine turtles. Uniquely, they kill their prey with a bite to the skull using their huge canines. The jaguar's bite is the strongest of all felids – twice as powerful as that of a lion.

A fight between jaguars is punctuated by hisses and growls

Communication and Voice

Fearsome and furtive, adult jaguars rely on silence and guile to catch their prey and are thus not given to extensive articulation. When females come into estrus, they communicate their fertility by marking territory with urinary scents and by vocalizations, which range from purrs, mews, and grunts to the jaguar's characteristic hoarse, cough-like roar. Males typically emit a series of deeper roars, repeated several times, to advertise their presence to females and to warn rivals off their territories. Clashes between males elicit much snarling and hissing.

KEY FACTS

Panthera onca
Local names: **Tigre**

 Size Shoulder height: 26–30 in (65–75 cm); Weight: up to 350 lb (160 kg).

Lifespan 12–15 years in the wild.
Population in Costa Rica Unknown.
Conservation Status NT.
Gestation Period 90–105 days.
Reproduction Females reach sexual maturity at two years and give birth to litters of two to four cubs every 18–24 months.

 Habitat From dry deciduous forest to seasonally flooded wetlands and lowland rainforest.

 Top Places to See Corcovado, Santa Rosa, Talamancas, Tortuguero.

Sighting Tips Look for the nesting sites of marine turtles and water holes, especially at dawn or dusk.

Friends and Foes The jaguar's only foe is mankind. The main threats are deforestation, illegal hunting, and persecution by farmers.

 Facts and Trivia A sacred animal for many pre-Columbian cultures, the jaguar featured prominently in tribal art. Ancient shamans wore jaguar skins.

A black panther is really a jaguar affected by melanism, or intense black pigmentation.

A crepuscular creature, the jaguar is most active around dawn and dusk.

Adult males mark their territory with urinary scents and scratch markings on trees.

Other Carnivores

Costa Rica supports about two dozen species of non-felid carnivorous mammals, although most are omnivorous to various degrees. A few are easily observed, while others are highly elusive or rare – the olingo, for example, is a creature of the night and not likely to be readily seen. On the other hand, the raccoon and the coati are diurnal and often become quite bold in approaching lodges and tourists in the hope of being fed.

Family

The gray fox and coyote belong to the Canidae family. The coati, raccoons, and olingo are members of the Procyonidae family, while the tayra and river otter are Mustelidae and are related to weasels.

The olingo has a dense, honey-colored coat

Olingo

*Species: **Bassaricyon Gabbii** • Best Seen: **Carara, Corcovado, La Selva, Selva Verde***

🄲 🐾 🐾 🐾   LC

This bushy-tailed arboreal mammal, with short legs and small rounded ears, is strictly nocturnal. Lively and furtive, it lives in the upper forest canopy, where it feeds on insects, fruit, and small vertebrates. Its fur is cream on the belly and dark brown around the midriff, and its tail makes up more than half of its 35-in (90-cm) length. The olingo is a popular (but illegal) pet, which causes it to be poached from the wild.

The tayra is as big as a medium-sized dog

Tayra

*Species: **Eira Barbara** • Best Seen: **Arenal, Braulio Carrillo, La Amistad***

🄾 🄲 🐾 🐾 🐾 🐾 🐾 🐾   LC

A forest-dwelling weasel, the tayra *(tolomuco)* averages 24–28 in (60–70 cm), plus tail. It is black except for a white throat, though its neck and head silver with age. Armed with large claws and powerful legs, this diurnal hunter is an expert climber capable of leaping between branches in pursuit of small monkeys, birds, and other prey. It also eats fruit, eggs, and honey.

IUCN status DD: Data Deficient; LC: Least Concern

White-Nosed Coati

*Species: **Nasua Narica** • Best Seen: **Arenal, Cahuita, Manuel Antonio***

🄾 🄲 🐾 🐾 🐾 🐾 🐾 🐾   LC

The white-nosed coati *(pizote* to the locals) is a cousin of the raccoon and commonly seen in Costa Rica from sea level to an altitude of about 11,500 ft (3,500 m). Females and juveniles forage in bands of up to 30 individuals; males are solitary. The coati's chestnut body contrasts with its silvery chest and white nose, which is long and pointed. Ringed with black and white, the long tail is held aloft while walking, and it aids balance when climbing trees.

A white-nosed coati tucking into a banana tree

Northern Raccoon

*Species: **Procyon Lotor** • Best Seen: **Cahuita, Santa Rosa, Tortuguero***

🄾 🄲 🐾 🐾 🐾 🐾 🐾 🐾   LC

Familiar to North Americans, the Northern raccoon *(mapache)* is found in most parts of Costa Rica. Mostly nocturnal, this omnivore also forages by day, using its dexterous front paws to manipulate objects. It can also rotate its paws backward to descend trees headfirst. It stands up to 12 in (30 cm) tall and has gray fur and a white face with trademark black mask.

Raccoons are highly intelligent and inquisitive

Crab-eating raccoons inhabit shoreline forests

Crab-Eating Raccoon
Species: **Procyon Cancrivorus** • *Best Seen:* **Manuel Antonio, Palo Verde, Terraba-Sierpe**

◯ⒸⓋⓎ   LC

Native to Central and South America, the crab-eating raccoon shares its Northern cousin's coloration, but its shorter fur gives it a smaller, leaner look. This coastal dweller favors shoreline forests, especially mangroves. Although it scavenges for birds' eggs, lizards, and fruits, its diet consists mainly of crabs and other crustaceans. Crab-eating raccoons are often seen begging or trying to steal tidbits from visitors at Manuel Antonio National Park.

The gray fox resembles a slender, long-eared dog

Gray Fox
Species: **Urocyon Cinereoargenteus** • *Best Seen:* **Guanacaste, Rincón de la Vieja, Santa Rosa**

Ⓒ Ⓨ   LC

The gray fox is easily recognized by its silvery coat, with white bib and rust-red underparts and neck; its large, alert ears; and its bushy, black-tipped tail. A stealthy, nocturnal predator, it hunts for small mammals and birds both on the ground and in trees, which it is able to climb thanks to the strong, curved claws on its hind paws. Although females expel males from the den after pups are born, the monogamous father continues to forage for food for his family. A territorial animal, the gray fox marks its turf with urine. The best time to see one is around dawn or dusk, and the best location is the lowlands of Guanacaste.

Coyote
Species: **Canis Latrans** • *Best Seen:* **Palo Verde, Rincón de la Vieja, Santa Rosa**

◯ⒸⓎⓎ   LC

Opportunistic hunters, coyotes often pair up to kill rodents and ground-nesting birds. Their diet also includes snakes and large invertebrates. Closely resembling the gray fox, a coyote is more robust and stands up to 26 in (65 cm) tall at the shoulder, which is crossed by black-tipped guard hairs. A coyote's howl is often heard around dusk.

A coyote letting out its unmistakable drawn-out howl

Neotropical River Otter
Species: **Lontra Longicaudis** • *Best Seen:* **Cahuita, Gandoca-Manzanillo, Palo Verde, Tortuguero**

◯ⒸⓎ   DD

Known in Costa Rica as *nutria*, this sleek, robustly built aquatic mammal inhabits lowland riverine and swampy habitats, where it feeds on fish, amphibians, and crustaceans. The Neotropical river otter requires unpolluted waters and healthy riparian vegetation. It has short legs, a long body, thick neck, and a flat head with tiny ears and a broad, thickly whiskered muzzle. Its pelt is dense and sleek. Its heavily clawed, webbed feet and powerful tail provide propulsion in the water. You are most likely to see one at Tortuguero or Gandoca-Manzanillo Wildlife Refuge, where small groups are frequently spotted playing.

The Neotropical river otter has a short, dense coat

Key to Field Guide icons *see p65*

Primates

Costa Rica has four of the 53 species of New World primates, which are limited to a spectrum of tropical forest. They differ from their Old World counterparts in having flat noses with side-facing nostrils, plus (in many species) strong prehensile tails that can grasp branches and aid maneuvering through the treetops. The Costa Rican species are small to mid-sized, mostly herbivorous, and arboreal – only capuchin monkeys are adept at foraging on the forest floor. Intelligent and entertaining, primates also have a complex social structure.

Family

Costa Rica's four diurnal primate species are all classified as New World Monkeys, or Platyrrhines ("flat-nosed"). White-faced and squirrel monkeys are in the Cebidae family; howler and spider monkeys belong to the Atelidae family.

Mantled Howler Monkey

Species: Alouatta Palliata • Best Seen: Manuel Antonio, Santa Rosa, Tortuguero

LC

The male howler monkey emits a distinctive loud roar

Weighing up to 23 lb (10 kg), the mantled howler monkey, or *mono congo*, is the largest Costa Rican primate and the most widespread, present in most national parks and reserves. These monkeys are named for the male's extraordinarily loud and drawn-out throaty roar, emitted at dawn and dusk and to intimidate interlopers. The call is made by passing air through an enlarged hyoid bone to amplify the sound in the howler's balloon-like throat. The mantled howler is black, but adult males have a chestnut-colored mantle on their flanks and back. Its long, prehensile tail acts as an extra arm for gripping branches. The howler monkey eats mostly leaves, fruit, and flowers, and it spends much of the day snoozing to digest its low-energy food source. It lives in troops of up to 20 animals and is the most resilient of the monkey species to forest disturbance due to its small home range and low-energy lifestyle.

A black-handed spider monkey swinging from a tree

Spider Monkey

Species: Ateles Geoffroyi • Best Seen: Arenal, Braulio Carrillo, Corcovado, Palo Verde, Santa Elena

EN

A gangly acrobat, the rust-colored spider monkey is named for its disproportionately long limbs, which are supremely adapted to life in the upper forest canopy. This monkey brachiates, or swings, beneath branches aided by its long prehensile tail, which is tipped by a palm-like pad and can support its entire weight. Its hands have long, hook-like fingers but only a vestigial thumb. One of several subspecies, Geoffroy's spider monkey has a black head and hands and a pale mask around the eyes and muzzle. Among the largest of New World monkeys, it can weigh up to 19 lb (9 kg). It lives in bands of up to 35 individuals but by day it forages for fruit and leaves in smaller groups. The spider monkey inhabits several forest habitats, from dry deciduous to montane cloud forest. It requires large tracts and is one of the first mammals to disappear due to habitat disturbance.

IUCN status EN: Endangered; LC: Least Concern; VU Vulnerable

White-Faced Monkey

Species: **Cebus Capucinus** • *Best Seen:* **Cabo Blanco, Cahuita, Manuel Antonio**

LC

This long-lived monkey is commonly called "capuchin" for its black cloak and cap and white chest, neck, and shoulders, which hint at the dress of the namesake Franciscan friars. Mischievous or malicious, depending on your point of view, this hyperactive and agile animal spends much of the day searching for food from ground to treetop, and it will snatch human belongings (such as bags left unattended on the beach) in its search for tidbits. An omnivore weighing 5.5–7.7 lb (2.5–3.5 kg), it eats everything from buds, fruits, and nuts to birds' eggs, insects, and small vertebrates. The white-faced monkey is the most intelligent of New World monkeys: it uses twigs to forage for insects, and stones to crack open crab shells; it even rubs itself with crushed millipedes to repel mosquitoes. Highly gregarious, this monkey lives in groups of ten to 35 members dominated by an alpha male and female. Territories tend to overlap, leading to hostile encounters that often result in infanticide by males that take over a group. The white-faced monkey is widely distributed throughout Costa Rica, where it lives in almost every kind of forest below 6,500 ft (2,000 m).

White-faced monkeys are easily identified by their coat

a squirrel monkey carrying a baby on its back

Squirrel Monkey

Species: **Saimiri Oerstedii** • *Best Seen:* **Corcovado, Golfito, Manuel Antonio**

VU

Handsome and tiny, the endearing squirrel monkey (called *mono tití* locally) is restricted in Costa Rica to the Central and Southern Pacific coastal forests, but it also extends into Panama. Unlike the other three local primates, its tail – which is far longer than its body – is not prehensile, and it is used purely for balance as the monkey scampers along branches on all fours. The most social of the species, the squirrel monkey lives in egalitarian groups of up to 100 members. Adult males share females, whose estrus is synchronized during a two-month mating season; rather than fighting, males engorge themselves to attract the females' attention. The squirrel monkey has short-cropped fur with an olive or orange body, white chest and face, and black mouth, hands, cap, and tail tip. Like the white-faced monkey, it is omnivorous but feasts primarily on fruit and insects. Being so small, it is preyed on by felids, raptors, and snakes. When predators are detected, male sentinels issue alarm calls, and the monkeys dive for cover. The species' population is recovering after a steep decline caused by deforestation.

Key to Field Guide icons *see p65*

Manatee

A large, lumbering marine mammal, the manatee is a placid aquatic herbivore and an exciting feather in the cap for nature lovers, who can encounter them in the backwaters of Tortuguero and Gandoca-Manzanillo. This distant relative of the elephant evolved from four-legged land mammals millions of years ago and today lives in warm brackish tropical and subtropical waters. Sometimes reaching lengths of more than 10 ft (3 m), manatees can remain underwater for long periods, surfacing for air at regular intervals.

A manatee calf can vocalize within a few hours of being born, thereby establishing an immediate, strong link with its mother. Although fully weaned after about a year, a calf will stay with its mother for another year or so, to learn about feeding and resting grounds and travel routes.

Family and Breeding

Although generally solitary, manatees are sometimes spotted in groups. Females can come into estrus throughout the year, and about two years after giving birth. Like their cousin, the elephant, male manatees form ephemeral mating herds around estrus females and compete for their turn at copulation. Male–female bonds do not form. Females give birth to a single baby – or, rarely, twins – about 13 months after impregnation. The calf nurses from nipples located behind the mother's flippers. Mother and calf form a strong bond, remaining together for two years during weaning.

Gentle and slow-moving, manatees face the greatest danger of injury and even death from fast-moving vessels. Every year, many of these plump marine mammals sustain nasty cuts from boat propellers and internal injuries from hull collisions. Boat traffic along the canals and lagoons of Tortuguero National Park scares them into the backwaters. Other threats to the manatee population include pesticides washing down from banana plantations.

What you Might See

Visitors who explore the lagoons of Tortuguero and Gandoca-Manzanillo by canoe are often pleasantly surprised to encounter manatees, which sometimes emerge alongside the vessel for an eye-to-eye encounter. Manatees swim at a leisurely 3–5 mph (5–8 km/h) and often pause to float nonchalantly.

The prehensile upper lip is used to gather food and eat, much like an elephant's trunk.

A manatee's paddle-shaped tail is efficient at providing propulsion through water.

IUCN status VU: Vulnerable

A manatee's diet includes a wide range of plant species

Feeding

Manatees are opportunistic browsers, with a varied diet consisting of more than 60 different aquatic plant species, including seagrasses, water hyacinths, and mangrove leaves. They spend the greater part of each day grazing and can eat up to 10 percent of their body weight daily. Lacking incisors and canine teeth, manatees rely on molars that, uniquely among mammals, are constantly replaced as they become worn down and fall out.

Manatees rely on a range of sounds to communicate among themselves

Communication and Voice

Manatees use a varied repertoire of chirps, squeaks, and grunts to communicate with one another. Variations in pitch and tone have specific meanings – for example, short, harsh squeaks indicate anger or annoyance, while squeals reveal alarm or fear. Hungry calves squeak until allowed to nurse, while calves separated from their mum will cry until she answers – from as far away as 197 ft (60 m). Smell, taste, and touch are also used for communication: during mating season, male manatees caress females and utter excited squeals.

KEY FACTS

Trichechus manatus

Local Name: **Sea cow, manatí**

 Size Length: up to 12 ft (3.6 m); Weight: up to 3,910 lb (1,775 kg).

Lifespan 55 years.
Population in Place 200+.
Conservation Status VU.
Gestation Period 13 months.
Reproduction Females first conceive at about five years of age, then give birth every 2–5 years until about 25.

 Habitat Shallow, marshy coastal lagoons and rivers bordering the Caribbean Sea.

 Top Places to See Barra del Colorado, Gandoca-Manzanillo, Tortuguero.

Sighting Tips
A trail of bubbles dribbling to the surface is a sure sign that a manatee is passing by below.

Friends and Foes
Crocodiles may occasionally strike at manatee calves that stray too far from their mothers.

 Facts and Trivia
Manatees belong to the Sirenia order, named for the sirens of Greek mythology. This is because the Spanish who first arrived in the New World thought these placid creatures were mermaids – that is, half-girl and half-fish.

Females in estrus often beach themselves to avoid overly amorous male suitors.

The manatee's thick gray skin is covered with coarse hair and was prized by indigenous people.

Small, widely spaced eyes are covered by a special transparent eyelid to aid underwater vision.

Baird's Tapir

The largest Neotropical land mammal, Baird's tapir has a thick hide and huge bulk, which help protect it against its only predators – jaguars and crocodiles. Sadly, this shy, reclusive creature fares less well against illegal hunters. The remote heights of the Cordillera Talamanca are a rare sanctuary with a stable population, but elsewhere numbers are dropping: it is estimated that fewer than 5,500 individuals remain in the wild. Baird's tapir is therefore listed as endangered.

With a barrel-shaped body and stocky legs, the tapir resembles the offspring of a horse and a pig. It has good hearing and a long, prehensile snout. Its keen sense of smell makes up for poor vision.

Family and Breeding

Adult tapirs mostly keep to themselves, although they are often seen with juveniles, and the bond between mother and calf is strong. Rival males fight to mate with a female. The excited winner initiates an elaborate courtship by spraying urine. The couple dances a quickening duet as they stand nose to tail, sniffing each other's genitals, before violent copulation in which each bites at the other. Females give birth to a single calf, weighing about 15 lb (7 kg). The calf is weaned for a year, then spends another year or two with the mother. Males do not contribute to raising their offspring.

The tapir has a thick, tough skin, particularly on its hind quarters, and it is covered with short, bristly, tightly packed hairs. Individuals that live at higher elevations, such as the páramo of Chirripó National Park, grow thicker coats as protection from the cold.

What you Might See

The water-loving tapir inhabits a wide range of habitats, from marshy grasslands and thick rainforest to high-mountain páramo. Chances of a sighting improve at marshy lagoons and high-mountain lakes, while tunnel-like tapir trails often lead to mud pools. If you see tapir, keep your distance, as they alarm easily and can react aggressively.

Tapirs enjoy cooling off in lakes and pools. Only their head remains above water.

Dark- or olive-brown, tapirs have a cream-colored throat and white-tipped ears.

A tapir feeding on leaves in the forest undergrowth

Feeding

Baird's tapir is a grazer-browser that feeds primarily at twilight and by night, using its prehensile snout to forage for and pluck leaves and fruit. Its preferred diet consists of fruit and berries, plus tender shoots and young leaves supplemented by aquatic vegetation. Weighing up to 880 lb (400 kg), it can devour one-tenth of its own body weight in vegetative matter daily. The tapir's tendency to follow well-worn paths that meander through the thick forest undergrowth makes it relatively easy to find – for both hunters and wildlife enthusiasts.

Baird's tapir using its sense of smell to read territorial markings

Communication and Voice

Solitary, unsociable, and territorial, tapirs mark their small home ranges with urine and dung. Except in breeding season, two tapirs that come into contact react aggressively by baring their teeth. If neither retreats, a fight can occur, with each trying to bite the other's hind legs – their sharp incisors can inflict serious wounds. Tapirs vocalize with shrills, snorts, squeaks, and whistles. These vary in pitch depending on meaning and are especially loud when the animal is sexually excited.

KEY FACTS

Tapirus bairdii
Local Name: **Danta**

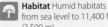 **Size** Shoulder height: 3.9–5 ft (1–1.5 m); Weight: up to 880 lb (400 kg).

Lifespan 30 years.
Population in Costa Rica Less than 1,000.
Conservation Status EN.
Gestation Period 13 months.
Reproduction Females typically conceive after two years and give birth every two years.

 Habitat Humid habitats from sea level to 11,400 ft (3,500 m).

 Top Places to See Corcovado, La Amistad, La Selva, Rincón de la Vieja, Tenorio.

Sighting Tips Tapirs mark well-tramped trails with urine and dung deposits. Their large, splayed-toe tracks are unmistakable.

Friends and Foes Tapirs are a tasty treat to jaguars, and large crocodiles can seize them at lagoons.

Facts and Trivia Baird's tapir is named for the American naturalist Spencer Fullerton Baird, who studied them in the 1840s.

Calves are rust-colored, with white spots and stripes serving as camouflage.

Active at dusk and in the night, tapirs shelter amid dense vegetation during the day.

The Tapir's hoofed toes are splayed to allow for extra mobility in land marshes.

Other Mammals

Costa Rica supports 212 mammal species. This figure includes approximately 100 species of bats. These are the only mammals in the world that have evolved for flight – their wings are really webbed forelimbs. Exclusively nocturnal, they navigate by emitting ultrasonic squeaks and track the echoes with special receptors. This is known as echolocation. Mammals that are active by day include rodents, ungulates, and the three-toed sloth, which is frequently seen.

Family

Costa Rica's mammals are grouped in 11 orders, including the felids. Anteaters, sloths, and tamanduas are in the order Pilosa. Bats belong to the Chiroptera order, while peccaries and deers are even-toed ungulates – hoofed animals with more than 220 species worldwide.

Three-Toed Sloth

*Species: **Bradypus Variegatus** • Best Seen: **Braulio Carrillo, Cahuita, Manuel Antonio, Tortuguero***

LC

The three-toed sloth – more accurately called "three-fingered" sloth, since the two-toed sloth, confusingly, also has three toes – can be seen in every kind of forest in Costa Rica. It has a round face with a blunt nose, black eye mask, and prominent forehead, and it is able to rotate its neck by 360 degrees. Sloths spend virtually their entire lives suspended by their hook-like claws, or curled up asleep in the forks of branches. Active by day, they feed exclusively on the leaves of several tree species, notably the cecropia. The three-toed sloth's thick, long gray fur runs from its belly to its back to facilitate the drainage of rain while hanging upside down. Green algae grow on the fur, providing natural camouflage and food for a species of moth that lives in the fur and lays its eggs in sloth dung. The sloth grows to about 2 ft (60 cm) in length but weighs no more than 15 lb (7 kg). It requires sunshine to digest the cellulose in its leafy low-energy diet, and its slow metabolism and minimal muscle mass result in very slow movements. Females in estrus scream to attract males, which have an orange patch and a black stripe between their shoulders.

IUCN status VU: Vulnerable; LC: Least Concern

Two-Toed Sloth

Species: Choloepus Hoffmanni • Best Seen: Cahuita, Corcovado, Tapantí-Macizo

🅲🐾🆅🐾🐾🐾   LC

This nocturnal animal has many similarities to its smaller three-toed cousin, but it has only two claws on its forelimbs, plus a more extensive diet that includes insects, fruit, and even birds' eggs. It has a cream-colored face and bulbous brown eyes. Although it crawls clumsily along the ground, it is a good swimmer. Females give birth to a single baby once a year and carry it clinging on their chests; if a baby falls, its calls are ignored and it is doomed – a meal for snakes, cats, or hawks.

Two-toed sloths are brown with pink noses

Northern Tamandua

Species: Tamandua Mexicana • Best Seen: Caño Negro, La Cruz, Santa Rosa

⭕🅲🐾🐾   LC

This semi-arboreal mammal, a dedicated eater of ants and termites, supplements its diet with tiny beetles and other insects. The tamandua has a coarse cream coat with a shoulder band and black flanks. It grows up to 35 in (88 cm) in length and uses its strong forearms and huge claws to tear open ant nests. Its elongated snout tapers to a tiny mouth, through which an extremely long, narrow tongue darts to lick up insects. Lacking teeth, it has a powerful gizzard for grinding its food. A long prehensile tail aids when climbing trees in its preferred habitats – lowland forests.

The northern tamandua is two-toned

Giant Anteater

Species: Myrmecophaga Tridactyla • Best Seen: Corcovado

⭕🐾🐾   VU

The largest of the three anteater species can exceed 7 ft (2.1 m) in length, half being its bushy tail and another 20 in (50 cm) its slender, curving snout, which provides a keen sense of smell. This gray, black, and white mammal shuffles along on its knuckles, like a chimpanzee. Its large front claws are perfect for ripping apart termite mounds, but also for defense – the anteater rears up on its hind legs to slash at attackers. This extremely rare animal has disappeared from most of its former range and is thought to be restricted to Corcovado.

The unmistakable profile of the giant anteater

Silky Anteater

Species: Cyclopes Didactylus • Best Seen: Braulio Carrillo, Corcovado, Monteverde

🅲🐾🐾🐾🐾   LC

Also called the pygmy anteater for its relatively small size, which rarely exceeds 18 in (45 cm), this nocturnal animal is arboreal by nature. During the day, it sleeps curled up into a ball high up a tree, and by night, it hunts for ants, termites, and beetles. Resembling a teddy bear, it has soft, honey-colored fur, a short pink snout, and a long prehensile tail. The silky anteater forages in a variety of forest types and nests in tree hollows, where it gives birth to a single pup.

The tiny silky anteater

For Key to Field Guide icons *see p65*

The agouti is quite relaxed in the presence of humans

Agouti

*Species: **Dasyprocta Punctata** • Best Seen: Corcovado, La Selva, Manuel Antonio, Monteverde*

LC

Known as *guatusa*, this large ground-dwelling rodent has grown so accustomed to humans that at many national parks it can be seen at close range, grooming or feeding. The agouti mostly eats palm nuts, which it buries for storage. Its chestnut-brown coat is glossy, and the male's rump hairs form a fan-shaped crest that is displayed during territorial disputes. Monogamous for life, the agouti breeds year-round. During courtship, the male sprays the female with urine.

Paca

*Species: **Cuniculus Paca** • Best Seen: Braulio Carrillo, Corcovado, Tortuguero*

L

A cousin of the agouti, the paca (called *tepezcuintle* in Costa Rica) is distinguished by its shiny dark-brown fur spotted with several parallel lines of white dots along its sides. If the agouti resembles a guinea pig, the paca is shaped like a giant tailless rat. A nocturnal animal, this herbivore enjoys a diet of seeds, roots, fruits, and flowers. A good climber and swimmer, where possible it flees to water to escape danger. It is illegally hunted for its tasty meat, and many *campesinos* (peasants) also raise pacas commercially.

The paca lives near mangrove swamps and river banks

The peccary bears a strong resemblance to the pig

Collared Peccary

*Species: **Pecari Tajacu** • Best Seen: Braulio Carrillo, Corcovado, Santa Rosa*

LC

One of two peccary species in Costa Rica, this large mammal is only distantly related to the pig, which it resembles. Standing up to 24 in (60 cm) tall, it is covered in thick gray bristles; it has short legs and a massive head tapering to a tiny snout used for sniffing out fruits, nuts, and tubers. It roams many lowland environments, from savanna to rainforest. The collared peccary typically lives in groups of up to 20 individuals. Herds of the more aggressive white-lipped peccary can contain more than 100 animals.

Cacomistle

*Species: **Bassariscus Sumichrasti** • Best Seen: Braulio Carrillo, Carara, Corcovado*

LC

Much smaller in size than its cousin, the raccoon, the cacomistle is also far rarer. Living in the upper levels of moist forests, it has been heavily impacted by deforestation – in Costa Rica it is listed as an endangered species. It has huge black eyes for vision while prowling at night for insects, small vertebrates, and fruit. With a narrow nose and extremely long, pointed ears, its face is catlike – indeed, cacomistle means "half-cat" in the Nahuatl language. At full stretch, it measures 3.3 ft (1 m) in length, equally divided between its body and its black-and-white hooped tail.

The cacomistle's tail makes up half of its body length

IUCN status DD: Data Deficient; LC: Least Concern

The Mexican tree porcupine has a bulbous snout

Mexican Tree Porcupine

Species: Sphiggurus Mexicanus • Best Seen: Rincón de la Vieja, Santa Rosa

LC

Porcupines belong to the Erethizontidae family of rodents. As its name suggests, the Mexican tree porcupine is arboreal and mostly nocturnal, with a prehensile tail that aids in maneuvering around the treetops. It inhabits most forest types but prefers drier habitats and is rare in rainforest. Covered almost entirely in thick quills mixed with white-tipped black fur, this porcupine has a small round head and a fleshy snout. It eats leaves, fruits, and seeds. Normally silent, it wails during breeding season and can emit a disagreeable, garlicky odor.

The red brocket deer has a distinctive rust-brown coat

Red Brocket Deer

Species: Mazama Americana • Best Seen: Arenal, Cahuita, Rincón de la Vieja

DD

Endemic to Central America, this small deer inhabits thick forests, where its rust-brown fur is camouflaged by dark shade. The red brocket deer's lower legs are edged with black, while its throat and inner legs are whitish. Juveniles have two rows of white spots running along each flank. Adult males can be up to 31 in (80 cm) tall at the shoulder, and they grow small, spike-like antlers. The red brocket deer dines mostly on fruits, but it also browses on leaves. A shy creature, it is less commonly seen than the white-tailed deer.

Kinkajou

Species: Potos Flavus • Best Seen: Corcovado, La Selva, Monteverde

LC

An arboreal mammal related to the cacomistle, raccoon, and olingo, the kinkajou is distinct among them for its prehensile tail. It uses its dexterous forepaws to hold and eat figs and other fruits and insects, and its long, extrudable tongue to scoop up honey and nectar. Kinkajous are social animals and sometimes forage in groups. They are hunted for their short golden fur, as well as for the illegal pet trade. Your best chance of seeing this nocturnal mammal is on a night tour.

A prehensile tail helps the kinkajou navigate the treetops

White-Tailed Deer

Species: Odocoileus Virginianus • Best Seen: Barra Honda, Caño Negro, Santa Rosa

LC

Slightly bigger than the red brocket deer, the white-tailed deer prefers grassland, wetlands, and dry deciduous forest over dense evergreen forests, and it is particularly active around dawn and dusk. It is gray-brown to rust in coloration and displays the white underside of its tail when alarmed. Capable of huge leaps, it relies on speed and agility to outwit cougars, coyotes, jaguars, and human hunters. Groups of up to ten individuals are frequently seen foraging together. Males spar for dominance in breeding season, when they lose weight due to a singular focus on mating.

A white-tailed deer at a water hole

Key to Field Guide icons *see p65*

The armadillo, with its distinctive banded armor

Nine-Banded Armadillo

Species: **Dasypus Novemcinctus** • *Best Seen:* **Arenal, Caño Negro, Santa Rosa**

LC

Of South American origin, the armadillo is protected by a bony shell of interlinked scales. Armed with powerful claws that have evolved for burrowing, it thrives only in soft-soil environments. It usually emerges at dusk to dig frantically for termites, grubs, and tubers. Although it typically ambles, it can flee quickly from danger and – being capable of holding its breath for several minutes – it can easily run along riverbeds or even swim across. The nine-banded armadillo can reach 42 in (110 cm) in length, nose to tail.

The opossum is a semi-arboreal marsupial

Common Opossum

Species: **Didelphis Marsupialis** • *Best Seen:* **Cahuita, Carara, La Selva**

LC

The opossum is the only marsupial in Costa Rica. A primitive yet adaptable creature, it inhabits a wide range of habitats below 6,600 ft (2,200 m), including urban environments. Active by night, it spends most of its time on the ground but can also climb trees in search of fruit and birds' eggs. Females give birth several times a year to tiny babies that emerge after only two weeks' gestation and climb into their mother's pouch to suckle.

IUCN status LC: Least Concern; NT: Near Threatened

Striped Hog-Nosed Skunk

Species: **Conepatus Semistriatus** • *Best Seen:* **Cahuita, Poás, Santa Rosa**

LC

This widespread medium-sized mammal belongs to its own family, the Mephitidae. A solitary creature that lives in habitats from lowland grassland and scrub to moist mid-elevation forest, the *zorrillo* (as it is known locally) emerges at night to hunt for fruit and small invertebrates. Including its long bushy tail, this black-and-white striped animal grows up to 20 in (50 cm) long. The skunk wards off potential predators by spraying a foul-smelling sulphurous chemical from its anal scent gland.

The skunk defends itself by releasing an offensive odor

Variegated Squirrel

Species: **Sciurus Variegatoides** • *Best Seen:* **Carara, Monteverde, San Gerardo de Dota**

LC

Related to the squirrels that are familiar to North Americans and Europeans, the variegated squirrel is endemic to Central America. This widespread rodent, the most frequently seen of five local squirrel species, has a copper-colored body with a black back and gray bushy tail, which typically curls along its back. It nests inside trees, and – unlike other squirrels – it feeds mostly on fruit. Bold by nature, it often scampers onto restaurant tables to steal patrons' fruit.

A variegated squirrel feeding on a coconut

The bulldog bat's wings can span 3.3 ft (1 m) across

Greater Bulldog Bat

Species: Noctilio Leporinus • Best Seen: Drake Bay, Gandoca-Manzanillo, Tortuguero

C 🐟

LC

Visitors to Tortuguero are virtually guaranteed a sighting of the greater bulldog bat, also known as "fishing" bat, swooping low over the lagoons to snatch fish with its long claws. Its reddish fur is water-repellent, and its narrow wings act as oars to gain speed and take off if it falls in the water. The greater bulldog bat can be seen wherever there are large bodies of water, including sheltered coves on both the Caribbean and Pacific shores. Like all bats, it uses echolocation to find prey.

A colony of Jamaican fruit bats roosting in a cave

Jamaican Fruit Bat

Species: Artibeus Jamaicensis • Best Seen: Arenal, Cahuita, Rincón de la Vieja

C 🌴 🏠 🕭 🍃 🐟 🌿

LC

One of the most important pollinators in the neotropics, this large bat has a huge wingspan – up to 16 in (40 cm) – although its body is usually no more than 4 in (10 cm) long. It has a short, broad snout topped by a nose leaf, and its gray-brown fur has a distinctive soapy smell. The bat snatches wild figs and other small fruits in flight and returns to its roost to eat the pulp. Like the Honduran white bat, it is one of 15 species that form a tent from large leaves; the Jamaican fruit bat prefers broad-leaf palms, but it also lives in hollow trees.

Honduran White Bat

Species: Ectophylla Alba • Best Seen: Cahuita, Hitoy-Cerere, Tortuguero

C 🏠

NT

This tiny bat averages less than 2 in (5 cm) in length. It has snow-white fur and orange nose, ears, legs, and wings. Mostly a fruit eater, it lives only in the Caribbean lowland rainforest, where it roosts communally, shoulder to shoulder, inside "tents" made by chewing the veins of heliconia leaves until they fold. Usually the group comprises a single male with his harem. Sunlight filtering through the leaf makes the Honduran white bat's fur appear green, providing camouflage.

Honduran white bats roosting together in a leaf

Common Vampire Bat

Species: Desmodus Rotundus • Best Seen: Barra Honda, Caño Negro, Santa Rosa

C 🏠 🕭 🍃 🐟 🌿

LC

Costa Rica has three vampire bat species that feed on the blood of cattle and other mammals and birds, usually while they sleep. This manner of eating bears a little resemblance to the way the eponymous vampire in Bram Stoker's novel *Dracula* feeds. A vampire bat typically crawls toward its victim, whose fur it trims with clipper-like teeth, then pierces the skin with two sharp fangs. Its saliva contains an anticoagulant substance called draculin, which permits it to suck up free-flowing blood. After feeding, the bat uses its powerful pectoral muscles to leap into the air and take flight.

The vampire bat has straw-like grooves in its tongue

Key to Field Guide icons *see p65*

Marine Mammals and Fish

Costa Rica's large pelagic animals include rays, sharks, dolphins, humpback whales, and other cetaceans. Whale- and dolphin-watching trips are a great way to see these creatures – whales are frequently seen in Golfo Dulce, Golfo de Nicoya, and in the warm waters surrounding Isla Caño and Isla Cocos. Scuba divers can enjoy close-up encounters with groupers, hammerhead sharks, whale sharks, and other marine creatures.

Family

Dolphins and whales are in the Cetacean order of air-breathing mammals that evolved for an aquatic life. Fish, on the other hand, belong to several dozen groups of loosely related marine vertebrates.

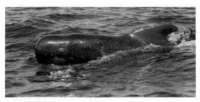
A short-finned pilot whale surfacing for air

Pilot Whale

Species: Globicephala Melas • Best Seen: Whale Marine National Park, Isla Caño

DD

An ocean nomad, this whale actually belongs to the dolphin family. It prefers deep waters, especially those at the edge of the continental shelf, where it feeds primarily on squid. Dark gray in color, the pilot whale is recognizable by its high, blunt forehead; sweeping dorsal fin set forward toward the rear of its head; and tiny tail flukes. It typically lives in groups of 10–30 individuals. Adult males can measure 16–20 ft (5–6 m), and females 11–17 ft (3.6–5.2 m).

Humpback Whale

Species: Megaptera Novaeangliae • Best Seen: Whale Marine National Park, Isla Caño, Drake Bay

LC

Twice a year (Dec–Mar and Jul–Oct), schools of humpback whales arrive in the waters off southwest Costa Rica to breed and give birth. These giants have long pectoral fins and a black-and-white tail fin; despite weighing up to 40 tons (36,000 kg), they perform spectacular leaps, or breaches. Males compose complex communal songs that are used in courtship.

A humpback whale performing an acrobatic breach

The bottlenose dolphin tracks its food by echolocation

Bottlenose Dolphin

Species: Tursiops Truncatus • Best Seen: Gulf of Papagayo, Whale Marine National Park, Golfo Dulce

LC

This playful and extremely intelligent creature with a gray body and pale-pink belly can grow to 12 ft (3.7 m) long and weigh up to 1,400 lb (635 kg), although those found in Costa Rican waters tend to be smaller. It mostly eats fish and squid, which it pursues at speeds up to 20 mph (30 km/h). Highly social, it typically lives in groups of several hundred individuals.

Spinner Dolphin

Species: Stenella Longirostris • Best Seen: Drake Bay, Gulf of Nicoya, Isla Caño

DD

This long, dark-gray mammal is named for its acrobatic displays, performed either singly or alongside a pod of fellow dolphins. Unusually long fins help power the spinner dolphin, which can leap high enough in the air to spin many times before splashing down in belly or back flops. It can even somersault. Spinner dolphins communicate by slapping the water and by trailing bubbles from their blowhole.

The slender spinner dolphin has a pencil-thin beak

IUCN status DD: Data Deficient; EN: Endangered; LC: Least Concern; NE: Not Evaluated; VU: Vulnerable

Intimidatingly large, the whale shark has a gentle nature

Whale Shark

Species: Rhincodon Typus • Best Seen: Gulf of Papagayo, Isla Caño, Isla Cocos

VU

This gentle giant – the world's largest fish – can grow to 40 ft (12 m), yet it is so docile that it will let swimmers touch it. It scoops up plankton and tiny sea creatures as it swims slowly, with its vast mouth open. Its gray upper body is marked with striped hoops interspersed with rings of pale spots; three ridges run along each flank. Whale sharks exist in large numbers around the Bat Islands, in the Gulf of Papagayo, and in the nutrient-rich waters around Cocos Island.

The unmistakable scalloped hammerhead

Hammerhead Shark

Species: Sphyrna Lewini • Best Seen: Gulf of Papagayo, Isla Caño, Isla Cocos

EN

The scalloped hammerhead, one of nine shark species named for a flattened cephalofoil head structure, inhabits Costa Rica's Pacific coastal waters and throngs around Isla Cocos. Its hammer-shaped head, lined with super-sensitive receptors for detecting prey, offers 360-degree binocular vision. Unlike most other sharks, hammerheads swim in huge schools that can number several hundred individuals. At night the group disbands, and individuals hunt solo for small fish. Females give birth to live young. Unlike several other hammerhead species, the scalloped hammerhead is not considered dangerous or aggressive to humans. Its population is threatened by fishing fleets, which capture hammerheads in nets and on lines, both inadvertently and deliberately, for the Asian food and medicinal trade.

Black Marlin

Species: Makaira Indica • Best Seen: Gulf of Papagayo, Central Pacific waters

NE

One of three marlin species in Costa Rican waters (along with the blue and striped marlins), the black marlin has a long, sharp upper jaw, or bill, which it uses to slash at small tuna and other prey. Its streamlined body is dark blue above and silvery-white below, with faint blue stripes. Capable of speeds up to 65 mph (100 km/h), it is the most highly prized game fish. However, local sport fishers practice catch-and-release, except for trophy-size specimens.

The black marlin, with its rapier-like upper jaw

Sailfish

Species: Istiophorus Platypterus • Best Seen: Gulf of Papagayo, Central Pacific waters

NE

Unlike its cousins the marlin and the swordfish, the sailfish has a huge dorsal fin that forms a retractable sail. Taller than the fish itself, this fin is laced with blood vessels and thought to aid in cooling and heating the fish as necessary. It is also useful when herding prey – groups of sailfish are known to corral schools of sardines and other fish. The sail is folded down for swimming. Like a chameleon, the sailfish can change body color and even flash iridescent hues using irregularly shaped cells containing crystals that control the distribution and absorption of pigment and light. Capable of incredible leaps, the sailfish is even faster under water than the black marlin.

The sailfish's dorsal fin runs the entire length of its back

Key to Field Guide icons *see p65*

Amphibians and Reptiles

Despite the fearsome reputation of toxic poison-dart frogs, venomous snakes with potentially lethal bites, and man-eating crocodiles, most of Costa Rica's amphibians and reptiles are perfectly harmless to humans. These cold-blooded creatures have variable body temperatures and depend on their surroundings for warmth, so they can frequently be spotted basking in the sun. Amphibians lay their eggs in fresh water, which they also need to stay moist. Prolific in warmer lowlands, they are relatively scarce at higher elevations.

Family

Reptiles are arranged in four orders, including Crocodilia, Squamata (snakes and lizards), and Testudines (turtles and tortoises). Amphibians belong to three orders: Anura (frogs and toads), Caudata (newts and salamanders), and the worm-like Gymnophiona.

Poison-Dart Frogs

Family: **Dendrobatidae** • *Best Seen:* **Barbilla, Braulio Carrillo, Corcovado, La Selva**

Most Species: Variable

Small (0.6–2.4 in/1.5–6 cm) and brightly colored, these ground-dwelling frogs are named for their toxic skin secretions, which derive from their diet of ants and tiny beetles. The poison varies in potency, and only two species of poison-dart frog found in Panama and Colombia are strong enough to kill humans. Costa Rica has seven species, including the red-and-blue Dendrobates pumilio and the green-and-black Dendrobates auratus. By day, poison-dart frogs hop about the moist forest floor, safe from predators thanks to their gaudy coloration, which serves to advertise their toxicity. Females lay their eggs in moist places. Newly hatched tadpoles typically hitch a ride on their mother's back to be carried to water, where they can feed. Dendrobates pumilio even deposits unfertilized eggs into the water as food.

The gaudily colored strawberry poison-dart frog

The charismatic red-eyed tree frog is a master of camouflage

Red-Eyed Tree Frog

Species: **Agalychnis Callidryas** • *Best Seen:* **Cahuita, Corcovado, La Selva**

LC

This arboreal frog has a lime-green body, blue sides streaked with yellow, orange toes, and red eyes with narrow black pupils. It measures 1.5–2.75 in (4–7 cm), but more than twice that with its limbs extended. An excellent climber, it moves slowly and stealthily, feeding on moths and other flying insects, which it snares with its long, sticky tongue. When in danger, it flashes its bright body parts to startle the predator and facilitate escape. The red-eyed tree frog is a nocturnal hunter, and by day it sleeps folded on the underside of large leaves, using suction cups on its feet to hang upside down. During breeding season (Oct–Mar), the forests at night resound with the croaking of males calling for mates.

IUCN status LC: Least Concern; NE: Not Evaluated

The glass frog's abdominal skin is transparent

Glass Frogs

Family: Centrolenidae • Best Seen: La Selva, Monteverde

C 🐸 🌿 🦎 🐦   Most Species: Variable

Named for their transparent bodies, glass frogs are nocturnal, mostly arboreal, difficult to spot in the wild, and generally small, rarely exceeding 3 in (7.5 cm). Although the upper body is green and often spotted, the abdominal skin is translucent, exposing the frog's internal organs, such as its heart, intestines, and liver. Some species are entirely transparent. Denizens of the humid forests of Costa Rica at most elevations, glass frogs are particularly common and diverse in montane cloud forests.

An anole lizard displaying its orange dewlap

Anoles

Family: Polychrotidae • Best Seen: Manuel Antonio, Rincón De La Vieja, Selva Verde

🌿 C 🐸 🌿 🦎 🐦 🌿   Most Species: Variable

Costa Rica has more than two dozen species of anoles, a common and diverse Neotropical lizard family that includes almost 400 species. They typically measure 3–8 in (8–20 cm) and have pointed snouts and long slender tails that they can break off to escape predators. Normally green or brown, anoles can change color depending on mood and temperature. Semi-arboreal and active by day, they stake out a territory around low-lying foliage. When an intruder is near, the male performs "push-ups" and displays the orange or red dewlap beneath its throat. If this does not scare away the intruder, a fight might ensue, in which the competitors bite at each other's necks.

Basilisk Lizard

Species: Basiliscus Plumifrons • Best Seen: Corcovado, Gandoca-Manzanillo, Tortuguero

⭕ 🌿 🦎 🦎   NE

Ranging from bright green to olive, the basilisk lizard is also known as the Jesus Christ lizard because it can dart across water thanks to its long, slender webbed toes, which create air pockets above the water and prevent it from sinking. It lives in lowland rainforests and usually close to streams – it is an excellent swimmer. It grows to about 2 ft (60 cm) in length. Males have crests atop their heads and backs, which they use to court females.

A basilisk lizard walking across a body of water

Gecko

Species: Hemidactylus Frenatus • Best Seen: Barra Honda, Cahuita, Santa Rosa

C 🌿 🌿 🦎 🦎   LC

Costa Rica has nine species of this adorable creature. The gecko is ubiquitous by night, its presence given away by its loud chirp, which is used by both sexes to attract mates and warn off competitors. One particular species, the house gecko, seems to find its way into every dwelling in Costa Rica. Measuring up to 6 in (15 cm), most geckos have velvety pinkish-gray skin with specks or stripes. They can scurry upside down across branches or ceilings thanks to their toe pads, which are covered with bristles, or setae, so fine they tap into electrical attraction at a molecular level. A devourer of mosquitoes, the gecko has such keen eyesight that it can detect color at night.

Geckos' toe bristles allow them to climb any surface

Key to Field Guide icons *see p65*

American Crocodile

Species: **Crocodylus Acutus** • *Best Seen:* **Barra del Colorado, Corcovado, Río Tárcoles, Tortuguero**

⬜🅲🆅🆅 VU

One of the largest members of the crocodile family – it can attain a length of 23 ft (7 m) – the American crocodile inhabits brackish tidal estuaries and lowland rivers from southern Florida to Venezuela. In Costa Rica, it is most populous in the lagoons of Tortuguero, on the Caribbean; the Tempisque and Tárcoles rivers; and Corcovado National Park, on the Pacific. Its broad, massive, olive-green body tapers to a narrow, elongated head. The American crocodile can remain submerged for more than one hour and is capable of rapid bursts of speed on land, where it spends long hours in the sun to heat its body. It primarily feeds on fish, but occasionally seizes unwary mammals that come to the rivers to drink. Males defend their aquatic territories against rivals. Females lay eggs in sandy nests in the dry season. Crocodiles are felicitous parents, and both male and female will guard the nest and young hatchlings to protect them from predators. American crocodiles use the ocean to migrate between rivers, and very rarely they have been known to attack surfers and swimmers. In recent years, they have even been spotted in Lake Arenal – at about 1,640 ft (500 m) elevation. How they got there is a mystery.

The crocodile's back features several lateral rows of raised scales that act like the keel of a boat.

The nostrils are located atop the snout, so the crocodile can breathe while under water.

The American crocodile can live to 80 years of age

The green iguana uses its well-developed dewlap in courtship displays

Green Iguana

Species: **Iguana Iguana** • *Best Seen:* **Corcovado, Manuel Antonio, Palo Verde, Santa Rosa**

⬜🅲🌸🐾🆅🆅🌿🐾 LC

The green iguana is a scaly, dragon-like lizard that can grow up to 6.6 ft (2 m), with its tail taking up half its length. Mature green iguanas can range in color from gray-olive to dark brown, although all juveniles are lime green. During the mating season (Nov–Dec), males turn bright orange and advertise their prowess as potential lovers from the treetops. The green iguana inhabits various low- and mid-elevation ecosystems throughout Costa Rica, and it roams on ground level, which it prefers on cold days to forest canopy. An agile climber, it eats flowers, fruits, and leaves. A spiny crest extends along its back, and it has a regenerative tail that it can discard to escape predators, which it detects with the aid of a rudimentary third eye atop its head. Females lay 20–70 eggs in nests in the ground, but newborns are left to fend for themselves.

IUCN status LC: Least Concern; NT: Near Threatened; VU: Vulnerable

Spectacled Caiman

*Species: **Caiman Crocodilus** • Best Seen: Caño Negro, Tortuguero, Gandoca-Manzanillo*

LC

Abundant throughout Costa Rica's Caribbean and Pacific lowland rivers and wetlands, this small olive-brown crocodilian is commonly seen basking in the sun along riverbanks. It grows up to 8 ft (2.5 m) in length and is easily identified by dark crossbands on its body and tail, and by a bony ridge resembling the bridge of a pair of spectacles between its eyes – hence its name. A nocturnal hunter, it eats mainly fish and amphibians. Caimans breed primarily in wet season. Females lay up to 40 eggs in nests scraped together from leaves, twigs, and sand; males help guard them. Raccoons prey on the nests, and baby caimans can be seized by herons and other birds of prey.

Spectacled caimans basking in the sun along a riverbank

The Mesoamerican slider turtle has an olive-green neck with yellow markings

Slider Turtle

*Species: **Trachemys Scripta** • Best Seen: Caño Negro, Palo Verde, Tortuguero, Gandoca-Manzanillo*

NT

The slider turtle, the most common of the eight species of freshwater turtles found in Costa Rica, has two subspecies: the ornate slider and the Mesoamerican, or Nicaraguan, slider, limited to the extreme north of the country. This medium-sized turtle – it grows to 24 in (60 cm) – has dark-olive skin striped with yellow markings, yellow eyes, and a yellow underside to its carapace. They are usually seen in or close to large ponds and rivers, or sunning on partially submerged rocks or logs, often piled up one atop the other. Slider turtles are omnivores and eat anything from insects and fish to aquatic vegetation. They mate in spring and fall, when they sink to the bottom of the river- or lake bed to copulate. Females can store sperm for several months. The population is at risk from illegal poaching for the pet trade.

Key to Field Guide icons *see p65*

Marine Turtles

Five of the world's seven marine turtle species nest on Costa Rican beaches. Although they differ in shape and size, they all share the same lineage. Sea turtles begin life as hatchlings when they emerge from their sandy nests and crawl to the sea. The nest's ambient temperature determines the gender of the hatchlings, only a tiny fraction of which will survive to adulthood. Males will never return to land, while females come ashore to lay eggs. Turtle populations have seen a sharp decline, and two species are on the verge of extinction.

Family

Each of Costa Rica's five marine turtle species is the only species in its genus, except the ridley, which is one of two species in the Lepidochelys genus. All belong to the Cheloniidae family, except the leatherback, the sole member of the Dermochelyidae family.

The leatherback turtle, with its teardrop-shaped body

Leatherback Turtle

Species: **Dermochelys Coriacea** • *Best Seen:*
Gandoca-Manzanillo, Playa Grande

 CR

The largest of the sea turtles, the leatherback can measure 6.5 ft (2 m) and weigh up to 1,200 lb (550 kg). It roams the world's oceans powered by massive front flippers. Its body is pewter-colored, pink underneath, covered with white blotches, and lined with seven ridges for hydrodynamic efficiency. Instead of a hard carapace, it has thick cartilaginous skin overlaying a matrix of small, polygonal bones and fatty flesh that permits it to resist the extreme cold of Arctic waters and the pressure of deep ocean dives. Backward spines in its throat aid in eating slippery jellyfish, its main food source. Female leatherbacks nest at night on both the Caribbean (Feb–Jul) and Pacific (Oct–Mar) shores of Costa Rica and prefer soft-sand beaches facing deep water, such as Pacuaré and Playa Grande. The female lays 50–100 eggs in a deep nest dug with her rear flippers, before filling in the pit by flinging sand with her front flippers. The leatherback matures at about 10 years and can live to 40 years or more. These turtles are listed as critically endangered due to ocean pollution, incidental capture by long lines and drift nets, and the poaching of eggs by animals and humans.

Loggerhead turtles feeding on algae

Loggerhead Turtle

Species: **Caretta Caretta** • *Best Seen: Gandoca-Manzanillo, Tortuguero*

EN

With the exception of its copper-colored shell, the loggerhead turtle is similar in size and appearance to the green turtle. The males fight to copulate with the females, which mate with several partners and can store sperm until ovulation. Like all turtles, the female loggerhead lays as many as 50–100 eggs, principally nesting on the Caribbean shores of Costa Rica, and more infrequently on the Pacific side. As an omnivore, the loggerhead turtle has a varied diet, but it mostly feeds on bottom-dwelling invertebrates, which it crushes with its powerful jaws.

IUCN status CR: Critically Endangered; EN: Endangered; VU: Vulnerable

The hawksbill's beak-like mouth is an effective weapon

Hawksbill Turtle

Species: Eretmochelys Imbricata • Best Seen: Gandoca-Manzanillo

⬤🄲🐢 CR

This delicate-looking mid-sized (up to 39 in/ 1 m in length) turtle is in fact extremely aggressive – it is named for its sharp beak-like mouth, which it uses to defend itself. It prefers shallow coastal waters and is frequently seen swimming around coral reefs. A solitary nester, the hawksbill turtle comes ashore in Costa Rica along both coasts; Atlantic and Pacific subspecies differ slightly in coloration. Adults eat all manner of sealife, including Portuguese man- of-war jellyfish, whose toxins make hawksbill meat unpalatable to humans. This turtle is targeted by hunters for its uniquely patterned, reddish-brown, and slightly iridescent carapace, which is used to make jewelry and trinkets. Artificial plastic with tortoise-shell patterns has only partially helped stem poaching, and today this beautiful creature is critically endangered. The hawksbill has large scales between its eyes, and the yellow-fringed scutes (plates) of its serrated, shield-shaped shell overlap.

Green Turtle

Species: Chelonia Mydas • Best Seen: Gandoca-Manzanillo, Pacuare, Tortuguero

⬤🄲🐢 EN

The green turtle is the largest of the shelled species and can grow up to 5 ft (1.5 m) in length. Named for the green layer of fat under its shell, it has a small round head and a broad, heart-shaped carapace closely resembling that of the smaller hawksbill turtle, though the green turtle's shell ranges in color from olive green to chestnut or ocher. Uniquely, this turtle is a herbivore and grazes on shallow-water sea grasses. It has separate Atlantic and Pacific populations, and in Costa Rica it is primarily found at Tortuguero National Park, which, between June and November, is the species' main nesting site in the western hemisphere. In common with other shelled turtles, the male has a hook on each front flipper with which he grasps the female during copulation. Females mate every two to four years and lay 100–200 eggs. The green turtle's population appears to have stabilized after being decimated for the turtle-soup industry.

The herbivorous green turtle has a heart-shaped shell

Olive Ridley

Species: Lepidochelys Olivacea • Best Seen: Camaronal, Ostional, Santa Rosa

⬤🄲🐢 VU

The smallest of Costa Rica's five turtle species, averaging 24–28 in (60–70 cm), the olive ridley is remarkable for nesting en masse at a few select locations worldwide. In Costa Rica, these include five or six beaches along the shores of Nicoya and Guanacaste, mainly at Ostional and Nancite. Each female nests up to three times per season. Synchronized arrivals take place as often as twice-monthly from July to December, peaking in August and September, when tens of thousands of female turtles arrive to lay eggs on the beach where they were born. The ridley's omnivorous diet includes algae, shrimp, and lobster.

Olive ridleys are thought to be the most abundant turtles

Key to Field Guide icons see p65

Snakes

Although snakes are present in most habitats in Costa Rica, seeing them is not easy as they are reclusive and mostly nocturnal. Most of the country's 135 recorded snake species are fairly harmless; 17 are venomous; and nine are classed as highly venomous. Pit vipers, for example, named for the heat-sensitive organs (pits) between their eye and nostril, can inflict lethal bites. It is wise to keep a safe distance regardless of the species.

Family

Costa Rica's snakes belong to the Squamata order, like their close relatives, the lizards, from which they descended. Costa Rica has nine families of snakes, with Colubridae the largest.

A brown vine snake slithering among the trees

Vine Snakes

Family: **Colubridae; Genus: Oxybelis** • Best Seen: **Caño Negro, Carara, Corcovado, Tortuguero**

 LC

Costa Rica has two species of the mildly venomous vine snake. These extremely slender brown or bright-green reptiles have adapted for a life in the trees, where they feed primarily on birds. Measuring up to 6.6 ft (2 m) yet barely 0.8 in (2 cm) thick, they have pointed heads and large eyes. Vine snakes live in humid habitats at lower elevations.

Boas

Family: **Boidae** • Best Seen: **Braulio Carrillo, Cahuita, Manuel Antonio, Santa Rosa**

LC

The thick-bodied boa constrictor is the largest snake in Costa Rica, growing to a length of 10 ft (3 m). Two smaller rainbow boa species also strangle their prey, and live only in moist areas. These wide-ranging snakes are semi-arboreal. All are patterned cream, gray, and brown, with darker saddles; they shine with a blue radiance when exposed to direct light.

A boa constrictor coiled around a tree branch

A young mussurana, recognizable by its bright-red skin

Mussurana

Species: **Clelia Clelia** • Best Seen: **Braulio Carrillo, Caño Negro, La Selva, Tortuguero**

LC

The mussurana is harmless to humans and remarkable for feeding on other snakes. People are known to keep one in the house as a measure against vipers, to whose venom it is resistant. Pink or bright red when young, mussuranas later turn dark gray with a cream belly, and can exceed 6.6 ft (2 m). They are found only in the Caribbean lowlands.

Yellow-Bellied Sea Snake

Species: **Pelamis Platurus** • Best Seen: **Golfo de Papagayo, Isla Caño**

LC

Often seen washed up on Pacific beaches, the yellow-bellied sea snake spends its entire life at sea, feeding on fish and eels, and propelling itself with its spatulate tail. Averaging 18–25 in (45–65 cm) in length, it is black above with a yellow belly. Although extremely venomous, this sea snake is docile and reluctant to strike.

The yellow-bellied sea snake swims in coastal waters

IUCN status LC: Least Concern

The Neotropical rattlesnake has thick brown scales

Neotropical Rattlesnake

Species: Crotalus Durissus • Best Seen: Barra Honda, Palo Verde, Rincón de la Vieja, Santa Rosa

C 🌿   LC

The only rattlesnake in Costa Rica, the *cascabel*, as it is known locally, is found solely on the Northern Pacific slopes. It prefers low-elevation dry forest, savanna, and scrub, for which it is well camouflaged, with a blotchy beige-and-brown skin patterned with dark triangles and diamonds. Twin stripes run along the top of its neck. When threatened, this stout snake vibrates its rattle and lifts the front third of its body off the ground in preparation to strike. Its venom is one of the most toxic of all rattlesnake species.

Female fer-de-lances are much larger than the males

Fer-De-Lance

Species: Bothrops Asper • Best Seen: Cahuita, Corcovado, La Selva, Tortuguero

C 🏠 🌿 🌿   LC

This large, highly venomous pit viper, called *terciopelo* (meaning "velvet") locally, is the most feared snake in Costa Rica, accounting for half of all bites and most fatalities. Growing to 8 ft (2.5 m) and about as thick as a man's arm, the fer-de-lance inhabits a wide range of lowland habitats and is common along riverbanks. It is easily identified by its skin pattern of diamonds and diagonal stripes in various shades of brown and by its large, flat, sharply triangular head (fer-de-lance means "spearhead" in French), which is pale yellow on the underside. Mostly nocturnal, it rests in leaf litter by day. Unpredictable when disturbed, it is aggressive and fast-moving in defense. Females give birth to 20–100 live young, which are fully envenomed and potentially as deadly as their parents.

Eyelash Viper

Species: Bothriechis Schlegelii • Best Seen: Braulio Carrillo, Cahuita, Corcovado, Tortuguero

⚪ C 🏠 🌿 🌿   LC

The sinister beauty and small size (22–32 in/ 55–80 cm) of this forest-dwelling pit viper belie its potentially lethal bite. Named for the large scales over its eyes, this nocturnal arboreal snake can be bright yellow, olive green, brown, and sometimes pink. It lives in moist forests up to 4,900 ft (1,500 m) and spends its days coiled up on branches; hikers should watch where they put their hands. Males compete for females by facing off with heads erect and attempting to push the other to the ground.

Eyelash vipers from the same litter can be of various colors

Coral Snakes

Family: Elapidae; Genus: Micrurus • Best Seen: Cahuita, Carara, Gandoca-Manzanillo, Tortuguero

⚪ C 🌿 🏠 🌿 🌿   LC

Distinctive for their black, red, and yellow/white banding, coral snakes possess the most potent venom of all New World snakes. Small – less than 3.3 ft (1 m) – and with tiny heads, they spend most of their time underground or in leaf litter, emerging to breed or hunt for frogs, lizards, rodents, and other prey. Unlike vipers, coral snakes have non-retractable teeth and hold on to a victim when biting. The rhyme "red on yellow, kill a fellow; red on black, friend of Jack," used to identify coral snakes in North America, does not apply in Costa Rica, where the order of the bands cannot be used as a gauge. Costa Rica has four species of coral snakes, across a range of lowland and mid-elevation habitats. Allen's coral snake is found only in the Caribbean lowlands.

A red-and-black coral snake in leaf litter

Key to Field Guide icons *see p65*

Birds

Boasting over 800 species grouped into 75 different families, Costa Rica's avifauna is exceptionally varied, exceeding that of the USA and Canada combined. More than 630 are resident species, although only six are endemic. Any part of the country is suited to successful birding, with many places offering the chance to see more than 100 species a day. Avian diversity peaks between October and April, when migrants flock in.

Family

A growing body of genetic and fossil evidence suggests that birds are most properly placed with crocodiles as the only living members of the Archosauria family, a group that also includes the extinct dinosaurs.

The colorful scarlet macaw is spectacular in flight

Scarlet Macaw

Species: Ara Macao • Relatives: Green macaw

LC

The smaller of Costa Rica's two macaw species, the scarlet macaw grows up to 36 in (90 cm) in length. It has a scarlet body and tail, turquoise rump, bright-yellow upper wings, and blue wing feathers. Today it occupies only a fraction of its former range throughout three-quarters of Costa Rica, being almost entirely restricted to Carara National Park and the Peninsula de Osa. Seasonally monogamous, the scarlet macaw emits loud, throaty squawks, especially when flying in pairs or flocking at clay licks. It nests in cavities in tall trees, where females lay one or two eggs (Dec–Apr).

Keel-Billed Toucan

Family: Ramphastos Sulfuratus • Relatives: Chestnut-mandibled toucan, collared aracari, emerald toucanet, fiery-billed aracari, yellow-eared toucanet

LC

Costa Rica has six of the 42 toucan species, a Neotropical family of short-bodied birds with colorful, oversize beaks. The most recognizable is the keel-billed toucan, with a black body, yellow bib, red abdomen, and rainbow-hued bill. The chestnut-mandibled toucan has a brown and yellow bill; the two aracari species have red, yellow, and black bills; and the toucanets have smaller, green bodies. Toucans – whose main food is fleshy fruit, supplemented by small reptiles, hatchlings stolen from nests, and eggs – eat by throwing their head back and dropping the food into their throat.

The toucan's beak is lightweight and serrated like a saw

The great green macaw, found in the northern lowlands

Great Green Macaw

Species: Ara Ambiguus • Relatives: Scarlet macaw

CR

The second largest of the world's 17 macaw species, the great green, or Buffon's, macaw is known locally as *lapa verde* or *guacamayo*. It sports a bright-red fuzzy forehead, lime-green plumage that merges into teal-blue wings, and a blue-and-scarlet tail. Its massive hooked beak is designed to break open the nut of the *almendro* tree, its main food. As a result of deforestation and poaching for the illegal pet trade, only an estimated 300 great green macaws remain in the wild, including about 50 breeding pairs.

IUCN status CR: Critically Endangered; LC: Least Concern

The cattle egret's S-shaped neck gives it a hunched look

Cattle Egret

Species: **Bubulcus Ibis** • *Relatives:* **Bare-throated tiger heron, great blue heron, green heron, snowy egret**

   LC

This graceful, snow-white heron species is ubiquitous in open lowland habitats, mainly grassland, where it accompanies cattle and feeds on insects and small creatures such as frogs and lizards. It stands up to 22 in (56 cm) tall and has a short, stout neck, which it keeps drawn in an S-curve or tucked between its shoulders. Juveniles have black beaks that turn yellow as adults. In breeding season, its legs and bill turn red, and both sexes sprout orange plumes on the neck and back. Male egrets woo a different mate each season and display by raising their bills skyward and shaking twigs. It is common to see colonies roosting together in trees, usually beside rivers. The cattle egret is easily confused with the larger snowy egret, which has a black bill and legs.

Blue-Crowned Motmot

Species: **Momotus Momota** • *Relatives:* **Broad-billed motmot, keel-billed motmot, rufous motmot, tody motmot, turquoise-browed motmot**

   LC

The most commonly seen member of the Momotidae family, the blue-crowned motmot is a low- and mid-elevation woodland species averaging 17 in (42 cm) beak to tail. It has a green body and wings, orange chest, and turquoise face with a black mask around its red eyes. Its long blue, bare-shafted tail with racket tips swings like a pendulum to warn predators. A heavy bill is good for skewering insects and lizards, but this bird also eats fruit and can even consume poison-dart frogs. Often living in colonies, the motmot makes its nest in a long tunnel that it carves from soil banks. Its call – "oot oot" – resembles that of an owl.

The blue-crowned motmot, with its distinctive tail

Montezuma Oropendola

Species: **Psarocolius Montezuma** • *Relatives:* **Chestnut-headed oropendola**

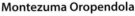   LC

A common resident of humid forests up to 3,300 ft (1,000 m), the oropendola is a deep-chestnut color, with a black head, turquoise cheeks, a pink wattle, an orange-tipped bill, and a bright-yellow tail. Averaging 20 in (50 cm), this bird lives in colonies of up to 60 individuals, choosing tall, free-standing trees in which females weave vines and twigs into pendulous nests that can be as long as 6.6 ft (2 m). When courting (Jan–May), the polygamous male makes rapid cooing calls and performs a complete somersault around a branch. A male will peck a female to ruffle her feathers prior to mating. The oropendola's diet consists of fruit, insects, and small vertebrates.

The Montezuma oropendola is a gregarious bird

Key to Field Guide icons *see p65*

Resplendent Quetzal

Catching a glimpse of the Resplendent quetzal – the largest and most striking member of the Trogon family and one of the most beautiful tropical birds – is the reason many people visit Costa Rica. The male, with its iridescent metallic-green feathers and arrestingly intense blood-red chest, bedazzles everyone who sees it in its mountainous cloud forest habitat, which ranges from southern Mexico to western Panama. It also features 24-in (60-cm) long tail feathers that it uses to impress females during mating displays. The female is less flamboyant.

The pit of the wild avocado fruit is too big to pass through the quetzal's digestive tract, so the bird vomits it up after digesting the pulp.

Feeding

Although the quetzal's mixed diet includes caterpillars, insects, and even small frogs and lizards, this bird is primarily a frugivore that relies on wild avocados (aguacatillos) and other fruits of the laurel family. The quetzal is an altitudinal migrant, and its seasonal movements – between 3,280 ft and 9,840 ft (1,000 m and 3,000 m) – are dictated by the fruiting of various laurel species at different times of year. The bird swallows the fruit whole and eventually regurgitates the pit, in the process becoming an important propagator of the laurel tree. The quetzal is threatened by deforestation at lower altitudes, to which it descends during the non-breeding season.

Young quetzals are fed larvae, insects, and worms

Family and Breeding

A solitary bird when not breeding, the Resplendent quetzal is monogamous and territorial in the breeding season (Feb–Apr). The couple use their beaks to hollow out nests in soft, dead, or rotten trees. The cock and the hen take turns incubating the pale-blue eggs – the male by day and the female by night. Hatchlings typically emerge after 18 days, to be fed insects, larvae, and worms by both parents. Eventually, the female abandons the nest, leaving her young in the care of the male. Fledglings leave the nest after about one month.

What you Might See

The quetzal initiates flight by dropping backward from its perch. Its flight is undulating, powered by intermittent and rapid wing beats. It feeds mid-flight on wild avocados. During breeding season, the male makes spiraling flights to drive competitors away from its nest site, which is often an abandoned woodpecker nest.

The male looks after the eggs by day and cares for the young when the female flees the nest.

The quetzal's small, convex wings are well adapted for flying through dense forests.

IUCN status NT: Near Threatened

The quetzal's wing feathers are unusually long and appear fringed. The male also sports a spiky crest of filamentous feathers extending down the face and partially covering its yellow beak. His two coverts – streamer-like main tail feathers – cross each other above the end of the tail.

The Aztecs and the Mayas worshiped the Resplendent quetzal as a living depiction of Quetzalcoatl, the plumed serpent god. The male's tail feathers, used in ceremonies, were considered more precious than gold, and only nobles and priests were allowed to wear them. The bird's name derives from the Aztec word quetzalli, meaning "long plume."

Communication and Voice

The male quetzal is a true showman that attempts to impress a potential mate by flaunting its extraordinary tail feathers in spectacular mid-flight displays. Loose and slender, the feathers ripple gracefully behind it like the long ribbons of a rhythmic gymnast as the quetzal flies upward then swoops down in a graceful arc. Male quetzals also vocalize with at least six distinct calls, including a repetitive and slightly slurred "kwuee, kwuee, kwuee", shrill calls that resemble a cat's meow, and the striking of a high-pitched tuning fork.

The male quetzal has several very distinct calls

KEY FACTS

Pharomachrus mocinno

Local Name: **None**

Size Body length: 14–16 in (36–40 cm); Tail (male): 24 in (60 cm); Weight: 7–8 oz (200–225 g).

Lifespan 8–10 years.
Population in Costa Rica 2,800–4,800.
Conservation Status NT.
Incubation Period 17–18 days.
Reproduction Females begin to reproduce in their second year and lay one or two eggs each season.

Habitat Humid subtropical forests and clearings above 3,300 ft (1,000 m).

Top Places to See Chirripó, La Amistad, Monteverde, San Gerardo de Dota.

Sighting Tips
The male's tail feathers are so long that they sometimes stick outside the nest.

Friends and Foes
Adults are weak flyers, and they must keep a wary eye out for raptors. Olingos and other arboreal mammals raid nests.

Facts and Trivia
The Resplendent quetzal is difficult to keep in captivity due to its fragility. There is only one known case of it being successfully bred.

Males' tail feathers begin to grow at three years, forming a train longer than its body.

The quetzal's iridescent plumage can vary from blue-violet to green-gold.

Quetzals are sedate birds and will perch motionless on branches for hours on end.

Black Vulture

Species: Coragyps Atratus • Relatives: King vulture, turkey vulture, yellow-headed vulture

LC

Known by Costa Ricans as zopilote, this black-feathered scavenger is present nation-wide below 6,600 ft (2,000 m). It stands 25.5 in (65 cm) tall and has a 5-ft (1.5-m) wing-span. The black vulture has a bald dark-gray head and a short hooked beak. It is frequently seen sunning with its wings outstretched, or hovering in the sky with its eye out for road kill and other carrion, its main food.

King Vulture

Species: Sarcoramphus Papa • Relatives: Black vulture, turkey vulture, yellow-headed vulture

LC

A relative of the Andean condor, with a 6.6-ft (2-m) wingspan, the king vulture is a large lowland forest dweller. It has a white body and black wing and tail feathers; its bare neck, face, and beak are gaily colored in red, yellow, black, and purple. Mature birds also have a wrinkled fleshy swelling atop their beaks. The king vulture soars high in the sky; a sighting would be considered a feather in the cap for any birder.

Harpy Eagle

Species: Harpia Harpyja • Relatives: Black hawk-eagle, crested eagle, ornate hawk-eagle

NT

By far the largest raptor in the Americas, this huge eagle is found in Costa Rica only in the Osa Peninsula and Talamancas. It is slate gray, with a white underside, black-and-white striped legs, and a pale-gray head crowned by an Elizabethan-style ruff. It hunts monkeys, sloths, and other prey in the rainforest canopy using its massive talons. The harpy builds a large nest high in a tree; females lay two eggs, but only the first is hatched.

Northern Caracara

Species: Caracara Cheriway • Relatives: Red-throated caracara, yellow-head caracara

LC

One of the most common birds of prey in Costa Rica, the northern caracara is a lazy hunter that prefers to scavenge carrion. It is often seen stalking crabs and eels washed up on beaches, or perched roadside awaiting a chance kill. Standing up to 23 in (58 cm), it is brown except for a cream chest and head capped in black, plus yellow legs and a red cere at the base of its sharply hooked gray beak.

Slaty-Tailed Trogon

Species: Trogon Massena • Relatives: Collared trogon, emerald trogon, violaceous trogon

LC

Like all of Costa Rica's 11 trogon species, this cousin of the resplendent quetzal (*see pp96–7*) has an iridescent-green body, a short bill, and a long tail. Its abdomen is blood red. The slaty-tailed trogon likes humid lowland forest and can spend hours motionless on a perch. It flies short distances on sallies to snatch insects and fruits on the wing, and it makes its home in rotten trees or termite nests.

Fiery-Throated Hummingbird

Species: Panterpe Insignis • Relatives: Green-crowned brilliant, rufous-tailed hummingbird

LC

One of the most colorful of Costa Rica's 54 hummingbird species, this handsome bird is found only in the highlands. It grows to 4.5 in (11 cm) in length and has scintillating green and blue plumage, an orange throat, and a blue chest. It uses its straight, black bill to feed on tiny insects and the nectar of bromeliads and epiphytes. Males aggressively defend their territories against competitors.

IUCN status LC: Least Concern; NT: Near Threatened; VU: Vulnerable

Three-Wattled Bellbird

Species: Procnias Tricarunculata • *Relatives:*
Bare-necked umbrella-
bird, snowy cotinga

VU

This elusive denizen of the
cloud forest is famous for
the male's distinctive three-
part vocalization, which
resembles the clang of a
bell. Growing up to 12 in
(30 cm) long, it has a copper-
colored body, a white head,
and three worm-like wattles
dangling from atop its
bill (hence its name). Its
population is in rapid decline,
but lucky birders might see
one in Monteverde.

Sunbittern

Species: Eurypyga Helias • *Relatives:*
Sungrebe

LC

The sole member of the
Eurypygidae family, this bird is
similar to a heron but with a
more horizontal posture and
shorter legs. The sunbittern stalks
small vertebrates and fish along
streams and ponds in lowland
forest. Its plumage – in multiple
shades of gray, black, and brown
– is broken up with linear
patterns for camouflage in
dappled sunlight. During
courtship, or when threatened, it
spreads its wings to display vivid
red, yellow, and black eyespots.

Great Curassow

Species: Crax Rubra • *Relatives:*
Black guan

VU

The great curassow is a large
ground bird with dark-brown or
black feathers and a black-and-
white striped head topped by a
prominent, forward-curling
crest. The male's plumage has a
lustrous blue sheen. Restricted
to national parks as a result of
hunting and deforestation, it
lives in lowland humid forests,
such as at La Selva Biological
Station. The curassow runs
rather than flies, and forages in
the undergrowth for fruits,
seeds, and insects.

Blue Dacnis

Species: Dacnis Cayana • *Relatives:*
Scarlet-thighed dacnis, yellow-
throated euphonia

LC

A characteristic passerine, this
brightly colored member of
the tanager family stands out
for its azure plumage and
turquoise cap, which contrast
against its black wings and eye
mask. The female is bright
green, with blue head and
shoulders. Common in the
Pacific lowlands, the blue
dacnis likes to hawk its insect
prey at the forest edge, but it
is also often seen feasting at
banana feeders placed in hotel
gardens to draw butterflies.

Green Honeycreeper

Species: Chlorophanes Spiza
• *Relatives: Gray-headed tanager,*
red-legged honeycreeper

LC

Preferring the forest canopy
and clearings, this 5.5-in
(14-cm) long bird has a cyan
body, teal wings, a black
hood, and a yellow beak.
The grass-green female has a
straw-yellow throat but lacks
the beautiful iridescence of
the male. Its sleek profile,
upright stance, and long,
decurved bill give it a haughty
posture. A fruit eater, it
supplements its diet with
nectar and insects, and it
often feeds in flocks.

Great Antshrike

Species: Taraba Major • *Relatives:*
Dusky antbird, russet antshrike,
scaled antpitta

LC

One of more than 30 related
birds that specialize in feasting
on ants and termites, the
great antshrike is a striking
two-tone bird with brilliant
red eyes. The male is black
with a white abdomen and
white wing bars; the female
is reddish. It typically hunts in
pairs, using its sharp, heavy
beak to pick at insects and
skewer larger prey as it skulks
about the dense forest
undergrowth. It wags its tail
feathers while it sings.

Key to Field Guide icons *see p65*

Anhinga

Species: Anhinga Anhinga • Relatives: Neotropic cormorant

☐ 🖐 🖐   LC

Commonly seen swimming with only its neck above the water surface, this large freshwater bird has evolved for diving in search of fish and amphibians. It dries out its feathers by perching on branches and spreading its wings. Mostly black, with a brownish neck and a yellow beak, the anhinga has wings streaked with silver feathers. It has a long bill and a very long, S-shaped neck that explains its more common name: snakebird.

Northern Jacana

Species: Jacana Spinosa • Relatives: Wattled jacana

☐ 🖐 🖐   LC

Jacanas are medium-sized wetland birds with long legs and huge elongated toes that enable them to walk atop floating vegetation. Unusually among birds, the female is not monogamous, mating with up to four males, each of which builds and defends its own nest and raises the young alone. With its chestnut body, black head and neck, and yellow bill, the Northern jacana is a handsome sight tripping across the water lilies at Caño Negro Wildlife Refuge.

Jabiru Stork

Species: Jabiru Mycteria • Relatives: Wood stork

☐ 🖐   L

The huge Jabiru stork is unmistakable thanks to its massive and intimidating black bill, which is upturned at the tip. Standing up to 5 ft (1.5 m) tall, it is a common sight along rivers and wetlands such as Palo Verde National Park, where it lives in large groups that forage for fish and amphibians. It is conspicuous for its snow-white body and wings, which contrast with the red band around its neck and its soot-black head and legs.

White Ibis

Species: Eudocimus Albus • Relatives: Glossy ibis, roseate spoonbill

☐ 🖐 🖐   LC

The sight of white ibis flying with necks outstretched is a genuine thrill for birders. Colonial by instinct, the white ibis nests communally, often with hundreds of other individuals. Its preferred habitats are mangroves and brackish marshes. Its long, downcurved bill and gray-pink face mask turn flush during mating season. The black tips of its wings can be seen only in flight – the bird is all white when at rest.

Roseate Spoonbill

Species: Platalea Ajaja • Relatives: Green ibis, white-face ibis

☐ 🖐   LC

Inhabiting shallow freshwater and brackish lagoons, this bird is named for its spatulate bill, which it sweeps from side to side in the water to sift aquatic beetles and vertebrates. This long-necked wader stands up to 31 in (80 cm) tall atop long legs. Its back, neck, and head are typically white, while its pink wing plumage derives from the shrimp in its diet. Like other members of the Threskiornithidae family, it lays eggs in a treetop stick nest.

Boat-Billed Heron

Species: Cochlearius Cochlearius • Relatives: Bare-throated tiger heron, tri-colored heron

     L

One of the oddest-looking members of the heron family, the boat-billed heron has a big beak that is far broader than it is deep, looking like an upturned boat. Its huge black eyes hint at its nocturnal nature. Gray, fawn, and white, this handsome bird lives in mangroves and at the edge of freshwater habitats, where it hunts frogs, crabs, and fish. It will crouch for hours, awaiting prey.

Bare-Throated Tiger Heron

Species: Tigrisoma Mexicanum • Relatives: Great blue heron, green heron

 LC

This elegant upright wader is up to 3 ft (90 cm) tall, with a long, thick neck and gray-brown feathers striped with black streaks. Juveniles have more pronounced "tiger stripes" against their orange plumage. The most wide-spread of several beautiful heron species, it is often seen standing motionless beside watercourses and ponds, ready to skewer fish and frogs with its long yellow bill.

Blue-Winged Teal

Species: Anas Discors • Relatives: Fulvous whistling duck, mallard

LC

A seasonal migrant, this small duck flocks to Costa Rica in the winter months to escape the snows of North America and to breed; it is usually among the first migrants to arrive in the fall. Mottled brown with a gray-blue head and a black beak, it is named for its sky-blue wing patches. The mallard, well known in temperate countries for the iridescent-green head of the male, is another among 16 duck species in Costa Rica.

Muscovy Duck

Species: Cairina Moschata • Relatives: American wigeon, Northern pintail

LC

Despite its name, this large non-migratory duck is native to Central America – indeed, the male's hissing call is one of the distinctive sounds of the wetlands. Reaching up to 34 in (86 cm) in length, this bird has an iridescent black-green plumage with white wing patches, white neck, and a bright-red, heavily wrinkled eye patch. An avid insect eater, it helps keep down mosquito populations by gobbling their larvae.

Blue-Footed Booby

Species: Sula Nebouxii • Relatives: Brown booby, masked booby

LC

A delight to watch, either in flight or performing its courtship dance, the blue-footed booby nests on rocky offshore islands from Nicoya to Isla del Coco. This long-winged seabird has fawn and white plumage and bright-blue feet, which the male displays – first one foot, then the other – to impress females while pointing its head and tail skyward. It feeds on fish and has nostrils that are sealed for diving.

Brown Pelican

Species: Pelecanus Occidentalis • Relatives: White pelican

LC

This large gray-brown seabird with a yellow head and crown nests in large groups on offshore islands and is visible up and down both Costa Rican coasts. Brown pelicans are often seen flying overhead in long V formations or skimming the ocean in single file. Their huge wings, ideal for gliding, are tucked in for plunging dives into the ocean, while the lower half of their massive hooked bill has an expandable pouch for scooping up vast quantities of fish.

Frigatebird

Species: Fregata Magnificens • Relatives: Great frigatebird

LC

An agile aerial pirate that feeds primarily by harassing other birds until they release or regurgitate fish, this huge iridescent-black seabird has a wingspan up to 85 in (215 cm) and the lightest weight-to-size ratio of any bird in the world. The frigatebird never lands on water, for which it is ill-suited. It has a forked tail, crooked wings, and a long, sinister beak. During courtship, roosting males inflate a red sac on their throat while females fly overhead.

Key to Field Guide icons *see p65*

COSTA RICA AREA BY AREA

Costa Rica at a Glance

Brimming with natural wonders, Costa Rica's incredibly diverse terrain offers lush rain- and cloud forests that host an array of colorful fauna, craggy mountains, smoke-spewing volcanoes, and stunning beaches in every shade, from gold to taupe to black. Wildlife and adventure activities abound, ranging from canopy tours and turtle-watching to scuba diving and whitewater rafting. It is best to concentrate on the national parks and other natural attractions; very few towns are of interest. This guide divides the country into seven regions; each area is color-coded as shown here.

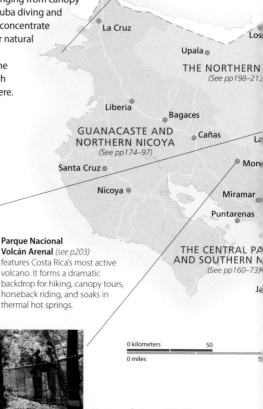

Parque Nacional Santa Rosa
(see pp188–9)

La Cruz

Los

Upala

THE NORTHERN
(See pp198–21

Liberia

Bagaces

**GUANACASTE AND
NORTHERN NICOYA**
(See pp174–97)

Cañas

La

Santa Cruz

Mon

Nicoya

Miramar

Puntarenas

**THE CENTRAL PA
AND SOUTHERN N**
(See pp160–73)

Ja

**Parque Nacional
Volcán Arenal** *(see p203)*
features Costa Rica's most active volcano. It forms a dramatic backdrop for hiking, canopy tours, horseback riding, and soaks in thermal hot springs.

| 0 kilometers | | 50 | |
| 0 miles | | | 5 |

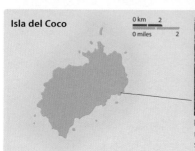

Monteverde *(see pp178–82)*
is famous for its cloud forest reserves, which draw birders eager for a sighting of Resplendent quetzals.

Isla del Coco

| 0 km | 2 |
| 0 miles | 2 |

Isla del Coco *(see p254)*, off the southwest coast, is remote and rugged. Hammerhead and whale sharks draw scuba divers.

◀ Meadows in the Costa Rica highlands

Parque Nacional Volcán Poás *(see p144)* is popular with Costa Ricans, who drive to the rim to peer into the crater of this smoldering volcano. On clear days the views are magnificent.

Barra del Colorado

Puerto Viejo de Sarapiquí

Tortuguero

da rlos)

THE CARIBBEAN
(See pp214–25)

Guápiles

anjo
Alajuela   SAN JOSÉ   Siquirres   Matina
(See pp106–33)
Heredia   SAN JOSÉ
Cartago   Turrialba   Puerto Limón

THE CENTRAL
HIGHLANDS
(See pp134–59)

Parque Nacional Tortuguero *(see p221)*, a pristine rainforest habitat, can be explored by boat along canals that offer excellent wildlife viewing. Green turtles nest on the seemingly endless beach.

epos

San Isidro de El General

THE SOUTHERN ZONE
(See pp226–45)

Buenos Aires   Potrero Grande

Golfito

Puerto Jiménez

Parque Nacional Corcovado
(see pp240–41)

Parque Nacional Manuel Antonio *(see pp172–3)* combines coral reefs, white-sand beaches, and lush forests full of wildlife that is easily spotted while hiking well-maintained trails.

Teatro Nacional *(see pp114–15)* is San José's major architectural draw. This bustling and amorphous city's attractions also include museums honoring pre-Columbian culture.

SAN JOSE

Nestled amid craggy peaks, the capital city enjoys a splendid setting and idyllic weather. Its magnificent Teatro Nacional and outstanding museums add to San José's attractions. The city's strongest draw, however, is its location in the heart of Costa Rica, which is ideal for hub-and-spoke touring. For many visitors, San José is their first experience of the country, providing an intriguing introduction to the pleasures that await farther afield.

Affectionately called *chepe* (the local nickname for anyone named José) by its inhabitants, San José is perched at an elevation of 3,800 ft (1,150 m), with the Poás, Barva, and Irazú volcanoes rising gracefully over the city to the north, and the rugged Talamanca Mountains to the south. Temperatures are a springlike 25° C (76° F) year-round, and the air is crisp and clear thanks to near-constant breezes.

Founded in 1737, San José grew very slowly through its first 100 years. Its creation on the eve of the coffee boom in the heart of coffee country, however, was advantageous. By 1823, the town had grown to challenge Cartago – the then capital – for supremacy. Following

a brief civil war, San José was named capital and quickly eclipsed other cities as prominent *cafetaleros* (coffee barons) imported skilled European artisans to beautify the city with fine structures. Since the 1960s, high-rise buildings and sprawling slum *barrios* (neighborhoods) have changed the profile of this city of one-third of a million people. Still, San José has its own charm. The main tourist sights, including the Teatro Nacional (National Theater), the gold and jade museums, and numerous plazas, are centered around the city core, within walking distance of one another. Everywhere, traffic squeezes tight at rush hour, when Costa Rican civility gives way to dog-eat-dog driving.

Varieties of fruit arranged temptingly in stalls at the Mercado Central

◄ Statues on the roof of San José's landmark Teatro Nacional

Exploring San José

Downtown San José features the city's top places of interest. The dazzling Teatro Nacional on Avenida 2, graced by Baroque and Neoclassical architecture, is San José's most remarkable building. The nearby Museo del Oro Precolombino, as well as the Museo de Jade Fidel Tristán Castro and the Museo Nacional in the east – all of which display pre-Columbian artifacts – are also major attractions. Another must-see is the Centro Costarricense de Ciencias y Cultura, to the northwest, with its superb rotating art exhibitions. Busts of prominent historical figures dot Parque España and Parque Nacional. The main historic quarter, Barrio Amón, boasts fine colonial structures along Avenida 9, while the suburb of Escazú offers excellent dining and a lively nightlife.

A quiet, tree-lined street in a residential locality of San José

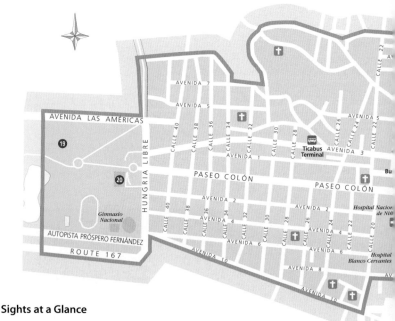

Sights at a Glance

Museums and Theaters

1 Teatro Mélico Salazar
3 *Teatro Nacional pp114–15*
4 *Museo del Oro Precolombino pp116–17*
10 Museo de Jade Fidel Tristán Castro
12 Centro Nacional de la Cultura
14 Museo Nacional
18 *Centro Costarricense de Ciencias y Cultura pp126–7*
20 Museo de Arte Costarricense
21 Museo de Ciencias Naturales "La Salle"

Historic Buildings

2 Catedral Metropolitana
6 Edificio Correos
8 Edificio Metálico
13 Asamblea Legislativa
16 Antigua Estación Ferrocarril al Atlántico

Parks and Theme Parks

7 Parque Morazán
9 Parque España
15 Parque Nacional
19 Parque Sabana
22 Parque Diversiones (Pueblo Antiguo)

Public Buildings

17 Universidad de Costa Rica

Markets and Neighborhoods

5 Mercado Central
11 Barrio Amón
23 Escazú

For hotels and restaurants in this area see pp252–61 and pp266–77

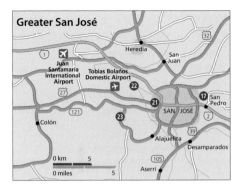

Greater San José

Heredia
San Juan
32
1
Juan Santamaría International Airport
Tobías Bolaños Domestic Airport
27
22
17 San Pedro
21
SAN JOSÉ
121
2
Colón
23
39
Alajuelita
Desamparados
105
Aserrí

0 km — 5
0 miles — 5

...etting ready for some angling at the man-made
...ake in Parque Sabana

ROUTE 108
18
CALLE CENTRAL
CALLE
RRIO PASA LA VACA
CALLE 10
8
7
AVENIDA 9
CALLE
AVENIDA
CALLE 6
AVENIDA 4
CALLE 4
AVENIDA 2
CALLE 2
Mercado Borbón
AVENIDA 3
Banco Nacional de Costa Rica
6
RIO CED
5
PLAZA LOS PRESENTES
Banco Central
Banco de Costa Rica
1
Iglesia La Merced
AVENIDA 8
CALLE 10
AVENIDA 6
CALLE 8
2
PARQUE CENTRAL
AVENIDA 8

ROUTE 108
BARRIO TOURNON
Río Torres
PARQUE ZOOLÓGICA SIMÓN BOLÍVAR
11
AVENIDA 13
Bishop's Castle
Casa Verde
AVENIDA 11
Hotel Don Carlos
Casa Amarilla
10
Legación de México
BARRIO ARANJUEZ
Hospital Calderón Guardia
8
9
AVENIDA
Radiográfica Costarricense
7
Iglesia El Carmen
12
Biblioteca Nacional
AVENIDA 3
PLAZA DE LA CULTURA
Tribunal Supremo de Elecciones
15
16
Gran Hotel
4
AVENIDA 1
13
3
Teatro Variedades
AVENIDA CENTRAL
14
La Caja
PLAZA DE LA DEMOCRACIA
BULEVAR RICARDO JIMÉNEZ
Iglesia La Soledad
BARRIO SOLEDAD
AVENIDA 6

0 meters — 500
0 yards — 500

Key

▢ Sight/place of interest

▭ Expressway

▭ Pedestrian street

Getting Around

The main sights, concentrated in downtown San José, are best explored on foot. To explore farther afield, take a taxi – this is a good way of getting around the warren of narrow, congested, one-way streets. Alternatively, you can rent a car, but do be prepared for the aggressive driving style of Costa Ricans (*see p309*). Jose Santamaría International Airport and Tobías Bolaños domestic airport are located 10 miles (17 km) northwest and 4 miles (6 km) west of downtown respectively. The international airport is well connected by airport taxis and buses to the city center; the domestic airport is served by taxis. For more details, see *pages 302–3 and 308–9*.

Street-by-Street: San José Center

Laid out in a grid of narrow, heavily trafficked one-way streets, San José's tightly condensed core contains the city's most significant sights. The main artery is the broad Avenida 2, which is thronged with honking taxis and buses threading past tree-shaded Parque Central. Running parallel to it and to the north is the Avenida Central, a pedestrian precinct lined with department stores, specialist shops, and places to eat. At the heart of this stroll-and-shop area lies the small concrete Plaza de la Cultura, which hums with activity all day – it is a popular meeting place for young people and is packed with hawkers as well as musicians and other entertainers.

❶ Teatro Mélico Salazar
Dating from the 1920s, this theater has a Neoclassical façade and a simple interior.

Avenida 2
This bustling avenue is lined with important buildings, including banks, between Calles 1 and 3. Traffic flows eastward on this four lane-wide avenue, which slopes downhill east of Calle 3.

Parque Central
Laid out in 1885 and shaded by palms and guanacaste trees, the compact central plaza has an unusual bandstand, which is supported by arches. Beneath it is the children's library, Biblioteca Carmen Lyra.

Bronze statue of a street cleaner

Statue of Pope John Paul II, made from marble by Jiménez Deredia.

La Curía (The Archbishop's Palace)

❷ ★ Catedral Metropolitana
The blue-domed Metropolitan Cathedral, built in 1871 in a simple Greek Orthodox style, features an elaborate altar.

Key

— Suggested route

0 meters
0 yards

Plaza de la Cultura
Created between 1975 and 1983, this is San José's main hub of social activity, despite its relatively austere layout.

The Gran Hotel, designed by architect Juan Joaquín Jiménez in 1930, is a city landmark *(see p248)*.

Clock tower

❸ ★ Teatro Nacional
The capital's finest architectural gem, the National Theater is renowned for its ceiling, which depicts a coffee harvest, and for its lavish tri-level, 1,040-seat auditorium. The theater was built in the early 1890s.

AVENIDA 1

AVENIDA

AVENIDA CENTRAL

CENTRAL

AVENIDA 2

CALLE 3

CALLE 7

❹ ★ Museo del Oro Precolombino
A subterranean modern structure, the Museum of Pre-Columbian Gold houses a superb collection of ancient gold adornments, as well as the National Coin Collection.

Teatro Vargas
supports independent theater groups.

Parque Mora Fernández is a palm-shaded plaza, lively with *marimba* music.

Statue of Juan Mora Fernández, Costa Rica's first president.

AVENIDA 4

La Caja (Social Security Building)

The horseshoe-shaped auditorium of Teatro Mélico Salazar

❶ Teatro Mélico Salazar

Map 1 C4. Calle Central and Ave 2.
Tel 2257-6005. 🚌 **Open** 8am–4pm
Mon–Fri. 📷 by appointment. 💻
🌐 teatromelico.go.cr

One of the city's landmarks, this theater was built in 1928 as the Teatro Raventós, and was renamed in 1986 after Manuel "Mélico" Salazar Zúñiga (1887–1950), a celebrated Costa Rican tenor. Designed by architect José Fabio Garnier, it has a Neoclassical façade adorned with fluted Corinthian pilasters. To the left of the entrance is a larger-than-life bronze bust of Zúñiga. To the right is a bas-relief plaque honoring José Raventós Gual, who had the theater built.

The handsome lobby, in checkered green-and-black tile, leads into a triple-tiered, horseshoe-shaped auditorium, which hosts theatrical and musical events, as well as folk dance shows. The auditorium has a striking parquet wooden floor beneath a wood-paneled ceiling, which is decorated with a simple mural and a wrought-iron chandelier.

❷ Catedral Metropolitana

Map 1 C4. Calle Central and Aves 2/4.
Tel 2221-3820. 🚌 **Open** 6am–noon
& 3–6pm Mon–Sat, 6am–9pm Sun.
🏛 ⛪

San José's pre-eminent church, the Metropolitan Cathedral was built in 1871 to replace the original cathedral, which

had been destroyed by an earthquake in 1820. Designed by Eusebio Rodríguez, the austere-looking structure combines Greek Orthodox, Neoclassical, and Baroque styles. Its linear façade is supported by an arcade of Doric columns and topped by a Neoclassical pediment with steeples on each side. Inside, a vaulted ceiling runs the length of the nave, supported by two rows of fluted columns. In a glass case to the left of the entrance is a life-size statue of Christ.

Although entirely lacking the ornate Baroque gilt of many other Latin American churches, the cathedral has many fine features, notably an exquisite Colonial-style tiled floor and beautiful stained-glass windows depicting biblical scenes. The main altar, beneath a cupola, comprises a simple wooden

Fountain on Avenida Central

base atop a marble plinth and supports a wooden figure of Christ and cherubs.

To the left of the main altar is the Capilla del Santísimo (Chapel of the Holy Sacrament), which has walls and ceilings decorated with wooden quadrants painted with floral motifs. The short gallery that leads to the chapel contains a glass- and-gilt coffin with a naked statue of Christ draped with a sash in the colors of the Costa Rican flag.

To the south of the cathedral is **La Curía** (The Palace of the Archbishop), built in 1887. This two-story structure has been remodeled, and is closed to the public. A small garden in front features a life-size bronze statue of Monseñor Bernardo Augusto Thiel Hoffman (1850–1901), the German-born second arch-bishop of Costa Rica. Hoffman lies buried in the crypt of the cathedral, alongside former president Tomás Guardia (see p47).

On the cathedral's north side is a contemporary marble statue of Pope John Paul II by Jiménez Deredia.

❸ Teatro Nacional

See pp114–15.

❹ Museo del Oro Precolombino

See pp116–17.

❺ Mercado Central

Map 1 B3. Calles 6/8 and Aves Central/1. **Tel** 2295-6104. 🚌
Open 6am–8pm Mon–Sat. ✏️

An intriguing curiosity, San José Central Market was built in 1881. The building, which takes up an entire block northwest of the Catedral Metropolitana, is itself rather uninspiring, but its warren of narrow alleyways, hemmed in by more than 200 stalls, immerse visitors in a slice of Costa Rican

Pillared façade of the austere Catedral Metropolitana

fe. This quintessential Latin American market thrives as a chaotic emporium of the exotic, with every conceivable item for sale, from herbal remedies and fresh- cut flowers to snakeskin boots and saddles for *sabaneros* (cowboys).

Toward the center, *sodas* (food stalls) offer inexpensive cooked meals sold at the counter. The market extends one block north to **Mercado Borbón**, which has stalls of butchers, fishmongers, and fruit sellers, and buyers crowded in as thick as sardines. Next to the market's entrance on the southeast corner, there are plaques honoring important political figures.

Pickpockets operate within the tightly packed alleys of the market. Remember to leave your valuables in the hotel safe when you venture out. It is best to tuck your camera well out of sight when it is not in use.

Edificio Correos

Map 1 B3. Calle 2 and Aves 1/3. **Tel** 2223-6918. **Open** 7:30am–pm Mon–Fri, 7:30am–noon Sat. **Museo Filatélico de Costa Rica: Tel** 2223-9766 (ext. 205). **Open** am–5pm Mon–Fri. **Closed** public ols.

he building housing the main ost office, or Correo Central, was completed in 1917. Designed by Luis Llach in eclectic style, it has a peagreen reinforced concrete façade, which is embellished with Corinthian pilasters. The arched

The Edificio Correos, featuring a blend of architectural styles

centerpiece is topped by a shield and supported by angels bearing the national coat of arms. The post office is abuzz with the comings and goings of locals picking up their mail at *apartados* (post office boxes) that fill the ground floor of the two-storey atrium.

Philatelists can view rare stamps in the small **Museo Filatélico de Costa Rica** (Philatelic Museum of Costa Rica), which takes up three rooms on the second floor. The first room has a fine collection of old telephones and telegraphic equipment that goes back more than 100 years.

The collection of stamps occupies the other two rooms, which also have exhibits on the history of philately in Costa Rica. The nation's first stamp, from 1863, is displayed here. Other

Statue of Juan Mora Fernández opposite Edificio Correos

exhibits include important and rare stamps from abroad, including the English Penny Black. The museum hosts a stamp exchange on the first Saturday of every month. The Edificio Correos is fronted by a pedestrian plaza shaded by fig trees. Towering over the plaza is a statue of the first president of Costa Rica, Juan Mora Fernández, who was in power from 1824 to 1828. Nearby, to the southwest of the Edificio Correos is another square, **Plaza Los Presentes**, which is dominated by *Los Presentes*, a contemporary monument in bronze. Created in 1979 by the well-known sculptor Fernando Calvo, the monument consists of statues of a dozen Costa Rican *campesinos* (peasant farmers). Shoeshines can be seen at work in the leafy plaza.

Los Presentes by Fernando Calvo, in Plaza Los Presentes, near Edificio Correos

❸ Teatro Nacional

Considered the finest historic building in San José, the National Theater was conceived in 1890, when Spanish-born prima donna Adelina Patti sidestepped Costa Rica while on a Central American tour due to the lack of a suitable venue. This spurred the ruling coffee barons to levy a tax on coffee exports to fund the building of a grand theater. Locals claim, disputably, that the structure was modeled on the Paris Opera House. Completed in 1897, it was inaugurated with a performance of *El Fausto de Gournod* by the Paris Opera. Declared a National Monument in 1965, the theater has a lavish Neo-Baroque interior, replete with statues, paintings, marble staircases, and parquet floors made of 10 species of hardwood.

La Danza de Vignami, painted on the ceiling of the auditorium

Teatro Café
The coffee shop adjoining the lobby is decorated in black and white tile, and has marble-topped tables. The ceiling is painted with a triptych.

KEY

① **A statue of Ludwig van Beethoven**, created in the 1890s by Adriático Froli, stands in an alcove.

② **The small garden** is formally patterned and features a life-size marble statue of a female flautist (1997) by Jorge Jiménez Deredia.

③ **Statue of Calderón de la Barca**, the 17th-century dramatist, by Italian artist Adriático Froli.

④ **Allegorical statues** of the Muses of Music, Dance, and Fame top the Neoclassical façade.

⑤ **The Palco Presidencial**, or presidential balcony, has a ceiling mural, *Alegoría a la Patria y la Justícia*, painted in 1897 by Roberto Fontana.

⑥ **The structure** was built with a steel frame.

⑦ **The exterior** of the building is of sandstone.

Entrance Lobby
With its pink marble floor and bronze-tipped Corinthian marble columns, the lobby hints at the splendors to come. The doors are topped by gilt pediments adorned with lions' faces. The wooden ceiling has a simple floral motif.

★ Coffee Mural
Depicting a coffee harvest, the huge mural on the ceiling of the intermezzo, between the lobby and the auditorium, was painted in 1897 by Milanese artist Aleardo Villa. The scene is full of errors, with coffee being shown as a coastal crop instead of a highland one.

VISITORS' CHECKLIST

Practical Information
Map 1 C4. Calles 3/5 and Ave 2.
Tel 2010-1100. Open 9am–4pm
Mon–Sat. 🖼 🎫 Shows:
Orquesta Sinfónia Nacional
(National Symphony Orchestra)
performances Mar–Dec: 8pm
Thu and Fri; 10:30am Sun.
🖥 9am–5pm Mon–Sat.
W teatronacional.go.cr

Transport
🚌 Cemeterio-Estadio.

★ Auditorium
Dominated by a rotunda ceiling with a mural of cherubs and deities, the red-and-gold auditorium has three floors, a horseshoe shape, and wrought-iron seats. The stage can be lowered and raised.

★ Foyer
A double staircase with gold-gilt banisters leads to the magnificent foyer, which features pink marble and a surfeit of crystals, gilt mirrors, and gold-leaf embellishments. Splendid murals show scenes of Costa Rican life.

❹ Museo del Oro Precolombino

Occupying the starkly modern subterranean space beneath the Plaza de la Cultura and managed by the Banco Central de Costa Rica, the Museum of Pre-Columbian Gold boasts a dazzling display of ancient gold items. The collection consists of more than 1,600 pieces of pre-Columbian gold dating back to AD 500. Most of the amulets, earrings, shamanic animal figures, and erotic statuettes exhibited here originated in southwest Costa Rica, attesting to the sophisticated art of the Diquis culture. The uses and crafting of these items are demonstrated with the help of models and other displays, which also depict the social and cultural evolution of pre-Columbian cultures.

★ Museo de Numismática
The National Coin Museum exhibits date back to 1502. The displays include coins, bank notes, and unofficial currency such as coffee tokens.

The First Coin
Costa Rica's first coin, called the Medio Escudo, was minted in 1825, when the country was part of the Federation of Central America (see p46).

Frog figurines, a traditional symbol of life for indigenous tribes, are among the gold displays.

Auditorium

★ El Guerrero
The most stunning piece is the life-size warrior adorned with gold ornaments, including a gold headband, chest disc (paten), amulets, and ankle rings. Gold objects were a symbol of authority.

Gold Craftsmanship
This section explains how pre-Columbian cultures utilized repoussé, the technique of decorating metal surfaces by hammering from the back.

Model of an Indian village

Third level

El Curandero (The Heale is a life-size model of "medicine man" performin a ritual healing usin medicinal plan

Golden Treasures
The main exhibition space, situated on the third level, is packed with golden objects of all sizes, from large gold chest discs to small, intricate pieces of jewelry.

VISITORS' CHECKLIST

Practical Information
Map 1 C4. Plaza de la Cultura, Calle 5 and Aves Central/2.
Tel 2243-4202. **Open** 9:15am–5pm daily. 🖼 📷 by appt. ✉
♿ 🅆 **museosdelbanco central.org**

Transport
🚌 all downtown buses.

Key

☐ Museo de Numismática

☐ Temporary exhibition gallery

☐ Pre-Columbian Gold Museum (introduction and orientation area)

☐ Pre-Columbian Gold Museum (exhibition of gold pieces)

☐ Nonexhibition space

Entrance

Foyer

Gift shop

First level

Second level

Gallery Guide

The museum occupies three floors below the plaza. Beyond the entrance, a broad foyer leads past a temporary exhibition space to the Museo de Numismática. Adjacent to this is a spiral staircase that descends to the second level. This floor offers an introduction to pre-Columbian culture and metallurgy, as well as temporary exhibitions that are changed every four months. The third level features an auditorium as well as the main gallery, which displays a permanent exhibition of ancient gold items.

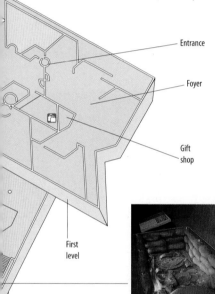

Finca 4 Site
This is a replica of a pre-Columbian grave unearthed in the 1950s. Discovered on a banana plantation in southeastern Costa Rica, the grave contained 88 gold objects.

Subterranean Vault
Accessed from Calle 5 by a broad staircase, the Gold Museum is housed in an underground space protected by steel doors.

Lost Wax Technique

Pre-Columbian groups, notably the Chibchas and Diquis of the Pacific southwest, were masterful goldsmiths, skilled in the use of the "lost wax" technique. Here, the desired form is carved in wax, then molded with clay and baked. The wax melts, leaving a negative into which molten metal is poured to attain the required result. Most pre-Columbian pieces were alloys of gold and copper, with the alloy called *tumbaga* being the most commonly used.

Gold shaman figurine

The intriguing Edificio Metálico, constructed entirely of metal

❼ Parque Morazán

Map 2 D3 Calles 5/9 and Aves 3/5.

Laid out as Plaza González Víquez on the site of an open-air reservoir in 1930, this small park was later renamed after Francisco Morazán (see p46). The Honduran-born Central American federalist served briefly as president of Costa Rica before being executed in 1842. Shaded by tabebuia (also called trumpet trees) that bloom in the dry season, the park is popular with office workers, school-children, and lovers, and hosts a cultural fair every Saturday, as well as occasional concerts.

The park's four ornate iron gateways are topped by Roman urns. At its center is the domed Neoclassical **Templo de Música**, built in 1920. Busts honor Morazán and other luminaries such as South American liberator Simón Bolívar (1783–1830). To the park's southwest is a bronze statue of former president Julio García, seated in a chair. Facing the park on the northeast, is an 11-ft (3.5-m) tall statue of another former president, Daniel Quiros, by Costa Rican artist Olger Villegas.

❽ Edificio Metálico

Map 2 D3. Calle 9 and Aves 5/7.
Tel 2222-0026.

Constructed entirely of prefabricated pieces of metal, this intriguing San José edifice, standing between Parque Morazán and Parque España, was designed by French architect Charles Thirio. The metal pieces were cast in Belgium in 1892 and shipped to Costa Rica for welding and assembly in situ. Since then, it has functioned as an elementary school, the Escuela Buenaventura Corrales y Julia Lang. A small bust of Minerva, the Roman goddess of wisdom, sits on top of its imposing Neoclassical façade. Take in a bird's-eye view of its exterior from the lobby of the Museo de Jade Fidel Tristán Castro across the street.

Carved pillars at Casa Amarilla

❾ Parque España

Map 2 D3. Calles 9/11 and Aves 3/7. Casa Amarilla: **Tel** 2223-7555. **Open** 8am–4pm Mon–Fri. by appointment.

Shaded by densely packed trees and bamboo groves, this leafy plaza is pleasantly full of birdsong. It was here, in 1903,

The Colonial-style pavilion in Parque España

that the Costa Rican national anthem, written by José María Zeledón Brenes (1877–1949) and Manuel María Gutiérrez (1829–87), was first performed

On the northeast corner, a quaint Colonial-style pabellón (pavilion), erected in 1947, is inlaid with sepia-toned ceramic murals of the apparition of the Lady of Los Angeles, the church of Orosi, and the cathedral of Heredia. A patinated life-size statue of conquistador Juan Vásquez de Coronado (see p44) stands at the southwest corner of the park. Brick pathways wind past busts of important figures, including Queen Isabel II of Spain (1830–1904) and philanthropist Andrew Carnegie (1835–1919). Facing the northwest side of the park is the ocher-colored, stuccoed **Casa Amarilla** (Yellow House). Designed by architect Henry Wiffield in an ornate Spanish Baroque style, it was completed in 1916 to house the Pan-American Court of Justice. In later years it served as the Presidential Residence and the Asamblea Legislativa. Today, the Foreign Relations Ministry has its offices here.

The most striking element of Casa Amarilla is the grand ornamental lintel above the front door. The grounds behind the ministry contain a section of the Berlin Wall; this can be viewed at the corner of Calle 13 and Avenida 9.

The towering building west of the Casa Amarilla is the **Instituto Nacional de Seguro** (INS or the National Institute of Insurance). In its front courtyard, paying homage to the institution of the family, is La Familia, a huge sculpture by Francisco Zúñiga (see p23).

The **Legación de Mexico**, 55 yd (50 m) east along Avenida 7, was built in 1924 and is a splendid example of Colonial-style architecture. The armistice of the 1948 War of Liberation was signed here.

⑨ Museo de Jade Fidel Tristán Castro

Map 2 D3. Calle 9 and Ave 7.
Tel 2287-6034. **Open** 8:30am–
30pm Mon–Fri, 11am–1pm Sat.
Closed public hols.

Located on the first floor of the
National Institute of Insurance
(INS) building, the Fidel Tristán
Castro Jade Museum contains
the largest collection of pre-
Columbian jade in the Americas.
It was founded by Fidel Tristán
Castro, the first president of the
INS, in 1977. The collection
consists of adzes, ceremonial
heads, and decorative pieces
from 500 BC to AD 800. There
are also *metates* (grinding tables
made of volcanic stone),
ceramics, and gold ornaments.
The Sala de Jade displays jade
pendants in kaleidoscopic hues
of green and blue, exquisitely
backlit to demonstrate their
translucent quality. The jade
pieces that make up this
collection did not come from
archaeological sites – they were
purchased from private
collectors who had bought
them from looters.

⑩ Barrio Amón

Map 1 C2. Calles Central/9 and Aves
7/13.

The richest architectural
collection in San José is the
complex of historic homes
in this residential *barrio*
(neighborhood), founded in
the 1890s by French immigrant
Amón Fasileau Duplantier. Once
on the verge of decay, the area
has now undergone restoration.
The most interesting places
are along Avenida 9; the stretch
between Calles 3 and 7 is lined
with beautiful ceramic murals
by local artist Fernando
Matamoros showing traditional
Costa Rican scenes.
Begin at Calle 11, where No.
30 is a two-story colonial
mansion boasting a life-size
campesino (peasant) in pre-cast
concrete gazing over the
wrought-iron railing. At Calle 7,
the **Hotel Don Carlos**
(see p252) was formerly the
residence of President Tomás

Detail of a ceramic mural showing a
traditional scene, Barrio Amón

Guardi *(see p47)* and is a curious
blend of Art Deco and
Neoclassical styles. One block
west, at the corner of Calle 5, is
the **Casa Verde**, a clapboard
building of New Orleans pine,
dating to 1910 and notable for
its soaring lounge spectacularly
lit by a stained-glass atrium.
The most audacious building
in this *barrio* is the **Bishop's
Castle** at Avenida 11 and Calle 3.
It was built in 1930 in ornate
Moorish style with turrets,
crenellations, keyhole windows,
a central dome, and a façade
decorated with glazed tiles
showing scenes from the novel
Don Quixote.

⑪ Centro Nacional de la Cultura

Map 2 D3. Calles 11/15 and Aves 3/7.
Tel 2255-3190 (ext. 210); Museo de
Arte y Diseño Contemporáneo: 2257-
9370. **Open** 10:30am–5pm Tue–
Sat. **Closed** public hols. 10am–
3pm Tue–Fri by appt.
W mci.go.cr

Immediately east of Parque
España, the rambling structure
of the National Center of
Culture takes up a block on the
site of the former Fábrica
Nacional de Licores (State Liquor

Factory). In 1994, the defunct
factory was converted into the
multi-faceted Centro Nacional
de la Cultura (CENAC), although
traces of the old distillery can
still be seen. The Ministry of
Culture is located here, as are
venues hosting the National
Theater Company and the
National Dance Company
(see p285). Most of the extant
buildings date to 1856, as does
the perimeter wall, whose
stone west gate is topped by a
triangular pediment. Note the
reloj de sol (sun clock), carved
into the perimeter wall to the
right of the southeast *portalón*
(gate) by architect Teodorico
Quirós *(see p23)*.
The **Museo de Arte y Diseño
Contemporáneo** (Museum of
Contemporary Art and Design)
occupies the southeast part
of the complex and features
permanent and rotating
exhibitions of art, architecture,
and ceramics in six rooms.
Evelia con baton, a sculpture
by Francisco Zúñiga, stands
in the west courtyard.

Detail on the façade of the Centro Nacional
de la Cultura

Jade Carving

Jade carving was introduced to the region by cultures
from the north around 500 BC and died out around AD
800, when it was replaced by gold. The indigenous
people used saws made of fiber string, as well as drills
and crude quartz-tipped chisels, to carve the semi-
precious stone into necklaces, pendants, and religious
figurines bearing replicas of animal motifs. No local
source is known to have existed: jade was traded from
Guatemala and neighboring regions.

Jade anthropomorphic figure

Street-by-Street: Around Parque Nacional

Commanding a bluff on the east side of downtown, Parque
Nacional, one of the city's largest parks, is a bucolic tree-
shaded retreat dotted with statues in the heart of San José.
Surrounding the park on three sides are the country's most
important government buildings, including the Legislative
Assembly complex. Also in the vicinity are many of Costa
Rica's significant cultural sights, such as the National Museum.
The area makes for pleasant strolling, especially with the
addition of a pedestrian precinct sloping south from Parque
Nacional, which is a lovely place to sit and relax.

Biblioteca Nacional
This modern-looking structure wa
erected in 1969–71 to house the
national library.

A fish pond,
stocked with koi,
runs along the
western side
of the park.

⑫ Centro Nacional de la Cultura
Occupying the site of the former State
Liquor Factory, the National Center of
Culture's attractions include the state-
of-the-art Museum of Contemporary
Art and Design.

*Epítome del
Vuelo* statue

Plaza de la Libertad Electoral
This small, semi-circular plaza honors the nation's
democracy. Neoclassical columns enclose a pink
granite statue, *Epítome del Vuelo* (1996), created by
sculptor José Sancho Benito.

**The Tribunal Supremo
de Elecciones** building
houses the government
body that ensures the
integrity of elections.

0 meters		100
0 yards		100

Key

━ Suggested route

★ Parque Nacional
entered on the impressive granite-and-bronze *Monumento Nacional*
392), this fine park is thick with trees and dotted with busts of several
tin American heroes.

Bulevar Ricardo Jiménez
This stretch of Calle 17 running
south of Parque Nacional is
a handsome palm-lined,
pedestrian-only causeway.
It is also known as the
Camino de la Corte.

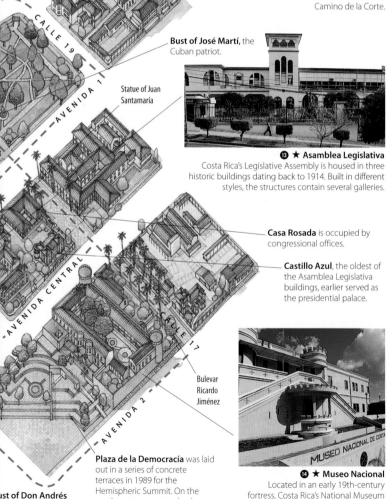

Bust of José Martí, the
Cuban patriot.

**Statue of Juan
Santamaría**

⓭ ★ Asamblea Legislativa
Costa Rica's Legislative Assembly is housed in three
historic buildings dating back to 1914. Built in different
styles, the structures contain several galleries.

Casa Rosada is occupied by
congressional offices.

Castillo Azul, the oldest of
the Asamblea Legislativa
buildings, earlier served as
the presidential palace.

**Bulevar
Ricardo
Jiménez**

⓮ ★ Museo Nacional
Located in an early 19th-century
fortress, Costa Rica's National Museum
traces the history of the nation from
pre-Columbian to contemporary times.

Plaza de la Democracía was laid
out in a series of concrete
terraces in 1989 for the
Hemispheric Summit. On the
southwest corner stands a bronze
statue of former president José
"Don Pepe" Figueres *(see p49).*

**ust of Don Andrés
ello**, a Venezuelan
tellectual.

⓭ Asamblea Legislativa

Map 2 E3. Calles 15/17 & Ave Central. **Tel** 2243-2000. 🚌 📷 compulsory: 9am; 2243-2547. Legislative debates: 9am–2:45pm Mon–Thu, 10am–noon Fri; by appt. 🖥 asamblea.go.cr

The country's seat of government is in an enclave of four buildings, covering an entire block. The main structure, **Edificio del Plenario**, built in 1958, serves as the congress building along with an adjoining edifice. A bronze statue of national hero Juan Santamaría *(see p138)*, torch in hand, stands in the north courtyard. The pink **Casa Rosada**, to the northeast, houses the offices of various political parties.

The Mediterranean-style **Castillo Azul** to the southeast was built in 1911 for Máximo Fernández, then a presidential aspirant. It served as the Presidential Residence until 1927, after which it was briefly the US mission. Since 1989, it has been used for official functions and contains government offices. Its six salons, boasting beautiful hardwood floors and Italian marble, include the Sala Alfredo González Flores, which is used for cabinet meetings, and the Sala Próceres de la Libertad, with its gilt-framed portraits of Latin American liberators such as Simón Bolívar.

Visitors are admitted to the Edificio del Plenario to witness legislative debates. Note that sandals are not permitted for men, nor bare legs for either sex.

Part of the Asamblea Legislativa complex in San José

Pre-Columbian stone spheres in the Museo Nacional

⓮ Museo Nacional

Map 2 E4. Calle 17 & Aves Central/2. **Tel** 2257-1433. 🚌 **Open** 8:30am–4:30pm Tue–Sat, 9am–4:30pm Sun. **Closed** public hols. 📷 ♿ 📷 🖥 museocostarica.go.cr

Dramatic and imposing, the crenellated, ocher-colored Bellavista Fortress – opposite the Legislative Assembly – was built in 1917 and served as an army barracks. Its exterior walls, with towers at each corner, are pocked with bullet holes from the 1948 civil war. Following his victory, José "Don Pepe" Figueres *(see pp48–9)* disbanded the army, and the fortress became the venue for the National Museum, which had been founded in 1887.

The entrance, on the west side, opens to a large netted butterfly garden with a snaking walkway that leads up to a landscaped courtyard displaying pre-Columbian *carretas* (ox-carts), stone *bolas* (spheres), and colonial-era cannons. The museum is arranged thematically in a counter-clockwise direction around the plaza. Rooms are dedicated to geological, colonial, archaeological, contemporary, and religious history. The displays start from the first arrival of humans in Costa Rica and go up to the formation of the nation and recent events: a key exhibit is the 1987 Nobel Peace Prize awarded to president Oscar Arias Sánchez *(see p49)*. The museum has a particularly impressive pre-Columbian

Bust of Don Andrés Bello in Parque Nacional

collection, notably of *metates* (grinding stones) and ceramics as well as spectacular gold ornaments displayed in the Sala de Oro, in the northeast tower. The Sala Colonial is laid out with rustic colonial furniture, and looks as a room would have looked in the 18th century.

The museum is approached via steps that lead up from the **Plaza de la Democracia**, which was laid out in 1989 to commemorate 100 years of Costa Rican democracy and received a much-needed facelift in 2009. The stepped plaza hosts a 1994 bronze statue of José Figueres; a crafts market occupies the western end.

⓯ Parque Nacional

Map 2 E3. Calles 15/19 and Aves 1/3. 🚌

The largest of San José's inner-city parks, laid out in 1895, this is also its most appealing, although it is to be avoided at night. The peaceful park is set on a gentle hill that rises eastward. Stone benches fringe the irregular paths that snake beneath flowering trees, swaying palms and bamboo groves. The massive *Monumento Nacional* is under towering trees at the center.

Cast in the Rodin studios in Paris and unveiled on September 15, 1892, it is dedicated to the heroic deeds of the War of 1856. Its granite pedestal has five bronze Amazons representing the

Children playing by a fish pond in Parque Nacional

entral American nations
epelling the adventurer William
Walker (see p47). Costa Rica
tands in the middle holding a
ag in one hand and supporting
wounded Nicaragua with the
ther; El Salvador holds a sword,
uatemala an axe, and
onduras an arch and shield.
ronze bas-reliefs to each side
epict scenes from the battles.
Busts dotted around the park
onor such Latin American
ationalists as the Mexican
evolutionary and priest Miguel
idalgo (1753–1811), the
enezuelan poet and intellectual
on Andrés Bello (1781–1865),
nd the Cuban patriot and poet
osé Martí (1853–95).
The park is surrounded by
nportant buildings. The
iblioteca Nacional (National
ibrary) is to the north, and to
he south, the pedestrianized
ulevar Ricardo Jiménez,
amed for the three-time
resident, slopes downhill three
locks to the building of the
ribunal of Justice.

⓰ Antigua Estación Ferrocarril al Atlántico

Map 2 F3. Calles 21/23 and Ave 3.

To the northeast of the
Parque Nacional is the former
Estación Ferrocarril al Atlántico
(Atlantic Railroad Station).
Built in 1908, this ornate
building, which resembles
a pagoda, later became the
terminus for the famous
"Jungle Train," discontinued in
1991 following a devastating
earthquake that destroyed
much of the railway line.
The building once housed
the Museo de Formas,
Espacios y Sonidos (Museum of
Form, Space & Sound), which
closed in 2007, when the
former station was earmarked
as the entrance for a new
presidential palace that is still
awaiting construction. For
the time being, rail buffs can
appreciate the vintage rolling
stock to the rear and east of
the building. This includes
Locomotora 59, a 1939 steam
locomotive imported from
Philadelphia for the Northern
Railway Company.
A bust of General Tomás
Guardia (see p47), under whom
the railroad was established
between 1871 and 1890, stands
in front of the building, next to
an obelisk commemorating
the abolition of capital
punishment in 1877.

Display of butterflies at San José's Museo de Insectos

⓱ Universidad de Costa Rica

Calle Central, San Pedro. **Tel** 2207-4000. Museo de Insectos: **Tel** 2207-5647. **Open** 1–4:45pm Mon–Fri. Planetario: **Tel** 2207-2580. **Open** for shows: 8:30, 9:30 & 10:30am Mon–Fri; 10am, 11am, 2pm & 3pm Sat.

The University of Costa Rica
imbues the suburb of San Pedro
with bohemian life. The campus
entrance is on Calle Central (off
Avenida Central), which throbs
with student bars and cafés. The
campus itself is not particularly
appealing, although numerous
busts and statues are sprinkled
about the tree-shaded grounds.
A botanical garden is located in
the southwest corner.
The **Museo de Insectos**, in
the basement of the Music
Department in the northeast
corner of the campus, boasts
a large display of butterflies,
beetles, spiders, wasps, and
other insects. A planetarium
hosts daily presentations in
Spanish. Call ahead to request
an English-language showing.

The ornate, pagoda-style exterior of the Antigua Estación Ferrocarril al Atlántico

⑱ Centro Costarricense de Ciencias y Cultura

Housed in a fortress-like building that served as the *penitenciario central* (central penitentiary) from 1910 to 1979, the Costa Rican Science and Cultural Center was inaugurated in 1994. The ocher façade, topped by salmon-colored crenellations, presents a dramatic sight at night, when it is illuminated. The center contains the Galería Nacional, whose airy exhibition halls feature paintings, sculptures, and other art forms by Costa Rica's leading exponents of avant-garde art. Also here is the Museo de los Niños, with dozens of thematic hands-on exhibits that provide children with an understanding of nature, science, technology, and culture. The center includes a youth center and auditorium. Scattered around the complex are models of various modes of transport.

Stained-Glass Ceiling
A skylit *vidriera* (stained-glass window) by Italian Claudio Dueñas lights the staircase to the Galería Nacional.

Museo Histórico Penitenciario
The old jail cells are preserved in their original condition in this area. Historic photographs show the jail in former years.

★ **Galería Nacional**
Occupying 14 large rooms upstairs, the National Gallery showcases rotating exhibits of contemporary works by local artists in spotlit rooms converted from former jail cells.

Sala Kaopakome
Named for an indigenous Bribri word meaning "Hall of Meetings," this space is used for artistic performances and other events.

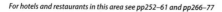

Genesis
This granite sculpture (1998) by Jorge Jiménez Deredia shows a woman evolving from an egg.

VISITORS' CHECKLIST

Practical Information
Map 1 B1. Calle 4 and 110 yd (100 m) N of Ave 9. **Tel** 2258-4929.
Open 8am–4:30pm Tue–Fri, 9:30am–5pm Sat & Sun. 🎫 📷 ♿ 🛗 🖥 Auditorio Nacional: **Tel** 2222-7647.
Ⓦ **museocr.org**

Transport
🚌 Sabana-Cemeterio along Ave 3. Best to take a taxi.

★ **Museo de los Niños**
The Children's Museum, dedicated to interactive education, is spread throughout 39 separate rooms, with exhibits on the themes of astronomy, Earth, Costa Rica, ecology, science, human beings, and communications.

Complejo Juvenil
Designed as a learning center for youth, the twin-level complex features a library, with books, audio cassettes, music CDs, interactive games and an Internet café.

KEY

① **The eastern wall** features paintings by contemporary artists such as Fabio Herrera.

② **The Auditorio Nacional**, the nation's premier auditorium, hosts performances of music and dance.

③ *Imagen Cósmica* (1998) by Jorge Jiménez Deredia is a bronze and marble sculpture.

④ **The entrance** is in the form of a medieval castle, with twin turrets.

⑤ **Escuela "El Grano de Oro"** has exhibits on the coffee culture and the history of coffee in Costa Rica.

⑥ **An electric train and carriages** date from 1928–30, when Costa Rica's rail system was electrified.

⑦ **Helicopter**

⑧ **Aircraft cockpit**

⑲ Parque Sabana

Calle 42/Sabana Oeste and Ave las Américas/Sabana Sur. 🚌 ♿

Officially named Parque Metropolitano La Sabana Padre Antonio Chapui, after the first priest of San José (1710–83), this park was the city's main airfield until 1955, when it was converted into a bucolic retreat and sports venue. The former airport buildings now house the Museo de Arte Costarricense. Looming over the park are the curving **ICE** (Costa Rican Institute of Electricity) tower to the north, and the strangely sloping **Controlaría de la República**, the government's administrative headquarters, to the south.

The park, which is accessed from downtown via the wide Paseo Colón, is popular with Costa Rican families, who picnic on weekends beneath the eucalyptus and pine groves. The park's facilities include jogging and cycling tracks, basketball, volleyball, and tennis courts, riding trails, a swimming pool, a gymnasium, soccer fields, and the National Stadium, completed in 2011. On the south side, a man-made lake is surrounded by modern sculptures. To the park's west, a cross honors Pope John Paul's visit to Costa Rica in 1983. It is best to avoid the park at night.

⑳ Museo de Arte Costarricense

Calle 42 and Paseo Colón. **Tel** 2256-1281. 🚌 **Open** 9am–4pm Tue–Sun. **Closed** public hols. 🎫 free on Sun. 📷 📹 🌐 musarco.go.cr

Costa Rica's leading museum of fine art, on the east side of Parque Sabana, is situated in the Colonial-style former airport terminal that closed in the 1950s. The Costa Rican Art Museum displays more than 3,200 important 20th-century works of art by Costa Rican sculptors and painters, as well as works by a smattering of foreign artists, including the Mexican Diego Rivera (1886–1957). Only a fraction of the museum's collection is on display, in rotating exhibitions that change yearly. Many of the works, most of which are privately owned, celebrate an archaic, pastoral way of life, best exemplified by *El Portón Rojo* (1945) by Teodorico Quirós Alvarado (*see p23*).

A highlight of the collection, and not to be missed, are Francisco Amighetti's wooden sculptures and woodcuts. On the second floor, the Salón Dorado has a bas-relief mural in bronze and stucco by French sculptor Louis Ferrón. Sweeping around all four walls, the panorama depicts an idealized version of Costa Rican history from pre-Columbian times to the 1940s. On the north wall is

View of the Museo de Arte Costarricense, San José

a representation of Christopher Columbus with Indians kneeling before him.

The **Jardín de Esculturas** (Sculpture Garden) at the back of the museum, exhibits works by prominent sculptors, and also displays pre-Columbian *esferas* (spheres) and petroglyphs. Most intriguing are the *Tres Mujeres Caminando*, Francisco Zúñiga's sculpture of three women, and the granite *Danaide*, a female curled in the fetal position, by Max Jiménez Huete.

㉑ Museo de Ciencias Naturales "La Salle"

Sabana Sur. **Tel** 2232-1306. 🚌 **Open** 7:30am–4pm Mon–Sat, 9am–5pm Sun. **Closed** public hols. 🎫 📷 📹

Located in the former premises of the Colegio La Salle school, the La Salle Museum of Natural Sciences was founded in 1960. Housing one of the most comprehensive collections of

Flags for sale in downtown San José

A spectacular bird diorama at Museo de Ciencias Naturales "La Salle"

SAN JOSE | 129

ative and exotic flora and fauna
the world, it boasts more than
0,000 items, from molluscs to
oths to manatees. A dinosaur
xhibit in the central courtyard
cludes a replica skeleton of a
rannosaurus Rex made of
sin. The fossil, shell, and
utterfly displays are particularly
oteworthy. Most exhibits are
dioramas that try to recreate
atural environments. Snakes are
oised to strike their prey. Fish
vim suspended on invisible
ire. The stuffed species are a bit
oth-eaten, and their contrived
ontortions often comic. Despite
is, the museum provides an
teresting introduction to
osta Rica's natural world.

Victorian-style Casa de Las Tías hotel in San Rafael de Escazú

raditional dance performance at Parque
versiones

Parque
Diversiones
Pueblo Antiguo)

mile (1.6 km) W of Hospital México,
Uruca. **Tel** 2242-9200. 🚌 **Open**
m–7pm Fri–Sun. 🚫🚼🚻
🌐 parquediversiones.com/
ueblo.htm

his splendid park, in Barrio La
ruca, 2 miles (3 km) west of
owntown, draws local families
ot only for the roller coasters,
ater slides, and other pay-as-
ou-go rides, but also for the
arvelous re-creations of
pical early-20th-century Costa
can settings in the adjoining
ueblo Antiguo (Old Village).
Pueblo Antiguo has three
ections: the coast, the capital
ty, and the countryside.
uildings in traditional
rchitectural style include a
hurch, a market, a fire station,

a bank, and a railway station.
There are several original
adobe structures, such as a
coffee mill, a sugar mill, and a
milking barn, which have been
moved here from the
countryside. A farmstead is
stocked with live animals.

Horse-drawn carriages, oxcarts, and an electric train offer
rides, and actors in period
costume dramatize the past.
Folkloric shows with music and
dance bring the place to life on
Friday and Saturday evenings.
Parque Diversiones has several
craft shops as well as a
restaurant that serves traditional
Costa Rican cuisine.

㉓ Escazú

2 miles (3 km) W of Parque Sabana.
🚌 🎭 Día del Boyero (Mar). Barry
Biesanz Woodworks: Barrio Bello
Horizonte. **Tel** 2289-4337. **Open**
8am–5pm Mon–Fri, 9am–3pm
Sat. 🚗 🎭 🌐 biesanz.com

This upscale district
lies west of Parque
Sabana and is
accessed by the
Carretera Prospero
Fernández. It exudes
an appeal that it
owes partly to its
blend of antiquity
and modernity, and partly to its
salubrious position at the foot
of Cerro Escazú mountain. The
suburb, which derives its name
from the indigenous word
itzkatzu (resting place), sprawls

Detail of church dome in San
Miguel de Escazú

uphill for several miles. It
is divided into three main
barrios – San Rafael de Escazú,
San Miguel de Escazú, and
San Antonio de Escazú.

Modernity is concentrated
in congested San Rafael de
Escazú, where an exquisite
Colonial-style church, designed
in the 1930s by architect
Teodorico Quirós Alvarado,
is encircled by high-rise
condominiums and US-style
malls. Half a mile (1 km) uphill,
in San Miguel de Escazú, admire
the colonial-era adobe houses,
each painted with a strip of
blue – many local residents
still firmly believe that this will
ward off witches.

San Antonio de Escazú,
farther uphill, is a farming
community. Time your visit
here for the second Sunday
of March, when flower-
bedecked *carretas* (oxcarts)
parade during Día del
Boyero (Oxcart Drivers'
Day), a festival
honoring the men
who drive the oxcarts.
**Barry Biesanz
Woodworks** is in
the barrio of Bello
Horizonte, in east
Escazú. This is the
workshop of Costa
Rica's leading
woodcarver and craftsman,
who creates elegantly beautiful
furniture, bowls, and boxes from
Costa Rica's hardwoods. His
works are available at the studio
and at upscale San José stores.

SAN JOSE STREET FINDER

The map below shows the area covered by the map on pages 108–9, as well as the city center area shown on the Street Finder maps on pages 132–3. It also shows the main highways used for getting around the potentially confusing area that is greater San José.

All map references for places of interest, hotels, and restaurants in San José city center refer to the Street Finder maps in this section. An index of street names and all the places of interest marked on the maps can be found on the facing page. Attractions located to the west of downtown are shown on the map on pages 108–9, while more distant places of interest are plotted on the inset Greater San José map on page 109.

The busy Calle Central, which runs north–south through the center of downtown San José

Scale of Maps 1–2

0 meters — 500
0 yards — 500

Key to Street Finder

- Major sight
- Place of interest
- Other building
- Bus station
- Hospital
- Police station
- Church
- Pedestrian street

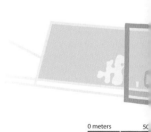

0 meters — 5(
0 yards — 500

Street Finder Index

THE CENTRAL HIGHLANDS

Shimmering volcanoes dominate the landscape of the Central Highlands as they tower over the country's central plateau – a broad valley at an altitude of around 3,300 ft (1,000 m). With steep slopes lushly covered by verdant forests and coffee bushes, the region offers glorious scenery. The climate is invigorating – one reason why two-thirds of the country's population live here today.

The mild climate and fertile soils of the *meseta central* (central plateau) attracted early Spanish colonial settlers. Pre-Columbian peoples had already occupied the region for about 10,000 years, although their most evolved community – Guayabo – was mysteriously abandoned before the Spanish arrival and overgrown by tropical jungle until discovered 100 years later. Today, the indigenous communities are relegated to the remote margins of the Talamanca Mountains.

Agricultural communities evolved throughout the valley and, eventually, farther up the mountain slopes. During the period of Spanish rule, these humble adobe villages were relatively isolated, and even larger urban centers, such as Alajuela and Heredia, garnered few

structures of importance. Earthquakes were responsible for the destruction of much colonial-era architecture, including some fine churches, and most of the surviving historically significant buildings are barely a century old.

The region has some stunning drives along roads that wind up the mountain-sides through green coffee plantations, dairy pastures, and, higher up, cool forests of cedar and pine. Most of the mountain forests are now protected, and national parks and wildlife refuges provide excellent opportunities for hiking and wildlife viewing. Sights and activities ranging from butterfly farms and coffee *fincas* to canopy tours and world-class whitewater rafting make the area a thrilling microcosm of the country's tourist attractions.

The striking Iglesia de Sarchí, standing in Sarchí's main square

◄ Coffee plantations on the slopes near the Volcán Poás, Central Highlands

Exploring the Central Highlands

Mountains surround this temperate region. Bustling Alajuela is a good base for exploring Volcán Poás, where it is possible to drive to the summit. Nearby is Heredia, a center of coffee production. To the northwest, the road to Sarchí and Zarcero makes a superb drive. Two other lovely drives are La Ruta de los Santos and the Orosi Valley. Costa Rica's main pre-Columbian site, the Monumento Nacional Guayabo, lies to the east of San José. For the more adventurous, Reventazón and Pacuare rivers are ideal for rafting, while the cloud-forested upper slopes of the Poás, Barva, and Turrialba volcanoes offer great hiking opportunities. Other options include coffee tours at plantations such as Café Britt and the Doka Estate.

The decorated interior of Iglesia de San José de Orosi

Orchid, Jardín Botánico Lankester

Sights at a Glance

Towns and Villages
1 Alajuela
3 La Guácima
5 Grecia
6 Sarchí
8 Zarcero
14 Heredia
16 Barva
17 San Isidro de Coronado
18 *Cartago pp147–9*
25 Turrialba

Sites and Buildings of Interest
4 Universidad de Paz
26 *Monumento Nacional Guayabo pp158–9*

Coffee Estates
10 Doka Estate
15 Café Britt

National Parks
11 Parque Nacional Volcán Poás
13 Parque Nacional Braulio Carrillo

20 Parque Nacional Los Quetzales
24 Parque Nacional Tapantí-Macizo la Muerte
27 Parque Nacional Volcán Turrialba
28 Parque Nacional Volcán Irazú

Areas of Natural Beauty
2 Zoo Ave Wildlife Conservation Park
7 El Silencio de Los Angeles Cloud Forest Reserve
9 Bosque de Paz Rain/Cloud Forest Biological Reserve
12 La Paz Waterfall Gardens
19 Jardín Botánico Lankester
21 San Gerardo de Dota
23 *The Orosi Valley pp152–4*

Tour
22 *La Ruta de los Santos p151*

Key
━━ Pan-American Highway
━━ Major road
── Secondary road
┅┅ Minor road
── Scenic route
━━ Provincial border
△ Peak

For hotels and restaurants in this region see pp252–61 and pp266–77

Panoramic view from the slopes of Volcán Irazú

0 km   10
0 miles   10

PARQUE NACIONAL
BRAULIO CARRILLO

Río Sucio

32

Alto Palma

PARQUE NACIONAL
VOLCÁN TURRIALBA

27

INSTITUTO
CLODOMIRO PICADO

7

Volcán Turrialba
10,950 ft

Volcán Irazú
11,260 ft

28

MONUMENTO
NACIONAL GUAYABO

26

PARQUE NACIONAL
VOLCÁN IRAZÚ

Pacayas

230

TURRIALBA

25

10

CATIE

CARTAGO

18

Río Reventazón

Lake Angostura

Río Pacuare

Cachí

Paraíso

19

BOTÁNICO
LANKESTER

Ujarrás

Hacienda
Atirro

23

Orosi

OROSI VALLEY

Hacienda
Grano de Oro

Chirripó
Abajo

2

Tapantí

24

PARQUE NACIONAL
TAPANTÍ-MACIZO
LA MUERTE

Río Pacuare

Río Grande de Orosi

Cortés

LA RUTA DE
LOS SANTOS

Santa María
de Dota

2

20

PARQUE NACIONAL
LOS QUETZALES

21

SAN GERARDO
DE DOTA

San Isidro
de El General

Getting Around

Juan Santamaría International Airport is on the outskirts of Alajuela, 1 mile (1.6 km) from the Pan-American Highway, which links the Central Highlands with the Pacific coast. It's easiest to explore the region by car. However, *rótulos* (directional signs) are few, and it's easy to get lost. Avoid nighttime driving and beware of potholes, sharp bends, and fog at higher elevations. Public buses run between most towns and to places of interest, but service can be erratic. Organized tours are available, and private guides and transfers can be arranged from San José.

View of a small town near Grecia

For additional map symbols *see back flap*

❶ Alajuela

Road Map D3. 12 miles (19 km) NW of San José. 45,000. Sat. Día de Juan Santamaría (Apr 11); Festival de Mangos (Jul).

Sitting at the base of Volcán Poás, this busy market town is Costa Rica's third largest city. The mango trees that shade the main square, Plaza del General Tomás Guardia, are the source of Alajuela's nickname, "City of Mangoes." Centered on a triple-tiered fountain with cherubs at its base, the plaza has a band-stand, and benches with built-in chess sets. It is dominated by the simple, domed **Catedral de Alajuela**, with a Classical façade and a magnificent barrel-vaulted ceiling adorned with frescoes. More interesting is the Baroque **Iglesia Santo Cristo de la Agonía**, five blocks east, which dates only from 1935. The interior boasts intriguing murals. The former jail, one block north of the main plaza, houses the **Museo Cultural y Histórico Juan Santamaría**, honoring the local drummer-boy who gave up his life torching William Walker's hideout in the War of 1856 (see pp46–7). Call ahead to arrange a screening of a video about the event. A bronze statue of Santamaría stands in tiny **Parque Juan Santamaría**, which is two blocks south of the main plaza.

On the southwest side of town, **Señor y Señora Ese** produces fine wooden crafts for sale and has artists' studios that can be visited.

Museo Cultural y Histórico Juan Santamaría
Ave 1 and Calles Central/2. **Tel** 2441-4775. **Open** 10am–5:30pm Tue–Sun. Tue–Fri.

Señor y Señora Ese
1.2 miles (1 km) SW of Alajuela. **Tel** 2441-8333. **Open** 8am–5:30pm daily. zooavecostarica.org

❷ Zoo Ave Wildlife Conservation Park

Road Map D3. Hwy 3, La Garita, 2 miles (3 km) E of Pan-Am Hwy. **Tel** 2433-8989. from San José (Sat–Sun at 8am) & Alajuela. **Open** 9am–5pm daily. zooavecostarica.org

With the largest collection of tropical birds in Central America, Costa Rica's foremost zoo covers 145 acres (59 ha). The privately owned zoo is one of only two in the world to display Resplendent quetzals. More than 60 other native bird species can be seen in large flight cages. Mammals are represented by deer, peccaries, pumas, tapirs, and the four native monkey species. Crocodiles, caimans, and snakes are among the dozens of reptile species found here.

Many of the animals and birds were confiscated from poachers, or rescued by the National Wildlife Service. Zoo Ave is also a breeding center and has successfully raised endangered species such as green and scarlet macaws. The breeding center and wildlife rehabilitation are off limits.

An enclosure at Zoo Ave Wildlife Conservation Park

A short distance away, the **Botanical Orchid Garden** delights with its walking trails, exhibitions, and hothouses where about 150 orchid species are grown. Bamboos, heliconias, and palms are also represented, and visitors can view a macaw breeding facility. The peaceful water gardens offer a relaxed setting with glimpses of koi fish, turtles, and an abundance of insects.

Botanical Orchid Garden
1 mile (1.6 km) W of Autopista General Cañas. **Tel** 2487-8095. **Open** 8:30am–4:30pm Tue–Sun. orchidgardencr.com

❸ La Guácima

Road Map D3. 7.5 miles (12 km) S of Alajuela. 15,500.

The sprawling community of La Guácima is renowned for the murals of butterflies that adorn its walls. Horse-lovers will find a visit to **Rancho San Miguel**, on the outskirts of La Guácima, worthwhile. This stable and stud farm raises Andalusian horses and offers horseback riding lessons, as well as a dressage and horsemanship show in the manner of the Lipizzaners of the Spanish Riding School at Vienna. It offers tours of its sustainable agriculture facility, including a bee farm and worm composting.

Rancho San Miguel
2 miles (3 km) N of La Guácima. **Tel** 2439-0003. **Open** 9am–5pm daily; by reservation. Shows: 7:30pm on Sat (Nov–Jul); by reservation only. josepabloferraro@ ranchosanmiguel.com

Interior of Alajuela's Museo Cultural y Histórico Juan Santamaría

Costa Rica's Colorful Butterflies

A lepidopterist's dream, Costa Rica has more than 1,250 butterfly species. The butterfly population increases with the onset of the rain from May to July, when breeding activity peaks. Most species of butterfly feed on nectar, although some prefer rotting fruit, bird droppings, and even carrion. Butterflies discourage predators through a variety of means. Many, such as the Heliconiinae, which eat plants containing cyanide, taste acrid; they advertise this to potential predators through distinct coloration – typically black striped with white, red, and/ or yellow – that other species mimic. Some are colored mottled brown and green to blend in with the background. Several butterfly species move seasonally between upland and lowland, while others migrate thousands of miles: the black-and-green Uranidae flits between Honduras and Colombia every year.

Butterfly "Farms"

These let visitors stroll through netted enclosures where dozens of species fly, forage, and reproduce. Some farms breed butterflies for export.

Caterpillars, the larvae of moths and butterflies, start feeding the instant they emerge from the eggs. These voracious eaters sport impressive camouflage and defenses. Many have poisonous spikes; one species even resembles a snake.

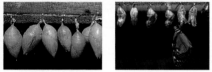

A chrysalid is created when a caterpillar attaches itself to a leaf or twig and its body hardens to form an encasement. Some caterpillars spin cocoons of silk; others roll leaves into cylinders, tying them with silken threads. They then pupate and emerge as butterflies.

Types of Butterflies

With 10 percent of all known butterfly species in the world, Costa Rica has lepidopteria ranging from tiny glasswings with transparent wings, to the giants of the insect kingdom, such as teal-blue morphos.

Morphos are dazzling, neon-bright butterflies whose iridescent upper wings flash with a fiery electric-blue sheen in flight. The wings are actually brown, not blue. The illusion is caused by the tiny, layered, glass-like scales on the upper wing. There are more than 50 species of this neotropical butterfly.

Morpho's wing

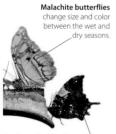

Malachite butterflies change size and color between the wet and dry seasons.

Swallowtails, found in open habitats and rainforest, have trailing hindwings.

Owl-eyes' hindwings resemble the startling face of an owl, including two huge black, yellow-ringed "eyes."

The postman feeds on poisonous passion flower leaves as a caterpillar, making the butterfly bad-tasting to predators.

Grecia's striking red-colored church, Iglesia de Grecia

❹ Universidad de Paz

Road Map D3. 8 miles (13 km) W of Escazú. 🚌 to Ciudad Colón, then by taxi. **Tel** 2205-9000. **Open** 8am–4:30pm Mon–Fri. 🅿 🖭 by appt. ♿ 🚻 Thu, Fri, Sat. 🌐 upeace.org

A United Nations institution, the University of Peace (UPAZ) enjoys an idyllic setting on 750 acres (300 ha) donated by the owners of Hacienda Rodeo, a cattle estate and forest reserve on which the campus is located. Founded in 1980, the university is dedicated to research and education for the promotion of peace.

The botanical gardens within the campus contain busts of famed pacifists such as Mahatma Gandhi, Russian novelist Alexey Tolstoy, and Henry Dunant, founder of the Red Cross. Particularly moving is the life-size statue *Peace Pilgrim* by Fernando Calvo, dedicated to Mildred N. Ryder (1908–81), who, from age 44 until her death, walked for the cause of world peace.

Trails lead into the **Reserva Forestal el Rodeo**, a 4.6-sq-mile (12-sq-km) primary forest reserve sheltering deer, monkeys, wild cats, and more than 300 species of birds.

❺ Grecia

Road Map C3. 11 miles (18 km) NW of Alajuela. 🚹 14,000. 🚌

A peaceful market town founded in 1864 and voted several times the nation's cleanest town, Grecia's claim to fame is the **Iglesia de Grecia**, made of rust-red prefabricated steel plates. Trimmed in white

filigree, the church has twin spires and a wooden interior with an elaborate marble altar.

Close to Grecia, the open-air **World of Snakes** displays 300 snakes of more than 50 species. Visitors are allowed to handle the non-venomous species.

🐍 World of Snakes
0.5 mile (1 km) SE of Grecia.
Tel 2494-3700. **Open** 8am–4pm daily. 🅿 🖭 🚻 🅿
🌐 theworldofsnakes.com

❻ Sarchí

Road Map C3. 18 miles (29 km) NW of Alajuela. 🚹 11,000. 🚌 ℹ Plaza de la Artesanía, Sarchí Sur. 🎉 Festival de las Carretas (Feb).

The country's foremost crafts center is set in the midst of coffee fields on the southern flank of Volcán Poás. The town is famous for its wooden furniture, leather rocking chairs, and hand-painted oxcarts, decorated with signature floral motifs and geometric designs.

Iglesia de Sarchí, which contains fine statuary by local artisans

The whitewashed buildings of Sarchí Norte, the town center, are graced by similar motifs. Don't miss the pink-and-turquoise **Iglesia de Sarchí** in the town plaza. One of its twin spires is topped by a trademark oxcart wheel.

Craft stores and *mueblerías* (furniture workshops) are concentrated in Sarchí Sur, 0.5 mile (1 km) east. A good place to buy souvenirs is **Fábrica de Carretas Joaquín Chaverrí** *(see p279)*. Decorative oxcarts of various sizes are painted in *talleres* (workshops) at the rear. More fascinating is **Fábrica de Carretas Eloy Alfaro**, the only remaining *taller* in the country that actually makes oxcarts. Sarchí is popular with tour groups – avoid visiting the town on weekends.

🏠 Fábrica de Carretas Joaquín Chaverrí
Sarchí Sur. **Tel** 2454-4411. **Open** 8am–6pm daily. 🅿 ♿ 🚻 🏠
🌐 sarchicostarica.net

🏠 Fábrica de Carretas Eloy Alfaro
164 yd (150 m) N of Sarchí Norte.
Tel 2454-4131. **Open** 6am–6pm Mon–Fri. 🅿 ♿ 🌐 fabricade carretaseloyalfaro.com

❼ El Silencio de Los Angeles Cloud Forest Reserve

Road Map C3. 20 miles (32 km) NW of Sarchí. **Tel** 2461-0300. 🚌 to San Ramón, then by taxi. **Open** 8am–5pm daily. 🅿 🚻 🏠 🍴 🌐 villablanca costarica.com

Providing easy access to a cloud forest environment, this 3-sq-mile (9-sq-km) reserve reverberates with the calls of aricaris, bellbirds, and three species of monkeys. Wild cats prowl the mist-shrouded forests, which range from 2,300 ft to 5,900 ft (700–1,800 m) in elevation and are accessed by a comprehensive network of trails classified by length and degree of difficulty.

Clouds swirl around the colonial farmhouse here, which sits atop the Continental Divide

The impressive topiary archway on the central path of Parque Francisco Alvardo, Zarcero

nd houses the Villablanca Cloud Forest Hotel & Spa (see p254). The hotel's tiny **La Mariana** Chapel has a high ceiling covered with hand-painted tiles, each devoted to a different female saint. Outside, an effigy of the black saint San Martín de Porres welcomes visitors.

Nearby **Nectandra Cloud Forest Garden** has well-maintained trails and landscaped gardens exhibiting the rich flora and fauna of Costa Rica.

Nectandra Cloud Forest Garden
16 miles (26 km) NW of San Ramón. **Tel** 2445-4642. 8am–5pm daily by appointment. **W** nectandra.org

Zarcero

Road Map C3. 14 miles (22 km) NW of Sarchí. 3,800. Feria Cívica (Feb).

This quiet mountain town, at an elevation of 5,600 ft (1,700 m), has a spectacular setting, with lush pastures and forested mountains all around. It is renowned for its cheese, called *palmito*.

At the heart of the town, the main attraction is **Parque Francisco Alvardo**, a spacious park with well-tended gardens and topiary features. Since 1960, gardener Don Evangelisto Blanco has been transforming the park's cypress bushes into various fanciful forms: an ox and cart, an elephant with

lightbulbs for eyes, a helicopter and airplane, a bullfight with matador and charging bull, and even a monkey riding a motorcycle. An Art Nouveau-style topiary archway frames the central pathway, which leads to a simple whitewashed church with a painted interior.

Bosque de Paz Rain/Cloud Forest Biological Reserve

Road Map C2. 9 miles (14 km) E of Zarcero. **Tel** 2234-6676. to Zarcero, then by taxi. **Open** 7am–5pm daily; only by appointment. **W** bosquedepaz.com

Set deep in the valley of the Río Toro on the northern slopes of Volcán Platanar, this 4-sq-mile (10-sq-km) reserve connects Parque Nacional Volcán Poás

(see p144) with remote Parque Nacional Juan Castro Blanco. Some 14 miles (22 km) of trails lead through primary and secondary forest, which span rain-sodden montane growth to cloud forest at higher elevations. The prodigious rainfall feeds the reserve's many waterfalls, as well as the streams that rush past a hummingbird and butterfly garden.

On clear days, *miradores* (viewpoints) offer fabulous vistas, as well as a chance to catch sight of sloths, wild cats, and howler, capuchin, and spider monkeys. A favorite of bird-watchers, the reserve has more than 330 species of birds, including resplendent quetzals and the loud three-wattled bellbirds.

Meals and accommodation are offered in a rustic log-and-riverstone lodge (see p253).

Traditional Oxcarts

The quintessential symbol of Costa Rica, the traditional *carreta* (oxcart) was once a regular feature on farmsteads and for transporting coffee beans. The wheels, about 4 ft to 5 ft (1.2–1.5 m) in diameter and bound with a metal belt, are spokeless. In the mid-19th century, the carts began to be painted in bright colors enlivened with stylized floral and geometric starburst designs. Metal rings were added to strike the hubcab and create a chime unique to the cart when in motion. Though still made in the traditional manner, almost all of today's *carretas* are purely decorative; miniature versions serve as liquor cabinets. Full-size oxcarts can cost up to $5,000.

A hand-painted oxcart, Sarchí

A vast expanse of coffee plants on the Doka Estate

⑩ Doka Estate

Road Map D3. Sabanilla de Alajuela, 7 miles (11 km) N of Alajuela. from Alajuela. **Tel** 2449-5152. 9am, 10am, 11am, 1:30pm, 2:30pm, and 3:30pm Mon–Sat; 9am, 10am, 11am, 1:30pm, and 2:30pm Sun; reservation recommended. 🗒
w dokaestate.com

Located on the lower slopes of Volcán Poás, this coffee *finca* was founded in 1929 by merchant Don Clorindo Vargas. Still owned by the Vargas family, the estate has some 6 sq miles (15 sq km) planted in coffee bushes and employs about 200 permanent employees; an additional 3,000 temporary workers are hired during the harvest season, which lasts October through January.

The Doka Estate, which still follows the time-honored tradition of drying coffee beans by laying them out in the sun, welcomes visitors eager to learn about coffee production and processing *(see pp32–3)*.

A guided tour of the *beneficio*, which dates from 1893 and is a National Historic Landmark, starts on a delicious note with a coffee-tasting session. The tour demonstrates the various stages involved in coffee production and ends in the roasting room. The estate offers splendid views down the slopes and across the valley. There is a small B&B nearby *(see p254)*.

⑪ Parque Nacional Volcán Poás

Road Map D1. 23 miles (37 km) N of Alajuela. from Alajuela and San José. 🅘 **Tel** 2482-2424.
Open 8am–3:30pm daily.
Closed during phases of volcanic activity. 🗒

The nation's most visited national park was inaugurated on January 25, 1971. Covering 25 sq miles (65 sq km), the park encircles Volcán Poás (8,850 ft/ 2,700 m), a restless giant that formed more than one million years ago and is ephemerally volatile, with peak activity occurring in an approximately 40-year cycle. The volcano had a minor eruption in March 2006, and a 6.2 Richter earthquake on January 9, 2009 devastated much of the immediate region.

The gateway to the park is the mountain hamlet of **Poasito**. The summit of the volcano is reached by an immensely scenic drive, which winds along coffee fields, horticultural gardens, and dairy pastures, with spectacular

Toucans at Parque Nacional Volcán Poás

views back down the valley. From the parking lot, a 5-minute walk along a paved path leads to the rim of one of the world's largest active craters. A viewing terrace grants visitors an awe-inspiring view down into the heart of the hissing and steaming caldera (collapsed crater, *see p207*), which is 895 ft (300 m) deep and a mile (1.6 km) wide. It contains an acidic turquoise lake, sulfurous fumaroles, and a 245-ft (75-m) tall cone that began to form in the 1950s. On clear days, it is possible to get magnificent views of both the Caribbean Sea and the Pacific Ocean.

The dormant Botos crater, to the southeast, is filled by the jade-colored **Botos Lake**, accessed by a trail that leads through forests of stunted myrtle, magnolia, and laurel draped with bromeliads and mosses. Over 80 species of birds such as fiery-throated hummingbirds, emerald toucanets and resplendent quetzals, have been identified in the forests. Mammal species include margays and the Poás squirrel, which is endemic to the volcano. Facilities at the national park include an exhibition hall for audiovisual presentations, a shop and a café. Clouds typically form by midmorning, so it is best to arrive early. Bring warm clothing; the average temperature at the summit is 12° C (54° F), but cloudy days can be bitterly cold. If possible, visit midweek – local

Botos Lake in a dormant volcano, Parque Nacional Volcán Poás

◀ A view of the magnificent crater of Volcán Poás

ielding blaring radios crowd
e park on weekends. Tour
perators offer guided
xcursions to the park.

La Paz Waterfall
Gardens

Road Map D2. Montaña Azul, 15 miles
4 km) N of Alajuela. **Tel** 2482-2720.
from San José. **Open** 8am–5pm;
t admission: 4pm. 🎫 🎫 🎫 🎫
🎫 **w** waterfallgardens.com

his multifaceted attraction's
ain draw is five thunderous
aterfalls plummeting through
eeply forested ravines on the
ortheast slopes of Volcán Poás.
aved pathways lead downhill
rough pristine forest to the
ascades, where spray blasts
sitors standing on viewing
atforms located above, below,
nd in front of the falls. Access to
e falls involves negotiating
etal staircases, but a shuttle
ns visitors back uphill.
The landscaped grounds
ature the **Hummingbird
arden**, which draws 26 species
f hummers – about 40 percent
f the nation's 57 species. As
any as 4,000 butterflies flit
bout the **Butterfly Garden**;
ores of macaws, toucans, and
her birds can be seen in a walk-
rough aviary enclosed by a
assive netted dome the length
f a football field; and jaguars are
highlight of a wild cat
xhibition. Other attractions
clude a walk-in ranarium
splaying poison-dart and other
og species; a serpentarium,
ith dozens of snake species;

e Butterfly Garden in La Paz
aterfall Gardens

and a re-creation of a traditional
farmstead with staff in period
costume. Renowned
ornithologists lead birding tours.
The park's restaurant has a
veranda with marvelous views
over the valley and forest. Deluxe
accommodations are available at
the Peace Lodge (see p254).

⑬ Parque Nacional
Braulio Carrillo

Road Map D2. Guápiles Hwy, 23 miles
(37 km) N of San José. 🚌 San José–
Guápiles. 🛈 Puesto Quebrada ranger
station, Hwy 32. **Tel** 2233-4533.
Open 8am–4pm Tue–Sun. 🎫 🎫

Named for Costa Rica's third
chief of state, this sprawling
185-sq-mile (480-sq-km)
park ranges in elevation from
120 ft (36 m) at La Selva in the
northern lowlands to 9,500 ft
(2,900 m) at the top of Volcán
Barva. The Parque Nacional
Braulio Carrillo is bisected
by the Guápiles Highway,
which links San José with
Puerto Limón; indeed, it
was the construction
of this highway that
prompted the
creation of the park in
1978 to protect the
capital's major watershed.
Despite its proximity to San José,
the park is one of the nation's
most rugged, with mountains,
dense rainforest cover, and
numerous waterfalls, plus it is
subject to torrential rains. It
protects five life zones, including

Margay at Parque
Nacional Braulio Carrillo

cloud forest at higher
elevations. Wildlife is diverse,
with 135 mammal species, 500
species of birds, and many
species of snakes.
The main entrance to the park
is the Quebrada González ranger
station, located 8 miles (13 km)
north of the Zurqui ranger
station (closed to visitors), near
the Rainforest Aerial Tram (see
p213). The most rewarding
hiking is around the summit of
Volcán Barva, on the west side of
the park and accessed by 4WD
via the Puesto Barva ranger
station above the village of
Sacramento. From here, a trail
leads through the spectacular
cloud forest to the crater.
The dormant Barva has at
least 13 eruptive cones, several
of which are filled with
lakes. Tapirs can be
frequently seen around
Danta and Barva Lakes.
Experienced hikers
can tackle longer trails,
taking several days,
which descend the
northern slopes via
deep canyons. There are
no facilities, and proper
equipment is
absolutely essential.
Note that there have
been instances of
armed robberies and theft from
cars parked near trailheads.
Hikers must report to the ranger
stations when setting out and
returning. Tour operators in
San José can arrange half-day
or full-day tours.

Stained glass at La Parroquia de la Inmaculada Concepción, Heredia

⓮ Heredia

Road Map D3. 7 miles (11 km) NW of San José. 42,500. by appointment. Sat. Easter Parade in San Joaquín de Flores (Mar/Apr).

A peaceful and orderly town founded in 1706, Heredia has a smattering of important colonial buildings at its heart and a bustling student life, owing to the presence of a branch of the University of Costa Rica (see p125). It is centered on Parque Nicolás Ulloa, popularly called Parque Central. Shaded by large mango trees, the park contains numerous busts and monuments. Dominating the park is the squat, weathered cathedral **La Parroquia de la Inmaculada Concepción**. Built in 1797, the cathedral has a triangular pediment, lovely stained-glass windows, and a two-tone checkerboard floor of marble.

On the north side of Parque Central, the forecourt of the municipality office features the *Monumento Nacional a la Madre*, an endearing bronze sculpture of a mother and child by Miguela Brenes. Adjoining the Municipalidad, to the west, the colonial-era **Casa de la Cultura** occupies the home of former president Alfredo González Flores (1877–1962). It is now an art gallery and a tiny museum. Nearby is **El Fortín**, an interesting circular fortress tower built in 1876.

Environs
A popular attraction in the lively town of Santa Barbara de Heredia, northwest of Heredia, is the **Ark Herb Farm**. Its orchards and gardens spread over 20 acres (8 ha). The farm exports medicinal herbs. North of Heredia, the steep upper slopes of Volcán Barva are popular

getaway spots for Josefinos for their crisp air and solitude. Tyrolean-style houses set amid cypress and pine forests can be rented at **Monte de la Cruz**, a reserve with trails. In July–August, **Hotel Chalet Tirol** (see p254) hosts the Credomatic Music Festival. To the southeast of Heredia is the environmental park **INBioparque**, with exhibits relating to conservation and bio-diversity, including various re-creations of natural habitats.

Label of a Café Britt product

🏛 Casa de la Cultura
Calle and Ave Central.
Tel 2260-4485. 9am–9pm daily.

🌿 Ark Herb Farm
Santa Barbara de Heredia, 3 miles (5 km) NW of Heredia. **Tel** 2239-2111. 8am–4pm Mon–Sat, by appt. 9:30am, by appt. arkherbfarm.com

🌿 INBioparque
3 miles (5 km) SE of Heredia. **Tel** 2507-8107. 8:30am–2pm Tue–Fri, 9am–3:30pm Sat & Sun. mandatory. inbioparque.com

Visitors admiring tropical flowers at Ark Herb Farm, near Heredia

⓯ Café Britt

Road Map D3. Santa Lucía, 0.5 mile (1 km) N of Heredia. **Tel** 2277-1600. organized transfers from San José mandatory; 9:30am, 11am, and 3pm. Concerts, lectures, films. coffeetour.com

A mecca for coffee lovers and one of the country's most visited tourist attractions, this *beneficio* (processing mill) roasts and packs gourmet coffees. Entertaining guided tours are led by *campesinos*, played by professional actors in period costume. The guides' homespun repartee unfolds a spellbinding love story along with a fascinating educational narrative on the history and production cycle of coffee, from the plantation to the cup. Visitors are led through the 6-acre (2.5-ha) coffee estates before taking a hard-hat tour of the packing facility, where they breathe in the tantalizing aroma of roasting beans. The tour ends in the coffee bar and dining room, after a multimedia presentation that highlights coffee's role in cultivating Costa Rican democracy and molding national identity. The factory store sells coffees, chocolates, souvenirs, and local crafts.

⓰ Barva

Road Map D3. 2 miles (3 km) N of Heredia. 4,900. from Heredia. Festival de San Bartolomé (Aug 24).

One of the country's oldest settlements, this quaint town was founded in 1613, with the official name San Bartolomé of Barva. Located at the base of Volcán Barva, the town contains many simple 18th-century adobe houses with traditional red-tile roofs.

The flower-filled and palm-shaded town square, laid out in 1913, is graced by the pretty **Iglesia de San Bartolomé de Barva**, erected in 1867 on the site of an Indian burial ground. It

placed two earlier churches
lled by earthquakes. On the
rtheast side is a grotto
edicated to the Virgin of Lourdes.
The **Museo de Cultura
opular**, on the outskirts of
arva, provides a portrait
late 19th-century life, with
riod pieces laid out in the
shion of the times. The
ilding is a former home of
-president Alfredo González
res. A part of the dung-and-
aw adobe masonry is
xposed to view. The kitchen
rves traditional meals.

Museo de Cultura Popular
nta Lucía de Barva, just S of Barva.
2260-1619. **Open** 8am–4pm
n–Fri, by appt. Sat & Sun.

San Isidro de oronado

ad Map D3. 6 miles (10 km)
of San José. 8,400.
stival de San Isidro Labrador
ay 15).

inging to the western
pes of Irazú volcano, San Isidro
Coronado is an agricultural
nter boasting the largest
thic church in the country.
e **Parroquia de San Isidro**,
hich soars over the town's
e-shaded plaza, was pre-
oricated in Germany in 1930
d erected in situ, being
mpleted in 1934.
San Isidro is a gateway to
zú Volcano National Park via
unbelievably scenic route
rough Rancho Redondo.
e road snakes along the
untainsides, granting
ectacular vistas over San
sé and the Central Highlands.

The Basílica de Nuestra Señora de los
Angeles, Cartago

⑱ Cartago

Road Map D3. 13 miles (21 km) E of
San José. 120,000. Corpus
Christi (May/Jun); Día de Nuestra
Señora de la Virgen de los Angeles
(Aug 2).

Costa Rica's first city and original
colonial capital was founded in
1563 by conquistador and
Spanish governor Juan Vásquez
de Coronado *(see p44)*. Named
for the Spanish word for
Carthage, it lost its capital status
to San José at the Battle of
Ochomogo in 1823. The city
was destroyed when Volcán
Irazú erupted in 1723. Most of
the subsequent colonial
structures were felled by violent
earthquakes in 1841 and 1910.
    Today the city has limited
appeal. However, Cartago
remains the nation's religious
capital, centered on the
Byzantine-style **Basílica de
Nuestra Señora de los Angeles**
(see pp148–9), dedicated to Costa
Rica's patron saint, La Negrita.
    Memories of the earthquake
of April 13, 1910, remain in the

ruins of the **Iglesia de la
Parroquia**, originally built in
1575 and destroyed five times
by earthquakes before its final
demise. The mossy ruins now
form the centerpiece of a small
garden adjoining the stark
central plaza. The **Museo
Municipal de Cartago**, in the
former army barracks, hosts
revolving art exhibitions.

Museo Municipal de Cartago
Ave 6 and Calle 2. **Tel** 2591-1050.
Open 9am–4pm Tue–Sat,
9am–3pm Sun.

⑲ Jardín Botánico Lankester

Road Map D3. 4 miles (6 km) E of
Cartago. **Tel** 2552-3247. from
Cartago. **Open** 8:30am–4:30pm daily.
jbl.ucr.ac.cr

Operated by the University of
Costa Rica as a research center,
these luxuriant botanical
gardens were founded in 1917
by English horticulturalist and
coffee-planter Charles Lankester
West. Covering 27 acres (11 ha),
they display almost 3,000
neotropical species in separate
sections dedicated to specific
plant families. The highlight is
the orchid collection, spread
throughout the garden. The
1,100 species are best seen in
the dry season, especially from
February to April. Pathways
snake through a bamboo
tunnel, a swathe of premontane
forest, a medicinal plant garden,
a cactus garden, a butterfly
garden, and a Japanese garden.
Visitors are given an orientation
talk before setting out on a
self-guided tour.

e weather-beaten ruins of Iglesia de la Parroquia, Cartago

Cartago: Basílica de Nuestra Señora de los Angeles

Named in honor of the country's patron saint, the Virgin of Los Angeles (also called La Negrita), Cartago's Cathedral of Our Lady of the Angels is Costa Rica's most important church. Legend has it that on August 2, 1635, a mulatto peasant girl called Juana Pereira found a small figurine of a dark-skinned Virgin Mary on a rock. The statue was put away in safe custody twice and mysteriously returned to the rock both times. The basilica was built to mark the spot. Destroyed in 1926 by a massive earthquake, it was rebuilt in 1929. The impressive Byzantine-style edifice features a stone exterior with a decorated façade and is topped by an octagonal cupola. A spring flowing beneath the basilica is considered to have curative powers.

Side Altar
The side altars contain a series of shrines to saints such as San Antonio de Padua, San Cayetano, San Vicente de Paul, and the black saint, San Benito de Palermo. There are also life-size statues of Jesus, Mary, and Joseph.

★ La Negrita Statue
The 8-inch (20-cm) high statue of Mary, the discovery of which supposedly led to the construction of the church, is installed in a shrine above the main altar. The shrine is encrusted with gold and precious stones.

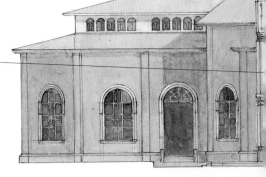

Façade
The façade has Moorish-style arches and fluted pilasters capped by angels.

The La Negrita Pilgrimage

Every August 2, devout Costa Ricans join in the Día de Nuestra Señora de la Virgen de los Angeles procession. Thousands walk the 15 miles (24 km) from San José to Cartago – many crawl much of the way on their knees; others carry crosses. Devotees descend to the subterranean Cripta de la Piedra to touch the rock and collect holy water from the underground spring. The statue of La Negrita is paraded through the city before being replaced in its shrine.

Pilgrims and tourists outside the church

The Ceiling
The wooden ceiling is centered on an octagonal, wood-paneled dome ringed by windows through which sunlight pours in, illuminating the nave and producing a sense of religious exaltation.

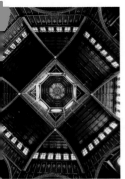

VISITORS' CHECKLIST

Practical Information
Calle 14/16 and Aves 2/4, Cartago. **Tel** 2551-0465.
Open 6am–7pm daily. ✝ regular services throughout the day. ♿

Transport
🚌 from San José (Calle 5 and Aves 18/20).

★ **The Nave**
The elaborate interior in the shape of a double cross is made entirely of hardwoods, painted with decorative floral patterns of white alabaster. Parabolic arches are supported atop clover-leaf-shaped wooden pillars.

KEY

① **The walls** are made of galvanized steel stuccoed with cement.

② **The Cripta de la Piedra** (Crypt of the Rock) is the subterranean shrine containing the rock where the La Negrita statue was supposedly found. Entered via a ramp to the rear of the basilica, it is filled with flickering votive offerings.

Stained-Glass Window
The basilica boasts several fine *vitrales* (stained-glass panes) depicting biblical scenes. The finest are in the Sacristy, in the southeast corner, and depict Jesus with various saints.

Cloud forest in the Parque Nacional Los Quetzales

⓴ Parque Nacional Los Quetzales

Road Map D3/D4. Pan-Am Hwy, 47 miles (76 km) SE of San José. 🚌 to Km 80, then hike. **Tel** 2200-5354. **Open** 8am–4pm daily. 🅿
🖥 sinac.go.cr

Bordering the Pan-American Highway is the Parque Nacional Los Quetzales, created in 2005 from the Los Santos Forest Reserve, the Biological Reserve of Cerro de las Vueltas, and various state properties. The park covers 12,355 acres (5,000 ha) of cloud forest, spread over the banks of the Río Savegre. This is one of the most biologically diverse regions in Costa Rica, with 25 indigenous species, 116 species of mammals, mangroves, and lagoons of glacial origins. One of the highlights, however, is the quetzals for which the park is named. Other birds that may be seen include sooty robins and hummingbirds.

Dantica Cloud Forest Lodge, which is just north of San Gerado de Dota, has trails running through primary cloud forest in which peccaries, deer, tapir, otters, ocelots, and pumas have all been sighted.

Dantica's three-room indigenous art gallery exhibits jewelry, textiles, ceramics, statues, and masks from such nations as Peru, Venezuela, and Colombia. There are also masks and natural-dye cotton bags produced by the Boruca indigenous group from southern Costa Rica.

🏨 **Dantica Cloud Forest Lodge**
Tel 2740-1067. **Open** 24 hrs. 🅿 🍴 🍽 🐾 🖥 dantica.com

㉑ San Gerardo de Dota

Road Map D4. 5.5 miles (9 km) W of Pan-Am Hwy at Km 80. 🏔 1,000. 🚌 to Km 80, then hike or arrange a transfer (call 8367-8141).

One of the best sites in Costa Rica for quetzal-watching, this small community is tucked into the bottom of a steep valley furrowed by Río Savegre. Go down a switchback from the Pan-Am Highway to reach the hamlet, which was first settled in 1954 by Don Efraín Chacón and his family. Today, the Chacóns' **Savegre Hotel Natural Reserve** protects around 1,000 acres (400 ha) of cloud forest and houses the Quetzal Education Research Center (QERC). This study center for quetzal ecology is the tropical campus of the Southern Nazarene University of Oklahoma. April to May is nesting season, when quetzals are most abundant. More than 170 other bird species are present seasonally.

Dramatic scenery, crisp air, and blissful solitude reward the few travelers who take the time to make the sharp descent into San Gerardo de Dota. Fruits grow in profusion in orchards surrounded by meadows and centenary oaks.

About 22 miles (35 km) of graded trails crisscross the forest, with options from very easy to technically challenging. Activities include guided treks from the frigid heights of Cerro Frío (Cold Mountain) at 11,400 ft (3,450 m) to San Gerardo de Dota at 7,200 ft (2,200 m). Other trails lead along the banks of the gurgling river, which is stocked with rainbow trout.

🏨 **Savegre Hotel Natural Reserve**
Tel 2740-1028. 🍴 🛏 🅿
🖥 savegre.com

Walking in the forest at Savegre Hotel Natural Reserve, San Gerardo de Dota

㉒ La Ruta de los Santos

South of San José, the Cerro de Escazú rise steeply from Desamparados to the town of Aserrí. Twisting roads then pass through San Gabriel, San Pablo de León Cortés, San Marcos de Tarrazú, Santa María de Dota, and San Cristóbal Sur in the steep-sided coffee country known as Tarrazú. These off-the-beaten-track communities – named for saints Gabriel, Paul, Mark, Mary, and Christopher – give this fabulously scenic drive through verdant highlands and valleys its apt name, "Route of the Saints."

Tips for Drivers

Tour length: 95 miles (153 km) round-trip.
Stopping-off points: Stop for a bite at the charming Vaca Flaca *(see p269)* or La Casona de Sara in Santa María *(see p270)*.
Information: Beneficio Coopedota. **Tel** 2541-2828.
W dotacoffee.com;
Beneficio Coopetarrazú.
Tel 2546-6098.
W cafetarrazu.com

① Desamparados
This town is dominated by its handsome church in Neoclassical style.

② Aserrí
The mountainside above Aserrí offers superb vistas across the valley toward Barva, Irazú, and Turrialba Volcanoes.

⑦ San Cristóbal Sur
This is the setting for the mountain farm where Figueres *(see p49)* prepared to launch the 1948 revolution that resulted in civil war.

⑥ Santa María de Dota
This tidy town's plaza has a granite monument commemorating those who died in the 1948 civil war. The Beneficio Coopedota accepts visitors – by reservation – for plantation tours.

③ San Gabriel
Occupying a mountain spur overlooking Río Tarrazú, this town is dominated by a white church with a domed roof.

④ San Pablo de León Cortés
The Iglesia de San Juan de la Cruz, built in 1997, towers above the plaza in this coffee center.

⑤ San Marcos de Tarrazú
Surrounded by coffee-covered slopes, the region's most important town boasts a fine church. Arrange a visit to Beneficio Coopetarrazú coffee mill in advance.

Key

⎯ Tour route
⎯ Highway
= Other road

0 km   3
0 miles   3

San José, Alajuela, 212, 209, Tarbaca, 209, 222, San Andreas, 226, 222, Emplame, Jardin, 226

㉓ The Orosi Valley

South of Cartago, the land falls away steeply into the Orosi Valley, a large gorge hemmed to the south by the Talamanca Mountains. Río Reventazón drains the valley and joins Lago de Cachí, also fed by other streams and raging rivers tumbling out of hills enveloped by cloud forest. Shiny-leafed coffee bushes cover the valley, which was an important colonial center and has two of Costa Rica's oldest religious sites. The ruins of the 17th-century church in the village of Ujarrás, set at the edge of Lago de Cachí, are the highlight of a visit to the valley. Orosi village is home to the country's oldest extant church. The valley's social life centers on this tranquil hamlet. Looping around the Orosi Valley is Route 224, which passes the main points of interest and makes for a perfect half- or full-day tour.

View of the spillways of Cachí Dam on Lago de Cachí

Cartago

Mirador U

Paraíso

224

Mirador de Orosi

Sanchiri

Río Aguacaliente

Orosi

224

Mirador de Orosi
Operated by ICT (Instituto Costarricense de Turismo), this *mirador* (viewpoint) offers stunning views over the valley and has picnic tables on lawns abuzz with hummingbirds.

KEY

① **Paradero Lacustre Charrara** offers picnic areas, a swimming pool, and recreational and sport facilities *(see p154)*.

② **La Casona de Cafetal**, a lakeside coffee *finca*, offers hiking trails and horseback rides.

③ **Monte Sky Mountain Retreat** protects a 139-acre (56-ha) area of cloud forest. Trails lead to waterfalls and offer a chance to spot quetzals. There are also facilities for tent camping. A 4WD vehicle is required to get here.

Río

Orosi
Surrounded by coffee plantations and peppered with waterfalls, the picturesque village of Orosi is known for the colonial-era Iglesia de San José de Orosi, which contains a small museum of religious art. Orosi has several thermal mineral springs called *balnearios (see p154)*.

For hotels and restaurants in this region see pp252–61 and pp266–77

jarrás
his village has all but vanished after being flooded in 1833. It is
nown for the ruins of the Iglesia de Nuestra Señora de la Límpia
oncepción, built in 1693 *(see p154)*.

VISITORS' CHECKLIST

Practical Information
Road Map D3. Cartago.
14,000. *i* 2533-3640 (Orosi
Tourism). Romería Virgen de
la Candelaria (3rd Sun of Apr),
Orosi Colonial Tourist Fair (Sep).
La Casona de Cafetal: **Tel** 2577-
1414. **Open** 11am–6pm daily.
Monte Sky Mountain Retreat:
Tel 2228-0010. **Open** 8am–
5pm daily.

Transport
 hourly from Cartago to Orosi.
Also to Cachí via Ujarrás.

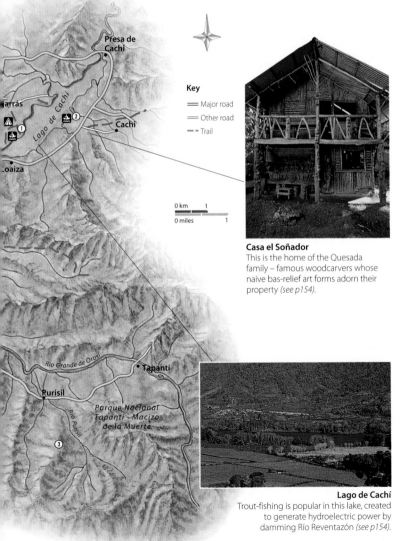

Key
— Major road
— Other road
-- Trail

Presa de
Cachí

Cachí

Lago de Cachí

jarrás

Loaiza

0 km   1
0 miles   1

Río Grande de Orosí

Tapantí

Purisíl

Río Purisíl

*Parque Nacional
Tapantí – Macizo
de la Muerte*

Casa el Soñador
This is the home of the Quesada
family – famous woodcarvers whose
naïve bas-relief art forms adorn their
property *(see p154)*.

Lago de Cachí
Trout-fishing is popular in this lake, created
to generate hydroelectric power by
damming Río Reventazón *(see p154)*.

For additional map symbols *see back flap*

Exploring the Orosi Valley

The first colonists arrived in the valley of Río Reventazón in 1564 to convert the indigenous Cabécar people who were led by a *cacique* (chief) named Orosi. The valley soon became an important religious center. It is the colonial relics that draw visitors to the region, but the scenery is no less appealing. Route 224, which encircles the valley, brings in an ever-increasing number of tourists.

Iglesia de San José de Orosi's interior, dominated by wood and terra-cotta

Ujarrás

8 miles (13 km) SE of Cartago.
Located at the edge of Lake Cachí and surrounded by coffee bushes, the hamlet of Ujarrás features the ruins of the **Iglesia de Nuestra Señora de la Límpia Concepción**, completed in 1693. The ruins stand in a charming garden awash with tropical flowers.

The site previously housed the shrine La Parroquia de Ujarrás. According to legend, a converted Indian found a wooden box containing a statue of the Virgin Mary. He carried it to Ujarrás, where it suddenly became too heavy for even a team of men to lift. The local priest considered this a sign from God that a shrine should be built here. When pirates led by Henry Morgan attacked the region in 1666, local inhabitants prayed at the shrine for salvation. A defensive force led by Spanish governor, Juan Lopez de la Flor, routed the pirates and in gratitude built a church in honor of the Virgen del Rescate de Ujarrás (Virgin of Rescue). Damaged in a flood in 1833, the church was thereafter abandoned. Every third Sunday in April, pilgrims walk to the shrine from Paraíso, which is 4 miles (6 km) to the west, in honor of the Virgin.

Orosi

5 miles (8 km) S of Paraíso. 🚌 8,862.
Balnearios Termales Orosi **Tel** 2533-2156. **Open** 7:30am–4pm: Wed–Mon. 🅿 🖼 Museo de Arte Religioso: **Tel** 2533-3051. **Open** 1–5pm Tue–Fri, 9am–5pm Sat & Sun. 🅿 🚻 🏛 ✉

Nestling neatly on the banks of Río Grande de Orosi, this small village is a coffee growing center. Mineral hot springs gush from the hillsides and can be enjoyed in orderly and well-maintained pools at **Balnearios Termales Orosi**. Orosi's pride is

Ruins of Nuestra Señora de la Límpia Concepción, Ujarrás

the beautifully preserved **Iglesia de San José de Orosi**, the oldest functioning church in Costa Rica. Built by Franciscans in 1743–66 and dominated by a solid bell tower, the whitewashed church has withstood several earthquakes, despite its plain adobe construction. The interior features a beamed ceiling, terra cotta floor, and simple gilt-adorned wooden altar. The Franciscan monastery adjoining the church is now the **Museo de Arte Religioso**, displaying period furniture and religious icons dating back three centuries. Most of the items – such as paintings, statuary, and altar pieces – come from Mexico and Guatemala.

🖼 Lago de Cachí

Paradero Lacustre Charrarra
1.6 mile (2 km) E of Ujarrás. **Tel** 2574-7557. **Open** 8am–5pm daily. 🅿 🚻 🖼 Casa el Soñador: 5 miles (8 km) E of Orosi. **Tel** 2577-1186. **Open** 9am–6pm daily.

This massive lake was created between 1959 and 1963, when the ICE (Costa Rican Institute of Electricity) dammed Río Reventazón. The Presa de Cachí (Cachí Dam) funnels water down spillways to feed massive hydro-electricity turbines. Visitors can enjoy kayaking, canoeing, and boating on the lake, arranged by local tour operators. The national tourist board operates **Paradero Lacustre Charrarra**, a recreational complex offering boating from the north shore. Horseback riding is also on offer.

On the southern shore is **Casa el Soñador** (Dreamer's House), the pretty bamboo-and-wood studio of sculptor Macedonio Quesada Valerín (1932–94). Carved figures representing the town gossips lean out of the upper-story windows and a bas-relief of Leonardo da Vinci's *The Last Supper* adorns the exterior. Macedonio's sons carry on their father's tradition of carving walking sticks, religious figures, and ornaments from coffee plant roots. The studio serves as an art gallery for the works of other local artists.

waterfall at Parque Nacional
Tapantí-Macizo la Muerte

Parque Nacional Tapantí-Macizo la Muerte

Road Map D3. 5.5 miles (9 km) of Orosi. **Tel** 2200-0090. Orosi, then by jeep-taxi. **Open** 8am–4pm daily.

South of the Orosi Valley, the vibrantly green Tapantí-Macizo National Park, created in 1982, protects 225 sq miles (583 sq km) of the Talamanca Mountains. Ranging in elevation from 3,950 ft to 8,350 ft (1,200–2,550 m). It features diverse flora, from lower montane rainforest to montane dwarf forest on the upper slopes. The national park is deluged with rains almost throughout the year, which feed the fast-flowing rivers rushing through it; February to April are the least rainy months, and the best time to visit.

Spectacularly rich in wildlife, the park has animals such as anteaters, jaguars, monkeys, tapirs, and even otters. Tapantí is a birder's heaven – more than 260 bird species inhabit its thick forests. Resplendent quetzals frequent the thickets near the ranger station, which has a small nature display.

Well-marked trails lace the rugged terrain. A particularly pleasant and easy hike is **Sendero La Catarata**, which leads to a waterfall. Fishing in the park is permitted from April to October.

Turrialba

Road Map E3. 27 miles (44 km) E of Cartago. 32,000.

This pleasant regional center squats in a broad valley on the banks of Río Turrialba at 2,130 ft (650 m) above sea level, against the base of Volcán Turrialba *(see p157)*. Once an important transportation hub midway between San José and the Caribbean, Turrialba had to forego that position with the opening of the Guápiles Highway in 1987, and cessation of rail service in 1991. Rusting railroad tracks serve as reminders of the days when the Atlantic Railroad thrived.

There is little of interest in the town; its importance lies in being a center for kayaking and rafting trips on the Río Reventazón and Río Pacuare, and serving as a good base from which to explore nearby attractions.

Wooden tortoise, Turrialba

Environs

The valley bottom southeast of Turrialba is filled by the 630-acre (255-ha) **Lake Angostura**, created by the building of a dam in 2000 to generate hydroelectricty. It lures several species of waterfowl and is a water sports center, although it is gradually being choked by water hyacinths. Río Reventazón (Exploding River) below the dam has Class III–IV rapids and is fabulously scenic, as is the nearby Río Pacuare, also favored by rafters *(see p156)*. **Hotel Casa Turire**, on the south shore of Lake Angostura, is a charming deluxe hotel offering biking, hiking, horseback riding, and many other activities *(see p254)*.

East of Turrialba, the **Centro Agronómico Tropical de Investigación y Enseñanza (CATIE)**, or Center for Tropical Agriculture Investigation and Learning, has trails through 3 sq miles (9 sq km) of landscaped grounds, forests, and orchards, which grow exotic fruits, plus a botanical garden. A lake attracts waterfowl. Guided tours provide fascinating insights into ecology and animal husbandry. Farther east is **Serpentario Viborana**, a serpentarium that exhibits several species of snakes, including boas and fer-de-lances. The guided tour includes a lecture on snake ecology.

Women in traditional dress can be seen at **Reserva Indígena Chirripó**, an incredibly scenic indigenous reserve in the Talamanca Mountains beyond Moravia del Chirripó, southeast of Turrialba.

Centro Agronómico Tropical de Investigación y Enseñanza (CATIE)
1.2 miles (2 km) E of Turrialba. **Tel** 2558-2000. 7am–4pm daily (Jardín Botánico). **catie.ac.cr**

Serpentario Viborana
Pavones, 5.5 miles (9 km) E of Turrialba. **Tel** 2538-1510. **Open** 9am–5pm daily. by appt.

Casa Turire, a delightful hotel near Turrialba

Whitewater Rafting

Costa Rica boasts rivers that are perfect for whitewater rafting. The best of the runnable rivers flow down from the mountainous Central Highlands to the Caribbean, cascading through narrow canyons churned by rapids, and interspersed with calm sections. Small groups paddle downstream in large purpose-built rubber dinghies, led by experienced guides. Trips can be anything from half a day to a week, catering to every level of experience: rivers are ranked from Class I (easy) to Class VI (extremely difficult). May, June, September, and October are the best months, when heavy rainfall gives rivers an extra boost. Rafting is organized by professional operators who provide gear, meals, and accommodations *(see p293)*.

Costa Rica's whitewater rivers offer an extraordinary combination of scenic beauty, wildlife sightings, and thrills. One of the finest rafting destinations, Río Reventazón (left) caters to enthusiasts of differing skill levels, with separate sections that have difficulty ratings ranging from Class II to V.

Rafters should wear T-shirts, shorts, and sneakers or sandals, and carry spare clothes.

Guides steer and give commands from the rear.

Safety gear such as life-jackets and helmets are mandatory.

Calm stretches provide ample scope for wildlife viewing – kingfishers, parrots, toucans, caimans, iguanas, and varieties of monkeys are among the easily seen fauna.

Rafting Down Rio Pacuare

Torrential Río Pacuare is ranked among the world's top five whitewater rivers. Rafting trips of varying duration take thrill-seekers on adrenaline-packed rides along thickly forested, wildlife-rich gorges, rushing currents, and amazing rapids.

Numerous waterfalls pour down the sides of the river's gorges. Some fall hundreds of feet, showering rafters with cool water on hot days.

Pounding rapids are found all along the length of the Rio Pacuare, and offer spectacular whitewater rides ranked Class III and IV in difficulty.

Riverside stops are arranged for hearty breakfasts and lunches. Overnight halts in wilderness lodges or tents on longer trips also offer opportunities for hiking and soaking in the scenery.

Monumento Nacional Guayabo

See pp158–9.

Parque Nacional Volcán Turrialba

Road Map D3. 15 miles (24 km) NW of Turrialba. to Santa Cruz, then by jeep-taxi. 2273-4335 (Volcán Turrialba Lodge). volcanturrialbalodge.com

The easternmost volcano in Costa Rica, the 10,950-ft (3,340-m) high Turrialba was dormant for more than a century following a period of violent activity in the 1860s. In January 2010, it became active again.

The volcano's name comes from the Huetar Indian words *turiri* and *abá*, which together mean "river of fire." Local legend says that a girl named Cira, lost while exploring, was found by a young man from a rival tribe, and they fell in love. When the girl's enraged father eventually found the two lovers and prepared to kill the young suitor, Turrialba spewed a tall column of smoke, signifying divine assent.

Established in 1955, the Turrialba Volcano National Park protects 5 sq miles (13 sq km) of land, much of which is covered in cloud forest of gnarled oak and myrtle trees.

Dirt roads go to within a few miles of the summit, which is then accessible by trails. Stamina is required for the switchback hike to the top. From there, in clear weather, it is possible to see the Cordillera Central and the Caribbean coast. A trail also descends to the floor of the largest crater, where sulfurous gases hiss out of active fumaroles. Access is granted only during inactive phases; the summit has been off-limits for the past few years.

There are no public facilities or transport in the park, but the privately run Volcán Turrialba Lodge (www.volcanturrialba lodge.com) on the western bank of the volcano at 9,200 ft (2,800 m), provides a base from which to explore the area.

Deep green lake in the largest crater of Parque Nacional Volcán Irazú

㉘ Parque Nacional Volcán Irazú

Road Map D3. 19 miles (30 km) N of Cartago. **Tel** 2200-5025. from Ave 2, Calles 1/3, San José, 8am daily. **Open** 8am–3:30pm daily.

Encircling the upper slopes of Volcán Irazú, this 7-sq-mile (18-sq-km) park was established in 1955. At 11,260 ft (3,430 m), the cloud-covered Irazú is Costa Rica's highest volcano, and historically its most active – the first written reference to an eruption was in 1723. Several devastating explosions occurred between 1917 and 1921, and it famously erupted on March 13, 1963, when US President John F. Kennedy was in the country to attend the Summit of Central America Presidents.

The name Irazú is derived from the Indian word *istarú*, which means "mountain of thunder."

The road to the summit winds uphill past vegetable fields. A viewing platform lets visitors peer down into a 985-ft (300-m) deep, 0.5-mile (1-km) wide crater, containing a pea-green lake. Four other craters can be accessed, but there are active fumaroles, and the marked trails should be followed. Although the volcano is often covered by fog, the cloud line is frequently below the summit, which basks in bright sunshine. Arriving early increases the chances of clear weather and good views. The lunar landscape of the summit includes a great ash plain called **Playa Hermosa**. Hardy vegetation, such as myrtle and the large-leaved "poor man's umbrella," maintains a tenuous foothold against acidic emissions in the bitter cold. Wildlife is scarce, although it is possible to spot birds such as the sooty robin and endemic volcano junco.

Signage at Parque Nacional Volcán Irazú

The **Museo Vulcanológico**, below the park, has displays that explain the action of volcanoes and profile the activity and ecology of Irazú.

Museo Vulcanológico 1 mile (1.6 km) below the park entrance. **Tel** 2305-8013. **Open** 8am–3:30pm daily.

㉖ Monumento Nacional Guayabo

Proclaimed a national monument in 1973, Guayabo, on the southern slope of Volcán Turrialba, is the nation's most important pre-Columbian site. Although minor in scale compared to the Mayan remains of Mexico, the 540-acre (218-ha) site, which is still shrouded in mystery, is considered to be of great cultural and religious significance. Believed to have been inhabited between 1500 BC and AD 1400, Guayabo is said to have supported a population as high as 10,000, before being abandoned for reasons unknown. The jungle quickly reclaimed the town, which was discovered in the late 18th century by naturalist Don Anastasio Alfaro. The peaceful site, most of which is yet to be excavated, has mounds, petroglyphs, walled aqueducts, and paved roads. Pottery, gold ornaments, flint tools, and other finds are displayed in San José's Museo Nacional *(see p124)*.

Petroglyphs
The most noteworthy of the petroglyphs scattered around the site are along the Sendero de los Montículos. The *Monolitho Jaguar y Lagarto* has a lizard on one side and, on the other, a spindly bodied jaguar with a round head.

Cisterns
Rectangular water tanks are situated in the western side of the settle-ment, and are spanned by a three-slab bridge.

Excavated Site

Initiated in 1968, excavation of the site was led by archaeologists from the University of Costa Rica. To date, only about 12 acres (5 ha) have been retrieved. Parts of the causeway and key structures have been rebuilt, and restoration work is ongoing.

Sendero de los Montículos
A 1-mile (1.6-km) self-guided trail leads from the entrance to a lookout, El Mirador Encuentro con Nuestros Origenes (The Encounter with Our Origins Lookout), before dropping down to the main archaeological site. Along the way, visitors can stop at 15 interpretive points that explain the social organization of the Guayabo tribe.

KEY

① **The stone aqueducts**, forming a network of covered and uncovered channels, continue to feed water into stone-lined cisterns.

② **Premontane rainforest** surrounding the site hosts hundreds of bird species, such as aracaris and oropendolas.

③ **The largest mound** – measuring 98 ft (30 m) in diameter and 15 ft (4.5 m) in height – is thought to have been a base for the house of the local *cacique* (chief).

Montículos (Stone Foundations)
Believed to date from AD 300–700, the circular and rectangular mounds of stone on the site were the foundations of conical wooden structures.

★ **Calzada** (Causeway)
The 21-ft (6.5-m) wide causeway is believed to have extended between 2.5 and 7.5 miles (4–12 km) from the main town. About 246 yd (225 m) have been reconstructed, including two rectangular stone structures thought to have been used as sentry posts.

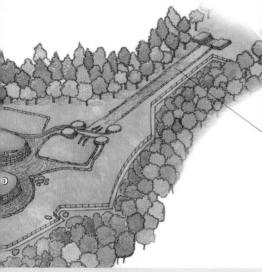

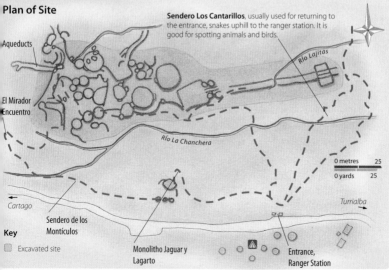

Plan of Site

Sendero Los Cantarillos, usually used for returning to the entrance, snakes uphill to the ranger station. It is good for spotting animals and birds.

Aqueducts

El Mirador Encuentro

Río Lajitas

Río La Chanchera

0 metres 25
0 yards 25

Cartago

Turrialba

Key

Excavated site

Sendero de los Montículos

Monolitho Jaguar y Lagarto

Entrance, Ranger Station

THE CENTRAL PACIFIC AND SOUTHERN NICOYA

ne white beaches are scattered along the shores of
ᵒuthern Nicoya, while the sun-drenched Central Pacific
ᵒastline is pummeled by non-stop surf and fringed
ᵗth forest. The region acts as a transition between two
ᶜosystems – the drier Meso-American to the north and the
ᵘmid Andean to the south – with flora and fauna of both
ᶜosystems. As a result, its wildlife reserves, such as Parque
ᵃcional Manuel Antonio, are among the nation's best.

angroves line the shores of the Gulf of
coya, which is studded with islands that
e important nesting sites for birds.
ᵣest areas, notably in Southern Nicoya,
ᵉre heavily denuded during the last
ᵉntury, but major conservation and
ᵣforestation efforts are now extending
ᵉ protected areas.
Spanish conquistadors explored the
ᵍion in the early 16th century and
ᵗablished short-lived settlements, which
l victim to tropical diseases and the
ᵣocious resistance of indigenous tribes.
ᵒwever, the Indians were swiftly
ᵉfeated. The principal city of the region,

Puntarenas, was founded in the early
1800s. It flourished due to the 19th-
century coffee trade, and developed into
the nation's main port for coffee exports
to Europe. In the early decades of the
20th century, bananas were planted
along the narrow coastal plain farther
south. They were replaced in the 1970s
by African oil palms, which today
dominate the economy and extend for
miles between the shore and forested
mountains. Jacó has now blossomed
as a beach resort for surfers, while the
town of Quepos retains its stature as a
major sportfishing base.

ᵃls waiting for the bus in a small town in Southern Nicoya

Palm trees shading the beach on Tortuga Island

Exploring the Central Pacific and Southern Nicoya

Beaches and national parks, teeming with wildlife, are the highlights of this region. The main town is the fishing port of Puntarenas, from where it is possible to take a day-trip by ferry to Isla Tortuga with its fabulous beach. Other fine beaches in Southern Nicoya await at off-the-beaten-track Montezuma and Malpaís, which are popular with surfers and budget travelers. Nearby Cabo Blanco is the site of the nation's oldest wildlife refuge. Inland from the Central Pacific coast, nature lovers can enjoy a crocodile safari on Río Tárcoles and hikes in Parque Nacional Carara, where scarlet macaws, monkeys, and other wildlife can be easily spotted. Major attractions along this coast are the lively surfing town of Jacó and the sportfishing center of Quepos, which gives access to Parque Nacional Manuel Antonio, one of the country's most popular wildlife parks.

Reserva Natural Absoluta Cabo Blanco

Sights at a Glance

Towns and Villages

❶ Puntarenas
❹ Tambor
❺ Montezuma
❼ Malpaís
❾ Jacó
⓬ Quepos

National Parks and Reserves

❷ Refugio Nacional de Vida
   Silvestre Curú
❻ Reserva Natural Absoluta Cabo
   Blanco
❽ Parque Nacional Carara
⓭ *Parque Nacional Manuel Antonio*
   pp172–3

Areas of Natural Beauty

❸ Isla Tortuga
⓫ Boca Damas
⓮ Valle del Río Savegre

Tour

❿ Santa Juana Mountain Tour

A riot of colors at the Tango Mar Resort in the fishing village of Tambor

For hotels and restaurants in this region see pp252–61 and pp266–77

...aming sportfishing boats lined up at Los Sueños Marina, near Jacó

An eye-catching sportfishing sign at Quepos docks

...tting Around

...ó and Quepos, in the Central Pacific region, and Southern
...oya's Tambor are linked by daily scheduled flights to Juan
...ntamaría International Airport and San José's Tobias Bolaños
...mestic airport. Puntarenas, Jacó, and Quepos are served by
...s from San José; several companies cater solely to tourists.
...untarenas is the gateway for ferries to Southern Nicoya. A
...gular car and passenger ferry service links it with Paquera;
...m here, a bus service operates to Montezuma along badly
...teriorated Highway 160. In the Central Pacific region, well-
...ved Highway 34 runs along the shore, linking all the major
...urist sights. Away from the coastal highways, most roads
... dirt tracks that can be treacherous during the wet season.
...WD vehicle is essential if you plan to drive around.

Key

━━ Pan-American Highway

━━ Major road

━━ Secondary road

┄┄ Minor road

━━ Provincial border

For additional map symbols *see back flap*

Fishing and excursion boats moored at the Puntarenas docks

❶ Puntarenas

Road Map B3. 75 miles (120 km) W of San José. 🚗 100,000. 🚌 🚢 Carnaval (last week of Feb); Festival de la Virgen del Mar (mid-Jul).

Often seen as a provincial backwater, the city of Puntarenas (Sandy Point) was once an important port. First settled in 1522 by the Spanish, Puntarenas later became the main shipping point for coffee beans, brought from the highlands in *carretas* (oxcarts). City fortunes waned in 1890, once the Atlantic Railroad was built, and many of its wooden structures are dilapidated. Today this slightly down-at-heel town exists on fishing, as attested to by rows of decrepit fishing boats moored at the wharves. It remains the main gateway for excursions to Isla Tortuga and for ferries to Paquera and Naranjo, on the Peninsula de Nicoya.

The town occupies a 3-mile (5-km) long, thin peninsula fringed on the south by a beach offering good views across the Gulf of Nicoya. A broad estuary runs along the north shore, where extensive mangrove forests are home to waterfowl such as roseate spoonbills, storks, pelicans, and frigate birds.

Puntarenas is favored as a *balneario* (bathing resort) by Josefinos who flock to the seafront boulevard, Paseo de los Turistas. The main draw in town is the **Museo Histórico Marítimo**, situated in the former 19th-century city jail. The museum has displays on indigenous cultures, maritime history, and the coffee era.

Environs

The sweeping sands of **Playa San Isidro**, 5 miles (8 km) east of town, are very popular with beachgoers from San José. During the weekend it can become crowded.

🏛 **Museo Histórico Marítimo**
Ave Central, Calles 5/7. **Tel** 2661-0387. **Open** 9:45am–5:15pm Tue–Sun.

Serene white beaches of Refugio Nacional de Vida Silvestre Curú

❷ Refugio Nacional de Vida Silvestre Curú

Road Map B3. 2 miles (3 km) S of Paquera. **Tel** 2641-0100. 🚌 Paquera–Cobano. **Open** 7am–3pm daily. 🅿 🏕 by appt. 🚻 🍽 🏕 🌐 curu.org

Part of a much larger privately owned hacienda, the seldom-visited 210-acre (85-ha) Curú National Wildlife Refuge has been set up to protect five distinct habitats extending inland from Golfo Curú. The majority of the hilly reserve is tropical deciduous and semi-deciduous forest populated by capuchin and howler monkeys, anteaters, agoutis, and sloths, as well as several species of wild cats and more than 220 species of birds. Endangered spider monkeys have also been successfully reintroduced. Since the number of visitors is low, it is possible to spot animals more easily than at many other refuges. Marked trails provide access.

Three beautiful beaches – **Playa Colorada, Playa Curú,** and **Playa Quesera** – are tucked inside the fold of green head-lands and extend along 3 miles (5 km) of coastline. Hawksbill and olive ridley turtles crawl ashore at night to nest in the sand. Whales and dolphins can sometimes be seen swimming in the warm offshore waters, while the mangrove swamps and lagoons that extend inland along Río Curú are good for spotting caimans.

❸ Isla Tortuga

Road Map B3. 2 miles (3 km) SE of Curú. 🚢 organized excursions. 🏊 🍽

This sun-bleached island – actually twin islets, Isla Tolinga and unoccupied Isla Alcatraz – offshore of Curú is run as a privately owned 765-acre (310 ha) nature reserve. Isla Tolinga, which has no overnight accommodation, is very popular for day-visits.

Isla Tortuga is rimmed by white beaches that dissolve into startlingly blue waters. Coconut palms lean over the beach.

Catamaran Manta Ray transporting visitors to Isla Tortuga

...aking on offer at Isla Tortuga, along with other beach activities and water sports

...e hilly interior is covered by ...ciduous forest, accessed by a ...ort but steep trail that leads ... the highest point of the ...and (570 ft/ 175 m). Signs ...oint out rare hardwoods, such ...*indio desnudo* (naked Indian). ...The preferred activity is to laze ... a hammock while sipping the ...and cocktail – *coco loco* (rum, ...oconut milk, and coconut ...ueur) – served in a coconut ...ell. The warm waters are great ... snorkeling. There are no jet ...is to break the blissful silence, ...ut visitors can choose from an ...ray of other water sports. ...Trips were pioneered in 1975 ... **Calypso Cruises**, which ...erates a 70-ft (21-m) ...otorized, high-speed ...tamaran that departs from ...ntarenas. Other companies ...fer similar excursions, which ...ually include hotel transfers, ...und-trip transportation, and ...ffet lunch. The 90-minute ...urney is its own reward – ...olphins and whales are ...equently spotted. A midweek ...sit is the best option, as ...eekends can get crowded.

...virons
...oobies, pelicans, frigate birds, ...d other sea birds nest on the ...attered islands that comprise ...e **Reserva Biológica Isla ...uayabo y Isla Negritos**, to ...e north of Isla Tortuga. Visitors ...e not allowed on shore. ...cursion boats pass between ...e islets that make up the ...ological reserve.

Calypso Cruises
2256-2727. 🞑 🞑
calypsocruises.com

❹ Tambor

Road Map B3. 11 miles (18 km) SW of Paquera. 🚌

A small, laid-back fishing village with a wide silver-gray beach, Tambor lines the aptly named Bahía Ballena (Whale Bay), where whales gather in mid-winter. Palm-fringed sands extend from the bay north to mangrove swamps. The village itself is somewhat somnolent, but two upscale resorts just outside town attract a large number of foreign beachgoers and Josefinos, most of whom fly in to the local airstrip. Visitors can play a round of golf or a game of tennis for a fee at the **Tango Mar Resort** *(see p256)*, which has a 9-hole golf course, or at the **Los Delfines Golf and Country Club**, which has an 18-hole course. Scuba diving for all abilities is on offer at the nearby **Playa Tambor Beach Resort and Casino**, which is affiliated to Barceló Los Delfines Club.

For a bird's-eye view of the area, take to the air in an autogyryro; trips are offered by **Ultralight Tours**. Alternatively, **Seascape Kayak Tours** offers guided sea kayaking trips of the bay and coastal mangroves from November to April.

🞑 **Los Delfines Golf and Country Club**
1 mile (1.6 km) E of Tambor.
Tel 2683-0294. 🞑 🞑 🞑 🞑 🞑

🞑 **Ultralight Tours**
Los Delphines Airstrip.
Tel 2683-0294.
🇼 ultralighttours.com

🞑 **Seascape Kayak Tours**
Tambor.
Tel 2747-1884.
🇼 seascapekayaktours.com

The lush greens of the golf courses of Tambor

Bright signs adorning shop fronts in Montezuma village

➎ Montezuma

Road Map: B3. 16 miles (26 km) W of Paquera. 🚌 from Paquera.

A favorite with budget travelers, this offbeat beach community has a laidback lifestyle, magnificent ocean vistas and beaches, and unpretentious yet hip bars. The compact village is tucked beneath precipitous hills and opens onto a rocky cove with fishing boats bobbing at anchor. Two superb beaches – Playa Montezuma and Playa Grande – unspool eastward, shaded by tall palms and backed by thickly forested mountains. Swimmers should watch out for the riptides. Sliding between treetops on the **Montezuma Waterfall Canopy Tour** is a safe, fun, and adrenaline-boosting activity, while **Finca Los Caballos** offers invigorating horseback rides in the hills abutting the Reserva Absoluta Nicolas Weissenburg. The reserve, however, has no public access. Clambering up the waterfalls to the west of the village is unsafe; instead, cool off in the pools at the base of the waterfalls.

🚡 Montezuma Waterfall Canopy Tour
1 mile (1.6 km) W of Montezuma.
Tel 2642-0808. **Open** daily. 🚡 🎫
8am, 10am, 1pm, and 3pm. 🖥
montezumatraveladventures.com

🐎 Finca Los Caballos
2 miles (3 km) NW of Montezuma. 🚕
2642-0124. 🎫 9am daily. 🚴 🏊
🖥 **naturelodge.net**

➏ Reserva Natural Absoluta Cabo Blanco

Road Map: B4. 6 miles (10 km) W of Montezuma. **Tel** 2642-0093. 🚌 Montezuma–Cabuya. Also taxis from Montezuma. **Open** 8am–4pm Wed–Sun and public hols. 🚶

Established in 1963 as the nation's first protected area, and elevated to the status of a reserve in 1974, the 4-sq-mile (10-sq-km) Cabo Blanco owes its genesis to the tireless campaign of the late Olof Wessberg and his wife Karen Morgenson; they also helped set up the Costa Rican National Park Service. Cabo Blanco was initially an "absolute" reserve, off-limits to all visitors, but today there is access to the eastern part of the tropical forests that cover the hilly tip of the Nicoya Peninsula. About 85 percent of the reserve is covered by rejuvenated secondary forest and pockets of lowland tropical forest. There are numerous monkeys, as well as anteaters, coatis, and deer. The 3-mile (5-km) long Sendero Sueco trail leads to the beautiful **Playa Cabo Blanco**; other beaches lie along the shore, but exploring should not be attempted when the tide is rising.

Offshore, the sheer walls of Isla Cabo Blanco are stained white by guano deposited by colonies of nesting seabirds, including frigate birds and brown boobies.

Activities in Montezuma

Cabo Blanco is accessed from the community of Cabuya, a mile (1.6 km) along a rough dirt road. It can also be entered at Malpaís. Tour operators nationwide offer excursions to the reserve.

➐ Malpaís

Road Map: B4. 6 miles (10 km) NW of Montezuma. 🚌 from Cóbano, 4 miles (6 km) N of Montezuma.

Its name may mean "bad land," but the Malpaís area's Pacific shoreline is unsurpassed for its rugged beauty. Until a few years ago, the region was unknown; today it is a famed surfers' paradise.

Named for their respective gray-sand beaches, three contiguous communities are strung along the dirt road that fringes the shore. Relaxed to a fault, they are characterized by colorful hotels, restaurants, and bars. The main hamlet is **Carmen**, from where the road runs 2 miles (3 km) south, through Santa Teresa, to the fishing hamlet of Malpaís, which gives the area its popular name. Beyond Malpaís, where vultures perch on fishing boats, the beach ends amid tidepools and fantastically sculpted rocks near the entrance to Cabo Blanco. A 4WD is required.

The best surf beach is **Playa Santa Teresa**, merging in the north with playas that are virtually uninhabited: Los Suecos, Hermosa, and Manzanillo. Santa Teresa boasts the understatedly deluxe Florblanca Resort (see p255), in stunning counterpoint to the budget options.

Surfer and sun-lovers on Playa Santa Teresa's Pacific shoreline

Arachnids and Insects of Costa Rica

Costa Rica hosts more than 300,000 species of insects, including more than 1,250 species of butterflies *(see p139)*. No one knows the exact number of beetle species or ants, which are in their thousands. Bees, wasps, and myriad other flying creatures buzz about, while an astounding profusion of other types of insects creep, crawl, or leap. Many advertise their toxicity with gaudy coloration. Others have adopted clever techniques of disguise to prey or avoid being preyed upon –swallowtail caterpillars, for example, camouflage themselves as bird droppings. Scorpions and other arachnids – from tiny jumping spiders to giant tarantulas – are ubiquitous too. Costa Rica celebrates its arachnid and insect diversity in butterfly gardens and insect museums around the country.

Army ants are nomadic and swarm by day, capturing small prey. At night, they build a bivouac nest with their bodies.

Golden orb spiders spin giant webs with a sticky, golden-yellow thread that is five times stronger than steel and three times more resistant than Kevlar.

Tarantulas are large, hairy terrestrial spiders that live in silk-lined burrows. Some species grow up to 12 in (30 cm) – large enough to prey on lizards, mice, and small birds.

Stinging hairs

Eight small eyes

Retractable claws

The praying mantis's prayer-like stance and gentle rocking motion belie its predatory behavior. Its forelegs are spiked for grasping as it devours its prey. A female will often eat the male during mating.

Rhinoceros beetles are named for the males' horns, which are used for fighting in mating season. Primarily fruit eaters, they grow up to 3 in (8 cm) in length but are harmless to humans.

Camouflage Techniques

Many arachnid and insect species adopt camouflage or mimicry to hide from predators or to ambush prey. Praying mantises resemble bright green leaves; the dead-leaf katydid looks like a dried, curled-up leaf; while stick insects can appear like twigs. Several palatable butterfly species have evolved to look like toxic Heliconid species.

A camouflaged praying mantis

Hiking through a lower elevation forest at Parque Nacional Carara

❶ Parque Nacional Carara

Road Map C3. 31 miles (50 km) SE of Puntarenas. **Tel** 2637-1054. 🚌 from San José and Jacó. **Open** May–Nov: 8am–4pm daily; Dec–Apr: 7am–4pm daily. 🅿 ♿ 🅆 sinac.go.cr

Occupying a climatological transition zone where dry northerly and humid southerly ecosystems meet, Carara National Park's forests are complex and varied. Despite its relatively small size – 20 sq miles (52 sq km) – the park offers some of the most diverse wildlife viewing in Costa Rica. Species from both the Meso-American and Amazonian environments are abundant, including the endangered spider monkey and the poison-dart frog. The birding is spectacular, with scarlet macaws being a major draw. They can be seen on their twice-daily migration between the forest and nearby coastal mangroves.

Carara's lower elevation forests have easy-to-walk trails that begin at the roadside visitor center; the longest is 5 miles (8 km) around. Guides can be hired to access pre-Columbian sites. Several tour operators in San José arrange day visits.

Environs

Carara is a Huetar Indian word for crocodile. The reptiles are easily seen from the highway as they bask on the banks of Río Tárcoles. Safaris are offered from **Tárcoles**, 2 miles (3 km) southwest of Carara. The

spectacular 600-ft (183-m) drop of **Catarata Manantial de Agua Viva** makes the waterfall popular with hikers who cool off in the pools at its base. Nearby, **Pura Vida Botanical Gardens** have walking trails through 30 lush acres (12 ha).

📷 Catarata Manantial de Agua Viva

Bijagual, 4 miles (6 km) E of Tárcoles. Tel 8831-2980. **Open** 8am–3pm daily. 🅿 🍴

🌿 Pura Vida Botanical Gardens

Bijagual. **Tel** 2645-1001. **Open** 8am–5pm daily. 🅿 🍴 ♿ 🖥 📷 🅆 puravidagarden.com

❾ Jacó

Road Map C4. 40 miles (65 km) S of Puntarenas. 🏠 8,000. 🚏 🚌 🎼 International Festival of Music (Jul–Aug).

Thriving on the surfer trade and that of Canadian "snowbirds" escaping the northern winter,

Jacó has evolved as the nation's largest and most party-oriented beach resort. Palms shade the 2-mile (3-km) long beach. Despite this, its gray sands are unremarkable, the sea is usually a murky brown from silt washed down by rivers, and riptides make swimming unsafe. There's no shortage of things to do, however – from crocodile safaris to horseback rides – and the nightlife is lively. Many of the nation's top surfers live here, although as a surf center, Jacó is best for beginners.

In town, **Pacific Bungee** offers the thrill of daredevil leaps, plus an adrenalin-charged catapult "ride". Outside town, the **Pacific Rainforest Aerial Tram** takes you on a 90-minute guided ride through the treetops on silent open-air gondolas. The modified ski lifts skim the forest floor, soar above giant trees, pass waterfalls, and give fabulous views along the Pacific coast. Guided tours such as the Poison-dart Frog Trail, are also offered along nature trails.

Environs

Sportfishing and excursion boats set out from Los Sueños Marina at **Playa Herradura**, a gray-sand beach tucked into a broad bay north of Jacó, with calm waters safe for swimming. This is also a great place for golf as there is a championship golf course.

Perched on a headland just north of Playa Herradura, **Hotel Villa Caletas** (*see p255*) is the

The gray sands of palm-fringed Playa Jacó

markable creation of French
esigner Denis Roy. A long
dgetop driveway lined with
oman urns has dramatic vistas
ut to sea and also provides a
riking entry to this deluxe
staurant and hotel. Musicians
erform in a Greek-style
mphitheater built into the
llside, a setting for the
ternational Festival of Music.
ne Serenity Spa offers
ampering treatments. A
inding track leads down to
aya Caletas, a rocky beach
ith a bar and grill. South of
có, **Playa Hermosa** is served
y dedicated surf hostels. Sand
ars provide consistently good
reaks swelling in from deep
aters offshore.

A guided horseback ride, part of the Santa Juana Mountain Tour

Pacific Bungee
e Pastor Diaz and Calle Las Brisas.
l 2643-6682. **Open** 9:30am–8:30pm
ily. W pacificbungee.com

Pacific Rainforest Aerial Tram
miles (3 km) E of Jacó. **Tel** 2257-
61. **Open** 9am–4pm Mon,
m–4pm Tue–Sun. 🐾 🎦 💻 📷
rainforestram.com

Santa Juana
ountain Tour

ad Map D4. 8 miles (11 km) E of
vy 34, 32 miles (50 km) S of Jacó.
l 2777-0777. 🚌 organized
ansfers. 🐾 🎦 7:30am daily. 🍽
inch included.) W sicomono.
m/tours

his educational tour takes
sitors deep into the Fila
nonta Mountains inland of
uepos. The tour is centered on
remote rural community at
e heart of an ecological

project, the purpose of which is
to engage individual local
families in ecotourism while
attempting to preserve
traditional rural customs.

There are several hiking trails
and a river walk, with waterfalls
and pools for bathing and
cooling off. Participants get
to visit butterfly-breeding,
animal-husbandry, and
reforestation projects; learn
about snakes at a serpentarium;
and visit an authentic sugar mill
powered by oxen. They can

A small lizard resting on a leaf in the depths
of the rainforest

even help pick coffee and
citrus, or fish for tilapia. A
guided horseback ride is
another option. A typical
campesino (peasant) lunch is
served at a restaurant offering
sensational views.

⓫ Boca Damas

Road Map D4. 33 miles (53 km) S
of Jacó. 🚌

Crisscrossed by countless
sloughs and channels, this vast
manglare (mangrove) complex
extends along the shoreline
between the towns of Parrita
and Quepos, at the estuary of
Río Damas. Coatis, pumas,
white-faced monkeys, and
several species of snakes
inhabit the dense forests.
Crocodiles and caimans lurk
in the tannin-stained waters.
Stilt-legged shorebirds and
boat-billed herons, with their
curious keel-shaped beaks,
pick among the mudflats in
search of molluscs.

Tour operators in Quepos
offer kayaking excursions.
Guides offer boat trips from
the small dock at Damas.

Crocodile Safari

Indiscriminate hunting during the past 400 years has resulted in a
decimation of the American *cocodrilo* (crocodile) population. Since
gaining protected status in 1981, however, crocodiles have managed
to make a comeback. They can be seen in rivers throughout the
Pacific lowlands, but are nowhere so numerous as near the mouth
of Río Tárcoles, where populations of more than 200 crocodiles per
mile have been counted. Boats depart from the village of Tárcoles,
near the mouth of the river, for 2-hour crocodile-spotting safaris
upriver. The reptiles, which grow up to 16 ft (5 m) in length, often
approach to within a few feet. Keep your hands in the boat. You can
also expect to see roseate spoonbills, scarlet macaws, and dozens of
other Costa Rican bird species.

Crocodiles seen from a bridge over Río
Tárcoles, Puntarenas

A relaxed cafeteria and ice-cream bar on a downtown Quepos street

⓬ Quepos

Road Map D4. 34 miles (55 km) S of Jacó. 15,000. Carnaval (Feb–Mar). **quepolandia.com**

Traditionally a game fishing base and center for the production of African palm oil, Quepos has blossomed as a tourist center and a gateway to Parque Nacional Manuel Antonio. The town buzzes both by day and at night, when its numerous bars and restaurants come alive.

On the north side of town, Boca Vieja village has wooden huts, which are linked by flimsy walkways that overhang the brown sands of **Playa Cocal**. In the hills to the south, quaint clapboard homes recall the 1930s, when the Standard Fruit Company established banana plantations. Panama disease killed them off, and today African oil palms dominate the coastal plains for miles around.

Environs
South of Quepos, a two-lane road winds over steep headlands to the hamlet of **Manuel Antonio**, fronted by **Playa Espadilla**, a wide scimitar of gray sand. At the north end of the beach is a lagoon with crocodiles. Restaurants, bars, and hotels line the route, including **El Avión**, a converted Fairchild C-123 transport plane, which was used by the CIA in the 1970s to run arms to the Nicaraguan Contras *(see p189)*.

Nearby, **Manuel Antonio Nature Park & Wildlife Refuge** offers easy walks through 40 acres (16 ha) teeming with sloths, raccoon-like coatis, leafcutter ants, and phenomenal birdlife.

The **Río Naranjo Valley** extends east of Quepos into the Fila Nara Mountains. The ruins of a Spanish mission, established in 1570, still stand by the roadside. Whitewater rafting trips are a popular excursion from Quepos.

Farther up the valley, **Rancho Los Tucanes** offers guided horseback and 4WD tours of its vanilla and pepper plantations. Trails lead through montane rainforest to the 295-ft (90-m) high Los Tucanos waterfall.

🗺 Manuel Antonio Nature Park & Wildlife Refuge
1 mile (1.6 km) S of Quepos. **Tel** 2777-0850. **Open** 6am–8pm daily; butterfly garden: 8am–4pm daily. 🌐 **sicomono.com/tour**

🗺 Rancho Los Tucanes
Londres, 7 miles (11 km) NE of Quepos. **Tel** 2777-0775. **Open** 7am–3pm daily. 🌐 **rancholostucanes.com**

⓭ Parque Nacional Manuel Antonio

See pp172–3.

⓮ Valle del Río Savegre

Road Map D4. 15 miles (25 km) SE of Quepos. from Quepos.

Cutting inland into the Fila San Bosco Mountains, the Río Savegre Valley is covered by plantations of African oil palms at its lower levels. Farther up the valley lies the rural community of El Silencio, where the local farmers' cooperative operates an ecotourist center called **Coopesilencio**. It offers horses for rides down rustic trails into nature reserve, and has a wildlife rescue center with scarlet macaws, deer, and monkeys.

Modeled on a South African safari camp, **Rafiki Safari Lodge** *(see p256)* is set atop a ridge overlooking the Savegre. It makes a great base for hiking, birding, and horseback riding, as well as for exhilarating whitewater rafting and kayaking trips on Río Savegre. A 4WD vehicle is essential for negotiating the rugged track, which is often inundated during the wet season.

🗺 Coopesilencio
25 miles (40 km) SE of Quepos. **Tel** 2787-5265. **Open** 9:30am–noon and 1–3:30pm daily. 🌐 **turismoruralcr.com**

Plantations of African oil palms in the Valle del Río Savegre

Sportfishing on the Pacific Coast

The ultimate draw for the game-fishing enthusiast, Costa Rica's waters witness the setting of new International Game Fish Association records every year. More anglers have claimed "grand slams" – both species of marlin and one or more sailfish in a single day – on the country's Pacific coast than in any other place on earth. In the wet season (May–November), fishing is best off the Golfo de Papagayo. In the dry season (December–April), when high winds in the Golfo de Papagayo make the waters dangerous, the best fishing is found farther toward the south, out of the year-round marinas of Quepos, Bahía Drake, and Golfito. Angling on the Caribbean coast is different: inshore fishing using light tackle is the norm here *(see p291)*.

Organized Fishing Trips

Sportfishing vessels often journey 20 miles (32 km) or more from shore to find game fish. Hooking a fish is only the beginning. The real sport lies in the fight that ensues.

Anglers strap themselves into the "fighting chair" to bring in larger species. Fights sometimes take hours and can tire the angler almost as much as the fish.

Charter shops and fishing lodges abound in Costa Rica. Apart from hiring out boats, they can also arrange fishing licenses for visiting anglers.

A catch-and-release policy is usually followed by sportfishing operators in Costa Rica. However, maritime laws designed to protect fish stocks from commercial over-exploitation are poorly enforced.

Deep Sea Fish

A wide variety of game fish await the keen angler on Costa Rica's Pacific coast. Angling is possible year-round, but there are prime areas and peak seasons for each species.

Yellowfin tuna are extremely powerful, weighing up to 350 lb (160 kg). They are found in warm currents year-round, but June–October is best.

Wahoo are long, sleek, and explosively fast fish that are found in northern waters between May and August.

Dorado (also called dolphinfish or mahimahi) have scales that flash a wide range of colors. This dramatic fighter is found from May to October.

Sailfish, hard-fighting giants up to 7 ft (2 m) long, and known for their spectacular leaps when hooked, are plentiful from December to April.

Blue marlins are considered the ultimate prize. The "Bull of the Ocean" puts up a fight like no other. Females weigh up to 1,000 lb (455 kg); males are smaller. August–December are generally the best months.

⓭ Parque Nacional Manuel Antonio

Named for a Spanish conquistador, and flanked by the ocean and forested hills, this beautiful park was inaugurated in 1972. Although it is the smallest in Costa Rica's park system, covering a land area of 6 sq miles (16 sq km), Manuel Antonio National Park has remarkable biodiversity, with abundant wildlife and magnificent beaches. Sightings of coatis, sloths, toucans, and scarlet macaws along the well-maintained trails are virtually guaranteed. This is one of the most visited parks in the nation: although there is a limit on the daily number of visitors, its wildlife is threatened by overuse, pollution, and unregulated hotel expansion.

Visitors queuing at the park entrance

Playa Espadilla Sur
A long swathe of coral-colored sand curling south from Manuel Antonio village, this beach connects with Playa Espadilla to the north.

Punta Catedral
This former island is now connected to the mainland by a *tombolo* (natural land bridge). The rocky promontory has tidal pools at its base and is encircled by a trail that ascends to a *mirador* (viewpoint).

Playa Manuel Antonio
This scimitar-shaped beach with soft white sands shelves into calm jade waters containing a small coral reef. Snorkeling is splendid, especially in the dry season. Green and Pacific ridley turtles sometimes nest here.

To Quepos

Quebrada Camaronera

Manuel Antonio

Playa Espadilla Norte

Playa Espadilla Sur

Punta Catedral

Isla Olocuita

The Manchineel Tree

Manchineel trees

Locally called *manzanillo*, or "beach apple," the manchineel tree is quite common on the beaches, causing problems for unwary visitors seeking its shade. This evergreen species (*Hippomane manicinella*), identified by its short trunk and bright green elliptical leaves, is very toxic. The sap and bark inflame the skin, while the small yellow apple-like fruit is poisonous. Moreover, if its wood is burnt, the smoke is an irritant to the lungs.

VISITORS' CHECKLIST

Practical Information
Road Map: D4. 100 miles (160 km) S of San José and 5 miles (8 km) S of Quepos. Tel 2777-5185. Open 8am–4pm Tue–Sun. Limited to 600 visitors a day.

Transport
from San José and Quepos.

Sendero Mirador
Ascending a hill and dropping past Playa Escondida, this muddy, 0.8-mile (1.3-km) long trail then rises to a *mirador* with great views toward Punta Catedral.

Monkeys
Capuchin monkeys and tiny squirrel monkeys are easily spotted throughout the park. Do not feed them – the illegal practice is a threat to their health and behavior.

Key

═══ Major road
─── Park boundary
─── Trail

Quebrada Azul
Quebrada Negra
La Catarata
Playa Escondida
② *Laguna Negra*
Río Naranjo
③ *Playa Playitas*
Punta Serrucho
Isla Mogote ④

0 meters 500
0 yards 500

KEY

① **Coral reefs** form a refuge for crabs, starfish, shrimp, and colorful fish. Dolphins and humpback whales are often seen in this area.

② **Laguna Negra's** brackish waters and mangrove swamps are an ideal home for the alligator-like caiman.

③ **Playa Playitas** is remote and, being a nesting site for marine turtles, is off limits to visitors.

④ **Isla Mogote** is a sacred site for the Quepoa Indians.

...ocky Islands
...n additional 212 sq miles ...50 sq km) of the park ...rotects 12 islands that host ...rge colonies of seabirds.

For additonal map symbols *see back flap*

GUANACASTE AND NORTHERN NICOYA

With its arid plains, men on horseback, rodeos, and bullfights, the province of Guanacaste is steeped in the hacienda heritage. The region stretches from the cloud-tipped volcanoes of the Cordillera de Guanacaste to the marshes of the Río Tempisque basin and the magnificent surf-washed beaches of Northern Nicoya – paradise for marine turtles and surfers.

A chain of volcanoes and mountains runs across this vast region, framing it to the east. To the northwest, the rugged Pacific shore, which is serrated by deep bays, has many of the nation's best beaches. Between mountain and coast lies a broad trough whose wetlands harbor crocodiles and waterfowl. To the southwest, the Nicoya peninsula enfolds the mangrove-fringed Gulf of Nicoya. Although the plains can be searingly hot, the mountains offer cool, beautiful retreats, while refreshing breezes caress the beaches.

In spring, the sparsely foliated deciduous forests of the plains explode in a riot of color while offering the advantage of relatively easy wildlife spotting. Thick evergreen cloud forests on the upper slopes of the mountains provide a splendid study in contrasts. The Chorotega culture was one of the region's most developed at the time of the Spanish arrival, and was quickly assimilated. While no great pre-Columbian architecture has been discovered, a tradition of superb pottery continues in the Guaitíl area. The predominant culture now is that of the *sabanero* (cowboy), tracing a lineage back to colonial days, when great haciendas were constructed. Raising or tending cattle is still the dominant occupation here, although many inhabitants cling to a way of life established in pre-Columbian times, earning their livelihood from fishing.

Sabaneros (cowboys) herding cattle at a ranch in Liberia

◀ Zipline canopy tour at Hacienda Lodge Guachipelín, Parque Nacional Rincón de la Vieja

Exploring Guanacaste and Northern Nicoya

The driest of Costa Rica's regions offers possibilities ranging from the spectacular cloud forests of Monteverde to the volcano parks of Rincón de la Vieja, Miravalles, and Guanacaste, and the beach-fringed Parque Nacional Santa Rosa. Birding is superb at Palo Verde, Lomas Barbudal, and near Cañas. To the north is Liberia, with its colonial buildings. Laid-back Playas del Coco to the west is a base for scuba diving, while Playa Flamingo is a sportfishing destination. Farther south is the surf center of Tamarindo, and Playa Grande and Ostional draw marine turtles. Guaitíl is famed for its traditional pottery, while Barra Honda attracts cavers.

Liberia's main plaza, flanked by trees

Sights at a Glance

Towns and Villages

2 Tilarán
3 Cañas
7 Liberia
15 Tamarindo
17 Nosara s Guaitíl
18 Sámara
19 Islita
20 Nicoya
21 Santa Cruz
22 Guaitíl

National Parks and Reserves

1 *Monteverde and Santa Elena pp178–9*
4 Parque Nacional Palo Verde
5 Reserva Biológica Lomas Barbudal
6 Zona Protectora Volcán Miravalles
8 Parque Nacional Rincón de la Vieja
9 Parque Nacional Guanacaste
11 *Parque Nacional Santa Rosa pp188–9*
16 Refugio Nacional de Vida Silvestre Ostiona
23 Parque Nacional Barra Honda

Areas of Natural Beauty

10 Bahía Salinas
12 Bahía Culebra

Beaches

13 Playas del Coco
14 Playa Flamingo

A mask at Rancho Armadillo, Playas del Coco

For hotels and restaurants in this region see pp252–61 and pp266–77

Cattle crossing a stream near Parque Nacional Palo Verde

Key

- ▬▬ Pan-American Highway
- ▬▬ Major road
- ▬▬ Secondary road
- ▭▭ Minor road
- ▬▬ International border
- ▬▬ Provincial border
- △ Peak

Getting Around

The Pan-American Highway runs the length of the region, connecting with the Nicaraguan border. Dirt roads connect the highway with Monteverde and other sights. Highway 21 links Liberia to Northern Nicoya, with feeder roads extending west to the principal beach resorts.

An efficient bus service connects towns along the Pan-American Highway, as well as several beach resorts, with San José, but bus travel between resorts requires time-consuming connections. Cars can be rented at Liberia and Tamarindo. Liberia has an international airport, while Tamarindo, Nosara, Tambor, and Sámara are served by domestic airports.

For additional map symbols *see back flap*

❶ Monteverde and Santa Elena

Known worldwide for its unique cloud forest reserve that helped promote Costa Rica's reputation for ecotourism, Monteverde boasts a pastoral alpine setting at an elevation of 4,600 ft (1,400 m), in the heart of the Cordillera de Tilarán. To the northwest is Santa Elena, which is the main commercial center. Several other reserves, incorporated within the Zona Protectora Arenal-Monteverde, are found in the area. Monteverde's fame has spawned all manner of attractions, including a variety of tours that permit visitors a monkey's-eye view of the forest canopy. However, even in the face of these ever-increasing services and attractions, Monteverde retains a bucolic charm.

Canopy Tours
Four canopy tours permit visitors to explore the canopy along a zipline or by rappeling.

Reserva Bosque Nuboso Santa Elena
Offering similar wildlife species to the Monteverde Cloud Forest Biological Reserve, the Santa Elena reserve is, however, less crowded (see p182).

Serpentario
This boasts close-up encounters with snakes that inhabit the local forests, as well as various other amphibians and reptiles (see p180).

Key

━━ Major road
━━ Other road
▬ ▬ Trail
▬ ▬ Park boundary

KEY

① **Bat Jungle** has a bat flyway.

② **Bajo del Tigre Trail** is a self-guided interpretative trail. Three-wattled bellbirds and quetzals are frequently seen.

③ **Finca Ecológico** has four trails through montane tropical forest.

④ **Monteverde Orchid Garden** displays one-third of Costa Rica's orchid species (see p184).

⑤ **Monteverde** is actually the name of the Quaker community of American extract, whose members live in scattered homes in the forests below the Monteverde reserve.

⑥ **The Friend's Meeting House** is the venue for meetings of Monteverde's Quaker community (see p180).

Monteverde Butterfly Garden
Dozens of butterfly species f about inside netted gardens this educational center, whic has displays spanning th insect world (see p180

Santa Elena
Located downhill of Monteverde, with the locality known as Cerro Plano lying in between, this is the area's main village, with a bank, bus stop, and other services.

La Lechería
Started by immigrant Quakers from the United States, the "Cheese Factory" is the foundation of the local economy. It offers visitors an insider's view of cheese-making *(see p180)*.

Pastures
Monteverde's lush rolling hills are fertile pastures for the cattle that are the source of the area's famous cheeses.

| 0 meters | 500 |
| 0 yards | 500 |

Sarah Dodwell
Watercolor Gallery

Reserva Biológica Bosque Nuboso Monteverde

Monteverde
⑤

La Lechería

Río Guacimal

Reserve Entrance

⑥ **Friend's Meeting House**

Sloth Sanctuary of Monteverde

Reserva Biológica Bosque Nuboso Monteverde
The world-famous Monteverde Cloud Forest Biological Reserve is the nation's foremost locale for viewing Resplendent quetzals – one among more than 400 species of birds found here *(see p181)*.

For additonal map symbols *see back flap*

Exploring Monteverde and Santa Elena

Cool and verdant Monteverde has its fair share of interesting sights, many of which are spread out along the winding dirt road that slopes gently upward from Santa Elena to the Monteverde Cloud Forest Biological Reserve. Other sights are tucked away off side roads, some of which are quite rugged and steep. Walking is a pleasurable option, but the heavily trafficked roads can be muddy or dusty, depending on the weather. It is always a wise idea to take along an umbrella. Dozens of hotels and restaurants line the route. A steeper dirt road leads northeast from Santa Elena to Santa Elena Cloud Forest Reserve, passing several key attractions along the route.

ⓩ Frog Pond of Monteverde
330 yd (300 m) SW of Santa Elena.
Tel 2645-6320. **Open** 9:30am–8:30pm daily. 🄰 🄲 🄰 🄳

The Frog Pond of Monteverde displays about 28 species of frogs and other amphibians, as well as snakes, salamanders, and lizards in large glass cases that attempt to replicate their natural environments. Several of Costa Rica's most intriguing *ranas* and *sapos* (frogs and toads) can be seen here, including poison-dart frogs, the endearing red-eyed tree frogs, transparent frogs, and huge marine toads. The best time to visit the Frog Pond is evening or night, when the frogs are most active and visitors can hear their distinctive calls.

ⓩ Serpentario
550 yd (500 m) S of Santa Elena.
Tel 2645-6002. **Open** 9am–8pm daily. 🄰 🄲 🄳
🅆 skyadventures.travel

Among more than 320 species of snakes shown behind glass in this snake house are the fearsome *terciopelo* (fer-de-lance, or *Bothrops asper*) and its nemesis, the terciopelo-eating *musarana* (*Clelia clelia*). Most species displayed here can be encountered in local forests. Also exhibited are turtles, iguanas, basilisk lizards, chameleons, and frogs. Although the educational labels are written only in Spanish, English-speaking guides are available.

Delicate orchids grown at the Monteverde Orchid Garden

ⓩ Monteverde Orchid Garden
0.8 mile (1.3 km) E of Santa Elena.
Tel 2645-5308. **Open** 8am–5pm daily.
🄰 🄲 🅆 monteverde orchidgarden.net

A great place to learn about orchids *(see p187)*, the Monteverde Orchid Garden has more than 500 local species. They are arranged in 22 groups along a winding self-guided trail labeled with educational signs. Visitors are each handed a magnifying glass to help them appreciate such diminutives as the liverwort orchid *(Platystele jungermannioides)*, the world's smallest flower.

ⓩ Monteverde Butterfly Garden
1.2 miles (1.8 km) S of Santa Elena.
Tel 2645-5512. **Open** 8:30am–4pm daily. 🄰 🄲 🄰 🅆 monteverde butterflygarden.com

With educational exhibits as well as butterfly arenas representing three distinct habitats, this nature center is an ideal locale for learning about the life cycle of the butterfly. The fascinating displays also include tarantulas, stick insects, giant rhinoceros beetles, and 5-in (13-cm) long caterpillars.

Educational videos are shown and a video "bug cam" gives visitors a larger-than-life real-time view of leafcutter ants inside a nest. The highlight of the hour-long guided tour is a large netted flyway where more than 40 species of colorful butterflies flit about amid dense foliage. Go midmorning, when the butterflies become active.

ⓩ Bat Jungle
1.75 miles (2.5 km) SE of Santa Elena.
Tel 2645-7701. **Open** 9am–7pm daily.
🄰 🄲 🅆 batjungle.com

Costa Rica boasts 109 species of bats (Monteverde alone has 65 of them), and you can learn all about these fascinating creatures at this exhibit. The highlight is a glass-walled flyway that is a habitat for eight bat species. Documentaries are shown, and you can don giant ears to gain a sense of a bat's phenomenal acoustic abilities.

The Quakers

The original settlers of Monteverde were 44 members of the pacifist Protestant religious group called Quakers. Hailing from Alabama, USA, where they had been jailed for refusing to be drafted, they arrived in Costa Rica in 1951, drawn by the fact that the country had abolished its army following the 1948 Civil War. They settled in the Cordillera de Tilarán, raising dairy cattle to produce the cheese that is now famous throughout the nation. The Quakers have been at the forefront of local conservation efforts in Monteverde.

Painting of a Quaker in traditional attire

The Golden Toad

In 1964 scientists discovered a new species of toad *(Bufo periglenes)* in the cloud forest above Monteverde. They named the brilliant orange creature *sapo dorado* (golden toad). In fact, only the male, which is 1 in (3 cm) long, is bright orange; the female is larger and speckled in patches of black, red, and yellow. Although abundant as recently as 1986, *sapo dorado* has not been seen since 1988 and is now considered extinct.

Golden toads, now extinct

La Lechería

miles (3 km) SE of Santa Elena.
el 2645-5436. **Open** 7:30am–5pm
aily (to 12:30pm Sun). 🐾 🞂 9am
nd 2pm. 🆆 **monteverde.net**

ounded by the original Quaker
ettlers of Monteverde in 1953,
he "Cheese Factory" today
roduces 14 types of
asteurized cheese, including
armesan, Gouda, and the
estselling Monte Rico. Guided
ours show visitors the
manufacturing process,
esulting in the production of
nore than 2,200 lb (1,000 kg)
f cheese daily. Visitors can buy
ajeta, a butterscotch spread,
nd cheeses on-site.

Reserva Biológica Bosque Nuboso Monteverde

miles (6 km) SE of Santa Elena.
el 2645-5122. **Open** 7am–4pm daily.
🞂 🞂 by reservation. 🞂 🞂 🞂
🞂 cct.or.cr

he dirt road that winds uphill
om Santa Elena ends at the
0-sq-mile (105-sq-km)

Monteverde Cloud Forest Biological Reserve, the jewel in the crown of the vast Arenal-Monteverde Protection Zone. Owned and operated by the Tropical Science Center of Costa Rica, the reserve straddles the Continental Divide and comprises six distinct ecological zones extending down the Pacific and Caribbean slopes. The upper elevation forests of the reserve are smothered by near-constant mists fed by sodden trade winds sweeping in off the Atlantic. On the more exposed ridges, trees are reduced to stunted dwarfs by the battering of the wind.

Iguana at Reserva Biológica Bosque Nuboso Monteverde

Wildlife abounds here. There are more than 150 species of amphibians and reptiles, and over 500 species of butterflies. More than 100 species of mammals include five wild cats – jaguars, jaguarundis,

pumas, margays, and ocelots. The umbrella bird and the endangered three-wattled bellbird are among the 400 species of birds. Quetzals are easily seen, the best viewing time being the April–May mating season, when they are especially active after dawn. Also easily spotted are humming-birds, which gather at feeders outside the visitor center; the reserve counts more than 30 species. Most wildlife, however, is elusive and difficult to detect. The reserve is crossed by 75 miles (120 km) of trails. A self- guided booklet corresponds to educational posts along the most popular trails, which are covered with wooden board-walks and are linked together to form what is colloquially called "the triangle." Sendero Chomogo is a steep trail leading to a *mirador* (viewpoint) atop the Continental Divide. From here, on rare days when the mists clear, visitors can see both the Pacific and the Caribbean. More challenging trails extend down the Caribbean slopes to the lowlands; these involve a full day's hike, with mud oozing underfoot. Rubber boots can be rented, along with binoculars. The driest months are between December and April. Hotels organize transport, and both taxis and buses operate from Santa Elena.

hike through Reserva Biológica Bosque Nuboso Monteverde

🅧 Reserva Bosque Nuboso Santa Elena

4 miles (6 km) NE of Santa Elena.
Tel 2645-5390. **Open** 7am–4pm daily.
🅐 🅑 7am, 11am, and 7pm, by
appointment. 🅓 🅔
🅦 **reservasantaelena.org**

Funded and run by the
community of Santa Elena, the
2-sq-mile (5-sq-km) Santa Elena
Cloud Forest Reserve is
dedicated to conservation and
education. The students of the
local high school play a vital role
in its development.

Set at a higher elevation than
the more famous and crowded
Reserva Biológica Bosque
Nuboso Monteverde *(see p181)*,
this magical green world is
cloudier and wetter. Spider and
howler monkeys are easily seen,
as are resplendent quetzals,
orange-bellied trogons,
squirrels, and agoutis. More
elusive are the tapirs, jaguars,
ocelots, pumas, and tayras,
which belong to the same
family as otters and weasels. On
clear days, there are fabulous
views toward Volcán Arenal in
the northeast. A self-guided
booklet is available for the
7 miles (11 km) of hiking trails.

🅧 Sky Walk/SkyTrek

3 miles (5 km) NE of Santa Elena.
Tel 2645-5238. **Open** 7am–4pm daily.
🅐 🅑 8am, 10am, and 1pm (Sky
Walk); 7:30am, 9:30am, 10:30am,
1:30pm, and 3pm (SkyTrek). 🅕 🅓 🅔
🅦 **skywalk.co.cr**; 🅦 **skytrek.com**

With high walkways, ziplines,
and suspension bridges, this
project on the edge of Reserva
Bosque Nuboso Santa Elena

A visitor trying the Sky Walk along the
cloud forest canopy

offers a variety of ways in which
to explore the cloud forest
canopy. Thrillseekers can try the
2-hour SkyTrek. Securely
harnessed, visitors slide
between treetop platforms
along ziplines that total a mile
(1.6 km) in length. Two
observatory towers offer
panoramic views of the
Guanacaste and Puntarenas
lowlands. The more sedate Sky
Walk is just as good for wildlife
viewing, with 3,300 ft (1,000 m)
of aerial pathways, including
five suspension bridges hung
between treetop platforms.

🅧 Selvatura Park

4 miles (6 km) NE of Santa Elena. **Tel**
2645-5929. **Open** 7am–5pm daily. 🅐
🅑 🅕 🅖 🅗 🅦 **selvatura.com**

Selvatura Park boasts 2 miles
(3 km) of treetop walkways
with eight suspension bridges

that meander through the
cloud forest canopy. Visitors
can also take part in a 14-
platform zipline canopy tour,
one of the longest in the whole
of Costa Rica, for a monkey's-
eye view of the upper
elevation forest.

A highlight of Selvatura Park
is the **Jewels of the Rainforest
Bio-Art Exhibition**, which
features a superb display of the
world's largest private insect
collection, put together by
entomologist Dr. Richard
Whitten. Beautifully laid out in
a riot of colors, thousands of
stick insects, butterflies, spider
wasps, beetles, moths, and
other insects are exhibited in
educational panels arranged
according to geographic
regions and themes. Other
exhibits in the Jewels collection
include giant crustaceans and
skulls of prehistoric creatures,
such as the saber-toothed tiger.
There are also human skulls,
ranging from Australopithecus
to Homo sapiens. Fascinating
videos about insect life are
shown in an auditorium.
Visitors can also watch
scientists at work in the
Selvatura laboratory via a
real-time video link.

Selvatura Park's other
attractions include a
hummingbird garden with
more than 14 species of
hummingbirds, a climbing wall,
guided nature walks, and a
domed, climate-controlled
butterfly garden with over 20
species of butterflies, including
the shimmering blue morphos

The entrance to Reserva Bosque Nuboso Santa Elena

Cloud Forests of Costa Rica

Named for the ephemeral mists that always envelop them, Costa Rica's cloud forests are typically found at elevations above 3,500 ft (1,050 m). More properly called montane tropical rainforests, they show extreme local variations in flora. On windswept, exposed ridges, trees and shrubs grow close to the ground as a form of protection, forming elfin forest with a primeval quality. More protected areas have taller vegetation typical of rainforests, with several levels *(see pp26–7)*. However, the lush canopies rarely reach 100 ft (30 m), although massive trees occasionally break through. Epiphytic plants such as orchids and bromeliads cling to branches, which also drip with lichen, fungi, mosses, and liverworts.

Pipers, found in moist areas, can have large leaves up to 20 in (50 cm) in size. Costa Rica has 94 species of pipers.

Swirling mists are created by humid Caribbean trade winds that condense as they sweep up to the Continental Divide.

Mosses breathe and draw water directly from the air through roots that hang from branches like an old man's beard.

Trees include guarumo, wild fig, and the huge zapote, with branches often weighed down by epiphytic plants.

Flora and Fauna

The constant interplay of sunshine, clouds, and rainfall in cloud forests produces flora of astounding diversity. Fauna is correspondingly abundant, although the mists and thick foliage hamper sightings.

Collared peccaries forage in large groups and are highly social. They use their long canines to defend themselves.

Prong-billed barbets have a telltale yodel but are reclusive and rarely seen. At night they sleep huddled together.

Howler monkeys are arboreal leaf- and fruit-eaters. Males are known for their intimidating, booming roars.

❷ Tilarán

Road Map: B2. 14 miles (22 km) E of Cañas. 🚗 7,700. 🚌 🎪 Feria del Día Cívica (Apr–Jun).

This neat little town, at an elevation of 1,800 ft (550 m) on the Continental Divide, has crisp air and a pretty plaza shaded by pines and cypress trees. It makes a delightful stop en route to and from Lake Arenal, although the only sight of note is the 1960s modern-looking, arch-roofed cathedral, decorated with marquetry. An agricultural town surrounded by undulating fields, Tilarán is known for its annual livestock show and rodeo.

❸ Cañas

Road Map: B2. 48 miles (77 km) N of Puntarenas. 🚗 19,000. 🚌 🎪 Feria Domingo de Resurrección (Mar/Apr).

This dusty cowboy town set dramatically in the lee of the Cordillera de Guanacaste is also known as Ciudad de la Amistad (City of Friendship). Surrounded by cattle haciendas in the searingly hot Tempisque basin, Cañas is most appealing for its *sabaneros* (cowboys). It sits astride the Pan-Am Highway, and serves as the gateway to Parque Nacional Palo Verde and Lake Arenal.

Environs

To the north, the **Centro de Rescate Las Pumas** (Puma Rescue Shelter) is a private facility for rescued wild cats. Some of the cats – which include jaguars, pumas, ocelots, margays, jaguarundis, and oncillas – are quite tame, having been raised by the late founder, Lilly Bodmer de Hagnauer. No guard rails prevent visitors from going up to the cages – caution is needed. Nearby, Río Corobicí is popular for rafting trips offered by **Safaris Corobicí**; small rapids add touches of excitement.

🐆 **Centro de Rescate Las Pumas**
Pan-Am Hwy, 3 miles (5 km) N of Cañas. **Tel** 2669-6044. **Open** 8am–5pm daily. 🅿 🌐 **centrorescate laspumas.org**

Bird-watching from canopied boats at Parque Nacional Palo Verde

🚣 **Safaris Corobicí**
Pan-Am Hwy, 3 miles (5 km) N of Cañas. **Tel** 2669-6091.
🌐 **safaricorobici.com**

❹ Parque Nacional Palo Verde

Road Map: B2. 26 miles (42 km) W of Cañas. **Tel** 2200-0125. 🚌 to Bagaces (14 miles/22 km N of Cañas), then by jeep-taxi. **Open** 8am–4pm daily. 🅿 🌐 **acarenaltempisque.org**

Palo Verde spreads over 50 sq miles (130 sq km), protecting a mosaic of habitats that includes mangrove swamps, marshes, savanna, and tropical dry forest at the mouth of Río Tempisque. Much of the vegetation consists of such drought-tolerant species as ironwood and sandbox, as well as evergreen *paloverde* (green stick) trees, which give the park its name.

Fauna is diverse and abundant. During the dry season (Dec–Apr), the trees burst into vibrant bloom. The ripening fruits draw monkeys, coatis, white-tailed deer, peccaries (wild hogs), pumas, and other mammals. In the wet season, much of the area floods and draws flocks of waterfowl to join herons, jabiru storks, ibis, roseate spoonbills and other stilt-legged waders. Palo Verde has more than 300 species of birds, including a large population of scarlet macaws and curassows. **Isla de Pájaros**, in the middle of Río Tempisque, is a major nesting site.

Wildlife viewing is best in the dry season, when the deciduous trees lose their leaves and animals collect near waterholes. Well-maintained trails lead to lookout points.

Several private wildlife refuges border the park to the west. **El Viejo Wildland Refuge & Wetlands** offers guided tours of Palo Verde's fringe forests and wetlands using amphibious all-terrain vehicles. The refuge includes a sugarcane estate and a traditional sugar-processing mill.

🐊 **El Viejo Wildland Refuge & Wetlands**
10 miles (17 km) SE of Filadelfia. **Tel** 2296-0966. 🅿 9am, 11am, and 1pm daily. 🅿
🌐 **elviejowetlands.com**

❺ Reserva Biológica Lomas Barbudal

Road Map: A2. 4 miles (6 km) SW of Pan-Am Hwy, 12 miles (19 km) NW of Bagaces. **Tel** 2200-0125. 🚌 to Bagaces, then by jeep-taxi. **Open** 8am–4pm daily (subject to change). 🅿 by donation. ⚠

Famous for its plentiful insect population, not least the 250 species of bees, the seldom-

Rare dry forests of Reserva Biológica Lomas Barbudal

sited Reserva Biológica Lomas Barbudal (Bearded Hills Biological Reserve) protects rare tropical dry forest. Established in 1986, the hilly, densely forested terrain hosts a similar array of wildlife to Parque Nacional Palo Verde. Trails span the 9-sq-mile (23-sq-km) reserve from the Casa de Patrimonio visitor center on the banks of Río Cabuyo. The best time to visit is during February and March, when the park's trees bloom in spectacular profusion.

Cloud-topped volcano, Zona Protectora Volcán Miravalles

Zona Protectora Volcán Miravalles

Road Map: B2. 16 miles (26 km) N of Bagaces. 🚌 from Bagaces.

This active volcano rises 6,650 ft (2,030 m) above the Guanacaste plains. Few visitors hike the trails at lace in the 42-sq-mile (109-sq-km) Miravalles Forest Reserve on the upper slopes. The main draw is **Las Hornillas** (Little Ovens), an area of steam vents and mud pools bubbling and hissing on the western slopes. The Institute of Electricity (ICE) produces power from the super-heated water vapor at **Proyecto Geotérmico Miravalles**. The fumaroles and mud pools are best viewed at **Las Hornillas Volcanic Activity Center**, where a short trail leads into an active crater. You can even wallow in warm, therapeutic mud before diving into a swimming pool. There are also horseback rides and a thrilling thermal waterslide that plunges you into a pool with magnificent volcano views.

On the lower slopes, **Río Perdido Activity Center** is set amid a dry-forest reserve laced with hiking and mountain biking trails. Ziplines and a challenge course span a river canyon, and there is whitewater rafting.

🔥 **Proyecto Geotérmico Miravalles**
17 miles (27 km) NE of Bagaces. **Tel** 2673-1111, ext 232. ⬤ by appt. ♨

🔥 **Las Hornillas Volcanic Activity Center**
1 mile (1.6 km) SE of Proyecto Geotérmico Miravalles. **Tel** 8839-9769. ⬤ 8am–5pm daily. ♨ 🍽 🚿
Ⓦ hornillas.com

🔥 **Río Perdido Activity Center**
San Bernardo de Bagaces, 20 miles (32 km) NE of Bagaces. **Tel** 2673-3600. **Open** 8am–6pm daily.
Ⓦ rioperdido.com

❼ Liberia

Road Map: A2. 16 miles (26 km) N of Bagaces. 🏛 42,000. ✈ 🚌 🎉 Día de la Anexión de Guanacaste (Jul 25).

Guanacaste's charming, historic capital, founded in 1769, is known as the White City for its whitewashed adobe houses with terra-cotta tile roofs. The loveliest houses are on Calle Real (Calle Central). The city is also known for its *puertas del sol* – double doors, one on each side of a corner, to catch both morning and afternoon sun. Liberia's cowboy tradition is celebrated at the **Monumento Sabanero**, on the main boulevard, and at **Museo de**

Interior of a colonial-era house on Calle Real, Liberia

Sabanero, where assorted cowboy items are housed in the venerable Casa de la Cultura. The main plaza has the modern **Iglesia Inmaculada Concepción de María**. Next door, the *ayuntamiento* (town hall) flies Guanacaste's flag, the only provincial flag in the country. Each July, locals celebrate Guanacaste's separation from Nicaragua in 1824. The Iglesia de la Ermita de la Resurección, familiarly known as **Iglesia de la Agonía**, is an engaging 1825 adobe colonial church, which features a small museum of religious art. Liberia is the main gateway to Parque Nacional Rincón de la Vieja *(see p186)* and the beaches of Northern Nicoya.

🏛 **Museo de Sabanero**
Ave 6 at Calle 1. **Tel** 2666-0135. ⬤ by appt.

⛪ **Iglesia de la Agonía**
Calle 9 and Ave Central. **Tel** 2666-0107. **Open** 2:30–3:30pm daily.

Cowboy Culture

Many Guanacastecos make their living as *sabaneros* (cowboys), also called *bramaderos* after the hardy Brahma cattle. Proud, folkloric figures, the *sabaneros* ride straight-backed in their elaborately decorated saddles, leading their horses in a high-stepping gait. The most important days of the year in Guanacasteco culture revolve around *topes* (horse shows) and *recorridos de toros* (bullfights), in which bulls are ridden and baited, but never killed.

Sabanero on a working ranch

The impressive Volcán Rincón de la Vieja

❽ Parque Nacional Rincón de la Vieja

Road Map: B1. 19 miles (30 km) NE of Liberia. **Tel** 2200-0399. 🚌 to Liberia, then by jeep-taxi. **Open** 7am–5pm daily; last admission: 3pm. 🚻 🏕 ⛺
🌐 acguanacaste.ac.cr

The dramatically beautiful Rincón de la Vieja volcano is studded with nine craters, of which only Rincón de la Vieja crater (5,900 ft/1,800 m) is active. The highest is Santa María (6,250 ft/1,900 m), while Von Seebach crater is filled with an acidic turquoise lake.

The park protects an area of 55 sq miles (140 sq km). The eastern slopes of the volcano are rain-soaked all year round; the western side has a distinct dry season, and ranges from deciduous forest at lower elevations to cloud forest below the stark moonscape summit.

Visitors can spot capuchin, howler, and spider monkeys, anteaters, sloths, kinkajous, and more than 300 species of birds, including quetzals and three-wattled bellbirds. Pea-green **Lago Los Jilgueros** is visited by tapirs.

The park offers superb hiking. Trails start at the park headquarters, the 19th-century **Hacienda Santa María**, and at **Las Pailas** ranger station. They lead past mud pools, hot sulfur springs, waterfalls, and fumaroles. The challenging 11-mile (18-km) summit trail requires a pre-dawn departure. The summit offers fabulous views as far as Lake Nicaragua.

Hikers must report to the ranger stations when setting out and returning. Both ranger stations can be reached from Liberia by jeep-taxis, and they are linked by a trail. The dry season from December to April is the best time to visit.

Environs

Several nature lodges on the western slopes of the volcano also operate as activity centers. On its southwestern flanks, **Hacienda Lodge Guachipelín** *(see p257)*, accessed from Liberia via Curubandé, is a working cattle ranch, specializing in horseback rides. Nearby, **Rincón de la Vieja Lodge** *(see p257)* has a 900-acre (364-ha) private forest reserve. Both lodges offer canopy tours. From Liberia, a road leads via Cañas Dulces to **Buena Vista Mountain Lodge & Adventure Center** *(see p257)* on the northwestern slopes. It offers horseback rides, a canopy tour, and a 1,300-ft (400-m) long water slide. **Hotel Borinquen**

Careta la Cangreja waterfall in the Parque Rincón de la Vieja

Mountain Resort Thermae & Spa nearby has bubbling mud pools and spa treatments.

🏨 **Hotel Borinquen Mountain Resort Thermae & Spa**
19 miles (30 km) NE of Liberia via Cañas Dulces. **Tel** 2690-1900. 🚻 ⚡
🍽 🌐 borinquenresort.com

❾ Parque Nacional Guanacaste

Road Map: A1. 22 miles (35 km) N of Liberia. **Tel** 2666-5051. 🚌 to Liberia, then by jeep-taxi. **Open** 8am–5pm daily with advance notice. 🚻 🏕 by reservation. ⛺
🌐 acguanacaste.ac.cr

This remote national park encompasses more than 325 sq miles (840 sq km) of reforested woodland and pasture extending to the top of Volcán Cacao (5,400 ft/1,650 m) and Volcán Orosi (4,900 ft/1,500 m). Facilities are few, but the rewards are immense, with a variety of habitats and superb wildlife viewing. Biological stations **Cacao**, **Pitilla**, and **Maritza** have spartan accommodations; Cacao and Maritza can be accessed only on foot or horseback.

Pre-Columbian petroglyphs can be seen at **Llano de los Indios**, on the lower western flanks of Volcán Orosi.

❿ Bahía Salinas

Road Map: A1. 38 miles (62 km) NW of Liberia. 🚌 to La Cruz, then by jeep-taxi.

Framed by cliffs to the north, salt pans to the east, and mangrove-fringed beaches to the south, this flask-shaped bay is swept by breezes from December to April. Fishing hamlets line its shores. Hotels at La Coyotera and Playa Copal serve as surfing centers. The Costa Rican Tourism Board visitor center in La Cruz has great views.

Frigate birds use the drafts around **Refugio Nacional de Vida Silvestre Isla Bolaños** to take off. A protected nesting site for pelicans and American oystercatchers, this island is off limits to visitors.

Costa Rica's Dry Forests

Dry deciduous forests once swathed the lowlands of the Pacific littoral from Mexico to Panama, covering most of today's Guanacaste and Nicoya. After the arrival of Columbus, the Spanish cleared vast areas of these forests to raise cattle, which still dominate the economy of the Pacific northwest. Today, only about 2 percent of the original cover remains, notably in the Tempisque basin, and Santa Rosa, Rincón de la Vieja, and Guanacaste National Parks. Recent conservation efforts, spearheaded by the US biologist Dr. Daniel Janzen, are returning large areas of savanna and ranchland to their original state. The intent is to link the existing patchwork and regenerate dry forest ecosystems.

The understory consists of short trees; above are stout-trunked, flat-crowned trees.

Grass and thorn scrub dominate at ground level.

Trees typically grow no higher than 40 ft (12 m) and are widely spaced.

The forest is relatively sparsely vegetated, with fewer species of flora.

The dry season sees the forest exploding in an outburst of color. Pink *pouí* blooms first, followed by bright orange *poró*, rose-colored *Tabebuia rosea*, vermilion *malinche*, and purple jacaranda.

Parque Nacional Santa Rosa *(see pp188–9)* protects the most important remnant of dry tropical forest in all Central America.

Guanacaste trees spread their wide-reaching branches close to the ground, providing precious shade in the searing midday heat. Such dry forest species have evolved to withstand the long seasonal drought by shedding their leaves.

Indio desnudo, or naked Indian, is named for its distinct copper-red bark, which readily peels to reveal an olive-colored trunk. Naked Indian is also called the *gumbo-limbo*.

White-tailed deer blend in well with the dun-colored grasses and dry forest. The best times to see them are dawn and dusk, when they emerge to search for food.

Thorny scrub, such as acacia, have long spikes to prevent birds and animals from eating their leaves and seeds.

⓫ Parque Nacional Santa Rosa

The country's first national park, inaugurated in 1971, Santa Rosa National Park covers 190 sq miles (492 sq km) of the Santa Elena Peninsula and adjoining land. It is divided into two sectors. To the north is the little-visited Murciélago Sector, with hidden beaches – notably Playa Blanca – accessed along a rugged dirt track. To the south, the much larger Santa Rosa Sector was the site of battles in 1856 and 1955, and boasts most of the sights of interest. The park protects the nation's largest stretch of tropical dry forest, as well as nine other distinct habitats. With 115 mammal species, including 20 types of bats, and 250 species of birds, the park is a superb wildlife-viewing area, especially in the dry season, when the deciduous trees shed their leaves.

Islas Murciélagos
The waters around these islands offer splendid scuba diving (see p292). Manta rays, grouper, and other large species are common.

Playa Nancite
This is one of three sites in Costa Rica where olive ridley turtles nest en masse in synchronized *arribadas (see p195)*, especially in September–October. Protected as a research site, it is off-limits to visitors except by permit.

Crocodiles
The mangroves at the northern and southern ends of Playa Naranjo harbor crocodiles.

KEY

① **Witch's Rock**, off Playa Naranjo, is renowned among surfers for the powerful, tubular waves that rise here and pump ashore.

② **Sendero Los Patos** leads to waterholes, which provide excellent opportunities for viewing peccaries and other mammals in the dry season.

③ **Centro de Investigaciones** is the main center for tropical dry forest research in Costa Rica.

④ *Tanquetas* (armored vehicles) lie half-buried in the undergrowth as rusting relics of an ill-fated attack launched by Nicaraguan dictator Anastasio Somoza against Costa Rica in 1955.

Playa Naranjo
A gorgeous white-sand surfing beach, Playa Naranjo has campsites with basic facilities. It is reached by an arduous dirt road that often gets washed out in wet season – check with rangers before setting out for the beach.

Río Calera

Playa Tule

Estacion Biológia Nancite

Playa Nancite

Estero Real

Bahía Naranjo

Peña Bruja

Playa Naranjo

Pacific Ocean

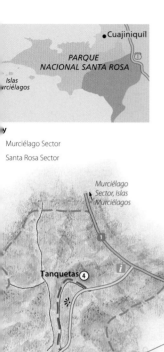

Cuajiniquíl

PARQUE NACIONAL SANTA ROSA

Islas rciélagos

y

Murciélago Sector

Santa Rosa Sector

Murciélago Sector, Islas Murciélagos

Tanquetas ④

Sector

de nes ③

La Casona

0 kilometers 2

0 miles 2

Sendero Indio Desnudo

Named for *indio desnudo* (naked Indian) or gumbo-limbo trees, this short trail features a monument to the Costa Ricans who fought in the battles of 1856 and 1955.

La Casona
Also called Hacienda Santa Rosa, this important monument is a replica built in 2001 after the 1663 original was destroyed by arsonists. The battle of 1856 against William Walker *(see p47)* was fought outside the hacienda, which now functions as a historical museum.

y

▦ Pan-American Highway

▢ Other road

▪ Trail

▸ Park boundary

The Contra Connection

Col. Oliver North

During the 1980s, the remote Murciélago Sector was utilized as a secret training ground for the CIA-backed Nicaraguan Contras in their battle to topple the Sandinista government *(see p48)*. An airstrip was illegally established here under the orders of Colonel Oliver North, a key player in the Iran-Contra scandal that shook the US in 1983–8. The road to the park entrance runs alongside the airstrip, which occupies land confiscated from Nicaraguan strongman Anastasio Somoza.

Visitors soaking up the sun on the wide gray-sand beaches of Tamarindo

⑫ Bahía Culebra

Road Map A2. 12 miles (19 km) W of Liberia.

Ringed by dramatic cliffs and fringed by beaches of varying hues, Bahía Culebra (Snake Bay) is the setting for Proyecto Papagayo, a controversial tourism project that has restricted access to the bay's sparkling waters. Spilling down the cliffs are big hotels, including the **Four Seasons Resort at Papagayo Peninsula** (see p256). Pre-Columbian settlements on the bay await excavation. **Witch's Rock Canopy Tour** has ziplines and a walkway through the dry forest canopy.

⚡ Witch's Rock Canopy Tour
23 miles (37 km) W of Liberia. **Tel** 2666-7101. **Open** 8am–5pm daily. 🅿
🅦 http://witchsrockcanopytour. com

⑬ Playas del Coco

Road Map A2. 22 miles (35 km) SW of Liberia. 🏔 3,000. 🚌 🎦 Fiesta Cívica (Jan); Festival de la Virgen del Mar (mid-Jul).

This wide beach combines the allure of a traditional fishing community with a no-frills resort. Although the pelican-patrolled beach is not particularly attractive, it is a favorite with Costa Rican families, and has a lively nightlife. Local outfitters offer sportfishing and scuba trips to Islas Murciélagos (see p188) and Isla Catalina, where schools of rays can be seen.

Environs
Secluded Playa Ocotal, west of Playas del Coco, has the region's best dive site. It is also a premier sportfishing destination. Playas Hermosa and Panamá, north of Coco, have exquisite settings, with Isla Catalina silhouetted dramatically at sunset.

⑭ Playa Flamingo

Road Map A2. 38 miles (62 km) SW of Liberia. 🏔 2,000. 🚌

With gently curving white sands cusped by rugged headlands, the gorgeous Playa Flamingo justifies its official yet less common name, Playa Blanca (White Beach). The large bay is a popular anchorage. Deluxe villas dot the rocky headlands. Most of the hotels are upscale timeshare resorts and, despite its fine beach, Flamingo is shunned by the off-beat and party crowd.

Environs
North of Playa Flamingo, the estuary of Río Salinas opens out at modestly appealing Playa Penca, where roseate spoonbills, egrets, and a rich variety of other birdlife can be spotted in the mangroves.

Southwest of Flamingo is **Playa Conchal** (Shell Beach), with its shining sands; the diamond-like sparkle of the sands is caused by crushed seashells. The beach slopes gently into turquoise waters, which are ideal for snorkeling and other water sports. For a fee, visitors can access **Westin Playa Conchal Resort & Spa** (see p258), which boasts a championship golf course.

⑮ Tamarindo

Road Map A2. 11 miles (18 km) S of Flamingo. 🏔 8,000. 🎦 🚌 🎦 International Festival of Music (Jul–Aug).

Formerly a sleepy fishing village, Tamarindo has rapidly developed into the region's premier resort. This hip surfers' haven is also a center for sportfishing, diving, and snorkeling. Tamarindo is popular with backpackers, but also boasts a cosmopolitan selection of restaurants and boutique hotels.

The area lies within **Parque Nacional Marino Las Baulas** (Leatherback Turtle Marine National Park), inaugurated in 1990. It protects 85 sq miles (220 sq km) of ocean and 1,100 acres (445 ha) of beach. **Playa Grande** – a prime nesting site of leatherback turtles between October and April, although their numbers have declined considerably. Pacific ridley, green, and hawksbill turtles occasionally nest here. During the nesting season, nobody is permitted on the beach after sundown, except guided groups by reservation.

The park also incorporates Playa Langosta, south of Tamarindo, and 990 acres (400 ha) of mangroves, which can be explored on boats.

Surfers heading for the water

⚡ Parque Nacional Marino Las Baulas
Tel 2653-0470. **Open** 6am–6pm daily.
🅿 🅲 compulsory on the beach; Oct–Feb: 6pm–6am daily.

For hotels and restaurants in this region see pp252–61 and pp266–77

Surfing Beaches of Northern Nicoya

Acclaimed as the "Hawaii of Latin America," Costa Rica offers world-class surfing and warm waters year-round. The greatest concentration of surfing beaches is in Northern Nicoya, where Pacific breakers pump ashore all year. Conditions are ideal between December and March, when the Papagayo winds kick up high waves. Dozens of beaches guarantee that surfers will find a fairly challenging ride on any day, while extremely varied tidal conditions provide breaks for every level of experience. Be warned, however: riptides are common and many surfers lose their lives every year; few beaches have lifeguards. Numerous villages and resorts have become surfers' havens and are heavily reliant on the waveboard trade, with scores of surf camps and surf shops.

① Playa Naranjo

This remote beach in the Golfo de Papagayo boasts a superb beach break, called Witch's Rock. Naranjo is accessed by 4WD or by boat from the resorts of Northern Nicoya.

② Playa Grande

Consistently high waves pump ashore onto this long, easily accessible beach. It is protected as part of a prime nesting site of the leatherback turtle.

④ Playa Nosara

Popular among surfers, Nosara has a fine beach break and a dramatic setting. It is backed by mangroves and has warm, rocky tidepools.

③ Tamarindo

The surf capital of Northern Nicoya, Tamarindo offers a rivermouth break, rocky point break, and beach breaks. It is also the gateway to nearby isolated surfing beaches such as Playas Langosta, Avellanas, and Negra.

0 km   10
0 miles   10

⑤ Playas Bejuco and San Miguel

Long slivers of silvery sand are washed by good surf. These remote beaches are oriented to budget travelers.

⑥ Playas Bongo, Arío, and Manzanillo

All three are as off-the-beaten-track as possible in Costa Rica. Just getting there is half the fun. Cracking waves, combined with the solitude, guarantee surfer bliss. Facilities are virtually nonexistent.

⑯ Refugio Nacional de Vida Silvestre Ostional

Road Map A3. 34 miles (55 km) S of Tamarindo. **Tel** 2682-0470. 🚌 from Santa Cruz and Nicoya via Nosara. **Open** 24 hrs daily. 🅿️ 📷 compulsory for the beach.

The setting for one of the most remarkable occurrences in nature, Ostional National Wildlife Refuge protects 4 sq miles (10 sq km) of land and sea around Playa Ostional. The beach is one of only a dozen worldwide where Pacific ridley turtles nest in synchronized *arribadas*. The best time to view them is during August and September. Green and leatherback turtles also nest here in smaller numbers. Ostional is the only place in Costa Rica where residents are legally allowed, under strict guidelines, to harvest eggs during the first 36 hours of an *arribada*.

Ostional is accessed by dirt roads that require 4WD during the wet season. The remote setting and the surrounding forests have shielded the area from development, though now there are a few hotels. Personal contact with turtles is forbidden, as are flashlights and flash photography.

⑰ Nosara

Road Map A3. 3 miles (5 km) S of Ostional. 🏨 5,000. ✈️ 🚌

This isolated community on the Nicoya coast comprises twin villages. **Bocas de Nosara**, 3 miles (5 km) inland, on the banks of Río Nosara, is a peasant hamlet where ox-carts still creak along dusty lanes. **Beaches of Nosara**, to the south, is a predominantly foreign settlement, with contemporary homes amid forests near the shore. The maze of roads comprising Beaches of Nosara backs onto the stunning **Playa Guiones**, a long, calm stretch of white sand and sun-warmed

A participant in a surfing competition at Playa Guiones, Nosara

tidepools in which monkeys can sometimes be seen enjoying a good soak. Strong tides rule out swimming, but the breakers are perfect for surfing. To the north, small **Playa Pelada** is encircled by steep cliffs. Nearby, **Reserva Biológica Nosara** protects 125 acres (50 ha) of tropical forest along the Río Nosara estuary. Over 250 bird species nest here, including wood storks, white-fronted parrots, and frigate birds. Crocodiles can be seen in the estuary.

Vultures, Nosara

🗺️ **Reserva Biológica Nosara**
Bocas de Nosara. **Tel** 2682-0035. 🅿️ 📷 by appointment. 📷 🖥️ 🏨 📧 🌐 lagarta.com

⑱ Sámara

Road Map A3. 16 miles (26 km) S of Nosara. 🏨 3,000. ✈️ at Carrillo. 🚌

Popular with backpackers, surfers, and middle-class Costa Ricans, Sámara is the most southerly of the beach resorts developed for tourism. At the southern end of Playa Sámara, at Matapalo, villagers eke out a living from the sea. Life revolves around lazing on the gray sands, or going surfing and riding. **Playa Carrillo**, 2 miles (3 km) south of Sámara, is a sportfishing center, while to the north, the **Flying**

Beach sign, Sámara

Crocodile Lodge and Flying Center offers flights by ultralight plane.

Flying Crocodile Lodge and Flying Center
Esterones, 3 miles (5 km) N of Sámar Tel 2656-8048. **Open** 7am–3pm dail 📷 🅿️ 🏨 📧 🌐 flying-crocodile.com

⑲ Islita

Road Map B3. 9 miles (14 km) S of Sámara. 🏨 1,000. ✈️ 🚌 to Sámara then by jeep-taxi.

Set in the lee of the soaring Punta Islita, this charming village is known for the **Hotel Punta Islita** *(see p256)*, a hilltop resort that houses the **Galería de Arte Contemporáneo Mar Anne Zürcher**. Artworks in varied media by established ar local artists are available here. Th hotel also supports the **Museo de Arte Contemporáneo al Ai Libre** (Open Air Museum of Contemporary Art), spread around the village – houses, individual trees, and even the soccer field have bee decorated with mura and other spontaneo aesthetic expressions Several rivers have to be forded along the rough dirt road linkin Islita to Sámara and Malpaís. The hotel als hosts The **Ara Projec** a breeding center and release site for green and scarlet macaws (www.thearaproject.org); the Lapa Lookout education cente has information for visitors.

Arribadas of Olive Ridley Turtles

The synchronized mass nestings called *arribadas* (arrivals), which are unique to the ridley turtle, are known to occur regularly at only a dozen or so beaches worldwide. Of these, three are in Costa Rica – Playa Nancite, Playa Ostional, and Playa Camaronal. *Arribadas* take place between April and December, peaking in August and September. Lasting between three and eight days, they happen at two- to four-week intervals, usually during the last quarter of the moon's cycle. On any one night, as many as 20,000 turtles congregate just beyond the breakers. Then, wave after wave of turtles storm ashore, even climbing over one another in a single-minded effort to find a nesting spot on the crowded sands. Millions of eggs are laid during each *arribada*, believed to be an evolutionary adaptation to ensure survival in the face of heavy predation.

Ridley turtles come ashore in groups numbering up to 100,000 turtles during a single *arribada*. Ridleys nest every year, sometimes as often as three times a season.

Hatchlings emerge together at night for the dangerous run to the sea and the safety it offers. Only about 1 percent survive to adulthood.

Flippers scatter sand on the nest to disguise it.

Females lay an average of 100 eggs each during an *arribada*.

The Nesting Process

Turtles seek sandy sites above the high-water mark in which to nest. Incubation typically takes around 50 days. The temperature of the nest affects the gender of the hatchling – cooler nests produce males, while warmer ones produce females.

Nests are scooped out to a depth of about 3 ft (1 m) using rear flippers.

Scientists tag ridley turtles during an *arribada* at Santa Rosa's Playa Nancite in an effort to track and study them.

Coatis, as well as raccoons and vultures, dig up turtle nests to feast on the eggs; less than 10 percent of turtle eggs hatch.

Commercial harvesting of eggs is legally done only by villagers of Ostional.

⑳ Nicoya

Road Map: A3. 44 miles (71 km) SW of Liberia. 🚌 21,000. 🚏 📅 Fiesta de la Yegüita (Dec 12).

Emanating sleepy colonial charm, Nicoya dates back to the mid-1600s, and is named after the Chorotega *cacique* (chief) who greeted the Spanish conquistador Gil González Davila in 1523. An advanced Chorotega settlement existed here in pre-Columbian times. Today, the town serves as the administrative center for the Nicoya Peninsula and bustles with the comings and goings of *campesinos* (peasants) and cowboys. Nicoya is also the gateway for Sámara and the Pacific beaches of the south-central Nicoya Peninsula.

Life centers around the old plaza, **Parque Central**. Built in 1644, the intimate, wood-beamed **Iglesia Parroquia San Blas**, located in the northeast corner of the plaza, has a simple façade inset with bells. Inside, a small museum has a display of historical artifacts and religious memorabilia.

Environs
Nature lovers can head about 17 miles (27 km) northeast to **Puerto Humo**, a riverside port town from where boats depart for Parque Nacional Palo Verde (*see p184*). Buses operate from Nicoya. Nearby, **Rancho Humo** is a nature conservancy with superb birdwatching in the wetlands adjoining Palo Verde. It offers hiking and guided tours by electric car and canopied boat.

🏞 **Rancho Humo**
Puerto Humo. **Tel** 2233-2233.
Open 7am–5pm daily. 🅿 📷 🚫
🌐 ranchohumo.com

㉑ Santa Cruz

Road Map: A2. 14 miles (22 km) N of Nicoya. 🚌 17,500. 🚏 📅 Fiesta Patronal de Santo Cristo (mid-Jan); Fiesta de Santiago (Jul 25).

Steeped in local tradition, Santa Cruz is Costa Rica's official La Ciudad Folklórica (National Folkloric City). Connected by Highway 160 to Tamarindo and the beaches of the north-central Nicoya Peninsula, this

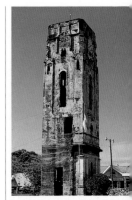
Ruined bell tower, Plaza Bernabela Ramos, Santa Cruz

center was founded in 1760. Many of the wooden colonial edifices that once graced its historic core were destroyed in a fire, but the overall ambience is still charming. **Plaza de los Mangos** serves as a focal point for the city's festivals, which draw visitors from miles around to enjoy traditional *marimba* music and dance. *Topes* (horse shows) and *recorridos de toros* (bullfights) also take place here

The architectural highlight of Santa Cruz is the landscaped **Plaza Bernabela Ramos**. On its east side is a modern church with fine stained-glass windows. Next to it is the ruined bell tower of a Colonial-style church which was destroyed by an earthquake in 1950. The plaza is a pleasant spot to relax and admire the statues, including that of Chorotega *cacique* Diría in the southwest corner, and a *montador* (bull-rider) on a bucking bull in the northeast.

The simple exterior of the Iglesia Parroquia San Blas in Nicoya

The Virgin of Guadalupe by Miguel Cabrera

Fiesta de la Yegüita
Also known as the Festival of the Virgin of Guadalupe, this fiesta blends Chorotega and Catholic traditions. According to legend, twin brothers were battling to death for the love of an Indian princess when a *yegüita* (little mare) intervened to stop the fight. The festival takes place every December and features traditional Costa Rican food, bullfights, rodeos, street processions, fireworks, music and dance, and ancient Indian rituals.

Statue of a bull-rider, Plaza Bernabela Ramos, Santa Cruz

Guaitíl

Road Map: A2. 7 miles (11 km) E of Santa Cruz. 🚌 1,500. 🚌

This small village offers the most authentic display of traditional culture *(see pp34–5)* in Costa Rica, with virtually the entire community deriving its income by making ceramics in pre-Columbian style. Guaitíl sits on the cusp between cultures – even the contemporary pieces draw inspiration from traditional Chorotega designs.

Headed by the matriarch of the family, most households have a traditional wood-fired, dome-shaped *horno* (oven) for firing pots and other ceramic objects. Visitors are welcome in the yards to watch artisans work the red clay dug from nearby riverbanks. The dusty lanes are lined with thatched stores and open-air shacks where the pottery is displayed.

A regeneration of Chorotega culture is now spilling over into the nearby villages as well. In San Vicente, the tiny **Ecomuseo de la Cerámica Chorotega** offers a historical and cultural profile on the production of clay pottery .

🏛 Ecomuseo de la Cerámica Chorotega

1 mile (1.6 km) E of Guaitíl. **Tel** 2681-1563. **Open** 8am–4pm Mon–Fri. 🚻

Parque Nacional Barra Honda

Road Map: B3. 11 miles (18 km) E of Nicoya. **Tel** 2659-1551. 🚌 Nicoya–Santa Ana village (0.5 mile/1 km from park entrance), then by jeep-taxi. **Open** 8am–4pm daily; last admission: noon; caving: 8am–1pm daily (Dec–Apr: to 2pm). 🚻 🚻 🚻 🚻 🚻 ⛰

One of the best spots for caving, this national park was established in 1974, and spreads over 9 sq miles (23 sq km). A tropical dry forest area, Barra Honda was used for raising cattle, but is now in the process of being reforested.

The park has excellent hiking. Trails lead to Mirador Nacaome lookout points atop Cerro Barra Honda (1450 ft/442 m), a massif

lifted up by powerful tectonic forces. Cerro Barra Honda is riddled with limestone caverns formed by the action of water over millions of years. Of the 40 caves discovered so far, 20 have been explored. **Santa Ana**, the largest cave, soars to a height of 790 ft (240 m). Inside **Cueva Terciopelo**, a dripstone formation called El Órgano (The Organ) produces musical tones when struck. **El Pozo Hediondo** (Stinking Well) is named for the droppings of the bats roosting there. Some caves have blind salamanders and blind fish, and most boast dramatic stalactites and stalagmites. Indigenous artifacts have been found in some caves.

Cave descents into Cueva Terciopelo are permitted; a licensed guide is compulsory. Guides are also compulsory for the Las Cascadas trail, which leads to waterfalls. Spelunkers enter Terciópelo via a 100-ft (30-m) ladder. Access to the other caves requires prior permission. Spelunking equipment and guides can be hired. Hikers

Puente de Amistad con Taiwan across Río Tempisque on Hwy 18

must report to the ranger station. A 4WD is needed to reach the park entrance. Jeep-taxis run from Nicoya.

Environs

The **Puente de Amistad con Taiwan** (Friendship with Taiwan Bridge) is a dramatic suspension bridge over Río Tempisque. It links Nicoya to the Pan-Am Highway.

A spelunker at Cueva Terciopelo, Parque Nacional Barra Honda

THE NORTHERN ZONE

The northern provinces are Costa Rica's flatlands – a gentle landscape quilted in pastures, fruit plantations, and humid rainforest. This wide-open canvas is framed by a dramatic escarpment of mountains. The extreme north of this perennially wet region is a world of seasonally flooded lagoons and migratory waterfowl, while the mountains in the south are cloaked in dense forests, which are protected in a series of national parks and wildlife reserves.

The rolling *llanuras* (plains) form a triangle, narrow to the west and broadening eastward, which extends north from the base of the *cordilleras* (mountain ranges) to Río San Juan, on the Nicaraguan border. The scenery is nowhere more splendid than around Lake Arenal, located on a depression between the Guanacaste and Tilarán Mountains. Volcán Arenal looms ethereally over the waters. Its near-constant eruptions and other local attractions have given a boost to the nearby town of La Fortuna, now a base for various adventure activities.

At the time of the Spanish arrival, the Corobicí peoples occupied the lower flanks of the mountains and were at war with their Nicaraguan neighbors.

During the colonial era, settlements were restricted to the main river courses, and were subject to constant plundering by pirates.

The region remained aloof from the rest of the country until the early 19th century, when a trade route was laid linking highland towns to a wharfside settlement – today's Puerto Viejo – which gave access to the Caribbean. Founded around that time, Ciudad Quesada grew to become the region's administrative center. The settlement campaign initiated in the 1950s led to the decimation of huge tracts of forest to make room for cattle farms as well as banana and citrus plantations. More settlements have since sprung up throughout the region.

Cloud-wreathed Volcán Arenal, the country's most active volcano

◄ An aerial tram taking visitors through the jungle at Arenal Theme Park near the Laguna de Arenal

Exploring the Northern Zone

The main gateway to the northern lowlands is Ciudad Quesada, a dairy town on the mountain flanks that fringe the region's southern border. La Fortuna, to the west, is a center for outdoor activities, from caving to horseback riding. The region's major attraction is Volcán Arenal, great for hiking and for soaking in the thermal waters of Tabacón. Nearby Lake Arenal offers fine fishing and world-class windsurfing. To the east of Ciudad Quesada are several private reserves – one of which includes the Rainforest Aerial Tram. Boats depart the nondescript town of Puerto Viejo de Sarapiquí for nature cruises along Río Sarapiquí. Caño Negro Wildlife Refuge, in the far north, is a superb birding and angling destination.

Stone figurine, Centro Neotrópico SarapiquíS

Sights at a Glance

Towns and Cities

❶ La Fortuna
❿ Ciudad Quesada (San Carlos)
⓬ Puerto Viejo de Sarapiquí

National Parks and Reserves

❸ Parque Nacional Volcán Arenal
❽ Refugio Nacional de Vida Silvestre Caño Negro
❾ Parque Nacional Volcán Tenorio
⓮ Refugio Nacional de Vida Silvestre Corredor Fronterizo

Areas of Natural Beauty

❷ Tabacón Hot Springs Resort and Spa
❹ *Laguna de Arenal pp204–5*
❺ Arenal Hanging Bridges
❻ Arenal Theme Park
❼ Cavernas de Venado
⓭ Selva Verde
⓯ La Selva Biological Station
⓰ Heliconia Island
⓱ Rara Avis
⓲ Rainforest Aerial Tram

Indigenous Site

⓫ Centro Neotrópico SarapiquíS

A cowboy at Selva Verde

For hotels and restaurants in this region see pp252–61 and pp266–77

...enal shrouded in mist

The hot springs at Tabacón, near Volcán Arenal

REFUGIO NACIONAL
DE VIDA SILVESTRE
...REDOR FRONTERIZO 14

Concho

Boca San Carlos

Río San Juan

Coopevega

Laguna Canacas

Trinidad

227

Río San Carlos

Boca Tapada

San Marcos

Pangola

Las Medias

Río Toro

Río Sarapiquí

H E R E D I A

250

PUERTO VIEJO
DE SARAPIQUÍ 12

SELVA VERDE

Pital

La Virgen de Sarapiquí

13   15

16   SARAPIQUÍ
HELICONIA ISLAND

LA SELVA
BIOLOGICAL STATION

CENTRO
NEOTRÓPICO
SARAPIQUÍS   11

41

CIUDAD
QUESADA
(SAN CARLOS)   10

140

Las Horquetas

141

17   RARA AVIS

Alajuela

RAINFOREST
AERIAL TRAM   18

Río Corinto

Guápiles

Getting Around

The towns of Upala and Los Chiles are access points for the Caño Negro Wildlife Refuge, which is reached by rough roads. Sansa and Nature Air offer flights to La Fortuna, which is linked by tourist buses with San José and key resorts beyond the region. Organized tours can be booked through tour operators and hotels. However, the best way of getting around is to rent a car. A 4WD is essential to reach Caño Negro and other sights away from the main roads. Many roads are prone to landslides, especially along the north shore of Lake Arenal and those that link La Fortuna and Upala.

...y

■ Major road

■ Secondary road

■ Minor road

– Track

■ International border

■ Provincial border

▲ Peak

For additional map symbols *see back flap*

❶ La Fortuna

Road Map C2. 81 miles (131 km) NW of San José. 🚌 12,000. 🚌

Volcán Arenal towers over this agricultural community and tourist hub, officially known as La Fortuna de San Carlos. Situated on a gentle slope, the picturesque town is laid out on a grid around a broad, landscaped plaza, which has a sculpture of an erupting volcano. A modern church stands on the plaza, its tall bell tower contrasting with Arenal behind. Numerous restaurants and hotels cater to the tourists who come here in search of adventure. Several agencies offer horseback rides, caving, fishing, biking, and rafting. A popular horseback trip is to Monteverde *(see pp178–9)*, but the ride is very demanding on the horses, so ensure you choose a well-kept animal.

Horseback riding in La Fortuna

Environs
The **Ecocentro Danaus Butterfly Farm and Tropical Garden** provides an educational introduction to the local fauna. It has a netted butterfly garden, a snake zoo, a frog garden, and a small lagoon stocked with waterfowl and caimans. **Arenal Natura** opened in 2010 with the best live frog, snake, and crocodile exhibits in the area. **Arenal Mundo Aventura** is a 2-sq-mile (5-sq-km) wildlife refuge and ecotour center with trails, rappeling, and canopy tours. Nearby, a steep, muddy trail leads to the base of **Catarata Río Fortuna**, a refreshingly cool, ribbon-like 210-ft (70-m) high waterfall. Swimming in the pools at its base is unsafe after heavy rains. Instead, visitors can soak in thermal waters at **Baldi Termae Spa**, which has landscaped outdoor pools and a swim-up bar and restaurant. Southeast of La Fortuna on Highway 142, **Hotel Bosques de Chachagua** *(see p260)* is a working cattle ranch with a 320-acre (130-ha)

One of the many buses that run from La Fortuna to various sights

private forest reserve at the base of soaring mountains. The reserve, which also welcomes day visitors, offers horseback rides into the forest and has hiking trails too.

🦋 Ecocentro Danaus Butterfly Farm and Tropical Garden
2 miles (3 km) E of La Fortuna.
Tel 2479-7019. **Open** 8am–4pm daily.
🚗 🅿 🌐 ecocentrodanaus.com

🦋 Arenal Natura
4 miles (6.5 km) W of La Fortuna.
Tel 2479-1616. **Open** 8am–7:30pm daily. 🚗 🅿 🌐 arenalnatura.com

🦋 Arenal Mundo Aventura
1 mile (1.6 km) S of La Fortuna.
Tel 2479-9762. **Open** 8am–5pm daily.
🚗 🅿 🖥 🌐 arenalmundo aventura.com

🏞 Catarata Río Fortuna
3 miles (5 km) SW of La Fortuna.
Tel 2479-8338. **Open** 8am–5pm daily.
🚗 🖥 🌐 arenaladifort.com

♨ Baldi Termae Spa
3 miles (5 km) W of La Fortuna. **Tel** 2479-2190. **Open** 10am–10pm daily.
🚗 ♿ 🌊 🖥 🌐 baldihotsprings.cr

❷ Tabacón Hot Springs Resort and Spa

Road Map C2. 8 miles (13 km) W of Fortuna. **Tel** 2519-1999. 🚌 from La Fortuna and Nuevo Arenal. **Open** 10am–10pm daily. 🚗 ♿ 🌊 📷 🅿
🌐 tabacon.com

Steaming-hot waters pour out from the base of Volcán Arenal and cascade through this lush landscaped *balneario* (bathing resort). Río Tabacón feeds a series of therapeutic mineral pools with temperatures that range from 27° to 39° C (80°– 102° F). Spa treatments are available. The main pool has a swim-up bar, and there is a splendid restaurant with views *(see p283)*. The *balneario*'s Gran Spa is a sumptuous alfresco full service spa. Volcanic mud wraps are a local specialty treatment.

The town of Tabacón is in the path of the main lava flow and was decimated in 1968 when Arenal erupted. Nonetheless, the resort is usually crowded on weekends and throughout the high season.

Environs
Arenal Waterfall Gardens & Club Río Outdoor Center offers landscaped thermal pools and cascades, plus a wild cat rescue center and an activity center.

🦋 Arenal Waterfall Gardens & Club Río Outdoor Center
6 miles (10 km) W of La Fortuna.
Tel 2401-3313. **Open** 8am–midnight daily. 🚗 🌊 🌐 thesprings costarica.com

The landscaped pools of the *balneario* at Tabacón

Panoramic view of Volcán Arenal and the San Carlos Plains

Parque Nacional Volcán Arenal

Road Map C2. 11 miles (18 km) W of La Fortuna. **Tel** 2461-8499. ⛟ to La Fortuna, then by jeep-taxi. **Open** 8am–4pm daily; last entrance: 3pm. ⛟ ⛟ **W** sinac.go.cr

Encircling the country's most active volcano, Arenal Volcano National Park spreads over 45 sq miles (120 sq km). Rising from the San Carlos Plains, the majestic Arenal is one of Costa Rica's most rewarding sights. Pre-Columbian tribes considered it the sacred "Home of the Fire God." Arenal ceased activity between the 13th and 16th centuries, and stayed inactive until July 29, 1968, when an earthquake re-awakened it. The perfectly conical 5,400-ft (1,650-m) high volcano now smolders incessantly and minor eruptions occur almost daily. At night it can look like a firecracker as it spews out red-hot lava, which pours down its flank. Witnessing an eruption is a matter of luck, as clouds often conceal the upper reaches; the dry season is the best for viewing. Ask to be woken if there is a nocturnal eruption. Trails cross a moonscape of choking lava scree on Arenal's lower western slopes. Hikers should note that access to some areas is restricted, and should observe the posted "no entry" zones. The volcano has already claimed several lives. The ranger station at the park entrance sells maps and has restrooms. Tour companies and hotels in La Fortuna offer guided tours.

The park also includes the dormant 3,800-ft (1,150-m) high Volcán Chato to the east. **Arenal Observatory Lodge** (see p261), midway up the western flank of Chato, has stunning views of Arenal and Lake Arenal. A museum provides an understanding of volcanology, and the restaurant offers grandstand views when Arenal erupts. Trails from the observatory lead through thick forests to Chato's summit, where a jade-colored lake shimmers in the crater. Canoes can be hired here.

Sign at Arenal
Observatory Lodge

❹ Laguna de Arenal

See pp204–5.

❺ Arenal Hanging Bridges

Road Map C2. 12 miles (19 km) W of La Fortuna. **Tel** 2290-0469. ⛟ to La Fortuna, then by jeep-taxi. **Open** 8am–4:30pm daily. ⛟ ⛟ ⛟ ⛟ **W** hangingbridges.com

A self-guided trail meanders through 620 pristine acres (250 ha) of primary forest and is punctuated by a series of 14 bridges suspended over ravines. The relatively easy, 2-mile (3-km) trail clings to the mountainside and offers close-up views of every level of the moist tropical forest, from ground to canopy. Guided walks include dawn birding and a night tour.

❻ Arenal Theme Park

Road Map C2. El Castillo, 14 miles (22 km) W of La Fortuna. **Tel** 2479-4100. **Open** 7:30am–5pm daily. ⛟ to La Fortuna, then by jeep-taxi. ⛟ ⛟ 7:30am and 3:30pm. ⛟ ⛟ ⛟ **W** skyadventures.travel

Aerial trams (teleféricos) whisk visitors up the northern slopes of the Cordillera de Tilarán at this private facility on the southern shore of Lake Arenal. The open-air carriages climb steeply through rainforest to a look-out point at 4,250 ft (1,300 m) from where visitors can enjoy fabulous views of the lake and the volcano. From the mirador, 2 miles (3 km) of ziplines connect treetop canopies and offer exhilarating rides across broad ravines.

Environs

The **Butterfly Conservatory** has a small, fascinating display of insects, scorpions, and snakes, as well as a butterfly garden and a medicinal herb garden. Tours take in the atrium habitats, laboratories, and greenhouses.

Butterfly Conservatory
El Castillo, 14 miles (22 km) W of La Fortuna. **Tel** 2479-1149. **Open** 8:30am–4:30pm daily. ⛟ ⛟ **W** butterflyconservatory.org

Open-air teleféricos touring the Arenal Theme Park

❹ Laguna de Arenal

Ringed by hills, with Volcán Arenal standing tall to the east, Lake Arenal has a breathtaking setting at an elevation of 1,800 ft (540 m). The 48-sq-mile (124-sq-km) lake fills a tectonic depression forming a gap between Tilarán and the Cordillera de Guanacaste, and was created in 1973 when the Instituto Costarricense de Electricidad (ICE) dammed the eastern end of the valley. The sole town is Nuevo Arenal, on the lake's north side. The easternmost shores are forest-clad, while huge swathes of verdant pasture lie to the south and west. The lake is swept by near-constant winds, providing windsurfers with world-class conditions. Archaeologists have identified pre-Columbian settlements beneath the waters.

Lucky Bug Gallery
This small shop attached to Restaurante Willy's Caballo Negro *(see p275)* sells an eclectic range of quality artwork and crafts.

Lago de Coter
The small lake features an activity center offering kayaking, swimming, and birding *(see p206)*.

KEY

① **Wind turbines** line ridges of the Continental Divide on the exposed western side of the lake, supplying electricity to the national grid *(see p206)*.

② **Tico Windsurf Center** *(see p206)*

③ **Toad Hall**, overlooking the lake, has a splendid gift store, café, and lovely accommodations.

④ **Presa Sangregado**, the 288-ft (88-m) long, 184-ft (56-m) high earthen dam that created the lake, generates a large portion of the nation's hydroelectric power.

⑤ **Rancho Margot** is a self-sufficient organic farm that also has a wildlife breeding center and trails into a rainforest reserve. Also on offer are kayaking and more extreme activities *(see p206)*.

The magnificent setting of Laguna de Arenal

VISITORS' CHECKLIST

Road Map B2. 11 miles (18 km)
from La Fortuna along Hwy 142.
Hotel-Tilawa: **Tel** 2695-5050.
W hotel-tilawa.com

Transport
🚌 from La Fortuna.

Arenal Hanging Bridges
series of suspension bridges are part of a 2-mile (3-km)
elf-guided interpretive trail through rainforest. The trail
ffers superb views of Volcán Arenal.

6 Arenal Theme Park
The Arenal Theme Park's "sky tram" consists of
open-air carriages, which ascend forest-
covered mountain slopes. Fabulous views of
the lake and volcano can be seen.

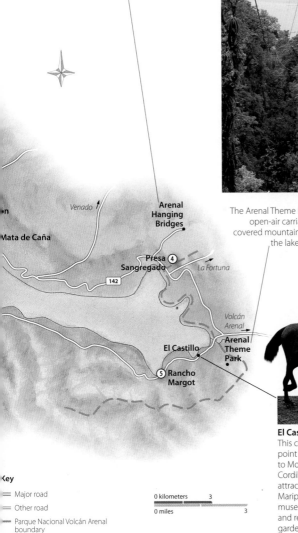

Venado

Mata de Caña

Arenal
Hanging
Bridges

Presa (4)
Sangregado

La Fortuna

142

Volcán
Arenal

El Castillo

Arenal
Theme
Park

(5) Rancho
Margot

El Castillo
This community is a starting
point for horseback rides
to Monteverde via the
Cordillera Tilarán. Other
attractions include Jardín de
Mariposas, which has a small
museum displaying insects
and reptiles, and a butterfly
garden (see p203).

Key

━━ Major road

━━ Other road

━━ Parque Nacional Volcán Arenal
boundary

0 kilometers   3

0 miles   3

Exploring Laguna de Arenal

Lake Arenal is encircled to the west and north by the winding Route 142, which links Tilarán with La Fortuna. East of Nuevo Arenal, the road deteriorates and is frequently blocked by landslides. A dirt road along the southeastern shore is impassable from the west at all times. The hotels and restaurants lining the northern shore make a pleasant break from driving. The greatest attractions of the area are the picture-postcard vistas, which can be best appreciated from Arenal's southwest shore. The lake is also a favored spot for sportfishing, windsurfing, and other water sports.

Visitors relaxing in the shade at the launch site of Tico Windsurf Center

Nuevo Arenal

24 miles (39 km) W of La Fortuna. 📷 2,200.

Replacing the old village, which was flooded in 1973 by the formation of the lake, this orderly town is a service center for the lake region. It has the only fuel station in the area, as well as several good restaurants. A dirt road, leading north through the Río Quequer Valley, links Nuevo Arenal with San Rafael on Highway 4.

A view of Lake Arenal

🎣 Rancho Margot

2 miles (3 km) W of El Castillo. **Tel** 8302-7318. 🚌 to La Fortuna, then by jeep-taxi. **Open** 8am–5pm daily. 🌐 📷 🚶 🌐 ranchomargot.org

The dirt road along the southeastern shore of Lake Arenal leads past Parque Nacional Volcán Arenal to Rancho Margot, a self-sustainable farm, hotel, and activity center beside the Río Caño Negro. Educational tours of the eco-oriented farm give fascinating insights, and visitors can also enjoy the wildlife rescue,

rehabilitation, and breeding center. Many sporting enthusiasts come here for activities such as kayaking, horseback riding, waterfall rappeling, and hiking in Rancho Margot's 375-acre (152-ha) forest reserve. There are also yoga and Spanish classes. Meals are served in a colonial farmstead.

Tico Windsurf Center

10 miles (16 km) SW of Nuevo Arenal. **Tel** 2692-2002. 🌐 ticowind.com

Swept by steady, strong northeasterly winds between November and March, Lake Arenal is rated as one of the finest windsurfing sites in the world. The Tico Windsurf Center, located southwest of Nuevo Arenal, caters to all levels of windsurfers and kitesurfers. In addition to hiring out sailboards, it offers multiday packages and beginners' and advanced lessons between the months of November and April. **Paradise Adventures** kicks up the adrenalin with wakeboarding and other watersports (tel 8856-3618; www.paradise-adventures-costa-rica.com).

🚤 Rain Goddess

Tel 8321-6189. 🌐 arenalhouseboattours.com

This 65-ft (20-m) private houseboat is furnished with deluxe accommodations in wood-paneled cabins. It can be rented for tailor-made itineraries that include fishing for *guapote* (rainbow bass) and other light-tackle game fish – Lake Arenal is considered a premier angling spot. The boat also has kayaks.

🦜 Lago de Coter

4 miles (6 km) NW of Nuevo Arenal. North of Lake Arenal, Lago de Coter occupies a basin in the Fila Vieja Dormida Mountains. The **Lake Coter Eco-Lodge** *(see p261)* is a center for activities such as canoeing, kayaking, horseback riding, and mountain biking. It also offers appealing accommodations. More than 350 species of birds have been recorded in the surrounding forests. A 3-sq-mile (9-sq-km) forest reserve nearby offers guided hiking and birding tours, as well as a zipline canopy tour.

Wind Turbines

Rising over emerald pastures on the western shores of Lake Arenal, two parallel ridge crests are dotted with over 100 wind turbines, each 120-ft (35-m) high. Situated near the village of Tejona, which has some of the highest average wind speeds in the world, this wind farm is the largest in Central America, with a projected annual production of up to 70 MW. Electricity is sold to the state-owned ICE (Instituto Costarricense de Electricidad).

Electricity-generating wind turbines on Lake Arenal's shores

Volcanoes in Costa Rica

Located in one of the world's most volcanic zones, Costa Rica has seven active volcanoes, and at least 60 that are either dormant or extinct. Volcanoes are created by plate tectonics – that is, the movement of the interlocking plates making up the earth's crust that ride on the magma (molten rock) in the mantle. Most volcanoes occur at the boundaries where plates meet or move apart, with magma bursting through cracks in the plate. Lying between 100 and 150 miles (160–240 km) inland of the subduction zone of the Cocos and the Caribbean plates, Costa Rica's volcanoes are concentrated in the northwestern and central regions. Most are steep-sided cones formed by silica-rich magma, and are highly explosive, with Arenal being the most active.

The Formation of Costa Rica's Volcanoes

Costa Rica's landmass sits on the Caribbean plate, beneath which the east-moving Cocos plate is being forced to form a subduction zone. The intense pressure melts the rocks – this viscous magma wells up to create volcanoes.

Cocos plate

Dormant volcanoes can have vents blocked by "plugs" of hardened lava.

The subduction zone is the region where a plate starts sinking below another.

The caribbean plate is the thicker continental plate.

The magma chamber feeds the volcano.

Lithosphere is the topmost part of the mantle.

Volcanic eruptions can be viewed at Arenal, which erupts every few hours during its active phases, oozing hot lava down its slopes. Lava blasted laterally from volcanoes appears as *nuées ardentes* (glowing clouds) – superheated avalanches of gas, ash, and rock that move downhill at astonishing speeds.

Smoke and ash are often steadily emitted by active volcanoes such as Volcán Arenal *(see p203)*. Smoking cinder blocks can sometimes be seen rolling down the slopes.

Bubbling mud pools and fumaroles (vents of steam), formed from rainwater superheated from below, are features of volcanoes such as Miravalles *(see p185)*.

Calderas are formed when the craters of volcanoes collapse, creating huge circular depressions. This caldera on 8,850-ft (2,700-m) high Volcán Poás is a mile (1.6 km) wide, still emits smoke, and contains a mineral lake *(see p144)*.

The wetlands of Refugio Nacional de Vida Silvestre Caño Negro

❼ Cavernas de Venado

Road Map C2. 1 mile (1.6 km) W of Venado, 24 miles (39 km) NW of La Fortuna. **Tel** 2478-9081. 🚌 from Ciudad Quesada. **Open** 9am–4pm daily. 🅿 🚻 🍴 🛍

Bioluminescent fungi help light the way for visitors scrambling through the underground passageways of these limestone caverns. Ten chambers, extending almost 2 miles (3 km), have been explored. Exquisite stalagmites, stalactites, and other subterranean formations fill the labyrinthine and narrow chambers, many of which contain marine fossils. **Cascada de La Muerte** is an underground waterfall that gushes during the wet season from May to November and after heavy rain. Bats flit about, blind fish swim in the underground streams, and small transparent frogs hop around in the ooze.

Guides lead 2-hour long explorations. Wilbert Solis, who owns the land on which the caves are located, supplies safety helmets, flashlights, and rubber boots. Come prepared to get covered in mud, and bring a change of clothes.

Agencies in La Fortuna offer tours. Venado is also accessible by a dirt road that begins at Hotel La Mansion Inn *(see p258)*, on the north shore of Lake Arenal. The village offers basic accommodation.

❽ Refugio Nacional de Vida Silvestre Caño Negro

Road Map C1. 65 miles (105 km) NW of La Fortuna. **Tel** 2471-1309. 🚌 from Upala. 🚤 from Los Chiles. **Open** 8am–4pm daily. 🅿 🚤

One of Costa Rica's main wetland conservation areas, Caño Negro Wildlife Refuge protects over 38 sq miles (98 sq km) of marshlands, lagoons, and *yolillo* palm forest. Most visitors come to fish for snook and tarpon, which thrive in Río Frío and other watercourses that feed Lago Caño Negro, a 3-sq-mile (9-sq-km) seasonal lake. Rare ancient garfish also inhabit the tannin-stained waters. The short dry season (Dec–Apr) is best for viewing crocodiles, caimans, and the large mammals that gather near permanent bodies of water. Monkeys and tapirs are numerous, while jaguars and other cats are more elusive. Lucky visitors may also see large flocks of migratory birds and waterfowl, including jabiru storks, Nicaraguan grackles, roseate spoonbills, and the largest colony of neotropic cormorants in Costa Rica.

Caño Negro village, on the west bank of Lago Caño Negro, is the only community within the reserve. The park headquarters is located here, as are several lodges that arrange guided tours and fishing

Neotropic cormorant

licenses. Boats can be rented in nearby Los Chiles, and agencies in San José offer tours, especially during the fishing season (Jul–Mar). Much of the area floods in the wet season, and access along the dirt roads can be a challenge.

❾ Parque Nacional Volcán Tenorio

Road Map B2. 7 miles (11 km) E of Bijagua. **Tel** 2200-0135. 🚌 from Upala, then by jeep-taxi. **Open** 8am–4pm daily. 🅿 🍴

Several nature lodges offer easy access to this 71-sq-mile (184-sq-km) park. Trails lead through montane rainforest to thermal springs and the **Pozo Azul**, a teal-blue pool at the base of the volcano. Local guides lead hikes in search of tapirs and other wildlife, but the summit trail is closed to all but scientists.

❿ Ciudad Quesada (San Carlos)

Road Map C2. 59 miles (95 km) NW of San José. 🏙 38,000. 🚌 *i* ICT, 75 yards N of Universidad Católica, 2461-9102. 🚌 Sat. 🎪 Feria del Ganado (Apr).

An important market center serving the local dairy and cattle industries, Ciudad Quesada is set amid pastures atop the mountain scarp of the Cordillera de Tilarán, at an elevation of 2,130 ft (650 m). The town, known locally as San

Mineral spring pools at Termales del Bosque, Ciudad Quesada

For hotels and restaurants in this region see pp252–61 and pp266–77

...los, is the administrative ...nter for the region, and is ...nous for its annual cattle fair ...d *tope* (horse show). The ...wn plaza and numerous ...abarterías (saddle-makers' ...rkshops) justify a visit here.

...virons

...ghway 140 slopes east, ...ssing **Termales del Bosque**, ...ere visitors can soak in ...ermal mineral springs and ...ve mud baths. Hiking trails ...e botanical gardens, and ...rseback rides and a zipline ...nopy tour are also on offer. ...Nearby, **La Marina Zoológica** is ...rivate, non-profit zoo that ...es in orphaned and rescued ...mals. Its numerous inhabitants ...lude jaguars, agoutis, ...onkeys, peccaries, and snakes, ...well as macaws, toucans, and ...ny other bird species. Tapirs ...bred for release into the wild.

...Termales del Bosque
...iles (6 km) E of Ciudad Quesada. ...2460-4740. **Open** 7am–10pm ...y. 🐾 ♿ 🖊 🖥 🗺
...termalesdelbosque.com

...La Marina Zoológica
...iles (10 km) E of Ciudad Quesada. ...2474-2202. **Open** 8am–4pm daily.
🖊 w zoocostarica.com

...man healing table and stones, Museo ...Cultura Indígena

Centro
...eotrópico
...arapiquíS

...ad Map D2. La Virgen de Sarapiquí, ...miles (47 km) N of Alajuela. **Tel** ...1-1004. 🚌 San José–Puerto Viejo ...Sarapiquí. **Open** 9am–5pm daily.
🖊 ♿ 🖊 🗺 w sarapiquis.org

...s broad-ranging ecological ...nter on the banks of Río ...rapiquí offers an enriching ...ight into indigenous cultures ...e pp34–5). The state-of-the-art

Parque Arqueológico Alma Alta at the Centro Neotrópico SarapiquíS

Museo de Cultura Indígena is dedicated to Costa Rica's living indigenous communities and the preservation of their artifacts. Its impressive exhibits include a large collection of masks, bark cloth paintings, and other decorative, domestic, and ritual objects, including shamanic healing sticks. An air-conditioned theater shows a 15-minute documentary.

The **Parque Arqueológico Alma Alta**, set in an orange orchard, is centered around four indigenous tombs, dating from the 15th century, and a representation of a pre-Columbian village. Indian guides offer tours of **Chester's Field Botanical Gardens**. Named for the naturalist Chester Czepulos (1916–92), the gardens have about 500 native species of plants renowned since pre-Columbian times for their medicinal use. The center also has a quality restaurant, hotel, library, and conference center.

Environs
The center adjoins the **Tirimbina Rainforest Reserve**, which protects 750 acres (300 ha) of mid-elevation premontane forest. It can be reached from Centro Neotrópico SarapiquíS by a 855-ft (260-m) long suspension bridge across Río Sarapiquí. A 325-ft (100-m) canopy walkway features among Tirimbina's 5 miles (8 km) of trails. Guided tours include a special "World of Bats" night walk. Adjoining Tirimbina, the **Sarapiquí Eco-Observatory** is a supreme

birding venue, with observation decks, trails, and guided tours.

Hacienda Pozo Azul is a working cattle ranch that offers whitewater rafting trips and canopy tours. The nearby **Snake Garden** allows visitors to get close to 70 snake species.

🚩 **Tirimbina Rainforest Reserve**
Tel 2761-0333. **Open** 7am–5pm daily.
🐾 🖊 w tirimbina.org

🚩 **Sarapiquí Eco-Observatory**
La Virgen de Sarapiquí. **Tel** 2761-0801.
Open 7am–5pm daily. 🐾 🖊
w sarapiquieco-observatory.com

🚩 **Hacienda Pozo Azul**
La Virgen de Sarapiquí. **Tel** 2438-2616.
Open 9am–6:30pm daily. 🖊 🖊 🖥
🖊 🗺 ⚠ w haciendapozoazul.
com

🚩 **Snake Garden**
La Virgen de Sarapiquí. **Tel** 2761-1059.
Open 9am–5pm daily. 🐾 ♿ 🖊 w
snakegarden@costarricense.co.cr

Horseback riding at Hacienda Pozo Azul, a working ranch

⓬ Puerto Viejo de Sarapiquí

Road Map D2. 52 miles (84 km) N of San José. 🏔 16,300. 🚌 ⛴

Positioned at the base of the Cordillera Central, on the banks of Río Sarapiquí, Puerto Viejo has functioned as an important river port since colonial days. Before the opening of the Atlantic Railroad in 1890, the town was the main gateway between San José and the Caribbean Sea. While the port trade has reduced, *pangas* (water-taxis) still connect the town to Parque Nacional Tortuguero *(see p221)* and Barra del Colorado via Río San Juan. Boats also set out on nature excursions.

Banana trees cover most of the Llanura de San Carlos flatlands around Puerto Viejo. **Bananero La Colonia**, a processing factory in the middle of banana fields, welcomes visitors.

Bananero La Colonia
3 miles (5 km) SE of Puerto Viejo. **Tel** 2768-8683. 🏞 📷 by appt. 📷
🌐 **bananatourcostarica.com**

Water-taxis on Río San Juan at Puerto Viejo de Sarapiquí

A verdant trail in the rainforests of Selva Verde

⓭ Selva Verde

Road Map D2. 5 miles (8 km) W of Puerto Viejo de Sarapiquí. **Tel** 2766-6800. 🚌 San José–Puerto Viejo via Vara Blanca. **Open** 7am–3pm daily. 🏞 📷 📷 📷 📷
🌐 **selvaverde.com**

One of the country's best private reserves, the 470-acre (190-ha) Selva Verde (Green Forest) reserve adjoins Parque Nacional Braulio Carrillo *(see p145)*. A prime destination for birders, the virgin low-elevation rainforest is home to over 420 bird species, including eight species of parrots. Ocelots, sloths, capuchin monkeys, and mantled howler monkeys are among the 120 species of mammals to be seen. Poison-dart frogs are numerous, as are snakes, although these are difficult to spot. Several of Selva Verde's 500 species of butterflies can be seen in a netted butterfly garden.

Guided canoe trips are offered on Río Sarapiquí, which runs through Selva Verde. Naturalist guides can be hired, and maps are provided for the well-maintained trails. The reserve also has a lodge with comfortable rooms.

⓮ Refugio Naciona de Vida Silvestre Corredor Fronteriz

Road Map C1. Bahía Salinas to Pun Castillo. **Tel** 2471-2191 (Los Chiles). 🌐 **refugio.fronterizo@sinac.go.c**

Intended as a biological corridor, the 230-sq-mile (590 sq-km) Frontier Corridor National Wildlife Refuge protects a wide strip of Costa Rican territory along the bord with Nicaragua, from Bahía Salinas on the west coast to Punta Castillo on the east. The eastern part of the refuge run along Río San Juan. Lined wit virgin rainforest, this broad riv flows 120 miles (195 km) east from Lake Nicaragua to Punta Castillo, and has long been disputed by the two nations.

Pangas link Puerto Viejo de Sarapiquí to Trinidad village, a the confluence of Ríos Sarapic and San Juan. The river trip through the reserve is splend for spotting sloths, crocodiles, and myriad birds, including oropendolas and rare chestnu bellied herons.

Environs

Boca San Carlos, 24 miles (39 km) upstream of Trinidad on F San Juan, has an airstrip and c also be reached by a dirt road is a gateway for river journeys into Nicaragua. Nearby, **Lagu del Lagarto** is a private reserv protecting 2 sq miles (5 sq km of virgin rainforest and swamp Elusive manatees inhabit the lagoons, and a nature lodge offers a good base for wildlife viewing. The restored, 17th-century, mossy hilltop f of **Fortaleza de la Inmaculac Concepción**, near the Nicaraguan hamlet of El Castillo, 25 miles (40 km) upstream of Boca San Carlos, worth a visit. Its small museu recalls the days when Spanis defenders fought back pirate and an English invasion fleet led by Lord Nelson.

🏨 **Laguna del Lagarto**
10 miles (16 km) S of Boca San Carlo **Tel** 2289-8163. 📷 📷 📷
🌐 **lagarto-lodge-costa-rica.com**

Freshwater Sharks

The presence of sharks in freshwater Lake Nicaragua has been a puzzle for centuries. In the 1970s, scientists tagged individual sharks with electronic monitors and found that they migrate along Río San Juan between the Caribbean Sea and the lake, a distance of 106 miles (169 km). These euryhaline sharks, capable of living in both fresh- and saltwater, are even able to navigate rapids.

Bull shark in the waters of Lake Nicaragua

Leaf-Cutter Ants

Present in most lowland and mid-elevation environments in Costa Rica, leaf-cutter ants are fascinating insects. They farm their own food, gathering leaves, petals, and other plant parts, and transport them to vast underground nests. They then compost the vegetation to farm a fungus whose spores feed the entire colony, which can number up to 10 million individuals. Ant societies are incredibly complex. Communities are divided into different-size castes, each with its own specialized task. Mature colonies produce reproductive ants, who mate with peers from other colonies. Virgin queens carry with them some fungus culture. Males die after mating, leaving fertilized females to start their own nests using the fungus culture.

Medaie carry leaves

Minors stand guard

Medium-sized ants, or medaie, cut the leaves and carry them back to the nest along trails that can exceed 656 ft (200 m). Each leaf shard may weigh three times more than the ant. Smaller siblings, or minors, hitch rides atop the shards and act as sentinels to ward off phorid flies.

Trees are often defoliated completely, in as little as 24 hours, by leaf-cutter ants. Scouts carry samples of trees, bushes, and flowers to foragers, who may reject them as unsuitable.

The major's powerful jaws are used to defend the colony from invaders and to carry away debris that is too large for smaller castes. Pre-Columbian people used the jaws as sutures to stitch together deep cuts.

The Phorid Fly

Tiny phorid flies (1–6mm) are the natural enemies of ants and can devastate whole communities. After mating, each female phorid fly seeks out an ant and swiftly deposits an egg in a fleshy crevice in the ant's thorax. The larva hatches inside the ant and eats it. Attacks can trigger panic in ant colonies.

Phorid fly, enemy of the leaf-cutter ant

The spongy fungal garden is cultivated by minims, the smallest ant caste. They mulch leaves into compost and smear the garden with antibiotic secretions to keep it free from the virulent Escovopsis mold.

Broad-billed motmot, La Selva Biological Station

⓯ La Selva Biological Station

Road Map D2. 2 miles (3 km) S of Puerto Viejo. **Tel** 2766-6565. 🚌 OTS shuttles from Puerto Viejo & San José. **Open** 8am–5pm by appt. 🅿 🕐 5:30am, 8am, and 1:30pm. ♿ 🚻 📷 🅿 🌐 ots.ac.cr

Created by the scientist Dr. Leslie Holdridge in 1954, La Selva Biological Station has been run as a private research facility by the Organization of Tropical Studies (OTS) since 1968. Scientific research at this 6-sq-mile (15-sq-km) reserve spans physiological ecology, soil science, and forestry, with over 1,000 tree species in the Holdridge Arboretum.

The predominant habitat is a vast swathe of lowland and premontane rainforest at the base of Parque Nacional Braulio Carrillo *(see p145)*. Snakes, although profuse, are rarely seen. More noticeable are poison-dart frogs, enameled in gaudy colors, and more than 500 species of butterflies, including neon blue morphos. Elusive jaguars and other big

cats prowl the forests, preying on monkeys, coatis, and deer, which are among La Selva's 120 mammal species. Peccaries are commonly seen around the research facility. About half of Costa Rica's bird species have been sighted here; the annual 24-hour La Selva Christmas Bird Count has become a pilgrimage for ornithologists from around the world. A basic bird-watching course is offered on Saturday mornings.

Access to the reserve is restricted to 65 people at any given time, and although it is open to the public by reservation, scientists and students get priority. Over 31 miles (50 km) of boardwalk trails crisscross La Selva, but precipitation can exceed 157 in (400 cm) in a year, and many trails are muddy. The gift shop has self-guiding booklets. OTS offers guided excursions from San José that include transport. Dormitory lodging is offered on a space-available basis.

⓰ Heliconia Island

Road Map D2. 5 miles (8 km) S of Puerto Viejo. **Tel** 2761-5220. 🚌 San José–Puerto Viejo de Sarapiquí via [Braulio Carrillo. **Open** 8am–5pm da 📷 🅿 by appointment. 🌐 heliconiaisland.com

This beautifully laid-out garden on the banks of Río Puerto Viejo was created in 1992 by the American naturalist Tim Ryan and is now run by Dutch owners. Hundreds of tropical plant species grow amid the lush 5-acre (2-ha) lawns. The garden specializes in heliconias, of which it has more than 80 species from around the world. Variou species of gingers thrive here, and also a superb collection of bamboos and orchids. Equally impressive are the palms, which includ the traveler's palm, nativ to Madagascar. It is so named because in an emergency, travelers can drink the water that is stored in its stalk.

Tropical heliconia

Hummingbirds hover as the sip nectar. Violaceous trogons and orange-chinned parakeet are among the more than 200 species of birds drawn to the exotic flora. Rare green macaw nest in *almendro* (almond) tre and are frequently sighted.

Guided tours impart fascinating trivia on tropical plant ecology. The torchlit nighttime tours are especially rewarding. The river has calm stretches safe for swimming, and the island has a restauran plus B&B hotel rooms.

Poison-Dart Frogs

The rainforests of Central and South America are inhabited by poison-dart frogs, so named because Indians use their poison to tip their arrows and blow-darts. About 65 separate species exist, although only three species are deadly to humans (none are found in Costa Rica). The frogs, which are no more than an inch (3 cm) long, produce the bitter toxin in their mucous glands and advertise this with flamboyant colors – mostly vivid reds, greens, and blues – to avoid being eaten by predators. Thus, unusually for frogs, they are active by day among the moist leaf litter. Several species of non-toxic frogs mimic their coloration. In captivity, poison-dart frogs tend to lose their toxicity, which they derive from their principal diet of ants and termites.

A colorful poison-dart frog

Rara Avis

ad Map D2. 17 miles (27 km) S of
erto Viejo. **Tel** 2764-1111. 🚌 San
sé–Las Horquetas. 🎫 🍽 ♿
🌐 rara-avis.com

is world-famous rainforest
serve was among the first
vate reserves in Costa Rica.
joining Parque Nacional
aulio Carrillo and La Selva,
e 4-sq-mile (10-sq-km) Rara
is is perched on the remote
rtheast slopes of Volcán Chato
an elevation of 2,300 ft (700 m).
The brainchild of entre-
eneur Amos Bien, who
eated it in 1983, Rara Avis
oneered the notion of
nerating income through
ologically sustainable
ntures in protected primary
ests. Its selective farming
ojects include a butterfly
m and philodendron and
chid cultivation.
Trails wander through pristine
d-elevation rainforest. The
odiversity is impressive, from
teaters, spider monkeys, and
rcupines to boa
nstrictors, coral
akes, red-eyed tree
gs, elusive jaguars
d pumas, and
most 400
ecies of birds,
:luding the umbrella
d, sunbitterns, and the
dangered great green
acaw. A rappeling system lets
u get eye-to-eye with canopy
vellers such as toucans and
ouchin monkeys. The park
s several waterfalls, but
ution is required when
imming in the pools that
m at their base.
Rara Avis is accessed by a
unting track that is often
ee-deep in mud. Transfers
m Las Horquetas, on
ghway 4, are by tractor-
awn canopied trailer, a
mpy 9-mile (14-km) journey
at takes an hour. Come
epared for heavy rainfall,
nich averages more than 200
:hes (500 cm) per year.
bber boots are provided for
kers. Two-night minimum
ys are required; accom-
odation is in a choice of
stic lodges.

**Porcupine in
Rara Avis**

Bananas

Costa Rica is the world's seventh
largest banana producer and its second
largest exporter. Plantations cover
195 sq miles (500 sq km) of the nation.
Massive tracts of protected rainforest
are felled each year to plant bananas,
and many chemicals are used to
maintain output. When washed out to
sea, these chemicals kill fish, poison the
waters, and foster the growth of plants
that choke estuaries and corals. As a
result of environmental campaigns, the
banana industry now follows more
ecologically sensitive practices.

Ripening fruit at a banana
plantation

⑱ Rainforest Aerial Tram

Road Map D3. Hwy 32, 25 miles (40
km) NE of San José. **Tel** 2257-5961. 🚌
San José–Guápiles. **Open** 9am–4pm
Mon; 6:30am–4pm Tue–Sun. 🎫 ♿
♿ 🍽 🏠 🌐 **rainforest
adventure.com**

Offering an alternative view
of the forest canopy, this
automated exploration system
was conceived by the
American naturalist
Dr. Donald Perry
while he was
involved in
scientific
investigation at Rara
Avis. Inaugurated in
1994, the Rainforest Aerial
Tram, also called "El
Teleférico," is the highlight of a
875-acre (355-ha) private nature
reserve on the eastern edge of
Parque Nacional Braulio Carrillo.
Visitors ride in open gondolas
that silently skim the floor of
the rainforest and then soar
above the trees on a 2-mile
(3-km) circuit. The 90-minute
tour is preceded by a video,
which describes the construction of the $2 million system,
and the flora and fauna to be
seen. A naturalist guide
accompanies each gondola
to assist visitors in spotting and
identifying wildlife. Howler and
white-faced monkeys are
occasionally seen at close
quarters, as are iguanas, sloths,
and snakes. Early morning and
late afternoon are the best
times to spot wildlife, but
visitors should keep in mind that
the main aim of the journey is
to learn about rainforest ecology.
Trails lead to Río Corinto, and
guided birding trips are offered,
along with frog and butterfly
exhibits. Accommodations are
in the form of cabins. Tour
agencies nationwide offer
package excursions.

Visitors taking a tour on a Rainforest Aerial Tram gondola

THE CARIBBEAN

nique within the country for its Afro-Caribbean culture,
his region is steeped in traditions brought by Jamaican
orebears, which lend a colorful, laid-back charm to the
amshackle villages that sprinkle the coast. One of Costa
ca's wettest regions, it extends along 125 miles (200 km) of
he Caribbean coastline between the Nicaraguan and Panamanian
orders. Stunning beaches line the shore, and primordial rainforest
erges with swampy lagoons in the north and rises into the rugged
alamanca Mountains in the south.

ter the closure of the port of Puerto
món to trade in 1665 *(see p45)*, the
panish made little attempt to settle the
gion. This drew pirates and smugglers,
ho induced slaves to cut precious
ardwoods for illicit trade. In the late
9th century, Jamaican laborers and their
milies arrived to build the Atlantic
ailroad and work on banana plantations.
ucceeding generations adopted a
ubsistence life of farming and fishing,
hich continues in today's Creole culture.
land, descendants of the original
digenous tribes live in relative isolation
designated reserves in the Talamanca
oothills, clinging to shamanism and
her traditional practices.

The region's only significant town is
Puerto Limón, located midway down
the coast. Northward, flatlands extend
to the Nicaraguan border. The coastal strip
is backed by swampy jungles and
freshwater lagoons that culminate in
Tortuguero National Park and Barra del
Colorado National Wildlife Refuge. A
network of canals, created in the 1960s
to link Puerto Limón with Barra, opened
up this otherwise virtually inaccessible
region. South of Puerto Limón, the shore
is lined with stupendous beaches.
The communities of Cahuita and Puerto
Viejo are popular with surfers and a
predominantly young crowd seeking
offbeat adventure.

ghtly colored wooden restaurant in the village of Cahuita

Gandoca-Manzanillo Wildlife Refuge, near Puerto Viejo

Exploring the Caribbean

With several national parks and wildlife refuges, the humid Caribbean has as its jewel Parque Nacional Tortuguero, with its dense rainforests, raffia palm swamps, and exotic range of fauna. Farther north, rain-sodden Barra del Colorado attracts anglers. The port town of Puerto Limón is a gateway to the villages of Cahuita and Puerto Viejo de Talamanca, vibrant centers of indigenous Afro-Caribbean culture. Parque Nacional Cahuita, which adjoins Cahuita village, also protects a small coral reef. Fine beaches extend south to Gandoca-Manzanillo, a coastal wetland harboring manatees and also an important nesting site for marine turtles. Several horticultural venues along Highway 32 exhibit tropical flora.

Entrance to a house in Puerto Limón

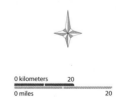

0 kilometers	20
0 miles	20

Key

━━ Major road

━ Secondary road

═══ Minor road

▬▬ International border

━━ Provincial border

--- Canal

Sights at a Glance

Towns and Villages

❸ Puerto Limón

❿ Cahuita

⓬ Puerto Viejo de Talamanca

National Parks and Reserves

❺ Parque Nacional Tortuguero

❻ Refugio Nacional de Fauna Silvestre
Barra del Colorado

❼ Veragua Rainforest Eco-Adventure

❾ Reserva Biológica Hitoy-Cerere

❽ Sloth Sanctuary

⓫ Parque Nacional Cahuita

⓭ Refugio Nacional de Vida Silvestre
Gandoca-Manzanillo

Areas of Natural Beauty

❶ Las Cusingas

❷ EARTH

Tour

❹ *Canal de Tortuguero Tour p220*

Indigenous Sites

⓮ Indigenous Reserves

Beach at Puerto Viejo de Talamanca

A picker cushioning a large bunch of bananas, Cahuita

Getting Around

Highway 32, linking San José to Puerto Limón, is heavily trafficked, particularly along the mountainous sections. A bus service provides easy access to Cahuita and Puerto Viejo de Talamanca. No roads penetrate to Tortuguero and Barra del Colorado, but both villages have airstrips serviced by daily scheduled flights from San José. Another popular option is to journey by canal – tour operators can make arrangements. An infrequent bus service connects the indigenous reserves along rough dirt roads – an uncomfortable, albeit cheap, ride.

For additional map symbols *see back flap*

Green honeycreeper, one of the species of birds found in Las Cusingas

❶ Las Cusingas

Road Map D3. 2 miles (3 km) S of Hwy 32, 37 miles (59 km) E of San José. 🚌 San José–Guápiles, then by jeep-taxi or hiking. 🛈 2382-5805. **Open** 8:30am–4:30pm daily. 🐾 🅿 ✎ 🐎

This botanical garden, spread over 35 acres (14 ha) near the less-than-appealing town of Guápiles, undertakes scientific investigation into tropical flora, fruits, and more than 80 species of medicinal plants. Hummingbirds, parrots, and scores of other birds flock to feed on the nectar and seeds. There are two short forest trails, one of which leads to Río Santa Clara and 10 sq miles (26 sq km) of protected forest. The visitor center, which includes a library, offers an introduction to reforestation, tropical ecology, and the use of medicinal plants.

Guided tours are offered, each about 2 hours long. A rustic family-size cabin with a wood-fired oven can be rented, and visitors can dine with the friendly Tico owners.

Environs

Acclaimed American-born artist Patricia Erickson welcomes visitors to her studio **Gallery at Home**, which displays her vibrant paintings inspired by scenes of Caribbean family life. To get there, turn south at Río Blanco; the studio is a short way down, on the left. Across the street, her husband Brian's **Muebles de Bamboo** offers a chance to watch bamboo furniture being made, using 32 different species grown in a bamboo garden.

Located on the borders of Parque Nacional Tortuguero and Refugio Nacional de Fauna Silvestre Barra del Colorado *(see p221),* **La Suerte Biological Field Station** offers superb opportunities for wildlife-viewing in a variety of habitats, including rainforests and marshes. Poison-dart frogs *(see p212)* and monkeys are abundant. This private research center specializes in residential workshops in tropical ecology, and offers overnight accom-modation. It can be accessed from Guápiles by buses via the community of Cariari.

🏛 **Gallery at Home**
330 yd (300 m) S of Hwy 32, 4 miles (6 km) W of Guápiles. **Tel** 2710-1958. **Open** by appt.

🏛 **Muebles de Bamboo**
Tel 2710-1958. **Open** 8am–5pm Mon– Fri, by appt. 🅆 brieri.com

📛 **La Suerte Biological Field Station**
La Primavera, 27 miles (43 km) NE of Guápiles. **Tel** 2710-8005. **Open** 9am–5pm daily. 🐾 🅿 ♿ ✎ 🐎 🅆 maderasrfc.org

Heliconia, Costa Flores

❷ EARTH

Road Map D2. 1 mile (1.6 km) E of Guácimo. **Tel** 2713-0248 (ext. 5002). 🚌 San José–Puerto Limón. **Open** 9am–4pm daily. 🐾 🅿 ♿ 🖥 📷 🐎 🅆 earth.ac.cr

One of the world's leading tropic research centers, the Escuela de Agricultura de la Región Tropical Húmeda (Agricultural College of the Humid Tropical Region) focuses on ecologically sustain-able practices. EARTH operates it own experimental banana plantation, banana processing plant, and paper-making plant that uses banana skins. There are guided tours and nature trails through the rainforest; horses ca also be hired.

Environs

More than 600 species of tropic flowers, including several varieties of heliconia, color the landscape at **Costa Flores**, the world's largest commercial farm for tropical flowers. Humming-birds zoom around the landscaped gardens, which are open only to cruise-ship groups. The **Finca Esperanzas** banana plantation of the Standar Fruit Co. offers tours of its farm and sorting plant, where Dole-brand bananas are packed. A shop sells banana-related souvenirs and tropical liqueurs made from bananas, coffee, and coconut.

🏵 **Costa Flores**
9 miles (14 km) E of Guápiles. **Tel** 2716-6430. **Open** 8am–4pm Mon–F by appt Sat & Sun. 🐾 🅿 ♿

📛 **Finca Esperanzas**
3 miles (5 km) E of Siquirres. **Tel** 276 8683. **Open** 9am–5pm Mon–Fri. 🐾

Sign for EARTH, a center for tropical research

st of Don Balvanero Vargas in Puerto
món's Parque Vargas

Puerto Limón

bad Map F3. 100 miles (160 km) E of
n José. 65,000.
ack Culture Festival (Sep); Día de las
lturas (Oct 12).

ocated in the bay where
hristopher Columbus and his
on Fernando anchored in 1502,
e port town of Puerto Limón
ad its origins in early colonial
ays. Used by pirates and
nugglers for trading
ahogany and other tropical
ardwoods, the settlement
rived on this illicit traffic under
e nose of the Spanish
uthorities. The town has a large
hinese population, whose
orebears arrived during the
880s as indentured laborers for
e construction of the Atlantic
ailroad. A small Chinese
emetery at the entrance to the
own honors this Asian heritage.
oday, the port handles most of
e nation's sea trade; the main
ighway into town is crowded
ith container trucks
roughout the day. The
aritime facilities have been
xpanded to serve cruise ships
lying the Caribbean coast.

Columbus supposedly landed
: **Isla Uvita**, half a mile (1 km)
ffshore. His landfall is
ommemorated by a bronze
ust, which was unveiled in
992, in time for the 500th
nniversary of his arrival in the
mericas. The bust faces **Parque**
argas, a tiny tree-shaded park
amed after Don Balvanero
argas, a former governor of
món province. The park, which

features a bust of Don Vargas,
is at the east end of the
pedestrian-only Avenida 2
(also known as El Bulevar).
Nearby, a beautiful mural by
artist Guadalupe Alvarez
depicts local history since
pre-Columbian days.

Puerto Limón has some
intriguing architecture, with
pretty filigreed iron balconies in
the style of New Orleans. To the
west of Parque Vargas, the
cream-colored stucco Belle
Epoque **Alcaldía** (Town Hall) is a
fine example. Other structures
are classics of the Caribbean
vernacular style, made of wood
and painted in lively tropical
pastels, with broad balconies on
stilts beneath which locals
gather to play dominoes. Visit
the lively **Mercado Central**, to
the north of the museum, for
everything from pigs' heads to
freshly caught fish. A dramatic

Detail of mural by Guadalupe Alvarez near
Parque Vargas

Shoppers outside Mercado Central in
Puerto Limón

post-modernist concrete
cathedral, **La Catedral del**
Sagrado Corazón rises over the
center of town with its crystal-
shaped 154-ft (47-m) spire.

Environs
Local surfers find their fun off
Playa Bonita, 2 miles (3 km)
north of town. This golden-sand
beach gets crowded on weekends with Limonenses, as the
town's inhabitants are known.
Swimming in the south end of
the bay is dangerous. A mile
(1.6 km) to the north of Playa
Bonita, **Moín** is where Costa
Rica's crude oil is processed and
bananas loaded for shipment
to Europe and North America.
Boats leave from here for
Tortuguero (see p220).

Mercado Central
Calles 3/4 and Aves Central/2.
Open 6am–6pm daily.

Carnaval

In the second week of October, Puerto Limón erupts into
kaleidoscopic color for Carnaval (see p39), a week-long
Caribbean Mardi Gras celebration
culminating on Día de las Culturas
(Columbus Day). Special buses bring
revelers from San José, and the city
packs in as many as 100,000 visitors.
Live reggae, salsa, and calypso get
everyone dancing. Other amusements
include beauty contests, bull-running,
desfiles (parades), street fairs, and
firework displays. The highlight is the
Grand Desfile, a grand parade of
flamboyant costumes and floats held
on the Saturday before October 12.
Most events take place on the docks.

Extravagantly dressed dancers
at Carnaval

❹ Canal de Tortuguero Tour

Travel along the Caribbean seaboard became possible with the building of the Tortuguero canal system in 1966–74. Four canals make up this 65-mile (105-km) long aquatic highway, which connects the port of Moín to Barra del Colorado village, and is lined with rainforest. Narrow in places, when the looming forest seems to close in on the water, the canal offers the chance of fascinating boating trips, with sightings of caimans and river turtles, and birds such as aracaris and kingfishers.

A tourist boat moving through the Tortuguero Canal

① **Caño de Penitencia**
Opening into Río Colorado, this canal links Tortuguero to Barra del Colorado. To the north, Caño de Palma canal offers an exhilarating shortcut through yolillo swamp and raffia palm forests.

⑤ **Laguna del Tortuguero**
At Tortuguero, the canal opens into a wide, 4-mile (6-km) long lagoon, whose banks are lined with nature lodges.

④ **Puesto Jalova**
The southern gateway to Parque Nacional Tortuguero is marked by a ranger station from where trails lead into the forest.

③ **Barra de Parismina**
This hamlet near the mouth of Río Parismina is considered Costa Rica's best spot to hook snook. Watch out for sand flats that beach unwary boats.

② **Caño Blanco**
Organized tour boats depart and arrive at this small dock on Río Matina, amid banana plantations. Roseate spoonbills are frequently seen on the banks.

① **Moín**
The terminus of the Tortuguero Canal is also Costa Rica's main banana-loading port. Private tour boats wait here for custom.

Tips for Trip

Tour boats: Most visitors travel on private boats owned by lodges. Carry warm clothing as it can be cold on the boat.
Time taken: 2.5 hours.
Stopping-off points: Parismina has fishing lodges and simple restaurants. Tour boats will stop on request.

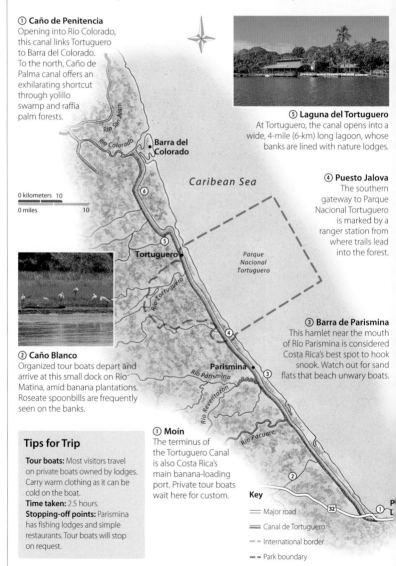

Caribbean Sea

Barra del Colorado

Río San Juan

Río Colorado

Tortuguero

Parque Nacional Tortuguero

Río Tortuguero

Parismina

Río Parismina

Río Reventazón

Río Pacuare

0 kilometers 10
0 miles 10

Key
— Major road
▬ Canal de Tortuguero
- - International border
– – Park boundary

A guide escorting a tour group through Parque Nacional Tortuguero

Parque Nacional Tortuguero

Road Map E2. 32 miles (52 km) N of Puerto Limón. Tel 2709-8086. from Pavona, Moín, and Caño Blanco. Open 6am–5:45pm daily; last admission: 5pm.

Created to protect the most important nesting site of the green turtle in the Western Hemisphere, the 73-sq-mile (190-sq-km) Tortuguero National Park extends along 14 miles (22 km) of shoreline and 19 miles (30 km) out to sea. The Canal de Tortuguero runs through the park, connecting a labyrinth of deltas, canals, and lagoons.

With 11 distinct life zones ranging from raffia palm forest to herbaceous swamps, the park offers one of the most rewarding nature experiences in the country. Although trails start from the ranger stations at the northern and southern ends of the park, this watery world is best seen by boat: the wide canals allow grandstand wildlife viewing, and silent approaches on the water permit unusually close contact with the fauna. River otters, caimans, and howler, spider, and white-faced monkeys are easily sighted, as are birds such as oropendolas, toucans, and macamars and other waterfowl. A guide is strongly recommended to avoid getting lost in the waterways and to identify wildlife that might otherwise

be missed. For most visitors, the star attraction is the green turtle, which nests between June and November. Three other species of marine turtles also come ashore throughout the year, although in lesser numbers. Entry to the beach is strictly regulated at night – only two tour groups are allowed each night, escorted by guides from the local cooperative.

Note that there are no roads to the park; access is by boat or small planes that land at Tortuguero village. Local lodges organize guided tours, and Tortuga Lodge (see p260) offers sportfishing.

Environs
The villagers of **Tortuguero**, to the north of the park at the junction of Laguna del Tortuguero and the Canal de Tortuguero, traditionally made their living by lumbering or by culling turtles. Today, tourism is the major source of employment, and locals

have learned a new ethic as conservationists. The **John H. Phipps Biological Station and Natural History Visitor's Center** has excellent displays on local ecology, especially marine turtles.

John H. Phipps Biological Station and Natural History Visitor's Center
550 yd (500 m) N of Tortuguero village. **Tel** 2709-8125.
Open 10am–noon and 2–5pm daily.

Refugio Nacional de Fauna Silvestre Barra del Colorado

Road Map E2. 21 miles (34 km) N of Tortuguero. Tel 2709-8086. from Tortuguero, Puerto Viejo de Sarapiquí, and Pavona. Open 8am–4pm daily. included with PN Tortuguero.

Connected to Parque Nacional Tortuguero by Caño de Penitencia, this 350-sq-mile (910-sq-km) refuge extends north to the border with Nicaragua. The flooded marshes, teeming rainforest, and vast raffia palm forests are home to an abundant wildlife, but despite this the refuge is virtually untapped as a wilderness destination. Crocodiles as well as birds such as jabiru storks and endangered great green macaws can be spotted, while tapirs, jaguars, and manatees inhabit the deep forests and swamps. The refuge's many rivers have populations of tarpon, snook, and garfish, and lodges catering to fishing enthusiasts are centered around Barra del Colorado at the mouth of Río Colorado.

Manatees

The endangered West Indian manatee (Trichechus manatus), or sea cow (see pp74–5), is found in lagoons and coastal habitats. With front flippers and a paddle-like tail, this hairless gray-brown mammal resembles a tuskless walrus. It feeds primarily on aquatic vegetation such as water hyacinths. Spending most of its time submerged, it is rarely seen. However, increasing encounters with manatees in Tortuguero and Barra del Colorado suggest that the population may be increasing.

West Indian manatee (Trichechus manatus)

Jesus Christ lizard, Veragua Rainforest Eco-Adventure

❼ Veragua Rainforest Eco-Adventure

Road Map F3. 18 miles (28 km) SW of Puerto Limón. **Tel** 2296-5056. 🚌 Puerto Limón–Liverpool, then by jeep-taxi. **Open** 9am–3pm daily. 🅿️ 🅲 🅿️
W veraguarainforest.com

This 3,200-acre (1,300-ha) reserve is used for ecological research by INBio, whose laboratory is open to visitors. You can walk through butterfly and frog gardens, view snake and insect exhibits, and hop aboard an aerial tram for a ride downhill to riverside trails, where poison-dart frogs hop about underfoot. For the more energetic visitor, there is a hike to a spectacular cascading waterfall, where the thundering spray can be felt. Try out the canopy zipline tour or visit the restaurant with its rainforest views. The entrance fee includes a guided tour. Visitors driving themselves to the park may need a four-wheel-drive vehicle.

❽ Sloth Sanctuary

Road Map F3. 5 miles (8 km) N of Cahuita. **Tel** 2750-0775. 🚌 from Puerto Limón to Cahuita and taxi from Cahuita. **Open** 7am–2pm Tue–Sun. 🅿️ 🅲 **W** slothsanctuary.com

This is the world's only center devoted to sloth research and rescue. The facility began in 1992 with the adoption of an orphaned three-fingered

sloth. Many more sloths soon followed and since then, the Sloth Sanctuary has become a leading research center on sloth ecology. Injured sloths, including those electrocuted while crawling along power lines, are treated at a "slothpital". Many are released into the wild, while others can be seen in enclosures. Visitors are led on guided tours that include an educational learning center, a sloth nursery, and the rehabilitation facilities where two- and three-toed sloths are cared for, alongside agoutis, coatis, monkeys, toucans, and other rescued animals. Trails lead into the 185 acre (75 ha) wildlife refuge composed of rainforest and marshland where caiman, river otter, and other aquatic creatures can be spotted.

❾ Reserva Biológica Hitoy-Cerere

Road Map F3. 28 miles (45 km) S of Puerto Limón and 12 miles (20 km) SW of Hwy 36 at Penshurst. **Tel** 2795-1446. 🚌 from Puerto Limón to Finca 12, further by jeep-taxi. **Open** 8am–5pm daily. 🅿️ **W** sinac.go.cr

Lying near the head of the Río Estrella valley and extending up the western flanks of the Talamanca Mountains, the 38-sq-mile (100-sq-km) Hitoy-Cerere Biological Reserve appeals to hardy hikers and nature lovers. It offers pristine rainforest

habitats fed by heavy rainfall. July, August, November, and December are the wettest months, when rivers thunder down the steep slopes. Large mammals thrive amid the dense forests, including all six of Costa Rica's cat species *(see pp66–7)*. Lucky visitors might even spot the extremely rare harpy eagle. Note that this isolated refuge offers minimal infrastructure.

Environs
Reserva Selva Bananito, bordering Parque Internacional de La Amistad *(see p231)*, protects 5 sq miles (13 sq km) of ecologically sustainable farmland and rainforest at the foothills of the Talamanca Mountains. It offers guided hikes and horseback rides, plus more adrenalin-charged activities, such as waterfall rappeling and a zipline ride to a 30-meter-tall (100-foot) canopy observation platform. A 4WD vehicle is required to get here. Overnight stays in the Caribbean-style lodge are recommended. Nearby, the Standard Fruit Co. offers cruise-ship groups an interesting **Banana Tour** at its Bananito farm, where Dole-branded bananas are produced and prepared for export.

🏞️ **Reserva Selva Bananito**
22 miles (35 km) SW of Puerto Limón. **Tel** 2253-8118. 🅿️ 🅲 🅿️ 🅴
W selvabananito.com

🍌 **Banana Tour**
Bananito, 22 miles (31 km) S of Puerto Limón. **Tel** 8383-4596. **Open** 9am–3pm daily. 🅿️ 🅲 🅿️ 🅴
W bananatourcostarica.com

❿ Cahuita

Road Map F3. 27 miles (43 km) S of Puerto Limón. 🏔️ 5,300. 🚌 🎭 Festival de la Cultura y el Ambiente Walter Furgerson (Jul); Carnavalito Cahuita (early Dec).

With its rich Afro-Caribbean heritage, Cahuita (meaning "mahogany point") is Costa Rica's most colorful village. Its inhabitants – a mix of folks with Jamaican and other

Ine of Parque Nacional Cahuita's many beaches

...fro-Caribbean heritage – live ...brightly-painted wooden ...ouses and shacks, some of ...vhich stand on stilts over the ...andy streets. Unlike many ...ther beach-focused villages, ...ich as neighboring Puerto ...iejo, Cahuita has been skipped ...y the tourist boom and stays ...ue to its laid-back Caribbean ...land roots. North of the ...llage are the black sands of ...alm-fringed Playa Negra, ...xtending north to the estuary ...f the Río Estrella and perfect ...or tidepooling and horseback ...des. The Festival de la Cultura ...el Ambiente Walter Ferguson, ...i July, celebrates Cahuita's ...iusical and cultural traditions.

nvirons
ree of Life Wildlife Rescue
enter & Botanical Gardens,
...cated toward the north end
...f Playa Negra, aims to
...romote conservation. The

center cares for wild creatures that have suffered due to loss of habitat, been injured, or even confiscated as illegal pets. Animals being rehabilitated for release back in to the wild cannot be viewed but others, including howler monkeys, peccaries, and white-tailed deer, are on show to the public. There are 12 acres (5 ha) of botanical gardens to explore, with a range of palms and diverse tropical plants.

One of Parque Nacional
Cahuita's snakes

🐾 **Tree of Life Wildlife Rescue Center & Botanical Gardens**
2 miles (3 km) N of Cahuita.
Tel 2755-0014. **Open** 9am–3pm
Tue–Sun. **Open** Nov–Aug. 🐾
w treeoflifecostarica.com

⓫ Parque Nacional Cahuita

Road Map F3. 27 miles (43 km)
S of Puerto Limón. **Tel** 2755-0461.
🚌 Puerto Limón–Cahuita. **Open**
6am–5pm daily (Kelly Creek);
8am–4pm Mon–Fri, 7am–5pm Sun
(Puerto Vargas). 🐾 at Puerto Vargas
ranger station; by donation at Kelly
Creek station. **w** sinac.go.cr

Situated immediately south of Cahuita is this 4-sq-mile (10-sq-km) park. Wildlife abounds, including armadillos, rodent-like agoutis, and anteaters, as well as toucans and green macaws. Crocodile-like caimans can be seen in freshwater rivers, while parrot fish, lobsters, and green turtles swim around a depleted coral reef off Playa Blanca. Swimming off Playa Vargas, farther to the south, is not advisable; waves pummel the long beach where marine turtles nest. A 4-mile (6-km) trail connects Cahuita village's Kelly Creek ranger station to the one at Puerto Vargas. Riptides may be present so check with rangers before swimming. A guide is obligatory for snorkeling.

Caribbean Culture

Rastafarian culture is widespread in Cahuita

Distinct in many ways from the Hispanic culture found elsewhere in Costa Rica, the culture of the Caribbean coast has close affinities with the English-speaking Caribbean islands. About one-third of the population trace their bloodline back to black Jamaicans whose own ancestors were

African. They first arrived in Costa Rica's Caribbean lowlands in the late 19th century to work on the Atlantic Railroad and banana plantations. Many people still speak a lilting English-based creole dialect, with parochial phrases familiar to the West Indies. The Latin music of the highlands here is replaced by the mellow riffs of Bob Marley, the Jamaican reggae superstar whose image adorns a lot of buildings in Cahuita. Many young males sport Rafastarian dreadlocks and smoke ganja (marijuana). The spicy local cuisine (see p264) is also distinct, not least for its use of chilies and tongue-searing peppers. Jerk (spiced and smoked) chicken, rondon ("rundown") of mackerel cooked in coconut milk, and fried sponge dumplings called johnnycakes all hark back to Caribbean island culture. What Happen: A Folk History of Costa Rica's Talamanca Coast and Wa'apin Man, both by Paula Palmer, provide fascinating accounts of the lives of early Afro-Caribbean settlers.

⑫ Puerto Viejo de Talamanca

Road Map F3. 8 miles (13 km) S of Cahuita. 🏔 5,000. 🚌 ℹ️ 2750-0398 (Talamanca Association for Ecotourism & Conservation/ATEC). 🌐 **ateccr.org**

One of the Caribbean coast's best surfing areas, Puerto Viejo de Talamanca is also a must-visit destination for offbeat travelers in Central America. Little more than a collection of stilt-legged shacks a decade ago, it has since expanded rapidly. Although electricity arrived in 1996, followed by a paved road in 2001 and later by malls, the village retains an earthy, laid-back quality.

Surfers come here between December and March to test their skills against the reef break La Salsa Brava, which can attain heights of up to 21 ft (6.5 m). The palm-fringed black sands of **Playa Negra** curl north from town. Inland of the beach, **Finca La Isla Botanical Garden** is an excellent place to explore the coastal rainforest along well-kept trails. Bromeliads are a specialty of this 12-acre (5-ha) garden, which also grows exotic fruits and ornamental plants. A self-guided booklet is available.

Puerto Viejo has some of the best budget accommodation in Costa Rica, as well as numerous outstanding eateries. Open-air bars and discos come alive at night, with revelers spilling onto the sands.

Detail of a statue at a lodge in Puerto Viejo

Tucuxi Dolphin

The rare *tucuxí* dolphin (*Sotalia fluviatilis*) – pronounced "too koo shee"– lives in the freshwater rivers and lagoons of Gandoca-Manzanillo and similar environments. This small species grows to 6 ft (2 m) in length and is blue-gray with a pink belly and long snout. It is shy and generally avoids boats, but is known to interact with its larger sea-going cousin, the bottle-nosed dolphin.

Tucuxí dolphin

Environs

A string of surfing beaches – **Playa Cocles**, **Playa Uva**, and **Playa Chiquita** – runs south from Puerto Viejo to the hamlet of Manzanillo. A paved road lined with hotels and *cabinas (see p249)* lies along the shore, with forested hills rising inland. **Crazy Monkey Canopy Ride** whisks you between treetops on a zipline. At Playa Chiquita, the **Jaguar Rescue Center**, where animals are rehabilitated, is not to be missed. Public transport in these areas is limited, but bicycles, scooters, and cars can be rented in Puerto Viejo.

🌿 Finca La Isla Botanical Garden
0.5 mile (1 km) NW of Puerto Viejo. **Tel** 2750-0046. **Open** 10am–4pm Fri–Mon. 🅿️ ✅

Crazy Monkey Canopy Ride
8 miles (13 km) S of Puerto Viejo. **Tel** 2759-9056. 🅿️ ✅ 8am & 2pm daily. 🌐 **almondsandcorals.com**

🌿 Jaguar Rescue Center
3 miles (5 km) S of Puerto Viejo. **Tel** 2750-0710. **Open** for guided tours by appt. only; 9:30am & 11:30am Mon–Sat. 🅿️ ✅ 🌐 **jaguarrescue.com**

⑬ Refugio Nacional de Vida Silvestre Gandoca-Manzanillo

Road Map F4. 8 miles (13 km) S of Puerto Viejo. **Tel** 2759-9001. 🚌 from Puerto Viejo de Talamanca. **Open** 8am–4pm daily. ✅ 🅿️ 🐟 🏕

Enclosing a mosaic of habitats, Gandoca-Manzanillo Wildlife Refuge is a mixed-use park occupied by settlements whose inhabitants live in harmony with the environment. Created in 1985, this 32-sq-mile (83-sq-km) reserve extends out to sea, protecting a coral reef and 17 sq miles (44 sq km) of marine habitat where several species of turtles breed. The Costa Rican conservation society **Asociación ANAI** runs a volunteer program for those who are keen to assist with research and protection of turtles. On land, the refuge has mangrove swamp, rare *yolillo* palm swamp and *cativo* forest, and tropical rainforest, all swarming with wildlife. Manatee and *tucuxí* inhabit the lagoons and estuaries. The waters are also important breeding grounds for sharks, game fish, and lobsters.

The beach at Refugio Nacional de Vida Silvestre Gandoca-Manzanillo

For hotels and restaurants in this region see pp252–61 and pp266–77

coastal trail and several inland ines – often overgrown and muddy – afford unparalleled opportunities for spotting mammals and an astounding versity of birds, amphibians, nd reptiles. The coast trail ads to Punta Mona (Monkey oint) and **Punta Mona Center**, n educational institution and hriving organic farm.

nvirons
quamor offers scuba diving nd snorkeling, plus kayaking nd a dolphin-spotting trip into andoca-Manzanillo Wildlife efuge. A local cooperative, **uias MANT**, also offers guided ips into the reserve, plus fishing nd snorkeling. **Finca Lomas**, un by ANAI, is an experimental rm inside the refuge.

sociación ANAI
anzanillo. **Tel** 2224-6090.
🔗 anaicr.org

🔟 **Punta Mona**
enter
miles (5 km) SE of
anzanillo. **Tel** 2614-
735. **Open** 8am–5pm
aily. 🌐🔲🔳🅆
untamona.org

quamor
anzanillo. **Tel** 2759-9012.
pen 7am–6pm daily.
🔗 greencoast.com/aquamor.htm

uias MANT
anzanillo. **Tel** 2759-9064.
pen 8am–5pm daily.

🔟 Indigenous
Reserves

oad Map F4. 🚌 to Bribri, then by ep-taxi. 🛈 ATEC: 2750-0398;
🔗 ateccr.org; Red Talamanca coturismo Comunitario:
🔗 redtalamanca@gmail.com

he indigenous Bribri and abécar peoples inhabit a eries of fragmented reserves n the Caribbean slopes of he Talamanca Mountains, urviving primarily through ubsistence agriculture. These vo related groups have anaged to retain much of neir culture, native languages, nimistic dances, and shaman-tic practices (see pp34–5).

Green iguanas raised on Reserva Indígena KeköLdi

Inside a house in the Reserva Indígena KeköLdi

The most accessible reserve is the **Reserva Indígena KeköLdi**, spread across 14 sq miles (36 sq km) in the hills southwest of Puerto Viejo. The reserve's local conservation projects include a farm where green iguanas are bred. The farm is located off the main road near Hone Creek, a 30-minute walk from Puerto Viejo. Farther south, beyond the regional administrative center of Bribri, is the **Reserva Indígena Talamanca-Bribri**. Centered on Shiroles, 11 miles (18 km) southwest of Bribri, this reserve encompasses the Valle de Talamanca, a broad basin carpeted by plantations of bananas. Trips to communities within the reserve are offered by **Albergue Finca Educativa Indígena**, an educational center and tourist lodge in Shiroles.

From Bambú, 6 miles (10 km) west of Bribri, a trip by dug-out canoe down Río Yorkín leads to **Reserva Indígena Yorkín**, where visitors housed in traditional lodgings gain an appreciation of indigenous culture.

Another reserve worth visiting in this area is the **Reserva Indígena Talamanca-Cabécar**, reached from Shiroles along rugged dirt roads that push up the valley of Río Coén. This remote settlement of the San José Cabécar is considered the most important center of shamanism and Indian culture. Guided hikes and overnight visits to the reserves are arranged by the Talamanca Association for Ecotourism and Conservation (ATEC) in Puerto Viejo de Talamanca, or by Red Talamanca Ecoturismo Comunitario. Note that the only place where a permit to visit is not required is the iguana farm in the Reserva Indígena KeköLdi.

Shamanism
The Bribri and Cabécar have a spirit-filled, animist vision of the world in which the shaman-healer – called *awá* by the Bribri and *jawá* by the Cabécar – is the central authority in the community. Shamanic tools include magic stones, *seteé* (medicine collars), *uLú* (healing canes), and a whole pharmacy of medicinal herbs. These are used along with ritual song and dance to cure a person who is ill, or to restore harmony within the community.

Instrument used in ritual music

A Bribri shaman feather

THE SOUTHERN ZONE

From world-class surfing and sportfishing to hardy mountain hikes and scuba diving with hammerhead sharks, Costa Rica's remote south is a setting for splendid adventures. Pre-Columbian relics lie smothered in jungles that offer some of the finest wildlife viewing in the nation. The country's largest indigenous communities live in isolated mountain retreats in this region.

Spanish conquistadors marched into the region to conquer the nomadic Chibchas and Diquis tribes, and to search in vain, as it turned out, for gold. The coastal area remained isolated and neglected throughout the colonial period and beyond. In 1938, the United Fruit Company arrived, and planted bananas across the valleys of the Sierpe and Coto-Colorado Rivers; banana plantations are still the economic mainstay of the region. To the north, the shore is hemmed by the thickly forested Fila Costanera Mountains, while waves crash upon gray-sand beaches. Farther south, the Peninsula de Osa is deluged with rains that feed a huge swathe of emerald green rainforest. The peninsula hooks around Golfo Dulce – a calm bay attracting dolphins and whales,

as well as sportfishing boats from the town of Golfito. Isla del Caño floats on the horizon. Considered sacred by pre-Columbian tribes, it contains ancient burial sites. To the southwest, uninhabited Isla del Coco is surrounded by teeming sealife.

The Talamancas, in the northeast of the region, rise to 12,530 ft (3,820 m) at the top of Cerro Chirripó. Here, the Boruca and Guaymí peoples struggle to maintain their cultures in remote communities threatened by logging and other commercial interests. Thick forests carpet the rugged peaks, forming a virginal environment where jaguars, tapirs, and other endangered species thrive. Between the two mountain ranges, the fertile Valle de El General is a breadbasket of agricultural produce.

hiker surveying the vast expanse of Parque Nacional Chirripó

◄ A makeshift bridge, close to San Gerardo de Rivas, in the rugged, unspoilt Parque Nacional Chirripó

Exploring the Southern Zone

The jungled shore of the Southern Zone is peppered with some of the country's finest beaches, including those at Bahía Drake, Zancudo, and Parque Nacional Marino Ballena. Surfers flock to Dominical and Pavones, while Golfito is a base for sportfishing. Whales and dolphins cavort in offshore waters, especially around Isla del Caño, while experienced divers can swim with hammerhead and whale sharks at remote Isla del Coco. Along the coast lie the rainforests of Parque Nacional Corcovado (on the Peninsula de Osa) and lesser-known sites such as the forest reserves Terraba-Sierpe and Barú. To the north, Chirripó offers an exciting hike to the summit.

Kayaking in Reserva Forestal del Humedad Nacional Terraba-Sierpe

Key

═══ Pan-American Highway

── Secondary road

┅┅┅ Minor road

▬▬▬ International border

── Provincial border

△ Peak

Sights at a Glance

Towns and Villages

② San Isidro de El General
⑧ Dominical
⑪ Palmar
⑯ Golfito
⑰ Zancudo
⑱ Pavones

National Parks and Reserves

④ *Parque Nacional Chirripó pp232–3*

⑤ Parque Internacional La Amistad
⑦ Refugio Nacional de Vida Silvestre Barú
⑨ Parque Nacional Marino Ballena
⑫ Reserva Forestal del Humedad Nacional Terraba-Sierpe
⑬ Reserva Biológica Isla del Caño
⑮ Parque Nacional Piedras Blancas
⑲ Parque Nacional Isla del Coco

Areas of Natural Beauty

① Cerro de la Muerte
③ Valle del Río Chirripó
⑥ Las Cruces Biological Station
⑭ *Peninsula de Osa pp240–41*

Indigenous Site

⑩ Reserva Indígena Boruca

For hotels and restaurants in this region see pp252–61 and pp266–77

Lush vegetation fringing aquamarine waters at Bahía Drake

MÓN

Cerro Punibeta
8,000 ft

5

INTERNACIONAL LA AMISTAD

Cerro Utyum
10,100 ft

Reserva
Indígena
Cabagra

Cerro Kamuk
11,650 ft

Cerro Nai
10,240 ft

PANAMA

enos Aires

Cabagra

Brujo

Cerro Bine
10,500 ft

Térraba

RESERVA
DÍGENA
ORUCA

Potrero Grande

Cerro Echandi
10,370 ft

PUNTARENAS

Reserva
Indígena
Curré

Santa
Elena

Río Colón

Alturas

Lucha

Piedra
Pintada

Venecia

237

San Vito

16

Sabalito

Piedras Blancas

6 **LAS CRUCES
BIOLOGICAL STATION**

15 **PARQUE NACIONAL
PIEDRAS BLANCAS**

237

Ciudad Neily

Playa
Cacao

16 **GOLFITO**

Coto 47

ulce

14

RNVS
Preciosa
Platanares

Pueblo
Nuevo

Santa
Rita

Gloria

Playa
Zancudo

17 **ZANCUDO**

Playa
Platanares

La Cuesta

238

PAVONES **18**

Cabo
Matapalo

Punta
Banco

Reserva
Indígena
Guaymí

Las Peñas

*Península
de Burica*

Colorful blooms outside a house near Parque
Nacional Chirripó

Getting Around

Palmar, Puerto Jiménez, Golfito, and
Ciudad Neily have domestic airports,
while charter planes serve smaller
airstrips. Major tourist sights can be
reached from San José by long-distance
bus. Local buses are the main form of
transportation in this region, although
more remote sights are accessible only
by jeep-taxi or cheap but uncomfortable
colectivos (pickup trucks).

Highway 2 (the Pan-American Highway)
is paved, as is Highway 16 through the
Valle de Coto Brus, but most connecting
routes are potholed dirt roads that are
covered with mud after rains. Many
nature lodges on the Osa Peninsula
and the Golfo Dulce shores can be
reached only by water-taxi.

For additional map symbols *see back flap*

Winding road in the valley of Cerro de la Muerte

❶ Cerro de la Muerte

Road Map D4. 31 miles (50 km) S of Cartago. 🚌 San José–San Isidro.

Cerro Buenavista is popularly called Cerro de la Muerte (Mountain of Death), in remembrance of the people who died of exposure while taking their produce to San José before the Pan-Am Highway was built across it.

The highway, connecting San José with the Valle de El General, passes below the actual summit (11,500 ft/ 3,500 m), which is buffeted by high winds. The vegetation is Andean *páramo* (grassland), with species that have adapted to the cold, boggy conditions. When the clouds part, there are superlative views.

The **Príncipe de la Paz**, a 10-m (30-ft) high statue of Christ, stands overlooking the road just after the descent from Cerro de la Muerte, about 4 miles (6 km) from San Isidro. Designed by the Costa Rican sculptor Francisco Ulloa, the statue was built as a symbol of peace in 1979, during the Nicaraguan civil war. Avoid this stretch of the Pan-Am Highway at night.

The **Mirador Vista del Valle** has a mountainside zipline tour with seven platforms.

🎿 Mirador Vista del Valle
Km 119, 5 miles (8 km) N of San Isidro. **🛈** 2200-5465. **Open** 8am–5pm daily. **🖥 w** valledelgeneral.com

❷ San Isidro de El General

Road Map E4. 51 miles (82 km) S of Cartago. **🚹** 41,200. **🚌** **🛈** Selva Mar, Calle 1 and Aves 2/4, 2771-4582. **🖥** Día de San Isidro Labrador (May 15). **w exploringcostarica.com**

The peaceful market town of San Isidro de El General sits at the base of Cerro de la Muerte and is the administrative center for Valle de El General. For tourists, it serves mainly as a refueling stop and as a convenient base for exploring Chirripó and Parque Internacional La Amistad. The only sight of interest in town is the modern, concrete cathedral. Built in 1967 on the east side of the plaza, the cathedral has stained-glass windows and a simple altar, which is dominated by a mural of San Isidro Labrador, patron saint of San Isidro.

Environs

Bird-lovers are in for a treat at **Los Cusingos Neotropical Bird Sanctuary**. Administered by the Tropical Science Center of Costa Rica, this 350-acre (142-ha) refuge for birds was founded by the eminent American ornithologist Dr. Alexander Skutch (1904–2004), co-author of the authoritative volume *Birds of Costa Rica*. More than 300 bird species have been noted in this sanctuary. Also of note are the Indian petroglyphs and Skutch's former home, maintained as if he still lived there.

The striking modern cathedral of San Isidro de El General

🦜 Los Cusingos Neotropical Bird Sanctuary
Quizarrá de Pérez Zeledón, 9 miles (14 km) SE of San Isidro. **🛈** 2253-3267 (Tropical Science Center). **Open** 7am–4pm daily (to 1pm Sun), by appt. **🖥 🖥 w cct.or.cr**

Works of art at the Museo el Pelicano, Valle del Río Chirripó

❸ Valle del Río Chirripó

Road Map E4. 6 miles (10 km) E of San Isidro. **🚌** from San Isidro.

This valley is scythed from the Talamanca Mountains by the turbulent Río Chirripó. Trout swim in the river's waters, and rapids provide kayaking thrills. A great place to stop in the valley is the fruit-and-coffee *finca* **Rancho La Botija** *(see p277)*, a popular destination for locals on weekends. Its attractions include an antique sugarcane mill, restaurant, and accommodation. Nearby, the roadside **Piedra de los Indios** (Rock of the Indians) bears pre-Columbian petroglyphs as well as some modern graffiti.

The scenery grows more dramatic and the climate more alpine as the road climbs into the mountains to reach **San Gerardo de Rivas**. Perching over the river gorge, this hamlet is the gateway to Parque Nacional Chirripó. Close by, **Museo el Pelicano** is a curiosity for its inspired stone and timber art by coffee farmer Rafael Elizondo Basulta. Nearby, **Aguas Termales** has natural thermal pools popular with local families seeking to counter

hiking trail at the Chirripó Cloudbridge Reserve

...e chilly mountain air. A steep
...ack, strewn with boulders,
...ads past the trailhead to
...e summit of Cerro Chirripó
...nd ends at the **Chirripó
...loudbridge Reserve**. The
...cally endemic parrot
...ountain snake can be seen
...t this private reserve; there are
...lso some good hiking trails.

Museo el Pelicano
...anaan, 10 miles (16 km) E of San
...dro. **Tel** 2742-5050. **Open** 8am–8pm
...aily.

Aguas Termales
...5 mile (0.8 km) NW of San Gerardo.
...el 2742-5210. **Open** 7am–6pm
...aily.

Chirripó Cloudbridge Reserve
...an Gerardo de Rivas, 12 miles (20 km)
...of San Isidro. **Open** 8am–4pm daily.
...**cloudbridge.org**

Parque Nacional Chirripó

See pp232–3.

Parque Internacional La Amistad

Road Map F4. to Guácimo, 66
...iles (107 km) SE of San Isidro, then
...y jeep-taxi. Estación Altamira HQ,
...1 miles (50 km) SE of Buenos Aires,
...730-9846. **Open** 8am–4pm daily.

...xtending into Panama, the
...ternational Friendship Park is
...ontiguous with other protected
...reas that form the Reserva de
...a Biosfera La Amistad (Amistad
...iosphere Reserve). It sprawls

over 675 sq miles (1,750 sq km)
of the rugged Talamanca
Mountains, and ranges from
elevations of 490 ft (150 m) to
11,650 ft (3,550 m) atop Cerro
Kamuk. This enormous park
spans eight "life zones," from low
montane rainforest to swampy
high-altitude grassland. The
diverse wildlife includes five cat
species and the endangered
harpy eagle.

With permits and a guide,
experienced hikers can cross
the Talamancas on a trail
that starts from the town
of Buenos Aires, 38 miles
(61 km) southeast of San
Isidro, and leads to Reserva
Indígena Talamanca-
Cabécar *(see p225)*.

The main ranger
station, a hostel, and an
ecology exhibition are at
Estación Altamira, the
recommended entry point. All the
official access points require 4WD.

Environs
East of Buenos Aires, **Reserva
Biológica Durika**, a 3-sq-mile
(9-sq-km) forest reserve, is a self-
sufficient holistic community
offering guided hikes, vegetarian meals, and rustic

accommodation. At **Finca
Coffea Diversa**, below Estación
Altamira, visitors can wander
among rows of flowering
shrubs and more than 200
coffee bush species. The rural
communities of Biolley,
Carmén, and Altamira are
enlivened with ceramic murals.

Reserva Biológica Durika
11 miles (18 km) N of Buenos Aires.
Tel 2730-0657.
durika.org

Finca Coffea Diversa
Altamira, 0.5 miles (1 km) W of
Estación Altamira. **Open** 8am–5pm
daily. **coffeadiversa.net**

❻ Las Cruces Biological Station

Road Map F5. 4 miles (6 km) S of San
Vito. **Tel** 2773-4004. San Vito–
Ciudad Neily. **Open** 8am–5pm daily.
ots.ac.cr

Ferns, Las Cruces
Biological Station

One of the world's leading
tropical research and
educational centers, Las
Cruces is run by the
Organization of Tropical
Studies (OTS). The center is
surrounded by a 580-acre
(235-ha) mid-elevation
forest, in which an
incredible diversity of
birds and mammals can
be seen along 6 miles
(10 km) of trails. Clouds
envelop the reserve, nourishing
the many ferns, palms,
bromeliads, and orchids laid out
in the 25-acre (10-ha) **Wilson
Botanical Gardens**, designed by
distinguished Brazilian landscaper
Roberto Burle-Marx. A riot of
color in even the rainiest of
weather, the collection extends
to greenhouses, where varieties
of tropical plants are propagated.

Pre-Columbian Petroglyphs

Costa Rica's pre-Columbian peoples left their legacy
etched on boulders. Significant finds include
Guayabo National Monument *(see pp158–9)*,
where jaguars, snakes, frogs, and birds of
prey symbolize creation, wealth, and power.
Piedra de Los Indios and Rancho La Bojita,
both in the Valle del Río Chirripó *(see p230)*,
have interesting petroglyphs, including a crude
map of the Talamanca region.

Petroglyph

➍ Parque Nacional Chirripó

Costa Rica's highest mountain, Cerro Chirripó (12,530 ft/3,820 m) is enfolded in the 194-sq-mile (502-sq-km) Chirripó National Park. Part of the Amistad Biosphere Reserve, the park protects three distinct "life zones" in rugged, virgin territory where wildlife flourishes with minimal interference from humans. As many as 60 percent of all wildlife species in Costa Rica are found here, including all six types of wild cats *(see pp66–7)* and many endemic species of flora and fauna. Glacial activity some 35,000 years ago carved small U-shaped valleys and deposited moraines, still visible today. Spring is the best time for hiking, although weather is always unpredictable, with frequent fog and rain.

COSTA RICA

THE SOUTHERN ZONE

PACIFIC OCEAN

Key

- ▢ Parque Nacional Chirripó
- ▢ Area of park illustrated

Cloud Forest Almost constantly shrouded in mist, the forests above 8,200 ft (2,500 m) are typified by dwarf blueberry trees festooned with epiphytes and mosses. Monkeys and quetzals are found in plenty.

Cordillera de Talamanca

Río Uran

Río Blanco

• Herradura

Río Chirripó

San Garado de Rivas ①

②

Refu Llano Bo

San Isidro de El General

Río Chirripó

KEY

① **The ranger station** in San Gerardo de Rivas has a trail map. Visitors must report here before setting out on the hike to the summit.

② **Sendero Termometro**, leading into cloud forest, is one of the steepest stretches of the trail.

③ **Monte Sin Fe** (Faithless Mountain) is reached by a steep uphill section called La Cuesta del Agua.

④ **Sabana de los Leones** (Savanna of the Lions) is named for the pumas frequently seen on the southern slopes.

⑤ **Centro Ambientalista El Páramo**, the sole lodging on the mountains, sleeps 40 people in bunks. It has solar-powered electricity and a communal kitchen, and rents out sleeping bags, blankets, and stoves. Kitchen staff can prepare cooked meals by reservation.

⑥ **Valle de los Conejos** (Valley of the Rabbits) is a marshy valley with a large rabbit population. It suffered from a devastating wildfire in 1992.

Hiking in the Park

Most visitors hike to the summit along a well-marked trail that ascends 8,200 ft (2,500 m) from the trailhead, near San Gerardo de Rivas. The 20-mile (32-km) hike to the top and back normally takes two days, with an overnight stay near the summit. Hire guide-porters in San Gerardo. An alternative route is from Herradura via Cerro Uran.

Hikers in Parque Nacional Chirripó

Serene Lago San Juan, Parque Nacional Chirripó

VISITORS' CHECKLIST

Practical Information
Road Map E4. 12 miles (19 km)
NE of San Isidro de El General.
🛈 Ranger station, San Gerardo
de Rivas; 2742-5083.
Open 6:30am–5pm daily;
reservations recommended.
No more than 40 people allowed
at a time. **Closed** May. 📷 📷
mandatory. 🛏 by reservation.

Transport
🚌 to San Gerardo de Rivas,
2 miles (3 km) from the park.

Tapirs

The park has the nation's largest
population of tapirs. Baird's tapirs
are often spotted drinking in
Lago San Juan, a short distance
west of the summit.

Río Chirripó

Valle de las
Morrenas

Cerro Laguna
12,340 ft

Cerro Nudo
12,340 ft

Laguna Los
Morrenas

Lago
Roja

upula
5 ft

Cerro Truncado
12,080 ft

Lago
San Juan

Cerro Chirripo
12,530 ft

Cerro Piramide 12,500 ft

Lago Ditkevi

tisqueros
12,135 ft

Cerro Nuevo
12,170 ft

Pico Noreste
12,280 ft

**Valle de
Los Conejos** ● 6

Cerro Páramo
12,500 ft

⑤

Cerro Terbi
12,340 ft

Cerro Crestones
12,210 ft

Talari

④

Río Terbi

Cerro Arno
11,155 ft

Cerro Chirripó

The views in every direction
from the summit are staggering in clear
weather. Hikers usually stay overnight at
Centro Ambientalista El Páramo, setting off
early morning for the last leg of the trek to
the top, which takes 90 minutes.

Los Crestones

Marking the end of a steep
1.2-mile (2-km) long climb called
La Cuesta de los Arrepen-
tidos (Repentants' Hill),
these dramatic
vertical rock
formations were
considered a
sacred site by
pre-Columbian
Indians.

Minor road

ark boundary

rail

eak

For additional map symbols *see back flap*

Zipline tour in Refugio Nacional de Vida Silvestre Barú

❼ Refugio Nacional de Vida Silvestre Barú

Road Map D4. 2 miles (3 km) N of Dominical. **Tel** 2787-0003. 🚌 Dominical–Quepos. **Open** 7am–5:30pm daily. 🐾🚣♿🚴📷🌿
W haciendabaru.com

A former cattle ranch and cocoa plantation, the 815-acre (330-ha) Hacienda Barú has varied habitats, including 2 miles (3 km) of beach that draw nesting hawksbill and olive ridley turtles. Turtle eggs are collected and incubated in a nursery for release. Barú has more than 310 bird species and several mammal species, such as jaguarundis and the arboreal kinkajous. There are butterfly and orchid gardens. Guided tree-climbing, canopy tours, kayak trips through the mangroves, hikes, horseback rides, and overnight stays in treetop tents are also on offer.

❽ Dominical

Road Map D4. 18 miles (29 km) SW of San Isidro de El General. 🏔 2,000. 🚌

The ultimate surfer's destination, this village thrives on the backpacker trade: the community consists mostly of foreign surfers who settled here. Its long beach extends south from the mouth of Río Barú to the fishing hamlet of Dominicalito. Non-surfers should beware of the dangerous riptides.

Environs
The thickly forested mountains south of Dominical, the Fila Costanera, are also called **Escaleras** (Staircase). Tour companies in Dominical offer hikes, plus all-terrain-vehicle and horseback trips into the mountains, where each Friday night (Dec–Apr), US expat Harley "Toby" Toberman shows movies at **Cinema Escaleras**, his private villa.

Highway 243 winds through the Río Barú valley, connecting Dominical to San Isidro. Tour companies offer trips to **Don Lulo's Nauyaca Waterfalls**, a dramatic, two-tiered waterfall that is a 4-mile (6-km) horseback ride away from the highway. Nearby, **Parque Reptilandia** exhibits dozens of snakes and other reptile species, including a komodo dragon from Indonesia. Guided tours offer an insight into reptilian behavior.

Signage for RNVS Rancho Merced

🎬 **Cinema Escaleras**
1.5 miles (2.5 km) NE of Escaleras. **Tel** 2787-8065.
Open from 5pm Fri.
W moviesinthejungle.com

🎬 **Don Lulo's Nauyaca Waterfalls**
Platanillo, 6 miles (10 km) E of Dominical. **Tel** 2787-0541. 🐎
🕗 8am and 2pm.
W cataratasnauyaca.com

🦎 **Parque Reptilandia**
Platanillo. **Tel** 2787-0343.
Open 9am–4:30pm daily. 🐾🌿
W crreptiles.com

❾ Parque Nacional Marino Ballena

Road Map D4. 11 miles (18 km) S of Dominical. **Tel** 2786-5392. 🚌 from Dominical. **Open** 6am–6pm daily. 🐾
🌿🚠 **W** sinac.go.cr

Created to protect the nation's largest coral reef, Whale Marine National Park stretches for 8 miles (13 km) along the shore of Bahía de Coronado, and extends 9 miles (14 km) out to sea. It is named after the humpback whales that gather in the warm waters to breed in the dry season between December and April. Several tour operators such as **Ballenas Aventuras**, offer whale-watching trips.

The park incorporates **Las Tres Hermanas** and **Isla Ballena**, which are important nesting sites for frigate birds, brown boobies, and pelicans. Hawksbill and olive ridley turtles nest on the palm-fringed beaches. Kayaking and scuba diving trips can be arranged.

Environs
To the north, **Refugio Nacional de Vida Silvestre Rancho Merced** offers city-slickers a chance to play cowhand; it also functions as a wildlife refuge. Nearby, the twin hamlets of **Tortuga Abajo** and **Ojochal** make a good base for exploring the area; Ojochal has several outstanding restaurants. Sustainably operated, **La Cusinga Lodge** offers great wildlife on its trails in the hilltops above pristine beaches.

🐎 **Refugio Nacional de Vida Silvestre Rancho Merced**
Uvita, 11 miles (18 km) S of Dominica
Tel 8861-5147. 🐎🚣
W ranchomerced.com

🐬 **Ballenas Aventuras**
Uvita, 11 miles (18 km) S of Dominica
Tel 2743-8362. 🐎
W bahiaaventuras.com

🏨 **La Cusinga Lodge**
3 miles (5 km) S of the Uvita bridge, between Km 166 and Km 167.
Tel 2770-2549. 🐎🌿🚣
W lacusingalodge.com

Surfers wading into the sea at the beach at Dominical

Costa Rica's Tropical Flowers

A luxuriant hothouse of bio-diversity, Costa Rica nurtures over 15,000 known plant species, including 800 types of ferns. Varieties of tropical flowers such as cannas, plumerias, and begonias flourish in the warm and humid regions, as do bromeliads and other epiphytes, which draw moisture and oxygen from the air. Cacti are found on the parched lowlands, while stunted dwarf forests and vivid clusters of pink, white, and lilac impatiens grow at higher elevations. Flowering trees color the tropical forests: the poinciana flames with vermilion blossoms, and the jacaranda drops its violet-blue, bell-shaped blooms to form spectacular carpets in spring.

Heliconias are known for their unusual bracts. The lobster-claw heliconia (right) has a yellow-tipped red bract. Costa Rica's 30 native species of heliconia thrive in areas with plenty of moisture.

Bracts are flowerheads atop huge stems that can grow up to 25 ft (8 m).

Large leaves are typical of heliconias, of which the banana plant is a member.

Passion flowers emanate a foul smell to attract pollinators, especially Heliconiinae butterflies.

The Aristolochia, or "Dutchman's pipe," gives off a fetid odor resembling that of rotting flesh. This draws flies, its principal pollinators.

Anthuriums have a distinctive heart-shaped spathe – usually red, white, or greenish – from which the flower spike protrudes.

Ginger lilies have large, hyacinth-like flowers rich in nectar. Introduced from Asia, these shoulder-high plants are common in landscaped gardens.

Bromeliads collect water in their tightly wrapped, thick, waxy leaves. Falling leaf matter decays inside this whorl, providing nutrients for the plant and creating a self-contained ecosystem.

Orchids

More than 1,400 species of orchids grow in Costa Rica, from sea level to the heights of Chirripó (see pp323–3). The greatest numbers are found below 6,000 ft (1,830 m). Orchids range from the 0.03-inch (1-mm) wide liverwort orchid (Platystele jungermannioides), the world's smallest flower, to others with pendulous 3-ft (1-m) long petals. All orchids have three petals and three sepals. Some have evolved unique features to attract specific pollinators: for example, the markings on certain orchids are visible only to insects that can see in the ultraviolet spectrum.

Detail of a mural showing various orchids

The bird of paradise flowers from a dramatic spathe with bright orange sepals and vivid blue petals. Set at right angles to the stem, the spathe looks like a bird's head.

⑩ Reserva Indígena Boruca

Road Map: E5. 22 miles (35 km) SW of Buenos Aires. 🚌 from Buenos Aires. 🎭 Fiesta de los Diablitos (Dec 31–Jan 2). **W** boruca.org

This is just one of several indigenous reserves – inhabited by the Boruca and Bribri – in the mountains hemming the Valle de El General. Located in the Fila Sinancra Mountains, the reserve is known for its Fiesta de los Diablitos, as well as its carved *jícaras* (gourds) and balsa-wood *máscaras* (masks). The women use traditional backstrap looms to weave cotton purses and shawls. The ridgetop drive to the hamlet of **Boruca** offers great views of the Río Terraba gorge. Local culture is showcased in the **Museo Comunitario Boruca**.

Reserva Indígena Térraba and **Reserva Indígena Curré** flank the Boruca reserve. **Reserva Indígena Cabagra**, home to the Bribri, can be accessed from the town of Brujo, 7 miles (11 km) southeast of Buenos Aires. With visitors demonstrating a growing interest in Costa Rica's indigenous cultures, these remote communities are gradually opening up to tourism.

🏛 **Museo Comunitario Boruca**
Boruca, 25 miles (40 km) SW of Buenos Aires. **Tel** 2514-0045. **Open** 9am–4pm daily. 📷

⑪ Palmar

Road Map: E5. 78 miles (125 km) SE of San Isidro de El General. 🏔 9,900. ✈ 🚌

Sitting at the foot of the Río Terraba valley, at the intersection of Costanera Sur and the Pan-Am Highway, Palmar is the service center for the region. The town straddles Río Terraba, which flows west through the wide Valle de Diquis. Pre-Columbian *esferas de piedra* (stone spheres) and a centenarian steam locomotive are displayed in the plaza of Palmar Sur. Palmar Norte is the town's modern quarter.

Reserva Forestal del Humedad Nacional Terraba-Sierpe

⑫ Reserva Forestal del Humedad Nacional Terraba-Sierpe

Road Map: E5. 11 miles (18 km) W of Palmar. 🚤 ℹ 2788-1212 (Tours Gaviota de Osa).

Created to protect the nation's largest stretch of mangrove forest and swamp, the Terraba-Sierpe National Humid Forest Reserve covers an area of 85 sq miles (220 sq km) between the deltas of the Sierpe and Terraba rivers. Countless channels criss-cross this vitally important ecosystem, which fringes 25 miles (40 km) of coastline.

Visitors kayaking in these quiet channels can see a variety of wildlife, including basilisk lizards, iguanas, crocodiles, and caimans, as well as monkeys, coatis and crab-eating raccoons. The birding opportunities are also excellent, with herons, egrets, and cotingas among the inhabitants. Guided boat and kayak tours are offered from Sierpe, 9 miles (14 km) south of Palmar.

⑬ Reserva Biológica Isla del Caño

Road Map: D5. 12 miles (19 km) W of Bahía Drake. ℹ 2735-5036 (PN Corcovado). 🚤 tours from Bahía Drake, Manuel Antonio & Dominical. **Open** 8am–4pm daily. 📷 **W** sinac.go.cr

Thrust from the sea by tectonic forces, the 805-acre (325-ha) uninhabited Isla del Caño was named a protected reserve in 1976, along with 10 sq miles (26 sq km) of surrounding waters. Today, it is administered as part of Parque Nacional Corcovado *(see p243)*. In the past, the island was considered to be sacred by the pre-Columbian Diquis peoples.

The coral-colored beaches are great for sunbathing. In the shallows, coral reefs teem with lobsters and fish, while dolphins, whales, and manta rays swim in the warm waters farther out. Diving is permitted in designated zones *(see p292)*. Terrestrial wildlife is relatively limited, although the lucky hiker might come across four-eyed foxes, brown boobies, and ospreys.

Mossy pre-Columbian tombs and granite *esferas* (spheres) are scattered along a trail running from the beachfront ranger hut to a lookout point. The trail winds past milk trees *(Brosimum utile)*, named for their drinkable milky latex.

Overnight stays are not permitted. Lodges in the Bahía Drake area *(see p242)* offer day trips and diving.

Fiesta de los Diablitos

At midnight on December 31, the Boruca gather to reenact the war between their ancestors and the Spanish conquistadors. At the

sound of a conch shell, men dressed in burlap sacking and devil masks pursue a fellow tribesman dressed as a bull. The *diablitos* (devils) drink *chicha* (corn beer) and perform theatrical skits recalling tribal events. After three days, the bull is symbolically killed, metaphorically freeing the tribe from colonial repression.

Borucas in devil masks

The Mangroves of Coastal Costa Rica

Costa Rica's shores contain five of the world's 65 species of mangroves – black, buttonwood, red, tea, and white. Mangroves are woody halophytes – plants able to withstand immersion in saltwater – and form swampy forests in areas inundated by tides. These communities are of vital importance to the maritime ecosystem, fostering a wealth of wildlife. The tangled roots buffer the action of waves, preventing coastal erosion. They also filter out the silt washed down by turbulent rivers: the accumulated mud extends the land out to sea. Threatened by the country's coastal development, this fragile ecosystem is now legally protected, with the Terraba-Sierpe reserve being the largest tract.

The Mangrove Ecosystem

Mangroves grow in mud so dense that there is little oxygen, and nutrients supplied by decomposing leaf litter lie close to the surface. Hence, most plants develop interlocking stilt roots that rise above the water to draw in oxygen and food.

Salt is expelled by mangroves in a variety of ways. A few species are "salt-excluders" that filter salt at root level, while some excrete it through special glands.

White mangroves have smooth, rounded leaves.

Black mangroves breathe through pneumatophores – roots that stick up from the mud.

Growth is fast – as much as 2 ft (0.6 m) in a year.

Red mangroves, like most other species, extract oxygen through spongy aerial roots via breathing cells called lenticels.

Pendulous seed pods drop to the mud and float away at high tide to begin a new colony far from its source.

Mangrove ferns grow toward the land part of the ecosystem.

The mudflats are rich in nutrients, forming a food source for marine creatures.

The Rich Fauna of the Mangroves

The microorganisms that grow in the nutrient-rich muds foster the growth of larger creatures such as shrimps and other crustaceans, which in turn attract various species of mammals, reptiles, and birds.

Aquatic nurseries for oysters, sponges, and numerous fish species, including sharks and stingrays, thrive in the tannin-stained waters. The roots protect baby caimans and crocodiles from predators.

Larger species, such as raccoons, coyotes, snakes, and wading birds forage for small lizards and crabs.

Birds, such as frigate birds and pelicans, and endemic species such as the yellow mangrove warbler roost atop mangroves.

The uninhabited Isla del Coco, covered in dense premontane forest ▶

⑭ Peninsula de Osa

Washed by warm Pacific waters on three sides, the isolated Osa Peninsula curls around the Golfo Dulce. The peninsula was a center for the pre-Columbian Diquis culture, whose skill as goldsmiths sent Spanish conquistadors on a futile search for fabled gold mines. Deluged by year-round rains, much of this rugged area remains uninhabited and trackless, and is covered with virgin rainforest. About half of Osa is protected within Parque Nacional Corcovado, the largest of the parks and reserves that make up the Corcovado Conservation Area. Those with a taste for adventure are richly rewarded with majestic wilderness and some of the most spectacular wildlife-viewing in the nation.

Bahía Drake
With a beautiful setting, Drake Bay is great for scuba diving and sportfishing centered on the small village of Agujitas (see p242).

Playa San Josecito
Backed by rainforest, this is a beautiful golden-sand beach with accommodations. Access is by boat or hiking trail.

KEY

① **Refugio Nacional de Vida Silvestre Punta Río Claro**, located inland of Punta Marenco, protects more than 400 bird species, four monkey species, and prime rainforest habitat adjoining Corcovado (see p243).

② **Dos Brazos**, a former gold mining center, welcomes visitors for gold-panning trips with community members.

③ **Cabo Matapalo** is popular with surfers.

④ **Laguna Pejeperrito** is inhabited by caimans, crocodiles, and waterfowl.

⑤ **Carate**, the gateway to Corcovado, is accessed by chartered planes to the small airstrip and a rugged dirt track.

Cerro Chocuaco
2,120 ft

Reserva Forestal
Golfo Dulce

Laguna
Chocuaco

Bahía
Drake

Playa
Cocalito

Playa
Caletas

Aguijitas

Punta
Marenco

**RNVS Punta
Río Claro**

Playa San
Josecito

**San Pedrillo
Ranger Station**

Río Aguijitas

*Parque
Nacional
Corcovado*

Río Corcovado

Río Sirena

Laguna
Corcovado

**Los Patos
Ranger Station**

Playa
Corcovado

*Pacific
Ocean*

**Sirena Ranger
Station**

Corcovado

Punta Río
Claro

Parque Nacional Corcovado
Sprawling Corcovado National Park protects one of the last original tracts of the Pacific coast's tropical rainforest in Meso-America. La Leona (left) is one of its four ranger stations. Crocodiles, tapirs, jaguars, and scarlet macaws are found in the park in large numbers (see p243).

Logging

The peninsula's large stands of precious hardwoods, such as mahogany, have suffered from excessive logging. Although restrictions have been placed on the activities of lumber companies, the cutting of protected tree species continues unabated.

Logging truck

Key

▬ Main road
▬ Minor road
▬ Trail
▬ Park boundary

Dolphins
Dolphins and humpback whales are frequently seen playing in the Golfo Dulce (Sweet Gulf).

Puerto Jiménez
The only town of significance on the Osa Peninsula, this is the starting point for visits to Corcovado, and a center for hiking, surfing, and similar activities, including kayaking through nearby mangroves *(see p243)*.

Pan-American Highway

245

Golfo Dulce

• La Palma
• arrigones
245
Agujas • Sandalo
Lalitas
Dos Brazos ②
ón
Puerto Jiménez ✈
*Playa Preciosa
Playa Platanares*
RNVS Preciosa Platanares
medal Lacustrino guna Pejeperrito
ation
rate ✈
④
Reserva Forestal Golfo Dulce
RNVS Pejeperro
Cerro Osa △ 1,050 ft
Playa Sombrero
245
③
Cabo Matapalo

kilometers 5
miles 5

Playa Platanares
A vital nesting site for marine turtles, the beach is fringed by wildlife-rich forest. A coral reef offshore is good for snorkeling.

Exploring Peninsula de Osa

The lush rainforests of Corcovado lie at the heart of the Osa Peninsula. Although tourism to the region is booming, travel into the interior is still a challenge. Highway 245 follows the eastern shore and a rugged dirt road links Rincón to Bahía Drake, but the only guaranteed access to the western shores is by boat or by small plane. Wilderness lodges line the coast.

Along the shore of sweeping Bahía Drake

Bahía Drake

Rocky cliffs and forested hills provide a compelling setting for the scalloped Drake Bay. Sir Francis Drake is said to have anchored the *Golden Hind* here in March 1579.

This is one of the most inaccessible areas in Costa Rica. In 2003, a dirt road was cut from Rincón, on Golfo Dulce, to Bahía Drake (pronounced "DRA-cay"), but the route is often impassable in wet weather, even for 4WD vehicles. Most visitors still arrive by boat from Sierpe *(see p236)*. The small village of **Agujitas**, toward the bay's southern end, survives largely on subsistence farming, fishing, and tourism.

Popular attractions include dolphin- and whale-watching trips on the bay. Snorkeling is another fun activity, especially in the southern bay, where the canyon of Río Agujitas can be explored by kayak. There are several budget accommodation options, as well as more expensive lodges that offer scuba diving and sportfishing. One such is **Aguila de Osa** *(see p260)*, which features snorkeling along with scuba diving and deep-sea angling. Among its other attractions are zipline tours and a treetop

observation walkway. You can also whiz between the treetops of primary and secondary rainforest with the **Corcovado Canopy Tour**, which has 11 ziplines ranging up to 400 m (1,312 ft) in length at 197 ft (60 m) above ground.

From Agujitas, a coastal trail leads south for 8 miles (13 km), via **Playas Cocalito**, **Caletas**, and **San Josecito**, to Parque Nacional Corcovado, passing by the **Refugio Nacional de Vida Silvestre Punta Río Claro**. This 2-sq-mile (5-sq-km) nature reserve adjoins Corcovado, and is home to much the same species of wildlife as can be seen in Corcovado. Guided hikes can be booked at Punta Marenco Lodge, which is nearby. Tapirs and crocodiles are frequently sighted while canoeing on **Laguna Chocuaco**, to the east of Agujitas; the local community cooperative offers trips.

⚡ Corcovado Canopy Tour
Los Planos, 8 miles (14 km)
SE of Agujitas. **Tel** 8810-8908.
Ⓦ corcovadocanopytour.com

⚡ Refugio Nacional de Vida Silvestre Punta Río Claro
Playa Caletas, 4 miles (6 km)
S of Agujitas. **ℹ** 8877-3535.
Open 8am–5pm daily. 🅰 🅲 🅳
🅴 **Ⓦ puntamarenco.com**

Puerto Jiménez

🅼 6,200.

The only settlement of significance on the peninsula, this dusty village is popular with backpackers. In the 1980s, Puerto Jiménez briefly blossomed on income from local gold and had a reputation as a "Wild West" frontier town, where carrying a gun was considered a good idea and prostitutes were paid with gold nuggets. Today, the town thrives on tourist money.

Various adventure activities are offered by local operators. Kayakers flock to the mangroves extending east along the shore of the Golfo Dulce to the estuary of Río Platanares. Home to crocodiles, caimans, freshwater turtles, and river otters, this ecosystem is protected within the 555-acre (225-ha) **Refugio Nacional de Vida Silvestre Preciosa Platanares**. The refuge lies along the shore of the lovely **Playa Platanares**, which has a small coral reef good for snorkeling. The beach is a nesting site for five species of marine turtles, best sighted from May to December. A small *vivero* (nursery) raises hatchlings for release into the jade-green water.

The shore south of Puerto Jiménez is lined with beaches. **Cabo Matapalo**, at the tip of the peninsula, and **Playa Sombrero** offer great surfing.

⚡ Refugio Nacional de Vida Silvestre Preciosa Platanares
2 miles (3 km) E of Puerto Jiménez.
🅰 by donation. 🅲 🅳 🅴

Locals on the main street of Puerto Jiménez

Lounging area on the beach at Parque Nacional Corcovado

⚑ Parque Nacional Corcovado
5 miles (40 km) SW of Puerto
Jiménez. **Tel** 2735-5036.
Open 8am–4pm daily. 🅿️ 🚻 🏊 ⚠️
🖥 sinac.go.cr

Considered the crown jewel
among the protected regions
of the humid tropics, this
165-sq-mile (425-sq-km) park
was created in 1975 to
preserve the largest Pacific
coast rainforest in the
Americas, as well as 20 sq
miles (52 sq km) of marine
habitat. Corcovado (meaning
"hunchback") has eight
distinct zones, including
herbaceous swamps, flooded
swamp forest, and montane
forest. The area receives up to
158 in (400 cm) of rainfall per
year, with torrential rains from
April to December.

Wildlife viewing is splendid
and among the most diverse
in Costa Rica. The park has
over 400 species of birds,
including the endangered
harpy eagle, and the largest
population of scarlet macaws
in Central America; bird-
watchers are guaranteed
sightings. Jaguars are spotted
more frequently here than at
any other park in the nation,

as are tapirs. Both species are
often seen on the beaches,
especially around dusk.
Corcovado is known for
its large packs of peccaries –
menacing wild hogs that
should be avoided. The
endangered *titi* (squirrel
monkey) is also found here.
There are more than
115 species
of amphibians
and reptiles.
Poison-dart
frogs *(see p212)*
are easily seen in
their gaudy livery,
but the elusive
lime-green red-eyed tree
frog and Fleischmann's
transparent frog are harder
to spot. The fortunate might
witness green, hawksbill,
leatherback, or Pacific ridley
turtles crawling ashore to
nest. However, the park is
understaffed and the wildlife
is under threat by poachers.

Although there are hotels and
organized tours close by, the
park is best suited to self-
sufficient hikers who enjoy
rugged adventures. There are
four official entry points and
ranger stations. **San Pedrillo**,

Small biplane used for
transport within Osa

to the west, is linked by a trail
from Bahía Drake. **Los Patos**, to
the east, can be reached from
La Palma, 12 miles (19 km)
northwest of Puerto Jiménez.
La Leona, to the south, is 1 mile
(1.6 km) west of the airstrip at
Carate, a hamlet 25 miles (40 km)
west of Puerto Jiménez; visitors
must then hike or ride a horse
from Carate. **Sirena**, the main
ranger station,
is 10 miles
(16 km) northwest
of La Leona and
16 miles (26 km)
southeast of San
Pedrillo. Poorly
marked trails connect the
stations; it is wise to hire a guide.

The coastal San Pedrillo–La
Leona trail passes the dramatic
100-ft (30-m) high **Cascada La
Llorona**. Be prepared to ford
rivers inhabited by crocodiles
on this two-day hike. The trail's
northern section is open only
from December to April. The
San Pedrillo–Los Patos trail
allows access to **Laguna
Corcovado**, where tapirs and
jaguars are often sighted.

There is no scheduled air
service to the airstrips near the
park, but air-taxis are offered by
charter companies.

Interesting attractions close
to Parque Nacional Corcovado
include the 105-acre (43-ha)
wetlands **Humedal Lacustrino
Laguna Pejeperrito**, 2 miles
(3 km) east of Carate, and the
865-acre (350-ha) **Refugio
Nacional de Vida Silvestre
Pejeperro**, 2.5 miles (4 km)
farther east. They are little
visited, but offer good
opportunities for spotting
birds, as well as crocodiles.

Gold Mining

Oreros (gold panners) had sifted for gold in the rivers of
the Osa Peninsula since pre-Columbian days. When
the United Fruit Company *(see p43)* pulled out of the
region in 1985, unemployed workers flooded the
peninsula, leading to a latter-day gold rush. This
short-lived gold rush caused major damage: trees
were felled, river banks dynamited, and exposed soils
sluiced. After violent clashes with the authorities, the
oreros were ousted in 1986. Some still work the outer
margins of Corcovado, while others earn their income
leading gold hunts for tourists.

Nuggets
of gold

⓯ Parque Nacional Piedras Blancas

Road Map E5. 28 miles (46 km) SE of Palmar. **Tel** 2741-8001 (Esquinas Rainforest Lodge). 🚌 from Golfito. **Open** 8am–4pm daily.

Split off from Parque Nacional Corcovado in 1991, this 55-sq-mile (140-sq-km) park protects the forested mountains to the northeast of Golfo Dulce. In the village of La Gamba, a cooperative runs the **Esquinas Rainforest Lodge** (see p261), which breeds the rodent-like *tepezcuintles* and offers hikes.

The emerald forests spill over the beaches – Playa Cativo and Playa San Josecito, which has the botanical garden **Casa de Orquídeas**, known for its large collection of orchids and ornamentals. Lining the shores are wilderness lodges. Boat trips, including water-taxi rides, from Puerto Jiménez and Golfito to the two beaches make for pleasant excursions.

🏵 Casa de Orquídeas
Playa San Josecito, 6 miles (10 km) N of Puerto Jiménez. **Tel** 8829-1247. **Open** 8am–5pm Sat–Thu by appointment. 🚻 🅿

Sign of the colorful botanical garden, Casa de Orquídeas

⓰ Golfito

Road Map F5. 48 miles (77 km) SE of Palmar. 🚹 10,900. ✈ 🚌
🌐 golfitocostarica.com

A sportfishing base, port, and administrative center for the southern region, dilapidated Golfito (Small Gulf) unfurls along 4 miles (6 km) of shoreline. Established by the United Fruit Company in 1938, the town's reign as the nation's main banana shipping port ended when the company pulled out of the region in 1985. The legacy of "Big Fruit" can

Stilt-legged house in Zona Americana, Golfito

be seen in the intriguing architecture of Zona Americana, the north end of town, which has stilt-legged wooden houses. The small plaza in Pueblo Civíl, the town center, abuts a busy water-taxi wharf. The **Museo Marino** nearby is worth a peek for its corals and seashells.

On weekends and holidays, Golfito is flooded with Ticos drawn to the Depósito Libre (Free Trade Zone) shopping compound created in 1990 to revive the town's fortunes.

The forested hills east and north of town are protected within **Refugio Nacional de Vida Silvestre Golfito**.

🏛 Museo Marino
Hotel Centro Turístico Samoa, just N of Pueblo Civíl. **Tel** 2775-0233. **Open** 7am–11am daily.

🏵 Refugio Nacional de Vida Silvestre Golfito
E of Golfito. **Tel** 2775-2620. **Open** 8am–4pm daily. 🅿 with local operators.

⓱ Zancudo

Road Map F5. 6 miles (10 km) S of Golfito (41 miles/66 km by road). 🚌 from Golfito. 🚤 water-taxi from Golfito.

This hamlet on the east shore of Golfo Dulce is known for its stupendously beautiful gray sand beach, caressed by breeze and surf. The 4-mile (6-km) long strip of sand is a spit, projecting from the shore. A mangrove swamp inland of the beach is good for spotting crocodiles, caimans, and waterfowl. Sportfishing centers offer superb river-mouth and deep-water fishing (see p291), while tarpon and snook can be hooked from the shore.

⓲ Pavones

Road Map B5. 7 miles (12 km) S of Zancudo. ✈ 🚌 from Golfito. 🚤 water-taxi from Golfito.

Known in the surfing world for its consistent 0.5-mile (1-km) 3-minute break, this small fishing village has blossomed due to the influx of young surfers. The waves peak between April and October. Coconut palms lean over the beautiful, rocky coastline.

Environs
Marine turtles nest along the shore. At **Punta Banco**, 6 miles (10 km) south of Pavones, the local community participates in the Tiskita Foundation Sea Turtle Restoration Project, which has a nursery to raise baby turtles for release. Nearby, **Tiskita Lodge** (see p261) offers fabulous vistas from its hillside perch. This lodge is part of a fruit farm that lures a wealth of bird- and animal life. Guided hikes are offered into a private reserve, where waterfalls tumble through majestic rainforest.

Reserva Indígena Guaymí, 9 miles (14 km) south of Punta Banco, is the remote mountain home of the Guaymí. Visits are discouraged.

A surfer wading ashore at Pavones

Parque Nacional Isla del Coco

Named a National Park in 1978, the world's largest uninhabited island is a UNESCO World Heritage Site. Of volcanic origin, the 9-sq-mile (23-sq-km) island is a part of the Galapagos chain. Torrential rainfall feeds spectacular waterfalls that cascade to the sea, while dense premontane moist forest carpets the land. The fragile ecosystem protects endemic fauna such as the Pacific dwarf gecko and Cocos anole, as well as 70 endemic plant species. A highlight is the huge colonies of seabirds, including magnificent frigate birds, noddies, and white terns. With waters of astounding clarity, the island is a world-renowned dive site *(see p292)*.

VISITORS' CHECKLIST

Practical Information
310 miles (500 km) SW of mainland. ℹ 2256-7476 (Fundación Amigos de La Isla del Coco); Permit needed to step ashore, which dive operators can arrange. 🚢 Dive Operators: Undersea Hunter: 2228-6613; Okeanos Aggressor: *see p301*. 🖥 cocosisland.org 🖥 islacoco@ns.minae.co.cr (Ranger station).

Transport
🚢 with dive operators (a 36-hr journey).

Isla del Coco, the "Dinosaur Island" of *Jurassic Park*

Bahía Chatham
The main anchorage has etchings carved into the cliff-face by sailors. Many of these date back centuries.

Bahía Wafer is a safe haven for yachters. Enclosed by sheer cliffs – which surround the entire island – it has a dramatic setting.

Coral reefs around the island contain 18 coral species and more than 300 species of fish.

Punta Maria

Cerro Yglesias 2,110 ft

Cascada Yglesias

Río Genio

Isla Montagne

Isla del Coco

Pacific Ocean

Isla Juan Bautista

Bahía Yglesias

Isla Muela

Cabo Dampier

Isla Manuelita

Isla Pájara

Bahía Weston

Isla Cáscara

Bahía Chatham

Bahía Wafer

Punta Rodriguez

Islas Dos Amigos

Red-footed Boobies
Virtually unafraid, these seabirds allow humans to approach within fingertip distance. Birds endemic to the island include the Cocos cuckoo and Cocos finch.

Cerro Yglesias, the highest point, is accessed by a steep, muddy trail. The mountain is tipped with coniferous forest.

km 1
mile 1

Key
— Trail
▲ Peak

Hammerhead Sharks
Congregating in their hundreds, these sharks provide an exhilarating experience for scuba divers. Also drawn by the huge fish population around the island are white-tipped sharks.

For additional map symbols *see back flap*

TRAVELERS' NEEDS

WHERE TO STAY

Costa Rica has an excellent selection of accommodations covering the entire country, with a wide choice for every budget. Even the remotest corners have inexpensive *cabinas* (cabins). The country's forté is the wilderness nature lodge, many in extraordinary settings, where guests can often view wildlife without having to leave their hammocks. Also on offer are special-interest lodgings catering to a particular activity, such as surfing or sportfishing.

Hotels range from self-catering *apartotels* (apart-hotels) to world-class luxury resorts and boutique hotels, which reflect the individuality of their owners. Additionally, there is no shortage of budget backpacker hostels. Costa Rican hotels rarely use the star-grading system. Instead, the country has adopted the Certificate for Sustainable Tourism (CST) system, which grades hotels by their cultural and ecological sensitivity, such as level of energy efficiency.

Warm interiors of one of the suites at the upscale Four Seasons in Bahia Culebra *(see p256)*

Chain Hotels

International chains such as **Best Western**, **Choice Hotels**, and **Quality Inn** are well represented in the low- and mid-range brackets. **Occidental** and **Marriott** offer reliable service and quality, while **Four Seasons** represents the deluxe end. **Hilton Hotels & Resorts** offers several all-inclusive options, in which all meals, entertainment, and facilities are provided for a set room rate at its Fiesta beach resorts.

Room cleaning and linen changing on a daily basis, as well as private bathrooms with showers, are standard in most establishments, and all chain hotels have at least one restaurant and bar. However, visitors should be aware that standards among budget-oriented chain hotels vary considerably and may not conform to their equivalents in North America or Europe. The more expensive options

usually offer a gourmet restaurant, gym, and casino or nightclub, and sometimes a tour agency and boutique shops.

Boutique Hotels

Costa Rica is acclaimed for its range of intimate boutique hotels, which are characterized by a charming originality and hospitality. Ranging from upscale, family-run bed-and-

Capitán Suizo, one of Costa Rica's many boutique hotels *(see p258)*

breakfasts and architectural stunners in the midst of coffee plantations to beach hotels inspired by a Balinese aesthetic, these exquisite lodgings can be found throughout the country.

Most of the boutique hotels are the creation of foreign entrepreneurs with artistic vision, and most benefit from the owners' hands-on management. They are usually lower priced than many chain hotels of similar standard and are of excellent value. Many also offer gourmet dining, and often a spa.

Wilderness Lodges

Nature lovers can choose between more than 100 wilderness lodges in the country. The majority are located close to, or within, national parks and wildlife reserves, or otherwise offer immediate access to regions of natural beauty. Guided hikes and other wilderness-related activities are generally available at these lodges.

Accommodations range from basic to modestly upscale although all have a degree of rusticity in common. The focus is on the nature experience, rather than the amenities offered. Several lodges have attained international fame, and therefore it is advisable to book in advance. Many of the more simple lodges, including those located within indigenous reserves, are run by community cooperatives. These offer opportunities to

◄ Resort hotel's swimming pool area illuminated in the evening

...rcovado Adventures Tent Camp, featuring furnished tents *(see p260)*

...ppreciate local culture and ...xperience nature from the ...cal perspective. **Cooprena** ...a promotion and booking ...gent representing many ...uch ecolodges.

...udget Hotels

...he country has thousands ...f simple budget accommo-...ations called *cabinas*, which ...ater to the mass of Tico (Costa ...can) travelers and backpackers. ...sually the term refers to a ...ow of hotel rooms, but it is ...sed loosely and can cover a ...ariety of accommodation ...ypes. *Cabina* is at times used ...terchangeably with *albergue*, ...ospedaje, or *posada*, all three ...erms for "lodging." *Albergue* ...ormally refers to simple rural ...odges, and *hospedaje* and ...osada are usually akin to ...ed-and-breakfasts.

...It is acceptable to ask to ...spect rooms before taking ...em. Services and furnishings ...re minimal, and bathroom accoutrements are usually limited to soap and towels; it is advisable to carry one's own sink plug and wash cloth. Many cheaper *cabinas* require that guests share bathrooms. Be prepared for cold water only; where hot water is available, it is typically heated by inefficient electric elements. Guests may also be asked to dispose of toilet paper in a wastebasket to avoid blocking the toilet drain. Take a padlock, and check that doors and windows are secure and that there are no holes or cracks that can be used by Peeping Toms.

Several budget hotels operate as members of International Youth Hostel Federation (IYHF). Most are run to a very high standard and have clean, single-sex dormitories. Some also have co-ed dorms. **Hostelling International Costa Rica** is the representative of the IYHF in Costa Rica and can help make reservations for hostels all over the country.

Apartotels and Motels

Ticos favor *apartotels,* which are basic, self-catering apartments with kitchens or kitchenettes and a small living and dining room; they are usually offered on long-term rentals. Rarely do they have restaurants or other facilities. San José has a large number of *apartotels;* they are also found in other towns and the major beach resorts.

Motels should not be confused with their North American or European equivalents. Found across the nation, they are no-frills places of convenience used mainly by lovers and rented by the hour.

Colorful decor at boutique hotel Xandari in Alajuela *(see p253)*

Camping

Visitors can camp in many of the national parks and wildlife refuges, including at ranger stations, where water, toilets, and occasionally showers are usually available. Some ranger stations prepare meals by arrangement; if not, carry provisions. A mosquito net and waterproof tent are also essential items to carry.

Outside the reserves, camping facilities are few except at major beach resorts. On weekends and public holidays, Tico families flock to beaches, where they camp on the sands. Avoid this illegal practice and camp only at designated sites. Hammocks can be bought or rented and hung almost anywhere. Campers always need to beware of theft and should never leave items unguarded.

...asa de las Tías *(see p253)*, Escazú

Hotel Groups

Several local hotels form groups and market themselves jointly based on their similarities. Ten of the finest boutique hotels of the country form the **Small Distinctive Hotels of Costa Rica**. This group offers a distinctive ambience in their excellent accommodations, which are located in diverse regions ranging from the capital city to remote mountains and beaches. **Greentique Hotels** represents three top-quality, nature-based hotels that operate according to sustainable practices. Several Swiss- and German-owned hotels are marketed collectively under the **Charming & Nature Hotels of Costa Rica** umbrella.

Specialized Lodging

Many places cater for a specific activity. Several nature lodges, for instance, are dedicated exclusively to sportfishing and offer all-inclusive packages. Some are in remote locations accessible solely by boat. Other resorts specialize in scuba diving, and offer diving lessons for beginners. Budget-oriented "surf camps" are often found at Costa Rica's many beaches. Some are quite sophisticated and offer various options, from outdoor dormitories with hammocks to private air-conditioned rooms. There are also plenty of health-oriented

El Sano Banano Beach Hotel, part of Ylang Ylang Beach Resort *(see p255)*

hotels, which range from rustic lodges to luxurious yoga retreats.

Many tour operators offer specialist tours for those interested in a particular activity *(see p288)*. By far the largest focus is on nature tourism: packages usually include stays at wilderness lodges and pre-arranged hikes, birding, and similar nature excursions.

Booking

It is best to book a place to stay well ahead of time, particularly for dry season travel (December–April). This is especially true around Christmas, New Year, and Easter. Reservations are also recommended for travelers following a pre-planned route. Advance bookings for

cabinas are not as critical except during peak months.

Many hotels in Costa Rica have a reputation for not honoring reservations, and for not issuing refunds. It is, therefore, advisable to make reservations through a travel agency or tour operator. If making a booking yourself, never send the request by mail, as the postal service is unreliable. Instead, use the phone or fax, or book online using the hotel's website. If a deposit is required, pay by cred card. In all cases, ensure that a written confirmation of the reservation is sent to you.

Prices and Payments

Regardless of hotel type, prices will be higher in the dry season than in the wet season (May–November). The more expensive hotels usually charge an additional premium for the peak season, which is the Christmas–New Year holidays, plus Easter. Rates can also vary according to the type of room. Hotels that depend on business travelers often have reduced rates for weekends and long stays. Tour operators may also be able to offer special deals. Many hotels offer discount schemes, such as special rates for surfers. A 16.39 percent tax is added to lodgings in tourist hotels. This is not always included in the advertised rate so check

The magnificent pool at Hotel Villa Caletas *(see p255)*, in Playa Herradurra

The tranquil Florblanca Resort set amid lush greenery, Malpaís *(see p255)*

when booking. Traveler's checks and credit cards are accepted in most hotels, with the exception of budget hotels, which usually only accept cash. Most places accept payment in US dollars.

Tipping

It is customary to leave a *propina* (tip) for the hotel staff at the end of the stay. The amount will depend on the type and quality of service, as well as the length of stay. Use your discretion. In general, it is normal to tip bellboys $1 and chambermaids $1 or more. Visitors should be aware that hotel wages among service staff in Costa Rica are often quite low and that tips in dollars often amount to a significant part of such workers' livelihoods.

Disabled Travelers

Only the more recently built hotels have access and purpose-built facilities for disabled travelers, including bathrooms with wheelchair access. Many wilderness lodges have level trails designed for wheelchairs. Hotel staff in all parts of Costa Rica will do everything they can to assist disabled travelers. **Shaka Beach Retreat**, in Malpaís, specializes in accommodation and surfing packages for disabled travelers.

Recommended Hotels

The lodging recommendations in this guide have been selected for their ambience, room and food quality, and/or good value. They span the spectrum across all price levels and types, from rustic, family-owned inns

and simple surfer retreats to wilderness nature lodges, deluxe beachfront resorts, and chic contemporary boutique hotels. Venues are listed by area, and within areas by price. Map references for hotels in San José refer to pages 132–3, while for the rest of Costa Rica, they refer to the road map at the end of the guide.

For the best of the best, look out for hotels featuring the DK Choice symbol. These establishments have been highlighted in recognition of an exceptional feature – a stunning location, notable architecture, magical ambience, exceptional facilities, or a combination of these. Most of these are very popular, so be sure to inquire regarding reservations well ahead of your visit.

DIRECTORY

Chain Hotels

Best Western
Tel 0800-011-0063, 1-800-780-7234.
W bestwestern.com

Choice Hotels
Tel 0800-011-0517, 1-877-424-6423.
W choicehotels.com

Four Seasons
Tel 2696-0000.
W fourseasons.com

Hilton Hotels & Resorts
Tel 800-445-8667, 1-800-774-1500. W hilton.com

Marriott
Tel 0800-052-1390, 1-888-236-2427.
W marriott.com

Occidental
Tel 2248-2323.
W occidentalhotels.com

Quality Inn
Tel 0800-011-0517, 1-877-424-6423.
W qualityinn.com

Wilderness Lodges

Cooprena
Tel 2290-8646.
W turismoruralcr.com

Budget Hotels

Hostelling International Costa Rica
Ave 8 and Calle 41, 1002 San José. Tel 2234-5486.
W hihostels.com

Hotel Groups

Charming & Nature Hotels of Costa Rica
W charmingnature hotels.com

Greentique Hotels
W greentique hotels.com

Small Distinctive Hotels of Costa Rica
Tel 2258-0150.
W distinctivehotels.com

Disabled Travelers

Shaka Beach Retreat
Tel 2640-1118.
W shakacostarica.com

Where to Stay

San José

CITY CENTER: Costa Rica Backpackers $
Budget   **Map** 2 F4
Ave 6, between Calles 21 & 25
Tel 2221-6191
Ⓦ costaricabackpackers.com
There are private rooms as well as dorms at this well-run hostel.

CITY CENTER: Kap's Place $
Budget   **Map** 2 E2
Calle 19, between Ave 11 & 13, Barrio Aranjuez
Tel 2221-1169
Ⓦ kapsplace.com
This cozy, colorful hotel is located in a peaceful residential area.

CITY CENTER: Pangea Hostel $
Budget   **Map** 1 C3
Ave 7 & Calle 3, Barrio Amón
Tel 2221-1992
Ⓦ hostelpangea.com
A popular backpackers' hostel, Pengea has its own airport shuttle service, a rooftop bar, and a pool.

CITY CENTER: Gran Hotel $$
Historical   **Map** 1 C4
Ave 2 & Calle 3
Tel 2221-4000
Ⓦ granhotelcostarica.com
Opened in 1928, this comfortable hotel has a restaurant and a spa.

CITY CENTER: Hotel Aurola Holiday Inn $$
Modern   **Map** 2 D3
Ave 5 & Calle 5
Tel 2523-1000
Ⓦ aurolahotels.com
There are stunning views from this high-rise hotel with a casino, gym, and spa.

CITY CENTER: Hotel Balmoral $$
Modern   **Map** 2 D3
Ave Central between Calles 7 & 9
Tel 2222-5022
Ⓦ balmoral.co.cr
Popular with business travelers, this hotel has a superb restaurant.

CITY CENTER: Hotel Don Carlos $$
Boutique   **Map** 2 D2
Calle 9 bis between Aves 7 & 9
Tel 2221-6707
Ⓦ doncarloshotel.com
A former presidential residence, this charming hotel is decorated with traditional arts and crafts.

CITY CENTER: Hotel Fleur de Lys $$
Boutique   **Map** 2 E2
Calle 13 between Aves 2 & 4
Tel 2223-1206
Ⓦ hotelfleurdelys.com
Choose from quaint, individually styled rooms in this beautiful converted mansion.

CITY CENTER: Hotel Kekoldi $$
Boutique   **Map** 2 D2
Ave 9 between Calle 5 & 7
Tel 2248-0804
Ⓦ kekoldi.com
A small Art Deco hotel, Kekoldi is in the historic Barrio Amón district.

CITY CENTER: Hotel Presidente $$
Modern   **Map** 2 D4
Ave Central between Calles 5 & 7
Tel 2010-0000
Ⓦ hotel-presidente.com
This is a tastefully furnished, minimalist hotel with a casino.

CITY CENTER: Hotel Santo Tomás $$
Boutique   **Map** 1 A2
Ave 7 between Calles 3 & 5
Tel 2255-0448
Ⓦ hotelsantotomas.com
In a converted 19th-century house, this hotel has a restaurant, garden, pool, and spa.

CITY CENTER: Hotel Villa Tournon $$
Modern   **Map** 2 D1
Ave 17 between Ave 15 & Calle 3
Tel 2233-6622
Ⓦ costarica-hotelvillatournon.com
An airy hotel with a piano bar, pool, and good business facilities.

CITY CENTER: Radisson Europa Hotel and Conference Center $$$
Modern   **Map** 1 C
Ave 17 & Autopista Braulio Carrillo
Tel 2010-6000
Ⓦ radisson.com
A popular conference venue, this comfortable hotel has two on-site restaurants and a fitness center.

EAST OF CITY CENTER: Hostel Toruma $
Budget   **Map** D
Ave Central between Calles 29/31
Tel 2234-8186
Ⓦ hosteltoruma.com
Clean dorms, as well as some private rooms, are offered in this charming former residence of a Costa Rican president.

EAST OF CITY CENTER: Hotel 1492 Jade y Oro $$
Boutique   **Map** D
Ave 1 2985, Calles 31/33
Tel 2225-3752
Ⓦ hotel1492.com
This family-run B&B on a quiet street offers personalized service and has a cozy lounge.

EAST OF CITY CENTER: Hotel Le Bergerac $$
Boutique   **Map** D
Calle 35 between Ave Central & 8, San Pedro
Tel 2234-7850
Ⓦ bergerachotel.com
Spacious wood-floored rooms, some with patios, can be found in this beautiful colonial house.

EAST OF CITY CENTER: Hotel Milvia $$
B&B   **Map** D
NE of Central Comercial M&N, San Pedro
Tel 2225-4543
Ⓦ hotelmilvia.com
In a 1930s plantation house, this cozy hotel has arty decor, period furnishings, and a tropical garden

EAST OF CITY CENTER: Boutique Hotel Jade $$$
Boutique   **Map** D
Calle 41, Barrio Dent
Tel 2224-2445
Ⓦ hotelboutiquejade.com
Near the university, this two-stor hotel has a cigar bar and a superb restaurant.

Façade of the Gran Hotel, in the heart of downtown San José

SCAZÚ: Casa de las Tías $$
B&B **Map** D3
*Calle León Cortes, 100 yards (100 m)
S of Mas X Menos*
Tel 2289-5517
W casadelastias.com
This Victorian-style cedarwood
house is set in lush gardens.

SCAZÚ: Costa Verde Inn $$
B&B **Map** D3
00 yards (200 m) S of Cementerio
Tel 2289-9509
W costaverdeinn.com
A delightful country inn with a
comfortable lounge and a garden.

SCAZÚ: Out of Bounds
Hotel & Tourist Center $$
Boutique **Map** D3
*Carretera John F. Kennedy, San Rafael
de Escazú*
Tel 2288-6762
W bedandbreakfastcr.com
The trendy Out of Bounds is
popular with adventure travelers.

SCAZÚ: Villa Escazú $$
B&B **Map** D3
*V of Banco Nacional, San Miguel
de Escazú*
Tel 2289-7971
W hotels.co.cr/villaescazu
A Swiss-style chalet, Villa Escazú
has log fires and lush gardens.

SCAZÚ: Alta Hotel $$$
Boutique **Map** D3
*Alto de la Paloma, 2 miles (3 km)
V of Escazú*
Tel 2282-4160
W thealtahotel.com
An upscale hilltop hotel, Alta has
an acclaimed restaurant.

SCAZÚ: Intercontinental
Real Hotel & Club Tower $$$
Luxury **Map** D3
*Autopista Prospero Fernández
& Blvd Camino Real*
Tel 2208-2100
W ihg.com
Amenities at this large, opulent
hotel include a pool, spa, fitness
center, and numerous restaurants.

WEST OF CITY CENTER: Gaudy's
Backpackers $
Budget **Map** D3
Ave 5 between Calles 36 & 38
Tel 2248-0086
W backpacker.co.cr
This friendly hostel is in a 1950s
modernist house in a quiet area.

WEST OF CITY CENTER:
Auténtico Hotel $$
Modern **Map** D3
Calle 40 & Avenida 7
Tel 2222-5266
W autentichotel.com
Close to Parque Sabana, this hotel
has chic decor and a lush garden.

Pool area of the deluxe Xandari boutique
hotel, Tacacori

WEST OF CITY CENTER: Best
Western Irazú Hotel & Casino $$
Modern **Map** D3
Ave 27, Barrio La Uruca
Tel 2290-9300
W bestwesternhotelirazu.com
This comfortable hotel is popular
with tour groups. It has airport
and downtown shuttle services.

WEST OF CITY CENTER: Crowne
Plaza Corobici $$
Modern **Map** D3
*Autopista General Cañas,
Sabana Norte*
Tel 2232-8122
W crowneplaza.com
A landmark hotel with dramatic
architecture, contemporary
furnishings, a spa, and superb
valley and mountain views.

WEST OF CITY CENTER: Hotel
Cacts $$
Budget **Map** D3
Ave 3 bis between Calles 28/30
Tel 2221-2928
W hotelcacts.com
A simple hotel, Cacts has quiet
rooms, some with shared
bathrooms. A good breakfast is
served on the rooftop terrace.

WEST OF CITY CENTER: Hotel
Parque del Lago $$
Modern **Map** D3
Paseo Colón between Calles 40 & 42
Tel 2247-2000
W parquedellago.com/index.php
A well-maintained, trendy hotel,
Parque del Lago has a delightful
bar-restaurant and is close to
Parque Sabana.

WEST OF CITY CENTER: Tryp
San José Sabana $$
Modern **Map** D3
Ave 3 between Calles 38 & 40
Tel 2547 2323
W tryphotels.com
Elegant decor and furnishings
feature in this high-rise hotel.
It has a great restaurant, a
nightclub, and a casino.

WEST OF CITY CENTER: Barceló
San José Palacio $$$
Modern **Map** D3
Autopista General Cañas
Tel 2220-2034
W barcelo.com
On the outskirts of the city, this
hillside hotel has large rooms, a
health club, and a pool.

DK Choice

WEST OF CITY CENTER: Hotel
Grano de Oro $$$
Boutique **Map** D3
Calle 30 and Ave 2
Tel 2255-3322
W hotelgranodeoro.com
Combining exquisite decor
and exemplary service with a
peaceful location, this popular
colonial-era mansion has eight
types of rooms, including a
sumptuous suite. Amenities
include rooftop Jacuzzis and a
splendid gourmet restaurant.

The Central
Highlands

ALAJUELA: Pura Vida Hotel $$
B&B **Map** D3
*Cruce de Tuetal Norte y Sur, 0.5 mile
(1 km) NW of Alajuela*
Tel 2430-2929
W puravidahotel.com
On a family-run former coffee
farm, this hotel consists of
cottages in hillside gardens. There
is a superb open-air restaurant.

ALAJUELA: Xandari $$$
Boutique **Map** D3
Tacacori, 3 miles (5 km) N of Alajuela
Tel 2443-2020
W xandari.com
A beautiful ridgetop hotel set in a
coffee estate, Xandari has sublime
valley views and colorful decor.

ATENAS: El Cafetal Inn $$
Boutique **Map** C3
*Santa Eulalia, 3 miles (5 km) N of
Atenas*
Tel 2446-5785
W cafetal.com
Rooms, cottages, and a bungalow
are offered at this country inn on
a coffee farm with nature trails.

BAJOS DEL TORO: Bosque del
Paz Lodge $$$
Wilderness lodge **Map** C3
9 miles (14 km) E of Zarcero
Tel 2234-6676
W bosquedepaz.com
This riverstone-and-timber lodge
is popular with birders. Meals are
included in the price. Advance
booking is essential.

For more information on types of hotels *see pp248–51*

Tree-lined entrance to the plantation-style Casa Turire, Turrialba

BAJOS DEL TORO: El Silencio Lodge & Spa $$$
Luxury   Map C3
10 miles (16 km) E of Zarcero
Tel *2761-0301*
[w] elsilenciolodge.com
Surrounded by rainforest, this ecofriendly lodge has spacious cabins, a spa, and gourmet cuisine.

EL ROSARIO DEL NARANJO: Vista del Valle $$
Luxury   Map C3
Calle Indio
Tel *2450-0800*
[w] vistadelvalle.com
Japanese-style cottages and condo-villas are offered at this coffee estate atop a canyon rim.

HEREDIA: Hotel Bougainvillea $$
Modern   Map D3
Santo Domingo de Heredia, 2 miles (3 km) E of Heredia
Tel *2244-1414*
[w] hb.co.cr
Set in tropical gardens, this hotel is adorned with modern art.

DK Choice

HEREDIA: Finca Rosa Blanca Coffee Plantation & Inn $$$
Boutique   Map D3
Santa Barbara de Heredia, 4 miles (6 km) NW of Heredia
Tel *2269-9392*
[w] fincarosablanca.com
This delightful family-run hotel has architecture inspired by Antoni Gaudí and individually decorated rooms with themed murals. Horseback rides and a guided tour of the estate's coffee farm are offered. There is a gourmet restaurant and a spa.

LA GARITA: Hotel La Rosa de América $$
Budget   Map C3
Barrio San José, 3 miles (5 km) W of Alajuela
Tel *2433-2741*
[w] larosadeamerica.com
Small cabins are set amid gardens at this cozy hotel.

MONTE DE LA CRUZ: Hotel Chalet Tirol $$$
Wilderness lodge   Map D3
6 miles (10 km) NE of Heredia
Tel *2267-6222*
[w] hotelchaleteltirol.com
Rustic cottages, modern rooms, and fine dining are offered in this Alpine-style hotel amid pine trees.

OROSI: Orosi Lodge $$
Budget   Map D3
200 yards (200 m) S of the plaza
Tel *2533-3578*
[w] orosilodge.com
This small colonial-style hotel has an open-air café offering free Wi-Fi.

OROSI: Rancho Río Perlas Spa & Resort $$
Modern   Map D3
1 mile (1.6 km) W of Orosi
Tel *2533-3341*
[w] hotelrioperlascr.com
In a secluded valley, this resort in lush gardens resembles a village with a chapel.

POÁSITO: Siempre Verde Bed & Breakfast $$
Budget   Map D3
Doka Estate, 7 miles (11 km) N of Alajuela
Tel *2449-5562*
[w] siempreverdebandb.com
A friendly, simple B&B, Siempre Verde is in a peaceful setting amid coffee fields and lovely gardens.

SALSIPUEDES: Mirador de Quetzales $$
Budget   Map D3
Km 80 on the Pan-Am Hwy
Tel *2381-8456*
[w] elmiradordequetzales.com
Spot quetzals from this rustic mountain lodge with cozy cabins.

SAN ANTONIO DE BELÉN: Costa Rica Marriott $$$
Luxury   Map D3
Ribera de Belén, 1 mile (1.6 km) E of San Antonio de Belén
Tel *2298-0000*
[w] marriott.com
Amid coffee fields, this sumptuous hotel's amenities include shops.

SAN GERARDO DE DOTA: Trogon Lodge $
Wilderness lodge   Map D
5 miles (8 km) W of the Pan-Am Hwy
Tel *2293-8181*
[w] trogonlodge.com
This wooden riverside lodge in a lush valley offers trout fishing.

SAN GERARDO DE DOTA: Dantica Lodge & Gallery $$
Luxury   Map D
3 miles (5 km) W of Pan-Am Hwy
Tel *2740-1067*
[w] dantica.com
Colonial-themed cabins with hip decor, forest views, and a gourmet restaurant feature here

SAN RAMÓN: Villablanca Cloud Forest Hotel $$
Luxury   Map C
Los Angeles , 7 miles (12 km) N of San Ramón
Tel *2461-3800*
[w] villablanca-costarica.com
This farmstead has cottages, a spa, nature trails, and gourmet dining

SANTA ANA: Aloft $$
Luxury   Map D
Forum 2 Business Park, Lindora
Tel *2205-3535*
[w] starwoodhotels.com
Neon decor and high-tech amenities abound at this hotel.

TURRIALBA: Volcán Turrialba Lodge $
Wilderness lodge   Map E
12 miles (19 km) NW of Turrialba
Tel *2273-4335*
[w] volcanturrialbalodge.com
A 4WD vehicle is needed to access this high-mountain lodge, perfect for horseback rides and hiking.

TURRIALBA: Hotel Casa Turire $$$
Boutique   Map E
Hacienda Atirro, 5 miles (8 km) SE of Turrialba
Tel *2531-1111*
[w] hotelcasaturire.com
This deluxe plantation-style hotel is on the shores of Lake Angostura

VARA BLANCA: Peace Lodge $$$
Boutique   Map D3
Montaña Azul, 15 miles (24 km) N of Alajuela
Tel *2482-2720*
[w] waterfallgardens.com
A hillside lodge with dramatic furnishings and huge bathrooms

VARA BLANCA: Poás Volcano Lodge $$$
Boutique   Map A2
14 miles (22 km) N of Alajuela
Tel *2482-2194*
[w] poasvolcanolodge.com
Antiques and hip furnishings decorate this mountaintop lodge

The Central Pacific and Southern Nicoya

JACÓ: Hotel Poseidon $$
Budget   Map C4
Calle Bohío
Tel 2643-1642
w hotel-poseidon.com
This modestly furnished hotel has a small pool and a fine restaurant.

JACÓ: Hotel Club del Mar $$$
Luxury   Map C4
Hwy 34, 1 mile (1.6 km) S of Jacó
Tel 2643-3194
w clubdelmarcostarica.com
Rooms, self-catering villas, a pool with a tapas bar, and watersports feature at this beachfront low-rise.

JACÓ: Vista Guapa Surf Camp $$$
Modern   Map C4
1 mile (1.6 km) NW of Jacó
Tel 2643-2830
w vistaguapa.com
Comfortable bungalows with ocean views, a communal TV lounge, and good surfing packages are offered here.

MALPAÍS: Malpaís Surf Camp & Resort $
Budget   Map B4
0.5 mile (0.8 km) S of Carmen
Tel 2640-0357
w malpaissurfcamp.com
Choose from camping, cabins, and bungalows at this well-run surfers' camp with a lively bar and plentiful activities.

MALPAÍS: Moana Lodge $$
Boutique   Map B4
2 miles (3 km) S of Carmen
Tel 2640-0230
w moanacostarica.com
African safari decor, log cabins, and lavish suites feature at this hotel set in tropical gardens.

MALPAÍS: Star Mountain Eco-Resort $$
Wilderness lodge   Map B4
1 mile (1.6 km) SE of Malpaís
Tel 2640-0101
w starmountaineco.com
Surrounded by a forest, this family-run ecolodge has an open-air restaurant.

MALPAÍS: Florblanca Resort $$$
Luxury   Map B4
Playa Santa Teresa, 3 miles (5 km) N of Malpaís
Tel 2640-0232
w florblanca.com
Spacious villas and a gourmet restaurant can be found at this serene beachfront resort.

MALPAÍS: Hotel Milarepa $$$
Modern   Map B4
Playa Santa Teresa, 3 miles (5 km) N of Malpaís
Tel 2640-0023
w milarepahotel.com
The Asian-inspired villas here have showers partly open to the sky. There is a gourmet restaurant.

MANUEL ANTONIO: Vista Serena Hostel $
Budget   Map D4
2 miles (3 km) SE of Quepos
Tel 2777-5162
w vistaserena.com
This spotless hostel offers lovely ocean views, an Internet café, a TV lounge, and hammocks.

MANUEL ANTONIO: Hotel Mono Azul $$
Modern   Map D4
1 mile (1.6 km) SE of Quepos
Tel 2777-2572
w hotelmonoazul.com
Well-equipped rooms, an airy restaurant, and three swimming pools, feature at this homey, ecoconscious hotel.

MANUEL ANTONIO: Hotel Si Como No Resort $$$
Luxury   Map D4
3 miles (5 km) S of Quepos
Tel 2777-0777
w sicomono.com
A range of delightful rooms, a spa, two restaurants, a cinema, and two pools are to be enjoyed at this ecofriendly hotel.

MANUEL ANTONIO: Makanda by the Sea $$$
Boutique   Map D4
3 miles (5 km) S of Quepos
Tel 2777-0442
w makanda.com
These spacious Japanese-style villas offer forest and ocean views. There is an open-air restaurant.

MONTEZUMA: Ylang Ylang Beach Resort $$$
Luxury   Map B3
Playa Grande, 0.5 miles (1 km) E of Montezuma
Tel 2642-0636
w ylangylangbeachresort.com
A romantic resort, Ylang Ylang is set in palm-shaded gardens accessed by a beach walk.

PLAYA ESTERILLOS: Alma de Pacífico $$$
Boutique   Map C4
Esterillos Este, 10 miles (16 km) SE of Jacó
Tel 2778-7070
w almadelpacifico.com
Gorgeous contemporary villas are set in gardens adorned with art and sculptures at this

beachside hotel. There is an excellent open-air restaurant and bar, a pool, and a spa.

PLAYA HERMOSA: Cabinas Las Arenas $$
Budget   Map C4
Hwy 34, 1 mile (1.6 km) S of Jacó
Tel 8729-4532
w cabinaslasarenas.com
Popular with surfers, this beachfront guesthouse has wooden cabins and camping.

PLAYA HERMOSA: Terraza del Pacífico $$
Modern   Map C4
Hwy 34, 1 mile (1.6 km) S of Jacó
Tel 2643-6862
w terrazadelpacifico.com
This beachfront resort has modestly furnished rooms, a spa, and adult and kids' pools.

DK Choice

PLAYA HERRADURA: Hotel Villa Caletas $$$
Luxury   Map C3
2 miles (3 km) N of Playa Herradura
Tel 2637-0505
w hotelvillacaletas.com
With a sublime mountaintop location and stunning decor, this French-run hotel exudes grandeur. The junior suites have Jacuzzis, and full suites have their own gardens. There are two acclaimed restaurants and a full-service spa. Live concerts are held in the amphitheater set in the cliff-face.

PLAYA HERRADURA: Zephyr Palace $$$
Luxury   Map C3
2 miles (3 km) N of Playa Herradura
Tel 2630-3000
w zephyrpalace.com
Costa Rica's plushest hotel offers themed rooms such as African Safari, Ancient Egypt, and more.

Illuminated pool area of the luxurious Florblanca Resort, Malpaís

PUNTARENAS: Doubletree Resort by Hilton Puntarenas $$$
Luxury   Map C3
Playa Puntarenas
Tel *2663-0808*
w doubletree3.hilton.com
Popular with Costa Rican families, this lively resort offers activities, sports, and live entertainment.

QUEPOS: Wide Mouth Frog $
Budget   Map D4
100 yards (110 m) E of the bus station
Tel *2777-2798*
w widemouthfrog.org
This backpackers' hostel has good dorms and some private rooms.

SAVEGRE: Rafiki Safari Lodge $$$
Wilderness lodge   Map D4
19 miles (30 km) SE of Quepos
Tel *2777-2250*
w rafikisafari.com
Luxurious tents have their own bathrooms at this African-style lodge in a valley, backed by forested mountains.

TAMBOR: Tambor Tropical $$$
Luxury   Map B3
0.5 mile (1 km) W of the airstrip
Tel *2683-0011*
w tambortropical.com
The wooden villas are set in tranquil gardens at this modern resort hotel with spa facilities and yoga classes.

TAMBOR: Tango Mar Resort $$$
Luxury   Map B3
3 miles (5 km) SW of Tambor
Tel *2683-0001*
w tangomar.com
Rooms, cabins, and villas are offered at this cliffside resort overlooking a gorgeous beach.

Guanacaste and Northern Nicoya

BAHIA CULEBRA: Four Seasons Resort $$$
Luxury   Map A2
Punta Mala, 27 miles (43 km) W of Liberia
Tel *2696-0500*
w fourseasons.com/costarica
There are excellent facilities at this chain resort in a stunning location with a golf course and spa.

CAÑAS: Hacienda La Pacífica $$
Wilderness lodge   Map B2
2.5 miles (4 km) N of Cañas
Tel *2669-6050*
w pacificacr.com
A rustic ambience is combined with modern amenities at this hacienda hotel on a working cattle ranch and reforestation project.

Pool with a shady thatched bar at the Doubletree Resort by Hilton Puntarenas

ISLITA: Hotel Punta Islita $$$
Luxury   Map B3
10 miles (16 km) S of Carrillo
Tel *2231-6122*
w hotelpuntaislita.com
At the top of a hill, this romantic resort has an infinity pool, a beach club, and a gourmet restaurant.

LIBERIA: Best Western Hotel & Casino El Sitio $$
Modern   Map A2
Hwy 21 and Pan-Am Hwy
Tel *2666-1211*
w bestwestern.com
This chain hotel has spacious rooms set around a landscaped courtyard with pools.

LIBERIA: El Punto Bed & Breakfast $$
Boutique   Map A2
Pan-Am Hwy, 100 yards (100 m) S of Hwy 21
Tel *2665-2986*
w elpuntohotel.com
In a former schoolhouse, this charming B&B has colorful, minimalist decor.

MONTEVERDE: Arco Iris Lodge $
Budget   Map C2
Santa Elena, E of bus stop
Tel *2645-5067*
w arcoirislodge.com
Stone-and-timber cottages feature at this superbly run lodge.

DK Choice

MONTEVERDE: Monteverde Lodge & Gardens $$$
Wilderness lodge   Map C2
0.5 mile (1 km) SE of Santa Elena
Tel *2257-0766*
w monteverdelodge.com
Set in gardens at the edge of a cloud forest, this modern hotel offers spacious, luxuriously furnished rooms. The bar overlooks a family-size Jacuzzi, and there is an elegant restaurant. Operated by Costa Rica Expeditions, it specializes in birding and nature hikes.

NOSARA: Lagarta Lodge $$
Wilderness lodge   Map A3
Punta Nosara, 2 miles (3 km) S of airstrip
Tel *2289-8163*
w lagarta.com
Superb coastal vistas and comfortable rooms are offered at this Swiss-run hilltop hotel.

NOSARA: Nosara Suites $$
Boutique   Map A3
Beaches of Nosara, 4 miles (6 km) S of the airstrip
Tel *2682-0087*
w cafedeparis.net
Choose from five stylish minimalist villas, some with lofts.

NOSARA: Harmony Hotel $$$
Boutique   Map A3
Playa Guiones, Beaches of Nosara
Tel *2682-4114*
w harmonynosara.com
Next to the beach, this resort has colorful rooms and bungalows.

NOSARA: L'Acqua Viva Hotel & Spa $$$
Boutique   Map A3
Playa Guiones, Beaches of Nosara
Tel *2682-1087*
w lacquaviva.com
This Indonesian-themed resort has Oriental furnishings. Ask for a room away from the road.

PLAYA AVELLANAS: JW Marriott Guanacaste Resort & Spa $$$
Luxury   Map A2
Hacienda Pinilla, 3 miles (5 km) S of Tamarindo
Tel *2681-2000*
w marriott.com
With a championship golf course, this is a sumptuous beachfront resort and residential complex.

PLAYA CARRILLO: El Sueño Tropical $$
Modern   Map A3
1 mile (1.6 km) SE of Carrillo
Tel *2656-0151*
w elsuenotropical.info
A comfortable hotel with themed rooms and an open-air restaurant.

PLAYA CONCHAL: Westin Conchal Resort & Spa $$$
Luxury   **Map** A2
miles (3 km) SW of Flamingo
el 2654-3300
🌐 westinplayaconchal.com
orgeous rooms, a golf course,
atersports, and a nature reserve
ature at this huge resort.

PLAYA FLAMINGO: Mariner Inn $
udget   **Map** A2
y the marina
el 2654-4081
🌐 marinerinn.com
his small inn has modest rooms
nd a lively restaurant-bar.

PLAYA FLAMINGO: Flamingo arina Resort $$$
uxury   **Map** A2
top hill in central Playa Flamingo
el 2654-4141
🌐 flamingomarina.com/en
here is a dive shop and activity
enter on-site at this hillside hotel.

PLAYA GRANDE: Hotel Bula ula $$
Modern   **Map** A2
end of Playa Grande
el 2653-0975
🌐 hotelbulabula.com
ear the beach, this cozy hotel has
open-air restaurant and bar.

PLAYA GRANDE: Hotel Las ortugas $$
Modern   **Map** A2
end of Playa Grande
el 2653-0423
🌐 lastortugashotel.com
otel rooms, villas for rent, and
excellent restaurant comprise
his beachfront resort.

PLAYA HERMOSA: Hotel La inisterra $$
Modern   **Map** A2
of Main Rd, at the S end
el 2670-0227
🌐 lafinisterra.com
njoy chic rooms, fine dining, and
cean views at this hilltop hotel.

PLAYA HERMOSA: Hotel Bosque el Mar Playa Hermosa $$$
uxury   **Map** A2
of Main Rd, at the S end
el 2672-0046
🌐 hotelplayahermosa.com
his elegant beachfront hotel has
superb restaurant and a pool.

PLAYA HERMOSA: Villas del ueño $$$
uxury   **Map** A2
of Main Rd, at the S end
el 2672-0026
🌐 villadelsueno.com
ovely spacious rooms, self-
ontained villas, a gourmet
estaurant, and two pools are

set in landscaped grounds at
this hotel run by friendly
Canadian hosts.

PLAYA NEGRA: Café Playa Negra $
Budget   **Map** A3
200 yards (200 m) S of the soccer field
Tel 2652-9351
🌐 cafeplayanegra.com
This is a small, tastefully furnished
hotel with an excellent restaurant.

PLAYA OCOTAL: El Ocotal Beach Resort & Marina $$$
Luxury   **Map** A2
2 miles (3 km) SW of Playas del Coco
Tel 2670-0321
🌐 ocotalresort.com
With superb bay views, this
modern hilltop resort specializes
in scuba diving and sportfishing.

PLAYA OSTIONAL: Tree Tops Bed & Breakfast $$
B&B   **Map** A3
San Juanillo, 3 miles (5 km) N of
Ostional
Tel 2682-1334
🌐 costaricatreetopsinn.com
The friendly owners serve superb
gourmet meals at this rustic,
thatched home above a cove.

PLAYAS DEL COCO: Hotel Puerta del Sol $$
Boutique   **Map** A2
400 yards (400 m) SE of the plaza
Tel 2670-0195
🌐 lapuertadelsolcostarica.com
There is a superb restaurant at
this charming Italian-run hotel.

PLAYAS DEL COCO: Rancho Armadillo $$$
Boutique   **Map** A2
1 mile (1.6 km) SE of Playas del Coco
Tel 2670-0108
🌐 ranchoarmadillo.com
Rooms have open-air showers at
this tranquil hacienda-style hotel.

RINCÓN DE LA VIEJA: Aroma de Campo $$
B&B   **Map** B1
Curubandé, 11 miles (18 km) E of
Pan-Am Hwy
Tel 2665-0008
🌐 aromadecampo.com
Belgian owners run this Tuscan-
style hacienda hotel. Gourmet
meals are served on a patio.

RINCÓN DE LA VIEJA: Buena Vista Mountain Lodge $$
Wilderness lodge   **Map** B1
17 miles (27 km) NE of Liberia via
Cañas Dulces
Tel 2665-7759
🌐 buenavistalodgecr.com
Flanking the volcano, this
ecolodge and activity center set
on a ranch has stone-and-timber

cottages, four restaurants,
thermal pools, horseback riding,
a water slide, and a zipline.

RINCÓN DE LA VIEJA: Rincón de la Vieja Lodge $$
Wilderness lodge   **Map** B1
17 miles (27 km) NE of Liberia via
Curubandé
Tel 2666-2441
This simple eclolodge and
activity center has wooden
dorms and cabins.

RINCÓN DE LA VIEJA: Hacienda Lodge Guachipelín $$$
Wilderness lodge   **Map** B1
14 miles (22 km) NE of Liberia via
Curubandé
Tel 2666-8075
🌐 guachipelin.com
On a working cattle ranch, this
lodge offers comfortable rooms
and lots of activities.

SÁMARA: Flying Crocodile Lodge $$
Boutique   **Map** A3
Playa Buena Vista, 5 miles (8 km)
S of Sámara
Tel 2656-8048
🌐 flying-crocodile.com
The colorful rooms and cabins
here are infused with arty motifs.

SÁMARA: Hotel Casa del Mar $$
B&B   **Map** A3
Playa Sámara, 200 yards (200 m)
E of the soccer field
Tel 2656-0264
🌐 casadelmarsamara.net
This modest beachside hotel has
a tropical garden.

SÁMARA: The Logan $$$
Boutique   **Map** A3
300 yards (300 m) uphill from the
soccer field
Tel 2656-2435
🌐 thelogansamara.com
An ecoconscious venue, The
Logan has four chic condo-villas
facing a saltwater plunge pool.

Pool in the delightful grounds of the
Rancho Armadillo, Playas del Coco

For more information on types of hotels see pp248–51

Bungalow at the forest edge in Rancho Margot, Laguna de Arenal

SANTA CRUZ: Hotel La Calle de Alcala $$
Modern   Map A2
150 yards (50 m) NE of Plaza de los Mangos
Tel *2680-0000*
W hotellacalledealcala.com
This delightful hotel has an open-air bar-restaurant surrounding a courtyard pool.

TAMARINDO: Hostel La Botella de Leche $
Budget   Map A2
200 yards (200 m) SE of Pacific Park Condos
Tel *2653-2061*
W labotelladeleche.com
Run by an Argentinian owner, this exceptional backpackers' hostel offers surfing lessons.

TAMARINDO: Hotel Arco Iris $$
Boutique   Map A2
400 yards (400 m) S of Pacific Park Condos
Tel *2653-0330*   **Closed** *2 weeks Oct*
W hotelarcoiris.com
Simple rooms with stone-walled bathrooms feature at this good-value hotel with gourmet dining.

TAMARINDO: Cala Luna Hotel & Villas $$$
Luxury   Map A2
Playa Langosta, 0.5 mile (1 km) W of Pacific Park Condos
Tel *2653-0214*
W calaluna.com
Villas have private terraces and pools at this beach resort.

TAMARINDO: Capitán Suizo $$$
Luxury   Map A2
Playa Langosta, 0.5 mile (1 km) W of Pacific Park Condos
Tel *2653-0075*
W hotelcapitansuizo.com
Spacious rooms and villas comprise this low-rise beach resort in lush gardens with a freeform pool.

TAMARINDO: Sueño del Mar Bed & Breakfast $$$
Boutique   Map A2
Playa Langosta, 0.5 mile (1 km) W of Pacific Park Condos
Tel *2653-0284*
W sueno-del-mar.com
Exuding romance and refined comfort, this gracious B&B has Colonial-style decor. Delicious breakfasts are served on the patio.

The Northern Zone

BIJAGUA: Celeste Mountain Lodge $$$
Boutique   Map B2
3 miles (5 km) NE of Bijagua
Tel *2278-6628*
W celestemountainlodge.com
Rooms have volcano views and dramatic minimalist decor at this French-run ecolodge. There is an open-air restaurant.

LA FORTUNA: Hostel Backpackers $
Budget   Map C2
200 yards (200 m) S of the plaza
Tel *2479-9129*
W hostelbackpackerslafortuna.com
Clean and efficient, with a pool and Wi-Fi zone, this is the best backpackers' option in town.

LA VIRGEN DE SARAPIQUI: SarapiquíS Rainforest Lodge $$
Wilderness lodge   Map D2
N of La Virgen de Sarapiquí
Tel *2761-1004*
W sarapiquis.org
Abutting a forest reserve, this pleasant, thatched ecohotel has two excellent restaurants.

LAGUNA DE ARENAL: Chalet Nicholas $$
B&B   Map B2
1 mile (1.6 km) W of Nuevo Arenal
Tel *2694-4041*
W chaletnicholas.com
This guesthouse has cozy rooms, organic meals, and forest trails.

DK Choice

LAGUNA DE ARENAL: Hacienda Toad Hall $$
Boutique   Map B2
5 miles (8 km) E of Nuevo Arenal
Tel *2692-8063*
W toadhallarenal.com
In a sublime setting with sweeping vistas of the lake, this hacienda-style hotel has romantic, individually styled rooms and suites adorned with antiques and fine art. A superb gift shop doubles as a café. Horseback rides are offered.

LAGUNA DE ARENAL: Lake Coter Eco-Lodge $
Wilderness lodge   Map B
4 miles (6 km) W of Nuevo Arenal
Tel *2289-6060*
W ecolodgecostarica.com
Duplex cabins here have volcano and lake views. The lodge is known for its wide-ranging activities, including kayaking.

LAGUNA DE ARENAL: Rancho Margot $
Wilderness lodge   Map B
1 mile (1.6 km) W of El Castillo
Tel *2479-7259*
W ranchomargot.com
A self-sustaining organic farm and ecolodge, Rancho Margot has dorms and bungalows at the forest edge.

LAGUNA DE ARENAL: Hotel La Mansion Inn $$
Luxury   Map B
5 miles (8 km) E of Nuevo Arenal
Tel *2692-8018*
W lamansionarenal.com
Hillside villas and spectacular lak views feature at this cozy hotel. Rates include horseback rides.

LAS HORQUETAS: Hacienda La Isla $
Boutique   Map D
2 miles (3 km) N of El Cruce
Tel *2764-2576*
W haciendalaisla.com
Rooms are charming and there is an open-air restaurant at this colonial hacienda.

LAS HORQUETAS: Rara Avis $$
Wilderness lodge   Map D
9 miles (14 km) W of Las Horquetas
Tel *2764-1111*
W rara-avis.com
Immerse yourself in tropical nature at this rustic lodge deep in montane rainforest. It offers a minimum two-day package with transport included.

MONTERREY: Leaves and Lizard Arenal Volcano Cabin Retreat $$
Wilderness lodge   Map C
Monterrey de Santo Domingo
Tel *2478-0023*
W leavesandlizards.com
The cabins and houses here boast volcano views. Nature trips are offered.

MUELLE: Tilajari Resort Hotel & Country Club $
Modern   Map C
12 miles (19 km) NW of Ciudad Quesada
Tel *2462-1212*
W tilajari.com
A range of sports facilities and activities are offered at this large resort hotel.

**ARQUE NACIONAL VOLCÁN
RENAL: Arenal Observatory
odge**
Wilderness lodge   Map C2
miles (8 km) SE of park entrance
el 2479-1070

W arenalobservatorylodge.com
verything from budget rooms to
llas plus guided hikes are offered
t this lodge close to the volcano.

**ARQUE NACIONAL VOLCÁN
RENAL: Arenal Nayara $$$**
uxury   Map C2
miles (8 km) W of La Fortuna
el 2479-1600

W arenalnayara.com
his hotel offers volcano views, an
cclaimed restaurant, and a spa.

**ARQUE NACIONAL VOLCÁN
RENAL: The Springs Resort
Spa $$$**
uxury   Map C2
miles (10 km) W of La Fortuna
el 2401-3313

W thespringscostarica.com
hermal springs, a wildlife refuge,
nd plush rooms are offered at
his dramatic six-story hotel.

**UERTO VIEJO DE SARAPIQUÍ:
elva Verde $$**
Wilderness lodge   Map D2
a Chilamate, 5 miles (8 km) W of
uerto Viejo
el 2766-6800

W selvaverde.com
ooms are spacious at this
colodge and reserve specializing
birding and nature trips.

**UERTO VIEJO DE SARAPIQUÍ:
a Selva Biological Station $$$**
Wilderness lodge   Map D2
miles (3 km) W of Puerto Viejo
el 2766-6565

W ots.ac.cr
un by the Organization of
ropical Studies, this lodge offers
uperb wildlife viewing.

he Caribbean

**ARRA DEL COLORADO: Silver
ing Lodge $$$**
Wilderness lodge   Map E2
/ of Barra del Colorado airstrip
el 8381-1403

W silverkinglodge.com
sportfishing lodge with spacious
abins linked by boardwalks.

AHUITA: Alby Lodge $$
&B   Map F3
00 yards (200 m) SE of bus stop
el 2755-0031

W albylodge.com
omantic, stilt-legged thatched
abins are set amid lawns here.
itchen facilities are available.

**CAHUITA: El Encanto Bed &
Breakfast Inn $$**
B&B   Map F3
Playa Negra, 0.5 (1 km) N of Cahuita
village
Tel 2755-0113

W elencantocahuita.com
In a Zen garden, this delightful
guesthouse has individually styled
rooms with excellent furnishings.

CAHUITA: Kelly Creek Cabins $$
Budget   Map F3
Next to Kelly Creek Ranger Station
Tel 2755-0007

W hotelkellycreek.com
This lovely Spanish-run
beachfront hotel has spacious,
sparsely furnished cabins with
verandas. There is no restaurant.

CAHUITA: Magellan Inn $$
B&B   Map F3
Playa Negra, 1.5 mile (2 km) E of
Cahuita village
Tel 2755-0035

W magellaninn.com
Close to the beach, this
romantic guesthouse is set in
lush landscaped grounds and
has simply furnished rooms.

PUERTO LIMÓN: Hotel Park $$
Budget   Map F3
Calle 1 and Avenida 3
Tel 2758-3476

W parkhotellimon.com
Simple rooms and a good
restaurant are offered at this
well-run hotel.

**PUERTO VIEJO DE TALAMANCA:
Rocking J's $**
Budget   Map F3
400 yards (400 m) E of the bus stop
on the road to Manzanillo
Tel 2750-0665

W rockingjs.com
A popular surfers' hostel, Rocking
J's has dorms, camping, and
private rooms. There is surfboard
and bicycle rental.

**PUERTO VIEJO DE TALAMANCA:
La Costa de Papito $$**
Luxury   Map F3
Playa Cocles, 1 mile (1.6 km) E of
Puerto Viejo
Tel 2750-0080

W lacostadepapito.com
Spacious wood cabins here are
surrounded by tropical gardens.
Breakfast is served on verandas.

**PUERTO VIEJO DE TALAMANCA:
Samasati Nature Retreat $$**
Wilderness lodge   Map F3
Hone Creek, 2 miles (3 km) NW of
Puerto Viejo
Tel 2224-1870

W samasati.com
This upscale yet rustic hotel
nestled in forested hills specializes
in yoga and holistic practices.

**PUERTO VIEJO DE TALAMANCA:
Le Caméléon Boutique
Resort $$$**
Boutique   Map F3
Playa Cocles, 1 mile (1.6 km) E of
Puerto Viejo
Tel 2582-0140

W lecameleonhotel.com
Minimalist design, white decor, a
spa, and state-of-the-art amenities
feature at this chic hotel.

**RESERVA SELVA BANANITO:
Selva Bananito Lodge $$**
Wilderness lodge   Map F3
16 miles (26 km) SW of Puerto Limón
Tel 2253-8118

W selvabananito.com
Specializing in adventure activities,
this rustic lodge has stilt-legged
cabins. Access is by 4WD vehicle.

TORTUGUERO: Miss Junie's $$
Budget   Map E2
100 yards (100 m) N of public dock
Tel 2709-8102

W iguanaverdetours.com
Run by a lovely family, this simple
hotel serves Caribbean soul food.
The verandas have rocking chairs.

Entrance to the Arenal Nayara, Parque Nacional Volcán Arenal

For more information on types of hotels *see pp248–51*

**TORTUGUERO: Laguna
Lodge** $$$
Wilderness lodge Map E2
*1 mile (1.5 km) N of Tortuguero
village*
Tel *2709-8082*
 lagunatortuguero.com
Specializing in nature excursions,
this riverside ecolodge has
botanical and butterfly gardens
and an atmospheric restaurant.

DK Choice

**TORTUGUERO: Tortuga
Lodge & Gardens** $$$
Wilderness lodge Map E2
3 miles (5 km) N of village
Tel *2257-0766*
W tortugalodge.com
Rooms are spacious and
elegant at this well-run eco-
and sportfishing lodge with
lush gardens and a fleet of tour
boats. It has gourmet dining, a
romantic open-air lounge bar,
and a beautiful infinity pool.
Trails access the rainforest.

The Southern Zone

BAHÍA DRAKE: Finca Maresia $$
Boutique Map E5
1 mile (1.6 km) E of Agujitas
Tel *2775-0279*
W fincamaresia.com
This modernist hilltop hotel
surrounded by rainforest has
Japanese-inspired cabins.

**BAHÍA DRAKE: Águila de
Osa Inn** $$$
Wilderness lodge Map E5
1 mile (1.6 km) S of Agujitas
Tel *2296-2190*
W aguiladeosa.com
Lovely, airy cabins overlook the
bay. The lodge has a fleet of sport-
fishing and scuba diving vessels.
There is an open-air restaurant.

**BAHÍA DRAKE: Corcovado
Adventures Tent Camp** $$$
Wilderness lodge Map E5
*Playa Caletas, 3 miles (5 km) SW of
Agujitas*
Tel *8384-1679*
W corcovado.com
Safari-style tents have shared
bathrooms. Rates include meals.

**BAHÍA DRAKE: La Paloma
Lodge** $$$
Luxury Map E5
*Playa Cocalito, 1 mile (1.6 km) S of
Agujitas*
Tel *2293-7502*
W lapalomalodge.com
Cabins have sunset views at this
clifftop lodge in lush grounds.

**CABO MATAPALO: Bosque del
Cabo** $$$
Wilderness lodge Map A5
12 miles (19 km) S of Puerto Jiménez
Tel *2735-5206*
W bosquedelcabo.com
Set in rainforest, this hotel has
ocean views. Rates include meals.

CABO MATAPALO: Lapa Ríos $$$
Wilderness lodge Map A5
9 miles (14 km) S of Puerto Jiménez
Tel *2735-5281*
W laparios.com
Wildlife viewing and gourmet
fare are highlights at this lodge
with bamboo bungalows.

CARATE: Lookout Inn $$$
Wilderness lodge Map A5
0.5 miles (1 km) E of Carate
Tel *2735-5431*
W lookout-inn.com
A hillside hotel with rooms, beach
bungalows, and jungle cabins.

CARATE: Luna Lodge $$$
Wilderness lodge Map A5
0.5 miles (1 km) N of Carate
Tel *8380-5036*
W lunalodge.com
Tents and thatched cabins are
offered here. Meals are included.

CIUDAD NEILY: Hotel Andrea
Budget Map B4/F
50 yards (50 m) W of bus station
Tel *2783-3784*
W hotelandreacr.com
A colonial-style hotel, Andrea
has modern rooms and
an airy restaurant.

**DOMINICAL: Cabinas San
Clemente**
Budget Map D
50 yards (50 m) W of soccer field
Tel *2787-0026*
Rooms range from basic to air-
conditioned options at this
backpackers' beachfront hostel
with a popular bar-restaurant.

DOMINICAL: Hacienda Barú $
Wilderness lodge Map D
2 miles (3 km) N of Dominical
Tel *2787-0003*
W haciendabaru.com
Close to the beach, this wildlife
refuge lodge has simple cabins
and a wide range of activities.

DOMINICAL: Waterfall Villas $$
Boutique Map D
*Platanillo, 5 miles (8 km) E of
Dominical*
Tel *2787-8378*
W waterfallvillas.com
Rooms have bamboo decor and
waterfall views at this deluxe
family-run riverside lodge.

ESCALERAS: Necochea Inn $$
B&B Map D
4 miles (6 km) SE of Dominical
Tel *8872-5782*
W thenecocheainn.com
This delightful inn has individually
styled rooms and suites.

**GOLFITO: Hotel Centro Turístico
Samoa**
Budget Map B4/F
1 mile (1.6 km) N of Pueblo Civil
Tel *2775-0233*
W samoadelsur.com
Large rooms and open-air dining
feature at this waterfront hotel.

**GOLFITO: Banana Bay
Marina** $$
Boutique Map B4/F
1 mile (1.6 km) S of the plaza
Tel *2775-1111*
W bananabaymarina.com
Rooms face the gulf and marina at
this small hotel with lovely decor.

**LAS CRUCES: Las Cruces
Biological Station** $$
Wilderness lodge Map F
4 miles (6 km) S of San Vito
Tel *2773-4004*
W ots.ac.cr
In the Wilson Botanical Garden,
this biological research station
offers spacious and cozy cabins.

Japanese-style room at the Finca Maresia, Bahía Drake

...opical grounds of the Casa Corcovado ...ngle Lodge, Playa San Josecito

...JOCHAL: Finca Bavaria $$
...&B **Map** E4
...5 mile (1 km) E of Playa Ballena
...el 8355-4465
🌐 finca-bavaria.de
...ooms have ocean views at this
...eaceful inn in hilltop gardens.

**...JOCHAL: The Lookout
...t Turtle Beach** $$
...outique **Map** E4
...aya Tortuga, 0.5 mile (1 km) NW
...f Ojachal
...el 2786-5074
🌐 hotelcostarica.com
...n a tropical hillside, these lovely
...ungalows have ocean views.

**...ARQUE INTERNACIONAL LA
...MISTAD: Finca Anael** $
...ilderness lodge **Map** F4
...eserva Biológica Durika, 11 miles
...8 km) E of Buenos Aires
...el 2730-0657
🌐 durika.org
...ccess to this mountain farm with
...ustic cabins is by 4WD vehicle.

**...ARQUE INTERNACIONAL LA
...MISTAD: La Amistad Lodge** $$
...ilderness lodge **Map** F4
...as Mellizas, 17 miles (27 miles) NE of
...an Vito
...el 2228-0405
...his remote mountain coffee farm
...ffers simple rooms and cabins.

**...AVONES: La Ponderosa Beach
...Jungle Resort** $$$
...odern **Map** B5
... miles (3 km) S of Pavones, on the
...oad to Punta Banco
...el 2776-2076
🌐 laponderosapavones.com
...hoose from cabins, suites, and
...illas at this popular surfers' resort.

...AVONES: Tiskita Lodge $$$
...ilderness lodge **Map** B5
...unta Banco, 3 miles (5 km) S of
...avones
...el 2296-8125
🌐 tiskita.com
...ature trails and wildlife viewing
...re the highlights at this ecolodge.

**PIEDRAS BLANCAS: Esquinas
Rainforest Lodge** $$$
Wilderness lodge **Map** A4/E5
Las Gambas, 6 miles (10 km) NE of
Golfito
Tel 2741-8001
🌐 esquinaslodge.com
Guided hikes and kayak tours are
offered at this community-run
ecolodge with cozy rooms.

**PIEDRAS BLANCAS: Playa
Nicuesa Rainforest Lodge** $$$
Wilderness lodge **Map** A4/E5
Playa Nicuesa, 9 miles (14 km) NW of
Golfito
Tel 2222-0704
🌐 nicuesalodge.com
Rooms have canopied beds and
garden showers at this upscale
waterfront ecolodge backed by
rainforest. Access is by boat.

**PLAYA PLATANARES: Iguana
Lodge** $$$
Luxury **Map** A4/E5
2 miles (3 km) E of Puerto Jiménez
Tel 8848-0752
🌐 iguanalodge.com
This hotel has rooms, bungalows
with garden showers, a gourmet
restaurant, and yoga classes.

**PLAYA SAN JOSECITO: Casa
Corcovado Jungle Lodge** $$$
Luxury **Map** E5
8 miles (13 km) S of Bahía Drake
Tel 2256-3181
🌐 casacorcovado.com
Access to this jungle-themed
hotel with deluxe cabins is only
by boat. It offers gourmet meals.

**PUERTO JIMÉNEZ: Cabinas
Jiménez** $$
Budget **Map** A4/E5
100 yards (100 m) W of soccer field
Tel 2735-5090
🌐 cabinasjimenez.com
The delightful cabins with
comfortable rooms and
verandas overlook the gulf.

**SAN GERARDO DE RIVAS: Monte
Azul Boutique Hotel** $$$
Boutique **Map** E4
Chimirol de Rivas, 6 miles (10 km) E of
San Isidro
Tel 2742-5222
🌐 monteazulcr.com
Chic villas and superb cuisine are
offered at this mountain lodge
and artistic retreat in lush gardens.

**SAN GERARDO DE RIVAS: Río
Chirripó B&B Yoga Retreat** $$$
Wilderness lodge **Map** E4
8 miles (13 km) E of San Isidro
Tel 2742-5333
🌐 riochirripo.com
In a fabulous riverside location,
this lodge has rich decor, tasteful
furnishings, and yoga classes.

**SAN ISIDRO DE EL GENERAL:
Rancho La Botija** $$
B&B **Map** E4
2 miles (3 km) E of San Isidro
Tel 2770-2146
🌐 rancholabotija.com
On a coffee estate with an
archaeological site, this family-run
hotel has a restaurant and a pool.

UVITA: Tucan Hotel $
Budget **Map** E4
100 yards (100 m) E of Hwy 34
Tel 2743-8140
🌐 tucanhotel.com
This hostel has a communal
kitchen and laundry facilities.

DK Choice

UVITA: Kurà Design Villas $$$
Boutique **Map** E4
In the hills, 2.5 miles (4 km) NE
of Uvita
Tel 8448-5744
🌐 kuracostarica.com
Six minimalist Cubist villas with
floor-to-ceiling glass walls and
chic decor feature at this
mountaintop ecohotel. A huge
sundeck and open-walled
lounge bar offer spectacular
coastal vistas. There is an infinity
salt-water pool and a restaurant.
Access is by 4WD vehicle.

**UVITA: Las Terrazas de
Ballena** $$$
Boutique **Map** E4
0.75 mile (1 km) NE of Uvita
Tel 2743-8034
🌐 terrazasdeballena.com
Three cozy thatched cabins are
perched on a forested mountain.

UVITA: Oxygen Jungle Villas $$$
Boutique **Map** E4
In the hills, 2 miles (3 km) NE of Uvita
Tel 8322-4773
🌐 oxygenjunglevillas.com
Glass-walled villas with divine
furnishings offer a pampering
retreat at this couples-only
mountainside hotel.

ZANCUDO: Cabinas Sol y Mar $
Budget **Map** B4/F5
1 mile (1.6 km) S of Zancudo village
Tel 2776-0014
🌐 zancudo.com
On the beachfront, this is an
informal hotel with a popular
open-air restaurant.

ZANCUDO: Oceano $
Budget **Map** B4/F5
400 yards (400 m) S of Zancudo
village
Tel 2776-0921
🌐 oceanocabinas.com
This endearing inn on a black sand
beach has free bicycle hire.

For more information on types of hotels see pp248–51

WHERE TO EAT AND DRINK

Remarkably cosmopolitan, the restaurants in San José and tourist enclaves offer a wealth of dining options. These span the globe, from Peruvian to Indian, with French and Italian cuisine especially well represented. In the countryside, food is based on traditional staples – rice and beans, accompanied by pork or chicken and tropical vegetables. Regional variations are prevalent, especially along the nation's eastern seaboard, where Afro-Caribbean dishes are infused with coconut milk and spices. Hot spices are rarely used elsewhere in Costa Rica. Small snack shops, called *sodas*, are found throughout the country, as are fast-food chain outlets, both American and local. Roadside fruit stalls are ubiquitous, with fresh fruits being an important part of the local diet *(see p264)*. Some vegetarian restaurants exist in San José and other major cities, and most other establishments will feature at least one vegetarian dish.

Restaurants and Bars

The capital city offers by far the greatest choice of places to eat, with a variety of cuisines for every budget and taste. Many of the finest gourmet restaurants are in deluxe hotels. There are a number of internationally renowned eateries presided over by award-winning chefs. Most of these specialize in conventional international cuisine. Hotels usually have their own restaurants, which in wilderness areas may be the only places to eat in the vicinity. The cheapest places to eat local dishes are the family-run *sodas,* small snack counters serving fixed-price menus and *casados* (set lunches, often referred to as *plato del día*, *plato ejecutivo*, or *comida corrida*).

Working-class males visit *cantinas* – neighborhood bars – where *bocas (see p264)* are served. These bars can be quite rough and women will generally not feel comfortable in these places. Visitors should stick to recommended bars in urban areas. Hotel staff can advise on places to avoid.

Chain Restaurants

All the principal American fast-food chains are conspicuous in Costa Rica, including Burger King, KFC, Pizza Hut, and McDonald's. There are also several homegrown companies as well, such as Burguí and Rosti Pollo, which compete with their American counterparts.

The main cities have a good selection of chain cafés, which serve light snacks and sometimes inexpensive buffets. An excellent option is Spoons, found in cities in the Central Highlands – it offers a wide range of salads, sandwiches, and hot meals at low prices. Musmanni is a nationwide *panadería* (bakery) chain selling freshly baked breads, confectionery, and sandwiches. Mexican fare is the specialty of Antojitos, which has outlets around San José. Bagelman's features bagels, sandwiches, and breakfast specials, while Pops is the local ice-cream chain.

Local Eating Habits

For the most part, Ticos (Costa Ricans) follow North American eating habits, with some differences. The typical *desayuno* (breakfast) consists of *gallo pinto (see p264)* served with fresh fruit juice and milky coffee. Extended families usually come together on weekends for brunch. Many businesses close at noon for *almuerzo* (lunch), which might last as long as 2 hours. The *merienda* (mid-afternoon coffee break) is still popular. Most restaurants close by 11pm, as the local preference is for early dining. Ticos are leisurely in the dining, and often linger at the table after finishing their meal, which can be frustrating if the restaurant is full. Many eateries close on Sunday.

Ticos rarely invite friends and acquaintances to dine at home, and prefer to extend invitations to restaurants. They seldom arrive at an appointed hour, except for important business occasions, and it is considered rude to arrive on time if invited for *cena* (dinner in a private home).

Paying and Tipping

Fixed-price menus such as *casados* normally offer better value than their à la carte equivalents. At *sodas*, it is possible to have a wholesome cooked meal for around 2000 colones. In elegant restaurants,

Tables in the garden courtyard at Café Park, San José *(see p268)*

Sano Banano Village Restaurant & Café *(see p271)*, Montezuma

three-course dinner with wine might cost around 15,000 colones per person. *Sodas* have no tax – in other places, the prices shown on menus usually include a 13 percent sales tax. An additional 10 percent service charge is often automatically added to the bill. Feel free to challenge this charge if service has been poor, and tip extra only for exceptional service.

Credit cards are accepted by most restaurants in cities and major resorts, but expect to pay in cash in rural areas, small restaurants, and *sodas*. VISA is the widely accepted card, followed by MasterCard and American Express; few places take Diners Club or traveler's checks.

Food Hygiene

Food is normally of a high standard nationwide, and tap water in most regions is trustworthy. If in any doubt, it is worth taking precautions by drinking only bottled water, fruit juices, or processed drinks. Bottled water is sold in all restaurants, hotels, and supermarkets. In restaurants and bars, order drinks without ice *(sin hielo)*.

Salads, vegetables, and fruits pose little problem, except in the Caribbean, Puntarenas, and Golfito, where hygiene can be questionable. To play safe, avoid salads and uncooked vegetables, and peel all fruits, especially those bought from open-air markets

and urban fruit stalls. Across the nation, milk and dairy products are pasteurized and are no cause for concern. Take care to avoid undercooked shellfish, meat, and fish.

Children

Costa Ricans love children and most restaurants welcome them. High-chairs are usually available, and many restaurants offer child portions; some even have special kids' menus. Many eating places, especially fast-food outlets and rural roadside cafés, have children's playgrounds.

Alcohol

Restaurants are usually licensed to sell beers and spirits, including *guaro*, the popular alcohol of choice. The more elegant restaurants serve a variety of international wines, although outside the Central Highlands quality often suffers due to poor

storage. Sale of alcohol is not permitted during election periods and three days (Thu–Sat) before Easter.

Smoking

Smoking is banned in all public venues in Costa Rica, including bars and restaurants.

Recommended Restaurants

The restaurants in this guide have been selected for their ambience, food quality, and/or good value. They span the spectrum across all price levels and cuisine types, from no-frills bargain-priced cafés and simple beachfront shacks to sumptuous temples of fine dining.

Restaurants are listed by area, and within these areas by price. Map references for restaurants in San José refer to pages 132–3, while for the rest of Costa Rica, they refer to the road map at the end of the guide. Many restaurants at key tourist venues close during low season or for special events, so it is always wise to call ahead or consult a restaurant's website before visiting.

For the best of the best, look out for restaurants featuring the DK Choice symbol. These establishments have been highlighted in recognition of an exceptional feature – a celebrity chef, exquisite food, or an inviting atmosphere, for example. Most of these are exceptionally popular among local residents and visitors, so be sure to reserve ahead.

The kitchen of Perla de Osa in Iguana Lodge, Playa Platanares *(see p277)*

The Flavors of Costa Rica

At Costa Rica's *ferias de agricultores* (farmers' markets), stalls are piled with glistening fruit, including exotics such as guayaba, marañón, and papaya. Tomatoes, peppers, and squash add their own bouquets and hues, as does a potpourri of herbs and spices. Pasture-fed cattle provide beef and fresh milk, while poultry roams free until ready for the pot. The warm waters off Costa Rica's shores deliver fresh fish and crustaceans glistening with brine. Caribbean and Creole are the main culinary styles.

Ripe papayas

One of the many *sodas* (foodstalls) found all over Costa Rica

Caribbean Cuisine

Making the most of local spices, cuisine along Costa Rica's Atlantic seaboard bears the zesty imprimatur of Jamaica, thanks to the many islanders who settled in the region. The sea's fresh bounty, such as shrimp and lobster, finds its way into curries and stews enlivened with chilies, ginger, and Scotch bonnet peppers. In Tortuguero, green turtle has long been a favorite meat, popularly used in stews, along with mackerel. *Pargo* (red snapper) is often "jerked" – spiced up with mouth-searing peppers and grilled over coals.

The milk of the versatile coconut forms a base ingredient for both cooking and in cocktails, while providing invigorating refreshment when drunk fresh from the shell. Local fruits such as citrus, papaya, and guava are jellied and candied with sugar, coconut, and cocoa.

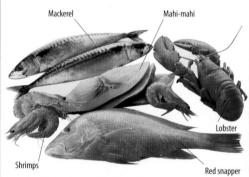
Mackerel

Mahi-mahi

Lobster

Shrimps

Red snapper

A selection of fresh seafood available in Costa Rica

Costa Rican Dishes and Specialties

Gallo pinto (fried rice and black beans) is the dish most associated with Costa Rica. It is commonly served as breakfast with scrambled eggs and slabs of local Monteverde cheese. At lunch it becomes *arroz con pollo*, with lightly seasoned stewed chicken or pork. This forms the basis of *casados* (set meals), served with vegetables such as carrots, yucca, cabbage, onions, *plátanos* (fried plantain), and a simple salad of lettuce, tomatoes, and hearts of palm. Rice dishes are enlivened by a splash of Salsa Lizano, a mildly spicy sauce made of vegetables. Countryfolk still favor traditional stews such as *sopa de mondongo*, made from tripe and vegetables, and a spicy meatball soup called *sopa de albóndigas*, from Guanacaste. Main meals are often preceded by *bocas*, tasty tidbits such as tortillas with cheese. Diners should be aware that any turtle eggs on offer may have been illegally harvested.

Scotch bonnet peppers

Ceviche is raw chunks of white fish marinated in citrus juice wit garlic, onion, and red and green peppers, served on crackers or lettuce leaves.

Well-stocked grocery store in San José

Guanacastecan Specialties

From the heartland of *comida criolla* (Creole cuisine), Guanacastecan fare revolves around *maíz* (sweet corn), introduced in pre-Columbian times by indigenous peoples. Succulent yellow sweet corn is eaten as a vegetable – cooked, boiled, or grilled – and, following ancient recipes, is ground into flour to form the base for tortilla and *tamale* dough. *Arroz* (rice) was brought by the Spanish from Asia. Today, it is a major crop in the lowlands and forms the chief accompaniment to the nation's cuisine, usually served alongside black beans, also grown in the lowlands. Brahma cattle graze the

pastures, producing highly prized steaks and ground beef. The seas off Nicoya are famous for game fish, such as

Vegetables at a *feria de agricultores* (farmers' market)

the flavorful dorado or mahi-mahi. Playas del Coco, Quepos, and Tamarindo are the main centers for sportfishing, while the port town of Puntarenas has a large shrimping and commercial fishing fleet.

On the Menu

Arreglados *(nationwide)*
Puff pastries filled with cheeses and/or meats.

Akee and codfish *(Caribbean)*.
Akee, blended with salted codfish and served with *callaloo* (similar to spinach) and fried dumplings called Johnny Cakes.

Cajetas *(nationwide)*.
A thick, nougat-like dessert made of coconut milk, sugar, orange peel, and other fruits.

Chorreadas *(Guanacaste)*.
Large corn tortillas served like pancakes and topped with *natilla* (sour cream).

Empanadas *(nationwide)*.
Turnover pastries filled with minced meat, potatoes, and onions, or cheese and beans.

Pan bon *(Caribbean)*.
Dark bread spiced with nutmeg and sweetened with caramelized sugar and candied fruits.

Rundown *(Caribbean)*.
Mackerel simmered in coconut milk with vegetables.

Tamales *(nationwide)*.
Steamed corn-dough pastries stuffed with minced beef and wrapped in banana leaves.

Filete de pescado grillé, grilled fillet of *corvina* (sea bass), is traditionally served with *ajo* (buttered garlic), rice, and mixed vegetables.

Olla de carne, a dish from Guanacaste, is a meat-and-vegetable stew with pumpkin-like chayote, corn, plantain, potatoes, and yuca.

Tres leches comprises layers of dense sponge cake soaked in condensed milk, evaporated milk, and cream, and topped with whipped cream.

Where to Eat and Drink

San José

CITY CENTER: Café de la Posada $
Argentinian   Map 2 E4
Calle 17 and Ave 2
Tel *2258-1027*
Run by Argentinians, the creative fare at this delightful café-restaurant includes *empanadas* (see p265), salads, quiches, and omelets, plus coffees and desserts.

CITY CENTER: Mama's Place $
Costa Rican   Map 1 B3
Calles Central/2 and Ave 1
Tel *2223-2270*   **Closed** *Sun*
A small diner run by an amiable Italian family, Mama's Place specializes in filling *casados*, pastas, and salads. It's a popular lunch spot among local workers.

CITY CENTER: Restaurante Casa China $
Chinese   Map 2 F3
Calle 25 and Aves 8/10
Tel *2257-8392*
Choose from a long list of dishes such as *dim sum* and Canton-style *congee* at this huge refectory-style restaurant in the Asociación China de Costa Rica.

CITY CENTER: Restaurante Vishnu $
Vegetarian   Map 1 C3
Calles 1/3 and Ave 1
Tel *2223-4434*
With several outlets throughout San José, this splendid budget option has an extensive menu and large portions. It focuses on health food, including vegetarian burgers, salads, fruit juices, and filling *casados*.

Kalú, a café, art gallery, and store in central San José

CITY CENTER: Spoon $
Costa Rican   Map 1 C3
Calles 5/7 and Ave Central
Tel *2217-2600*
This simple venue is popular for its good-value *casados* (see p264), submarine sandwiches, salads, and baked goods. There are outlets all over the city.

CITY CENTER: Balcón de Europa $$
Continental   Map 2 D3
Calle 9 and Aves Central/1
Tel *2221-4841*   **Closed** *Mon*
The French-born chef-owner at this informal restaurant with wood-paneled decor prepares hearty Continental dishes and pastas. Try the mixed plate with lasagna, tortellini, and ravioli.

CITY CENTER: Café Gourmet $$
International   Map 1 C4
Parque Mora Fernández, Ave 2
Tel *2221-4000*
The simple *arroz con pollo* (chicken with rice) is good value and filling, and there are excellent buffet options at this inviting patio restaurant in front of Teatro Nacional. There is live piano music.

CITY CENTER: Café Mundo $$
International   Map 2 E2
Ave 9 and Calle 15
Tel *2222-6190*   **Closed** *Sun*
Located in a handsome remodeled colonial mansion with patios and themed spaces, the menu here ranges from pastas and pizzas to surf 'n' turf. Be sure to leave room for dessert – try the tiramisu.

CITY CENTER: Kalú $$
International   Map 2 D2
Calle 7 and Ave 11, Barrio Amón
Tel *2221-2081*   **Closed** *Sun*
Part café, part art gallery, and part store, Kalú's avant-garde decor is matched by its sensational global fusion cuisine. Try the cream of squash soup and *gnocchi malbec*.

CITY CENTER: La Cocina de Leña $$
Costa Rican   Map 2 D1
Centro Comercial El Pueblo, Barrio Tournon
Tel *2256-5353*
Decorated in the style of a Costa Rican farmstead, this rustic restaurant serves fantastic traditional fare prepared in a wood-fired oven. Try the *olla de carne* (meat-and-vegetable) soup and cornmeal *tamales* (see p265) in plantain leaf.

CITY CENTER: La Criollita $
Costa Rican   Map 2 D
Calles 7/9 and Ave 7
Tel *2256-6511*   **Closed** *Su*
The menu in this lovely eatery with a stained-glass ceiling has Costa Rican and full American breakfasts, snack lunches, and simple, well-executed entrées. Try the garlic shrimp.

CITY CENTER: Tin Jo $
Oriental   Map 2 D
Calle 11 and Aves 6/8
Tel *2221-7605*
With a low-lit, dark ambience, this homey restaurant spans the Orient with its wide-ranging menu, offering great-value Chinese, Thai, Indonesian, Indian, and Japanese dishes.

DK Choice

CITY CENTER: La Esquina de Buenos Aires $$$
Argentinian   Map 2 D4
Calle 11 and Ave 6
Tel *2223-1909*
Re-creating the ambience of a Buenos Aires bodega, this warm and inviting restaurant is run by an Argentinian who delivers hearty meat dishes. Also on offer is splendid seafood, such as fillet of sole in blue cheese with boiled potatoes. The large wine list is heavy on Malbecs.

CITY CENTER: La Terrasse $$
French   Map 1 E
Ave 9 & Calle 15, Barrio Otoya
Tel *8939-8470*   **Closed** *Su*
Owned and run by native French chef Patricia Richter, this intimate restaurant with exquisite decor and terrace dining offers a changing menu. The beef stew provençal, when available, is a highlight.

CITY CENTER: Nuestra Tierra $$
Costa Rican   Map 1 E
Ave 2 and Calle 15
Tel *2258-6500*
Decorated to look like a farmstead, this rustic open-air restaurant serves creative dishes such as *corvina* (fish) in mango sauce. Staff in folkloric dress provide attentive service.

Samosas at Taj Mahal, Escazú

EAST OF CITY CENTER: Bagelmen's $
Café **Map** D3
Calle 33 and Ave 2
Tel 2212-1314
Bagelmen's specializes in sandwiches, bagels, and baked goods. The bagels are made to an original New York recipe. Breakfasts include *gallo pinto (see p.264)* along with many American favorites. There is free Wi-Fi.

EAST OF CITY CENTER: Café Ruiseñor $$
International **Map** D3
Calles 41/43 and Ave Central
Tel 2225-2562 **Closed** Sun
With indoor dining and a shaded patio, this airy brasserie is great for soups, salads, seafood (try the trout *veracruz*), and meat dishes. The cappuccinos and espressos are good too.

EAST OF CITY CENTER: Olio $$
Mediterranean **Map** D3
Calle 33, Aves 3/5, Barrio Escalante
Tel 2281-0541 **Closed** Sun
The expansive menu at this romantic, Bohemian tapas restaurant with brick walls and minimalist decor spans the Mediterranean from Spain to the Levantine. Try the Greek mezze plate or the chicken Vesuvio.

EAST OF CITY CENTER: Jürgen's Grill $$$
International **Map** D3
Boutique Hotel Jade, N of Autos Subaru Dealership, Barrio Dent
Tel 2283-2239 **Closed** Sun
A fashionable contemporary restaurant, Jürgen's Grill offers a creative French-influenced menu with attentive service. Delicacies include poached salmon with dill sauce, and grilled tilapia fish with Dijon mustard sauce. There is also a cigar lounge. No shorts, tank tops or flip flops are allowed.

ESCAZÚ: Giacomin $
Café **Map** D3
Calle del Llano, San Rafael de Escazú
Tel 2288-3381 **Closed** Sun
Specializing in homemade chocolates and gourmet coffees, this café also serves light snacks and gluten-free baked goods, including croissants and paninis. Terrace seating overlooks a landscaped garden.

ESCAZÚ: Chez Christophe $$
French **Map** D3
Plaza de la Paco
Tel 2224-1773 **Closed** Mon
This popular bakery serves omelets, quiches, and pastries. Try the fruit tarts and coffee éclairs. The French toast is to die for. The popular Sunday brunch includes delicious waffles.

ESCAZÚ: Taj Mahal $$
Indian **Map** D3
0.5 mile (1 km) W of Paco Plaza
Tel 2228-0980 **Closed** Mon
Costa Rica's only Indian restaurant, Taj Mahal serves biryanis, tandoor dishes, *tikka masala, naan* bread, and many vegetarian dishes. The rack of lamb is a specialty.

ESCAZÚ: L'ile de France $$$
French **Map** D3
Ave Escazú, 100 yards (100 m) E of CIMA Hospital
Tel 2289-7533
Chef Jean Claude conjures divine, refined dishes in a chic contemporary setting. Try the coq au vin, terrine of shrimp, or seafood bisque with cognac. There is a formal dress code.

ESCAZÚ: La Monastere $$$
French **Map** D3
4 miles (6 km) W of Escazú
Tel 2288-8515 **Closed** Sun
High above Escazú, this fashionable restaurant in a former chapel has a monastic theme; staff dress in habits. The menu includes *escargot*, and sea bass with crab, caviar, and champagne.

ESCAZÚ: La Luz $$$
International **Map** D3
The Alta Hotel, Alto de las Palomas, 2 miles (3 km) W of Escazú
Tel 2282-4160
An upscale restaurant with elegant contemporary decor in mock-Tudor style, La Luz serves gourmet nouvelle cuisine. Try fiery garlic prawns in tequila-limebutter sauce. It offers a great Sunday brunch

ESCAZÚ: Saga $$$
International **Map** D3
Ave Escazú, 100 yards (100 m) E of CIMA Hospital
Tel 2289-6615
This suave, modern restaurant serves gourmet fare such as deep-fried calamari and seafood risotto with coconut. For dessert, try the rice pudding with strawberries.

WEST OF CITY CENTER: Antojitos $
Mexican **Map** D3
W of Sabana Oeste, Rohrmoser
Tel 2231-5564
A lively, family-friendly restaurant, Antojitos serves traditional favorites and grilled meats. Sip on a delicious margarita while mariachis entertain you.

WEST OF CITY CENTER: Marisquería La Princesa Marina $
Seafood **Map** D3
Sabana Oeste, SW corner of Parque Sabana
Tel 2296-7667
For the perfect meal, try the ceviche appetizer followed by *corvina al ajillo* (garlic sea bass) at this simple canteen-style open-air restaurant.

WEST OF CITY CENTER: Sabor Nicaragüense $
Nicaraguan **Map** D3
Calle 20 and Aves Central/1
Tel 2248-2547
Good-value Nicaraguan and Costa Rican staples are served at this family-run restaurant. The *sopa de mondongois* (tripe and vegetable soup) is a must-try.

WEST OF CITY CENTER: Fogo de Brasil $$
Brazilian **Map** D3
Ave las Américas, Calles 40/42
Tel 2248-1111
A carnivore's delight, the staff in Brazilian dress deliver all-you-can-eat charcoal-broiled meats to the table. There is also a sushi buffet and a pasta bar. The *caipirinha* cocktails are delicious.

For more information on types of restaurants *see page 262–3*

WEST OF CITY CENTER:
La Bastille
French   **$$**
        Map D3
Calle 22 and Paseo Colón
Tel *2255-4994*   **Closed** *Sun*
The elegant, semi-formal
La Bastille serves *escargot*,
onion soup, and other highly
regarded French cuisine. Smart
dress is recommended.

WEST OF CITY CENTER:
Lubnan
Lebanese/Middle Eastern **Map** D3 **$$**
Calles 22/24 and Paseo Colón
Tel *2257-6071*   **Closed** *Mon*
With authentic Levantine dishes
such as falafel and *shish* kebabs,
this small, popular restaurant has
a party atmosphere. There is a
belly dancing show on Thursdays.

WEST OF CITY CENTER: Machu
Picchu
Peruvian   **$$**
        Map D3
Calle 32 and Aves 1/3
Tel *2283-3679*   **Closed** *Sun*
A popular seafood restaurant,
Machu Picchu serves quality
Peruvian dishes, from ceviche to
picante de mariscos seafood
casserole, best accompanied
with a pisco sour cocktail. The
decor features Peruvian art.
Service is excellent.

WEST OF CITY CENTER: Park
Café
International   **$$$**
        Map D3
Calle 44, Sabana Norte
Tel *2290-6324*   **Closed** *Sun & Mon*
Michelin-starred chef Richard
Neat delivers mouthwatering
dishes made with local
ingredients at this fine bistro
in the courtyard of an antique
shop. Reservations are essential.

WEST OF CITY CENTER:
Restaurante Grano de Oro **$$$**
French/Costa Rican   **Map** D3
*Hotel Grano de Oro, Calle 30 and
Aves 2/4*
Tel *2255-3322*
In San José's premier boutique
hotel, this elegant restaurant's
superb dishes blend French and
Costa Rican flavors. Delicacies
include poached mahi-mahi with
leeks and salmon soufflé. Service
is excellent.

WEST OF CITY CENTER: Sash **$$$**
Lebanese   **Map** D3
*Centro Comercial Plaza Mema,
Rohrmoser Blvd*
Tel *2230-1010*   **Closed** *Sun*
Try the ground garbanzo
hummus, baba ghanoush, and
seasoned lamb ribs at this
colorful restaurant with alcove
seating. There is a belly dancing
show on Friday evenings.

The Central Highlands

ALAJUELA: Xandari **$$$**
Continental/Costa Rican **Map** D3
Tacacori, 3 miles (5 km) N of Alajuela
Tel *2443-2020*
Set amid coffee plantations
with gorgeous views, this
romantic restaurant serves
healthy gourmet dishes made
with fresh local ingredients.
There is a good wine list.

CIUDAD CARIARI: Sakura **$$$**
Japanese   **Map** D3
*Wyndham Herradura Hotel, 0.5 mile
(1 km) SE of San Antonio de Belén*
Tel *2209-9800 (ext. 7060)*
Teppanyaki grills and an
oustanding sushi bar make up
the quality Japanese fare here.
Try the rainbow *maki maki* rolls.

HEREDIA: Inka Grill **$**
Peruvian   **Map** D3
*Centro Comercial Paseo de las Flores,
1 mile (1.5 km) SE of Heredia*
Tel *2560-1758*
A well-run chain restaurant,
Inka Grill provides classic,
mouthwatering dishes such
as mixed seafood ceviche and
other delights such as chili
chicken stew.

HEREDIA: Spoon **$**
International   **Map** D3
Plaza Heredia, Calle 9 and Ave 6
Tel *2263-2159*
Part of a countrywide long-
standing chain and popular
with university students, this
small restaurant-style café is
noted for its good-value *casados*,
salads, sandwiches, cakes, and
pastries such as strawberry-
chocolate tart.

Romantic, candle-lit dining room at
Xandari, Alajuela

HEREDIA: El Tigre Vestido **$**
International   **Map** D
*Finca Rosa Blanca Coffee Plantation
& Inn, Santa Barbara de Heredia,
4 miles (6 km) NW of Heredia*
Tel *2269-9392*
On a coffee estate, this restaurant
offers alfresco gourmet dining.
The menu includes Central
American dishes made from
estate-grown ingredients. Try the
pupusas (stuffed flat breads) and
eggplant lasagna.

DK Choice

HEREDIA: La Lluna
de Valencia
Spanish   **$$**
        Map D3
*San Pedro de Heredia, 2 miles
(3 km) NW of Heredia*
Tel *2269-6665* **Closed** *Mon–Wed;
mid-Dec–mid-Jan*
La Lluna's flamboyant Catalan
owner oversees the making of
superb paellas and other classic
dishes in the open kitchen of
this restaurant in a wooden,
rustic building. Try the octopus
in wine washed down with
sangria. There is live traditional
music during dinner.

HEREDIA: Restaurante Don
Prospero **$**
Costa Rican   **Map** D
*Café Britt, Santa Lucía, 0.5 mile
(1 km) N of Heredia*
Tel *2260-2748*
Part of the Café Britt coffee
processing site *(see p146)*, this
informal open-air restaurant
serves healthy dishes made using
organically grown vegetables, and
delicious desserts and coffees.

HEREDIA: Vitrales Bar &
Restaurant **$**
International   **Map** D
*Hotel Bougainvillea, 0.5 mile (1 km)
E of Santo Domingo de Heredia*
Tel *2244-1414*
Contemporary artworks adorn
the walls of this airy, good-value
restaurant, known for its
popular Sunday brunch. Dishes
include tuna carpaccio and
sautéed chicken with curry
sauce. The service is excellent.

LA GARITA: Fiesta del Maíz **$**
Costa Rican   **Map** C
*Hwy 3, 0.5 mile (1 km) W of
Pan-Am Hwy*
Tel *2487-5757*   **Closed** *Tue*
A no-frills roadside restaurant,
Fiesa del Maíz specializes in
traditional corn-based dishes,
such as *chorreadas* and *tamales*.
It is especially popular on
weekends, when *gallo pinto* is
on the menu.

GARITA: Restaurant Focaccia $$$
Italian   Map C3
Martino Resort and Spa
Tel 2433-8382   **Closed** Mon
Made using fresh vegetables
from the hotel's gardens, the
excellent fare at La Focaccia,
includes rosemary focaccia,
shrimp in white wine sauce, and
penne with salmon and vodka.

MONTE DE LA CRUZ: Baalbek Bar & Grill $$
Lebanese   Map D3
Los Angeles de San Rafael, 2 miles
(3 km) S of Monte de la Cruz
Tel 2267-6683   **Closed** Mon
This upscale Middle Eastern-
themed restaurant combines
superb countryside views with
top-class cuisine. The menu
features baba ghanoush and
other Mediterranean favorites.
There are hookahs in booths and
belly dancing on Friday nights.

MONTE DE LA CRUZ: Los Aroleses $$
French/Cost Rican   Map D3
6 miles (10 km) NE of Heredia
Tel 2267-6222
Located within the Hotel Chalet
Tirol, this wood-beamed alpine
restaurant offers cozy candlelit
dining. Try the shrimp in fennel
and Pernod.

OROSI: Orosi Lodge $
Café   Map D3
W of the Plaza
Tel 2533-3578   **Closed** Sun
In a small lodge, this charming
open-air eatery serves light
breakfasts, pizzas, snacks, homemade desserts, and ice cream
sundaes. It has Wi-Fi, as well as a
foosball table and a 1950s jukebox.

OROSI: Restaurante Coto $
Costa Rican   Map D3
In the N side of the Plaza
Tel 2533-3032
This traditional open-air
restaurant has a wood-fired oven.
The cheap casados ensure it
busy round the clock. The
menu includes excellent roast
chicken and pork dishes, garlic
sea bass, and local trout.

OROSI: La Casona del Cafetal $$
Costa Rican   Map D3
6 miles (10 km) E of Orosi Village
Tel 2577-1414
The beautiful lakeside setting on
a coffee plantation is the main
draw of this lovely restaurant. It
serves crêpes, soups, salads, and
traditional dishes such as tilapia
fish with mushrooms and trout
with pesto sauce. There is also an
all-you-can-eat Sunday buffet.

Cozy interior of the café at Orosi Lodge

POÁSITO: Steak House El Churrasco $$
Costa Rican   Map D3
At the junction for Vara Blanca
Tel 2482-2135   **Closed** Mon
Popular dishes at this rustic yet
elegant restaurant include grilled
tenderloin and tongue in tomato
sauce. Try the bean dip with
jalapeños, and the tiramisu.

SABANA REDONDO: Freddo Fresa $
Costa Rican   Map D3
Main Rd, Jaulares
Tel 2482-1495
The delicious homemade treats
at this rustic mountain lodge
with a log fire include potato
picadillo made with corn, sweet
red pepper, and coriander, as well
as fresh strawberry shakes.

SABANA REDONDO: Restaurante Jaulares $
Costa Rican   Map D3
12 miles (19 km) N of Alajuela
Tel 2482-2155
On the slopes of Volcán Poás and
resembling a rustic farmstead,
Jaulares serves traditional dishes,
steaks, and pizzas fired in a
wood-burning horno (oven).
There is live music on weekends.

SAN ANTONIO DE BELÉN: El Rodeo $$
Costa Rican   Map D3
4 miles (6 km) S of Alajuela
Tel 2293-3909
Equestrian paraphernalia lend
this timber-beamed restaurant
a unique ambience. Sample
authentic cuisine, such as corn
tortillas with sliced tongue and
tenderloin in jalapeño cream.

SAN GERARDO DE DOTA: Comida Típica Miriam $
Costa Rican   Map D4
2 miles (3 km) NE of San Gerardo
de Dota
Tel 2740-1049
Offering a real campesino (peasant)
experience, this delightful little
family-run restaurant with a cast-

iron stove, is located above
Dantica Lodge. It serves hearty
country fare, including fresh trout.

SAN GERARDO DE DOTA: Restaurant Le Tapir $$$
International   Map D4
3 miles (5 km) W of Pan-Am Hwy
Tel 2740-1067
Dantica Cloud Forest Lodge's
restaurant features glass walls, a
cozy cast-iron stove, and great
forest views. Highlights on the
menu include grilled zucchini
with tomato sauce, and trout
fillet with fresh herbs.

SAN JOSÉ DE LA MONTAÑA: Las Ardillas $$
Costa Rican/International Map D3
6 miles (10 km) N of Heredia
Tel 2266-0015
This wood-and-stone lodge's
rustic ambience is enhanced by a
huge hearth and its pinewood
setting. It specializes in local
roasted meat dishes prepared in
a wood-burning oven, as well as
many international favorites.

SAN PABLO DE LEÓN CORTÉS: Bar Restaurante Vaca Flaca $
Costa Rican   Map D3
25 miles (40 km) SE of San José
Tel 2546-3939
The decor at this rustic restaurant
along the Ruta de los Santos
includes cowhide seats, mounted
deer heads, and old rifles. Simple
traditional local dishes are on
the menu, as well as burgers
and sandwiches.

SAN RAMÓN: El Sendero $$
Costa Rican/Central
American   Map C3
Villablanca Cloud Forest Hotel
& Nature Reserve, El Silencio de
Los Angeles
Tel 2461-3800
El Sendero is worth the drive for
its traditional regional cuisine
and creative gourmet dishes, as
well as the view of the Arenal
volcano. The decor emphasizes
the hotel's hacienda heritage.

SANTA ANA: Bacchus $$$
French/Italian **Map** D3
*Casa Quitirrisí, 218 yards (200 m) N
of Montes Gas Station*
Tel 2282-5441 **Closed** Mon
In a refurbished century-old
house, this stylish bistro's menu
includes baked mushroom-and-
polenta ragout and pizza cooked
in a wood-fired oven. There is an
extensive wine list.

SANTA ANA: Product C $$$
Seafood **Map** D3
100 yards (100 m) N of Red Cross
Tel 2282-7767 **Closed** Mon
Sustainable dishes using fish
hand-caught in the Gulf of Nicoya
are served at this restaurant that
doubles as a fish market. Savor
carpaccio of trout with capers or
marinated octopus ceviche.

**SANTA MARÍA DE DOTA: Soda
La Casona de Sara** $
Costa Rican **Map** D3
*50 yards (50 m) E of Beneficio
Coopedota*
Tel 2541-2258
Overseen by a charming
matriarch, this simple family-run
restaurant serves hearty fare from
the open kitchen, where diners
peek into the simmering pots
and make their choice. Try the
fresh fruit *batidos* (shakes).

**SARCHÍ: Restaurante Las
Carretas** $
Costa Rican/International **Map** C3
*Adjacent to Fábrica de Carretas
Joaquín Chaverrí, Sarchí Sur*
Tel 2454-1633
At this homey restaurant with
rustic charm in a contemporary
setting, the extensive menu
ranges from soups, salads, and
burgers to Italian dishes and local
favorites. There is alfresco dining
in good weather.

**TURRIALBA: Hotel Casa
Turire** $$$
Costa Rican/International **Map** E3
*Hacienda Atirro, 5 miles (8 km)
SE of Turrialba*
Tel 2531-1111
In a classy hotel, this elegant
restaurant opens to a landscaped
courtyard with fountains. Sample
locally inspired dishes, followed
by delicious desserts and estate-
grown coffee.

**VARA BLANCA: Restaurante
Colbert** $$$
French/Costa Rican **Map** D3
14 miles (22 km) N of Alajuela
Tel 2482-2776
Crêpes, light snacks, and Costa
Rican cuisine *à la français*, such as
tilapia fish in tomato sauce are
served at this French-run café.

Elegant interior of the restaurant at Hotel Casa Turire, Turrialba

The Central Pacific and Southern Nicoya

DK Choice

JACÓ: Taco Bar $
International **Map** C4
*Behind Multicentro Costa Rica,
off Ave Pastor Díaz*
Tel 2643-0222
A casual, open-air establishment,
Taco Bar offers excellent-value
delicious and varied food, from
the tacos and all-you-can-eat
salad bar to Japanese-inspired
fare. Try the specialty fish tacos
with spicy coconut shrimp.
Service is good and there's a
lively ambience.

**JACÓ: Bar Restaurante
Esperanza** $$
International **Map** C4
Calle Bohío and Ave Pastro Díaz
Tel 2643-3326
This spacious tropical-themed
restaurant with a skylight, a large
bar, and shaded outdoor dining
serves dishes ranging from
gallo pinto to mussels in garlic
and olive oil.

**JACÓ: Clarita's Sports Bar &
Grill** $$
American **Map** C4
*Off Ave Pastor Díaz, at the N end
of Jacó*
Tel 2643-2615
A good choice for groups and
parties, this lively open-air
American-style bar-restaurant
serves all the favorites, from
omelets to burgers and burritos

**JACÓ: Hotel Poseidon Bar y
Restaurante** $$
International **Map** C4
Hotel Poseidon, Calle Bohío
Tel 2643-1642
Decorated with Oriental rugs
and wooden carvings, this small
restaurant is known for its hearty

breakfasts and creative fusion
fare, such as filet mignon with
Béarnaise-jalapeño sauce.

MALPAÍS: Rancho Ituana
Brazilian/International **Map**
*Playa Santa Teresa, 1 mile (1.6 km)
N of Carmen*
Tel 2640-0095
A colorful, laid-back restaurant,
Rancho Ituana's menu has dish
ranging from Indonesian to
Brazilian. There is a traditional
barbecue on Thursday evening
It is known for its full moon and
New Year parties.

**MALPAÍS: Zwart Art Studio
Café**
Café **Map**
*200 yards (200 m) N of soccer field,
Playa Santa Teresa*
Tel 2640-0011
The health-conscious menu at
this trendy, minimalist café
includes granola parfait,
wholewheat sandwiches, Gree
salad with feta, and fresh ahi
tuna. Finish with a decadent
warm brownie and ice cream.

MALPAÍS: Buenos Aires $$
International **Map**
Hotel Brisas del Mar, Santa Teresa
Tel 2640-0941 **Closed** Me
Enjoy gourmet fare at this
open-air hilltop restaurant.
The weekly changing menu
typically features calamari with
chipotle aioli appetizer, and sea
bass with capers and olives.
They also serve complimentary
pitta bread with dips.

**MALPAÍS: Nectar Bar &
Restaurante** $$
International **Map**
*Playa Santa Teresa, 3 miles (5 km)
N of Carmen*
Tel 2640-0232
Dine by candlelight at
Florbanca Resort's open-air
restaurant on gourmet nouvell
cuisine with Latin and Asian
influences. It also has excellent

h taco lunches and fish-of-
e-day specials, along with a
shi bar.

**ANUEL ANTONIO: Café
ilagro** $
entral American **Map** D4
miles (5 km) S of Quepos
2777-0794 **Closed** May–Nov:
n & all eves
eat sandwiches, pastries,
ffees, and teas are best
joyed on the rear patio at this
hall, charming roadside café. It
so has a souvenir store.

**ANUEL ANTONIO: Ronnie's
ace** $
sta Rican **Map** D4
mile (1.6 km) W of Marlintini's
2777-5120
rving traditional dishes and
afood specialties, this simple
en-air restaurant is on a hilltop
ith spectacular ocean vistas.
elicious sangria and desserts,
ich as caramelized pumpkin in
ne juice, are highlights.

**ANUEL ANTONIO:
arlintini's** $$
ternational **Map** D4
mile (1.6 km) S of Quepos, on the
ad to Manuel Antonio
2777-7474
n elevated roadside bar-
staurant, Marlintini's specializes
fresh seafood, but also has
ntinental favorites such as
rk chops and steaks. Its lively
ar features more than two
zen martini-based cocktails
us live music.

**ANUEL ANTONIO: Claro
ue Si** $$$
ternational **Map** D4
tel Si Como No Resort, 3 miles
km) S of Quepos
2777-0777
outhwatering health-conscious
afood dishes made using local
gredients with Caribbean and
ternational flavors are served
this fine-dining, open-air
staurant. Try the avocado salad,
d seafood and spinach ravioli.
ere is an extensive wine list.

ANUEL ANTONIO: La Luna $$$
ternational **Map** D4
ia Hotel, 2 miles (3 km) S of Quepos
2777-9797
e typical gourmet fusion
shes at this chic, contemporary
staurant with world-class
rvice include gorgonzola and
ndried tomato tart, tequila-
e scallops, and ginger and
nko-crusted tuna. It has
bulous ocean views and also
fers a good Sunday brunch and
oking classes with local chefs.

**MANUEL ANTONIO: Le
Papillon** $$$
International **Map** D4
Hotel La Mariposa, 3 miles (5 km)
S of Quepos
Tel 2777-0355
This acclaimed restaurant serves
French-inspired cuisine in a lovely
alfresco setting. Dishes range
from gallo pinto to chicken breast
in mustard and French wine. The
ocean views are breathtaking.

**MANUEL ANTONIO:
Restaurante Gato Negro** $$$
Mediterranean **Map** D4
Hotel Casitas Eclipse, 3 miles (5 km)
S of Quepos
Tel 2777-0408
The menu at this elegant
restaurant has a wide range of
homemade pastas, as well as an
extensive wine list. It offers a
warm, romantic ambience and
splendid views of Manuel
Antonio National Park.

**MANUEL ANTONIO: Sunspot
Poolside Bar & Grill** $$$
International **Map** D4
Makanda by the Sea, 3 miles (5 km)
S of Quepos
Tel 2777-0442 **Closed** Mon
Fresh ingredients are hallmarks
of the gourmet innovative
cuisine at this cozy open-air
restaurant with a romantic
poolside setting. Try the signature
blue cheese and bacon pizza.

MONTEZUMA: Bakery Café $
International **Map** B3
200 yards (200 m) E of the Village Sq
Tel 2642-0458 **Closed** Sun
Close to the main beach, this
simple café with alfresco dining
on a wooden deck is a great
choice for vegans and
vegetarians. It has organic
dishes, including delicious
banana breads and soy burgers.

**MONTEZUMA: El Sano Banano
Village Restaurante & Café** $
International **Map** B3
W side of the Plaza
Tel 2642-0638
Try the popular scrambled tofu
breakfast and curried veggies at
this natural-foods restaurant,
which also serves fresh fruit
juices and shakes. There are free
movie screenings every night.

**PLAYA HERRADURA: El Nuevo
Latino** $$
International **Map** C3
Los Sueños Marriott Ocean & Golf
Resort, 1 mile (1.6 km) W of Hwy 34
Tel 2630-9000
Seafood and gourmet Latin
fusion dishes are served at this
informal restaurant with lovely

pool views in the Marriott resort.
Try the lobster croquettes and
plantain-crusted red snapper.

**PLAYA HERRADURA: Steve
N' Lisa's Paradise Café** $$
International **Map** C3
1 mile (1.6 km) S of Parque Nacional
Carara
Tel 2637-0954
Perched beside Highway 32, this
long-standing and popular diner
offers a large menu of snacks and
international dishes. The menu
features excellent burgers, tuna
melt sandwiches, pastas,
seafood, and steaks.

**PLAYA HERRADURA: El Mirador
and El Anfiteatro** $$$
International **Map** C3
Hotel Villa Caletas, 2 miles (3 km)
N of Playa Herradura
Tel 2637 0505
Creative gourmet dishes are
served in a sublime mountaintop
setting, perfect for watching the
sunset. There is live music in the
classical amphitheater.

**PUNTARENAS: La Yunta
Steakhouse** $$
Steakhouse and Seafood **Map** C3
Paseo de los Turistas
Tel 2661-3216
This venerable two-story
wooden restaurant with a
shaded veranda overlooking the
Gulf specializes in grilled steaks,
plus seafood such as sea bass
with tropical fruit sauce.

QUEPOS: El Patio Café $
Central American **Map** D4
On the shorefront road
Tel 2777-4982
Popular with locals, this colorful
café serves excellent breakfasts,
ranging from granola with fruit
and yogurt to gallo pinto, as
well as homemade breads and
desserts, fruit shakes, and coffees.

Terrace dining area at El Anfiteatro, Hotel
Villa Caletas, Playa Herradura

For more information on types of restaurants see pages 262–3

QUEPOS: Dos Locos $$
Mexican   **Map** D4
Calle Central and Ave 5
Tel *2777-1526*
From *chimichangas* (deep-fried
burritos) and *flautas* (cylindrical
stuffed tortillas) to *quesadillas*,
Dos Locos offers all the classics,
as well as American breakfasts.
The lively decor plays on a cactus
and sombrero theme.

QUEPOS: El Gran Escape $$
International   **Map** D4
W of the bus station
Tel *2777-0395*   **Closed** *Tue*
The menu at this popular
restaurant in an old wooden
building features a wide variety
of dishes, from light snacks to
fresh seafood, steaks, and locally
inspired coconut chicken curry.

QUEPOS: Escalofrío $$
Italian   **Map** D4
Calle Central and Ave 5
Tel *2777-1902*   **Closed** *Mon*
Excellent pastas and pizzas
cooked in a wood-fired oven
are served at this family-friendly
restaurant. Try the sausage with
gorgonzola cheese and onions.
Leave room for delicious
homemade gelato.

**QUEPOS: Rainforest
Restaurant** $$
International   **Map** D4
*Hotel Mono Azul, 2 miles (3 km)
S of Quepos*
Tel *2777-1548*
The globe-spanning menu at
this hilltop hotel-restaurant has
good vegetarian options. Staples
include enchiladas, filet mignon,
pork chops, beef stroganoff, and
mahi-mahi dishes.

**TAMBOR: Restaurante
Arrecife** $$
International   **Map** B3
*Hotel Costa Coral, 1 mile (1.6 km)
W of the Airstrip*
Tel *2683-0105*
The extensive menu at this
restaurant with colorful
contemporary decor ranges

from light snacks and seafood
such as ceviche and *corvina* fish
with heart-of-palm sauce, to
burgers and chicken in orange
sauce. They also have karaoke.

Guanacaste and
Northern Nicoya

CAÑAS: Hacienda La Pacífica $$
International   **Map** B2
2.5 miles (4 km) N of Cañas
Tel *2669-6050*
In a historic hacienda, this
wonderful restaurant has a rustic
yesteryear ambience. Locally
grown organic rice accompanies
dishes such as jumbo garlic
shrimps and tenderloin pepper
steak. Bring mosquito repellent.

**CAÑAS: Restaurante Rincón
Corobicí** $$
Costa Rican   **Map** B2
*Pan-Am Hwy, 3 miles (5 km)
N of Cañas*
Tel *2669-6262*
The broad-ranging menu at this
multi-decked roadside restaurant
near the Río Corobicí features
local staples, including seafood.
Try the garlic sea bass and
delicious homemade lemonade.

ISLITA: 1492 Restaurante $$$
International   **Map** B3
*Hotel Punta Islita, 6 miles (10 km)
S of Carrillo*
Tel *2656-2020*
There are fabulous coastal vistas
from this romantic and elegant
gourmet restaurant. Local
ingredients are conjured
into mouthwatering dishes
influenced by Pacific Rim and
European tastes.

LIBERIA: Café Europa $$
German   **Map** A2
Hwy 21, 12 miles (19 km) W of Liberia
Tel *2668-1081*
This small roadside café-bakery
offers delicious pastries and
breads baked on site by the

German owner. Also available ar
burgers and German-inspired he
dishes such as breaded veal cutle

LIBERIA: Restaurante Jauja $
International   **Map** A
Ave Central and Calle 10
Tel *2665-2061*
This restaurant with rattan
furnishings and patio seating
offers a good fixed-price lunch
menu. Dinner specials include
dishes such as *dorado* (mahi-
mahi) with papaya sauce. Finish
with apple strudel with ice crea

DK Choice

**LIBERIA:
The Green House** $$$
International   **Map** A2
1 mile (1.5 km) W of Liberia
Tel *2665-5037*
With stunning glass-walled
minimalist architecture, this
restaurant serves delectable
gourmet fare, from tuna *tataki*
salad to tropical Thai-style fish
with curry coconut and onion.
It also offers great *huevos
rancheros* and pancake
breakfasts. There is a sushi bar
and live music on Friday nights.

MONTEVERDE: Café Cabure $
Argentinian   **Map** C
*Paseo de Estella, 2 miles (3 km) E of
Santa Elena*
Tel *2645-5020*   **Closed** *Su*
The eclectic menu at this café
and chocolate shop with terrace
seating offers salads and wraps,
plus chocolate-inspired dishes
and drinks. The shop sells divine
homemade chocolates and
flavored truffles. Wi-Fi is availabl

**MONTEVERDE: Garden
Restaurant** $$
Costa Rican/International **Map** C
*Monteverde Lodge, 1 mile (1.6 km)
SE of Santa Elena*
Tel *2645-5057*
Creative Costa Rican cuisine, suc
as shredded duck *empanadas*
and coconut and macadamia-
crusted sea bass, as well as goo
wines, feature at this restaurant
overlooking lush gardens. There
is a cozy bar with a hearth.

MONTEVERDE: Sofia $$
International   **Map** C
1 mile (1.6 km) E of Santa Elena
Tel *2645-7017*
An acclaimed fine-dining venue
Sofia combines Costa Rican
ingredients with global
inspirations to provide superb
fusion cuisine, such as tenderlo
with chipotle butter sauce and
chicken with guava reduction.

Alfresco dining area at Restaurante Jauja, Liberia

NOSARA: Luna Bar & Grill $$
International   Map A3
Playa Pelada, Beaches of Nosara
Tel *2682-0122*
This hip beachfront bar overlooks a cove and offers gourmet snacks such as sushi rolls and lentil soup. There are spectacular sunset views from the terrace, and world music to dance to.

NOSARA: Marlin Bill's $$
American   Map A3
*Beaches of Nosara, 4 miles (6 km)
S of the airstrip*
Tel *2682-0458*
This family-friendly open-air restaurant and bar serves classic favorites such as pork loin chops, blackened tuna salad, and key lime pie. Popular with expats, the bar has a large-screen TV for watching American football.

NOSARA: Pizzería Giardino Tropicale $$
Italian   Map A3
*Beaches of Nosara, 4 miles (6 km)
S of the airstrip*
Tel *2682-4000*
Known for its wood-fired pizzas, Giardino Tropicale also serves ravioli, spaghetti, and excellent seafood including carpaccio of sea bass. The charming rustic setting has shaded wooden decks.

NOSARA: Restaurante Vista del Paraíso $$$
International   Map A3
In the hills, 1 mile (1.6 km) E of Beaches of Nosara
Tel *2682-0637*   **Closed** *Sun*
The French-trained Texan chef at this small ridgetop restaurant with sensational coastal views prepares a diverse menu of dishes such as baked goat's cheese salad and Napoleon of beef tenderloin.

PLAYA CONCHAL: El Oasis $$
International   Map A2
Hotel Brasilito, NW corner of the plaza, Brasilito
Tel *2654-4596*
Close to the beach, this alfresco restaurant has a varied menu. Specialties include fish 'n' chips and "shrimp on the barbie." Warm croissants and *huevos rancheros* are part of the breakfast menu.

PLAYA FLAMINGO: Angelina's $$$
International   Map A2
*Centro Comercial La Plaza,
W of the Marina*
Tel *2654-4839*   **Closed** *Mon*
Local ingredients are used in the creative, globally inspired dishes at this stylish restaurant. Choose from gourmet pizzas, delicious fried calamari, seared ahi tuna, and oven-roasted pork tenderloin. There is a large wine list.

PLAYA FLAMINGO: Marie's Restaurante $$$
International   Map A2
*Centro Comercial La Plaza,
W of the Marina*
Tel *2654-4136*
A popular open-air restaurant with a thatched roof, Marie's specializes in hearty favorites ranging from fish 'n' chips to burritos. It has a wide choice of coffees as well as ice cream sundaes. It also offers dance lessons on Wednesday nights.

PLAYA GRANDE: Hotel Las Tortugas $$
International   Map A2
*W of El Mundo de la Tortuga,
N end of Playa Grande*
Tel *2653-0423*
Las Tortugas serves light meals such as burgers and salads, as well as steaks and seafood in a relaxed atmosphere with friendly service. For dessert, the apple pie and ice cream is a must-try.

PLAYA GRANDE: The Great Waltini $$$
International   Map A2
Hotel Bula Bula, S of El Mundo de la Tortuga, S end of Playa Grande
Tel *2653-0975*   **Closed** *Mon*
Snacks and gourmet dishes are served at this small restaurant with a shaded deck overlooking a garden. Try the delicious shrimp and crabcakes followed by duckling with red wine and raspberry reduction. There is an excellent cocktail list.

PLAYA HERMOSA: Ginger $$$
International   Map A2
Main road in village center
Tel *2672-0041*   **Closed** *Mon*
Run by Canadian chef Anne Hegney Frey, this chic contemporary restaurant is known for its striking minimalist design and fantastic tapas. Try the ginger rolls, fried calamari, or ginger ahi tuna.

PLAYA HERMOSA: Niromi Restaurant $$$
International   Map A2
Hotel Playa Hermosa, S end of Playa Hermosa
Tel *2672-0046*
An alfresco beachfront restaurant in an upscale hotel, Niromi serves gourmet dishes such as lamb chops in mint sauce and Costa Rican-style seafood such as coconut shrimp. It is set in a lovely garden amid Guanacaste trees and overlooks the beach.

Ginger, a contemporary tapas restaurant near Playa Hermosa

PLAYA HERMOSA: The Bistro $$$
International   Map A2
*Atop the hill, W of the Main Rd,
S end of Playa Hermosa*
Tel *2670-0227*
Refined French-inspired Costa Rican cuisine is served on a hilltop terrace at the restaurant in Hotel La Finisterra. Try the filet mignon with peppercorn sauce. There is sushi on Friday evenings.

PLAYA NEGRA: Café Playa Negra $
International   Map A3
S of Los Pargos Plaza
Tel *2652-9143*
At this small, charming café near the beach, the Peruvian owner-chef offers light dishes ranging from pancakes and French toast to ceviche, quiches, and pastas. Leave room for the delicious lemon pie. Wi-Fi is available.

PLAYA OCOTAL: Father Rooster Bar & Grill $$
International   Map A2
2 miles (3 km) W of Playas del Coco
Tel *2670-1246*
This rustic beach restaurant has a lively bar and a fun ambience. The menu focuses on bar staples such as burgers and *quesadillas*. The cocktails are delicious. Activities include volleyball.

PLAYA OSTIONAL: Tree Tops Bed & Breakfast $$$
International   Map A3
San Juanillo, 8.5 miles (14 km) NW of Nosara
Tel *2682-1334*
Three-course lunches and five-course dinners are served at this rustic B&B overlooking the ocean. The owner-chef conjures local ingredients into divine dishes such as red snapper with sherry and curry cream sauce.

For more information on types of restaurants *see pages 262–3*

PLAYAS DEL COCO: Andre's Beach Bar Restaurant $
Pizzeria   **Map** A2
SE corner of the soccer field
Tel 2670-2052   **Closed** *Mon*
This simple roadside canteen serves delicious thin-crust wood-fired pizzas at great prices, best enjoyed with an iced imperial beer, a cocktail or a fresh fruit smoothie. There is free Wi-Fi.

PLAYAS DEL COCO: Restaurante Sol y Luna $$
Italian   **Map** A2
Hotel Puerta del Sol, SE of the plaza
Tel 2670-0195   **Closed** *Tue*
Sample delicious homemade pasta and homegrown basil dishes at this cozy restaurant with an exquisite garden. Leave room for the decadent moist chocolate cake.

PLAYAS DEL COCO: Café de Playa $$$
International   **Map** A2
0.5 mile (1 km) E of the Village Center
Tel 2670-1621
An eclectic menu of gourmet dishes, from penne pastas to jumbo shrimp in rum sauce, as well as sushi, is served at this beachfront café-restaurant. There is an impressive wine list.

SÁMARA: Restaurante Las Brasas $$
Mediterranean   **Map** A2
On the NE corner of the soccer field
Tel 2656-0546
The menu at this open-air restaurant is laden with Spanish specialties such as gazpacho and paella. Seafood, steaks, and pastas are also available.

SÁMARA: Ristorante Gusto $$
International   **Map** A3
N side of soccer field
Tel 2656-0252
Savor delicious Italian and fusion dishes such as pasta carbonara, tuna tartare, and

chicken curry in a coconut bowl at this romantic and stylish Italian-owned restaurant in the village center. World music plays in the background.

TAMARINDO: Panadería La Laguna del Cocodrilo $$
French   **Map** A2
E of Tamarindo Diría and Plaza Colonial
Tel 2653-0255
Superb croissants, sweet and savory pastries, and *empanadas* are produced at this congenial bakery-café. It has a popular all-you-can-eat breakfast buffet.

TAMARINDO: Volcano Brewing $$
Brewpub   **Map** A2
5 miles (8 km) N of Tilaran
Tel 2653-1262
Hearty pub fare such as burgers and chicken wings are served at this beachfront pub with delicious beers available on tap. Health-conscious dishes include spinach tilapia fish.

TAMARINDO: Bamboo Sushi Club $$$
Japanese   **Map** A2
Opposite Hotel Tamarindo Diría
Tel 2653-0082   **Closed** *Sun*
Enjoy exquisite cuisine in a delightful tropical setting at this classy open-air sushi bar. The simple menu features fresh nigiri and sashimi, including a 40-piece Love Boat.

TAMARINDO: Capitán Suizo $$$
International   **Map** A2
Capitán Suizo Hotel, 0.5 mile (1 km) SW of Plaza Colonial
Tel 2653-0075
A fusion of fine European and tropical cuisine is served in this tranquil beachfront restaurant with a poolside bar. Typical dishes on the daily-changing menu include sea bass in mango sauce and tilapia fish in caper sauce.

TAMARINDO: Dragonfly $$$
International   **Map** A2
100 yards (100 m) NE of Hotel Pasatiempo
Tel 2653-1506   **Closed** *Sun*
Relish inspired Latin–Asian fusion cuisine in this romantic open-air restaurant under a canvas sail roof. Try the Thai chicken salad and panko-crusted pork loin with brandy and Dijon cream sauce.

TAMARINDO: El Jardín del Edén $$$
Mediterranean   **Map** A2
Hotel Jardín del Eden, SE of Tamarindo Diría
Tel 2653-0137
This romantic restaurant serves delicious Mediterranean-inspired dishes such as lobster in lemon sauce, and jumbo shrimp in whiskey.

TAMARINDO: Seasons by Shlomy $$$
Mediterranean   **Map** A2
Hotel Arco Iris
Tel 8368-6983   **Closed** *Sun mid-Sep–Oct*
The menu changes daily at this chic restaurant serving delights such as stuffed rigatoni with shrimp in creamy tomato sauce, and Lebanese-style chicken in red wine and spices.

VOLCAN MIRAVALLES: Río Perdido Activity Center $$$
Guanacastecan   **Map** B2
San Bernardo de Bagaces, 15 miles (24 km) NE of Bagaces
Tel 2673-3600
Inspired gourmet dishes that pay homage to the local tradition are served at this exciting activity center on Miravalles Volcano. Try the pumpkin squash soup.

The Northern Zone

LA FORTUNA: Choza de Laurel $$
Costa Rican   **Map** C2
400 yards (400 m) NW of the church
Tel 2479-7063
In the style of an old farmhouse, this rustic restaurant with a wood-fired oven and beams adorned with garlic cloves serves good-value *casados* as well as rotisserie chicken and grilled meats.

LA FORTUNA: Rancho La Cascada $$
International   **Map** C2
NW corner of the plaza
Tel 2479-9145
A spacious restaurant with an informal ambience and a huge thatched roof, Rancho Las

Chef presenting a dish at Seasons by Shlomy, Tamarindo

For key to prices *see page 266*

Selection of desserts on display at Ave del Paraíso, Tabácon

Cascada serves Italian favorites such as pastas and pizzas as well as Costa Rican staples including *gallo pinto* and *corvina al ajillo* (garlic sea bass).

LA FORTUNA: Restaurante Luigi $$
International Map C2
Luigi's Hotel, 2 blocks W of the Plaza
Tel 2479-9636
Flambé dishes are a specialty of this elegant restaurant with a pleasant terrace. The menu includes local seafood, beef stroganoff, pizzas, and pastas.

LAGUNA DE ARENAL: Tom's Pan German Bakery $
German Map B2
Nuevo Arenal, SE of the Plaza
Tel 2694-4547
This rustic, German-run bakery-café serves pastries, strudels, and cakes, as well as noodles, goulash, sauerkraut, and bratwurst. It also serves American breakfasts.

LAGUNA DE ARENAL: Mystica Lodge $$
Italian Map B2
10 miles (16 km) W of Nuevo Arenal
Tel 2692-1001
With rough-hewn timber furniture and flowers on every table, this informal yet elegant Italian restaurant in the intimate Mystica Lodge specializes in wood-fired pizzas and delicious ravioli dishes.

LAGUNA DE ARENAL: Rancho Margot $$
Costa Rican Map B2
5 miles (8 km) SE of Arenal National Park
Tel 2479-7259
The kitchen at Rancho Margot is supplied by its own fully-sustainable organic farm. The menu focuses on healthy dishes

made using seasonal ingredients and homemade dairy produce. There is a popular Sunday buffet.

LAGUNA DE ARENAL: Restaurant Willy's Caballo Negro $$
International Map B2
1 mile (1.6 km) W of Nuevo Arenal
Tel 2694-4515
A delightful German-owned café-restaurant overlooking a pond with waterfowl, Willy's Caballo Negro is well known for its schnitzels. Try the eggplant Parmesan or veal cutlet in spicy onion and bell pepper sauce. It has its own art gallery.

LAGUNA DE ARENAL: Toad Hall $$
International Map B2
4 miles (6 km) E of Nuevo Arenal
Tel 2692-8063
Attached to a marvelous art gallery and gift shop, this café-restaurant with lake views is an excellent breakfast and lunch spot. Try the pancakes with fresh fruit, or the grilled chicken salad. It has great fresh fruit smoothies.

DK Choice

LAGUNA DE ARENAL: Gingerbread $$$
International Map B2
2 miles (3 km) E of Nuevo Arenal
Tel 2694-0039 **Closed** Sun & Mon
Resembling a Tuscan villa, this restaurant is attached to a boutique hotel whose Israeli owner is a talented chef. His daily-changing menu uses local ingredients and ranges from sushi to jumbo shrimp with couscous and lentils. Choose between dining on the shaded patio or in a private booth in the cool interior.

PARQUE NACIONAL VOLCÁN ARENAL: Restaurante Heliconias Arenal Kioro $$$
International Map C2
4 miles (6 km) W of La Fortuna
Tel 2479-1700
Flowing lava can be seen through a wall of glass directly above this fine-dining restaurant. Try the *pejibaye* cream soup, octopus cocktail, or sea bass in caper sauce.

TABACÓN: Ave del Paraíso $$$
International Map C2
Balneario Tabacón, 8 miles (13 km) W of La Fortuna
Tel 2460-6229
Overlooking steaming hot springs and with dramatic volcano views, this cheery restaurant offers

Costa Rican staples and other wide-ranging dishes, from *gallo pinto* to *corvina* fish in apple and chili pepper sauce.

The Caribbean

CAHUITA: Café Choco Latte $
International Map F3
50 yards (50 m) SE of the bus stop
Tel 2755-0010 **Closed** Mon
The delightful open-air Café Choco Latte is a great breakfast spot – try the *gallo pinto* or granola and yogurt. The lunch menu has burritos, sandwiches, and vegetarian dishes.

CAHUITA: Miss Edith's $
Jamaican Map F3
200 yards (200 m) NW of bus stop
Tel 2755-0248
Sample spicy Caribbean classics such as rundown (fish stew) at this colorful family-run restaurant with shaded terrace seating. Homemade ice cream is served on weekends.

CAHUITA: Café Cocorico $$$
Italian Map F3
50 yards (50 m) N of the plaza
Tel 2755-0409 **Closed** Wed
Delicious gnocchi, pastas, pizzas, seafood, and homemade ice cream are served at this small, open-air eatery. Films are shown nightly on giant screens.

CAHUITA: Cha Cha Cha $$$
International Map F3
W of Cahuita Plaza
Tel 2755-0476
The wide-ranging menu at this charmingly rustic restaurant includes grilled squid salad, spicy coconut honey wings, and sea bass with shrimp and basil sauce.

GUÁCIMO: Restaurant Río Danta $
Costa Rican Map E2
Hwy 32, 3 miles (5 km) W of Guácimo
Tel 2760-0330
This roadside restaurant has forest trails, good for spotting poison-dart frogs. The menu features traditional fare along with pastas, steaks, and seafood.

MANZANILLO: Bar & Restaurante Maxi $
Caribbean Map F3
Manzanillo village
Tel 2759-9086
A simple, beachfront restaurant, Maxi is always lively and draws a young crowd. Caribbean seafood and filling *típico* (typical) dishes feature on the menu. Beach service is by request.

Open-air dining at Stashu's Con Fusion, Puerto Viejo de Talamanca

PLAYA COCLES: La Pecora Nera $$$
Italian   **Map** F3
2 miles (3 km) SE of Cocles
Tel *2750-0490*   **Closed** *Mon*
Run by a friendly Italian owner-chef, this unpretentious restaurant serves mouthwatering gourmet fare that belies the offbeat locale. Choose from gnocchis, bruschettas, pizzas, and calzones.

PUERTO LIMÓN: Restaurante Brisas del Caribe $
Costa Rican   **Map** F3
Calles 0/1 and Ave 2
Tel *2758-0138*
This restaurant on Parque Vargas is known for its excellent-value seafood dishes, lunchtime *casados*, and large buffet of *típico* (typical) fare, served cafeteria-style.

PUERTO VIEJO DE TALAMANCA: Bread & Chocolate $
Café   **Map** F3
Calle 215 and Ave 69
Tel *2750-0723*   **Closed** *Mon*
Start the day with cinnamon-oatmeal pancakes for breakfast at this friendly café. For lunch, try the grilled sandwiches, or crispy sautéed potatoes with jerk barbecue sauce. It has excellent cakes and pastries.

PUERTO VIEJO DE TALAMANCA: Café Rico $
International   **Map** F3
50 yards (50 m) W of Casa Verde Lodge
Tel *2750-0510*   **Closed** *Thu*
Hearty, healthy breakfasts and lunches are served at this rustic open-air café. The menu includes granola with fruit and yogurt, *huevos rancheros*, and *gallo pinto*.

PUERTO VIEJO DE TALAMANCA: Restaurante Tamara $
Caribbean   **Map** F3
Ave 71 and Calle 217
Tel *2750-0148*   **Closed** *Wed*
A Jamaican-themed restaurant painted in bright Rastafarian colors, Tamara serves such *típico* (typical) dishes as fried fish with *patacones* (plantain), along with burgers and fresh-fruit smoothies.

PUERTO VIEJO DE TALAMANCA: Chile Rojo $$
Asian   **Map** F3
Centro Comercial Puerto Viejo
Tel *2750-0025*
Located upstairs in a small mall, this restaurant serves excellent Asian-inspired fare. Try the Thai fish-and-coconut soup and fiery green curry. There is an all-you-can-eat sushi and buffet on Monday nights.

PUERTO VIEJO DE TALAMANCA: Salsa Brava $$
International   **Map** F3
E end of Puerto Viejo village
Tel *2750-0241*   **Closed** *Mon*
Excellent ceviche, Caesar salad with chicken teriyaki, and ice-cream sundaes are menu highlights at this informal thatched beachfront restaurant with a globe-spanning menu.

PUERTO VIEJO DE TALAMANCA: Veronica's Place $
Vegetarian   **Map** F3
Above Color Caribe, on Main St
Tel *2750-0263*
Health-conscious dishes feature at this charming restaurant in a creaky clapboard mansion with colorful Caribbean decor. The menu includes omelets, *gallo pinto*, and other Caribbean dishes. There are vegan options too.

PUERTO VIEJO DE TALAMANCA: Stashu's Con Fusion $$$
International   **Map** F3
400 yards (400 m) E of Puerto Viejo village
Tel *2750-0530*   **Closed** *Wed*
Organic dishes made to order with a choice of sauces are offered at this hip open-air restaurant with live music on Sundays. The macadamia-crusted fillet of snapper in white chocolate and lemon cream sauce is a must-try.

TORTUGUERO: Buddha Café $$
Mediterranean   **Map** E2
50 yards (50 m) W of the public dock
Tel *2709-8084*
Italian-owned, this urbane riverside restaurant with decks over the lagoon serves savory and sweet crêpes, lasagna and pizzas, and delicious fruit shakes.

DK Choice

TORTUGUERO: Miss Junie's $$
Caribbean   **Map** E2
At the N end of the village
Tel *2709-8102*
Named for its village matriarch owner who serves delicious traditional dishes, this air-conditioned restaurant is a dining institution. The menu includes jerk chicken, lobster in curry and coconut milk, *pan bon* (bread laced with caramelized sugar), and ginger cakes. Reservations are essential.

The Southern Zone

BAHÍA DRAKE: Águila de Osa Inn $$$
International   **Map** E5
0.5 mile (1 km) S of Agujitas
Tel *8840-2929*
Flavorful seafood and pasta dishes are served at this circular, thatched restaurant in the Aguila de Osa Inn, with bay views. Reservations are essential for non-guests.

CABO MATAPALO: Brisas Azul $$$
International   **Map** A5
Lapa Rios, 9 miles (14 km) S of Puerto Jiménez
Tel *2735-5130*
Choose from eclectic gourmet dishes prepared by perfectionist local chefs. Try the pineapple honey ginger salad and coconut crusted fish.

CIUDAD NEILY: Hotel Andrea $$
International   **Map** B4/F5
23 miles (37 km) E of Golfito
Tel *2783-3784*
In a colonial-style hotel, this eatery serves classics, from onion soup to filet mignon. The breakfast menu has *huevos rancheros* and pancakes with honey.

DOMINICAL: San Clemente Bar & Grill $
American/Mexican   **Map** D4
Immediately S of the soccer field
Tel *2787-0055*
American and Tex-Mex favorites are served at this open-air venue. It also offers excellent seafood

uch as mahi-mahi with honey and orange sauce. There is a lively bar with a pool table and TV.

DOMINICAL: ConFusione $$
International   **Map** D4
400 yards (400 m) S of police station
Tel 2787-0244
Delicious gourmet tapas are served at this elegant restaurant. Creative fusion dishes include penne with shrimps and capers in vodka sauce. There is live music.

DOMINICAL: Palapas $$$
Italian   **Map** D4
Hotel Cuna del Ángel, 5 miles (8 km) S of Dominical
Tel 2787-4343
This acclaimed restaurant serves excellent gourmet cuisine, including seafood. Try the tomato-basil soup and grilled garlic sea bass with creamy basil sauce. The flambé desserts are superb.

GOLFITO: Le Coquillage $$
International   **Map** B4/F5
Hotel Centro Turístico Samoa, N of Pueblo Civil
Tel 2775-0233
Encircling a bar shaped as a ship's prow, the wide-ranging menu at this open-air restaurant includes pizzas, pastas, and seafood such as garlic sea bass. There are fun pool tables and dart boards.

OJOCHAL: Villas Gaia $$
International   **Map** E4
Playa Tortuga, 0.5 mile (1 km) W of Ojochal
Tel 2786-5044
The vast menu at this open-air roadside restaurant with colorful, casual decor includes soups, salads, and snacks, plus exotic dishes such as macadamia-crusted fish fillet. There is tapas on Friday nights.

OJOCHAL: Citrus $$$
International   **Map** E4
200 yards (200 m) E of Costanera Sur
Tel 2786-5175   **Closed** *Sun & Mon*
Raising local dining standards to unimagined heights with its award-winning dishes, this sublime fusion restaurant serves delights such as coconut-milk tuna ceviche and wine-steamed mussels. There are flamenco and belly-dancing shows.

OJOCHAL: Restaurante Exótica $$$
International   **Map** E4
Ojochal village
Tel 2786-5050   **Closed** *Sun*
A cozy restaurant with bamboo screens and tree-trunk slab tables, Exótica is acclaimed for its creative tropical cuisine. Try

the fish fillet with banana curry sauce. There is an extensive wine list.

PAVONES: Café de la Suerte $
International   **Map** B5
N side of plaza
Tel 2776-2388   **Closed** *Sun*
A friendly Argentinean lady runs this simple open-air café specializing in vegetarian dishes, such as hummus. There are also excellent sandwiches and breakfasts consisting of omelets and granola with yogurt and fruit. The fruit shakes are delicious.

PUERTO JIMÉNEZ: Restaurante Carolina $
Costa Rican   **Map** A4/E5
100 yards (100 m) SE of the soccer field
Tel 2735-5185
Popular with backpackers, this good-value restaurant in the heart of town serves well-prepared and filling traditional dishes, including *gallo pinto*, and seafood, served al fresco.

DK Choice

PUERTO JIMÉNEZ: Perla de Osa $$
International   **Map** A4/E5
Iguana Lodge, Playa Platanares, 2 miles (3 km) E of Puerto Jiménez
Tel 8848-0752
A colorful beachfront restaurant with hammocks and a delightful ambience, Perla de Osa offers eclectic dishes including Caesar salad, grilled chicken club sandwiches, *empanadas*, and fish tacos. The Friday Night Pasta event draws a huge local crowd for the live salsa music. The bar serves fresh fruit smoothies and exotic tropical cocktails.

SAN GERARDO DE RIVAS: Café Blue $$$
American–Asian   **Map** E4
Monte Azul Boutique Hotel, Chimirol de Rivas
Tel 2742-5222
A chic open-air restaurant in a forested valley, Café Blue serves exotic fusion fare cooked to perfection. The three-course dinner might include chayote soup, pork loin with green curry, and lemon cheese pie.

SAN ISIDRO DE EL GÉNERAL: Café Trapiche $
Costa Rican   **Map** E4
Rancho La Botija, 4 miles (6 km) SE of San Isidro
Tel 2770-2146   **Closed** *Mon*
Choose from a simple menu of traditional dishes and some international options, such as

steak, pasta, and seafood, at this rustic farmstead with endearing country decor.

SAN ISIDRO DE EL GÉNERAL: Taquería Mexico Lindo $
Mexican   **Map** E4
Calle Central and Ave 2
Tel 2771-8222   **Closed** *Sun*
Popular with ex-pat Mexicans, this restaurant serves excellent-value authentic burritos, enchiladas, and vanilla flans. The cheerful dining area is festooned with *piñatas* (papier-mâché vessels).

SAN VITO: Pizzería Liliana $$
Italian   **Map** F5
50 yards (50 m) NW of the plaza
Tel 2773-3080
Choose from a selection of splendid pizzas and other staples at this simple restaurant in the center of town. The homey cooking is great value for money. Meals can be enjoyed al fresco on the small patio.

UVITA: Baker Bean $
Costa Rican   **Map** E4
100 yards (100 m) N of Banco de Costa Rica
Tel 2743-8990   **Closed** *Sun*
Surprisingly gourmet fresh-baked fare is served at this small roadside café. Try the spinach and cheese *empanadas*, and bagels with cream cheese. There is free Wi-Fi.

ZANCUDO: Oceano $$
American   **Map** B4/F5
400 yards (400 m) S of Zancudo village
Tel 2776-0921
The American owners prepare excellent *huevos rancheros*, burgers, and other similar staples at this tiny restaurant with charming diced-log tables. There is a popuar brunch.

The colorful beachside restaurant Perla de Osa, Puerto Jiménez

For more information on types of restaurants *see pages 262–3*

SHOPPING IN COSTA RICA

For many visitors, shopping is one of the thrills of a trip to Costa Rica. There is a good range of quality *artesanías* (crafts) stores, and most hotels have stores selling coffee, beautiful earthenware pottery in pre-Columbian style, handwoven hammocks, and souvenirs such as bowls and animal figures made of exotic hardwoods. San José has several art galleries, craft stores that stock a range of products including *molas* (reverse-appliqué cloth) from Bahía Drake and Sarchí leather rockers, and city malls that offer a vast choice of boutiques and jewelry stores. Across the country, bustling *mercados* (markets) are full of trinkets, piles of spices and herbs, *talabarterías* (saddle-makers) and *zapaterías* (shoe-makers), while colorful roadside stalls are piled high with fruits and vegetables. Indigenous crafts are increasingly appearing on the market. Note that it is illegal to buy or export pre-Columbian artifacts.

Palm-leaf baskets and hats for sale at a roadside stall

Opening Hours

Shops in San José are usually open from 8am to 6pm, Monday to Saturday. Large US-style malls are open on Sundays, but may close on Mondays. Outside San José, many *tiendas* (shops) close for lunch, typically between noon and 1:30pm. Shops in many tourist resorts remain open all week long, often until 9 or 10pm. Department stores and supermarkets everywhere stay open during lunchtime and often into the evening. Street markets and *mercados* usually open at around 6am and close by 2 or 3pm, although street stalls often stay open late.

Paying and Prices

Cash will be needed to pay for goods bought directly from craftsmen and at street stalls and markets. However, most stores accept VISA, and to a lesser degree, MasterCard and American Express, as well as US dollars. Credit card payments are sometimes subject to a small surcharge. Torn dollar bills are usually refused by shopkeepers. Some shops accept traveler's checks. A 13 percent sales tax will be added to the cost of most consumer goods in shops.

While leather goods are less expensive here than in most other countries, in general prices are relatively high. Items in galleries and hotel gift stores are sold at a fixed price. However, a certain amount of bargaining is expected at craft markets and *mercados*. The local artisans' cooperative markets have the best prices, and being government-regulated, ensure that a large slice of the profit goes directly to the craftsman. In general, larger stores and local export companies will arrange to have purchases shipped to the buyer's home.

Art Galleries

San José has numerous art galleries selling paintings, sculptures, prints, and other artworks by leading artists. Many of the best are found in the area around Parque Morazán *(see p120)* and **Centro Comercial El Pueblo**, which has over a dozen galleries. Two good outlets are the **Andrómeda Gallery** and **Kandinsky**. For more avant-garde art works, try **TeoréTica**, in Barrio Amón, which has a comprehensive selection, or **Galería 11–12**, which is located in the upscale western suburb of Escazú.

Many professional artists live in Monteverde. Manco Tulio Brenes sells his lovely paintings and sculptures at **Artes Tulio**. In

Centro Comercial El Pueblo, San José

Shelves of colorful objects in a San José craft store

the Caribbean lowlands, it is worth dropping in at Patricia Erickson's **Gallery at Home** (see p218), from where the artist sells her vibrant Afro-themed paintings.

Craft Stores

The variety of *artesanías* available in Costa Rica is quite large. Quality craft stores sell a range of products, from woodworks, which are created out of exotic hardwoods such as rosewood, ironwood, and purpleheart, to nature-themed books and tapes to Guatemalan weavings and embroideries.

The town of Sarchí (see p140) in the Central Highlands is the main source of crafts, and produces leather rocking chairs, handmade furniture with bas-relief carvings, and brightly painted miniature *carretas* (oxcarts; see p141). Here, the **Fábrica de Carretas Joaquín Chaverrí** (see p140) offers the largest and best selection of crafts. Nearby, the **Plaza de la Artesanía** also has several craft shops.

Toad Hall sign, Lake Arenal

Many store owners pride themselves on seeking out the finest quality crafts. One such place worth seeking out is **Lucky Bug Gallery** (see p204), on the north shore of Lake Arenal. A huge array of crafts are displayed at shops along Highway 21, not far from Liberia's Daniel Oduber International Airport.

In San José, the **Boutique Annemarie**, in the Hotel Don Carlos, has a fabulous array of crafts at fair prices, as does **Kiosco SJO**, which sells upscale jewelry, clothes, and craft items made by leading Latin American artisans.

Visitors who like browsing open-air markets should head to the **Mercado de Artesanías Nacionales**. This artisans' market houses a broad range of craft stalls under one roof. All the major tourist venues, especially the popular beach resorts such as Jacó and Tamarindo, are lined with stalls selling crafted items. The competition is intense, and bargaining is normal.

Indigenous Crafts

Although Costa Rica does not have as strong an indigenous craft tradition as other Latin American nations, it has many unique handicrafts to offer visitors. The Boruca tribe of **Reserva Indígena Boruca** (see p236) make balsa-wood masks and bas-relief wall hangings, available at a discount if bought directly from the artists. When buying directly from the craftsmen, bear in mind that their margin of profit is usually quite low. Many of the finest examples of Boruca art are also available in quality crafts stores in San José, and at **Coco Loco Arts & Crafts** in Chachagua near La Fortuna. Coco Loco also sells some fabulous contemporary pottery and marble carvings by leading artists.

Intriguing indigenous pottery comes from **Guaitíl** (see p197), where ocher vases, bowls, plates, and animals emblazoned with traditional Chorotega motifs are sold at the potters' roadside stalls. Many venues also sell the colorful hand-stitched *m olas* of the Kuna Indians of the San Blas islands of Panama. At **Molas y Café**, in Atenas, you can sometimes see Kuna members at work.

The two best commercial outlets for indigenous arts and crafts are **Galería Dantica** and **Galería Namú**, which sells an excellent selection of palm-leaf baskets, Boruca masks, Huetar carvings, and colorful, embroidered Guaymí clothing.

Pottery wares lining a street in Santa Ana, near San José

Woodworks

Popular items sold in stores specializing in woodwork include figurines, kitchen utensils, bowls, and jewelry boxes. Some of the finest wooden bowls and boxes are produced by **Barry Biesanz Woodworks** *(see p129)* – it is possible to buy directly from his Escazú studio. Biesanz's works have been gifted by the government of Costa Rica to many visiting dignitaries.

Gold jewelry on sale, Museo del Oro Precolombino store

Jewelry

Skilled goldsmiths craft exquisite jewelry using both modern designs and pre-Columbian motifs such as frogs and birds, often incorporating semi-precious stones such as lapis lazuli, onyx, and jade. It is best to buy from reputable stores, such as San José's **Esmeraldas y Diseños**, which also offers demonstrations of jewelry design. Most deluxe hotels and large malls also have jewelry stores. For good-quality jewelry in 14-carat gold, the **Museo del Oro Precolombino** store *(see p117)* is worth a visit. Items sold at streetside jewelry stalls are usually gold-washed, not pure gold.

Coffee

Several *beneficios* (coffee-processing factories) are open to visitors and will ship bulk purchases of vacuum-packed coffee. Among these are the Café Britt airport gift stores and the Café Britt *beneficio* *(see p146)*, which has a well-stocked craft store. Many regional varieties of coffee are sold at hotel gift shops, where traditional Costa Rican coffee-strainers called *chorreadores* are

also often available. Domestic-quality coffee is sold at shops in San José's **Mercado Central** *(see p112)*, where it is roasted on the spot; ask for *granos puros* (whole beans) rather than *café traditional*, which is coffee ground very fine and mixed with sugar.

Garments

Traditional Guanacasteco (from Guanacaste) dresses and blouses, such as those worn by dancers of Fantasía Folklórico *(see p285)*, are sold at the Mercado Central *(see p112)* in San José. The **Museo Comunitario Boruca** sells colorful indigenous skirts, while Fundación Neotrópica's **Tienda Heliconia**, in the suburb of Curridabat and at Poás Volcano National Park, sells good-quality T-shirts.

Other Specialty Stores

The suburb of Moravia in San José is known for its leatherwork. Belts and purses are an excellent buy, as are cowboy boots, which range in design from classical to trendy. A wide selection of cowboy boots is sold by *zapaterías*

(shoemakers) in Barrio México, northwest of downtown San José. Ciudad Quesada (San Carlos) *(see p208)* is the best place to go if you are looking for ornate saddles – a wide variety is available. It is worth keeping in mind that leather costs significantly less than in Europe or North America.

The capital city has several cigar outlets, which stock Cuban cigars. The **Cigar Shoppe**, in the city center, and the **Tobacco Shop**, in the Centro Comercial El Pueblo, are recommended. Don't buy cigars on the street; the boxed cigars may look genuine, but they are almost always cheap fakes. However, US citizens should note that it is illegal for them to bring home Cuban products, even if purchased in Costa Rica.

Beautiful orchids in sealed vials are available at airport gift shops and in various botanical gardens such as **Jardín Botánico Lankester** *(see p147)*, near Cartago.

Many artists produce stunning *vidriera* (stained glass). A good source is **Creaciones Santos** in San Miguel de Escazú.

One of the many specialty leather stores in Costa Rica

Stalls selling fresh produce and other articles at Mercado Central, San José

Markets and Malls

Every town has its *mercado central* (central market), selling everything from cowboy hats to medicinal herbs. Good buys at San José's Mercado Central include embroidered *guayabero* shirts (summer shirts for men), and cowboy boots made of exotic leathers. Town markets can be dark warrens, and quite crowded, especially on Saturdays; shoppers should watch out for pickpockets. Not many shopkeepers speak English. Most towns also have *ferias de agricultores* (farmers'

markets) on weekends, which sell all kinds of fresh produce. These usually start at dawn and are frequented by locals.

Malls are found only in big towns. **Mall San Pedro** in San José and **Multiplaza** in Escazú have many boutiques selling local and international brands.

DIRECTORY

Art Galleries

Andrómeda Gallery
Calle 9 and Ave 9,
Barrio Amón, San José.
Tel 2223-3529.

Artes Tulio
Monteverde.
Tel 2645-5567.

**Centro Comercial
El Pueblo**
Barrio Tournon.
Tel 2221-9434.

Galería 11–12
Plaza Itzkatzu, Escazú.
Tel 2288-1975.

Kandinsky
Centro Comercial,
Calle Real, San Pedro,
San José. **Tel** 2234-0478.

TeoréTica
Calle 7 and Aves 9/11,
San José.
Tel 2233-8775.

Craft Stores

Boutique Annemarie
Calle 9 and Ave 9,
San José.
Tel 2221-6707.

Kiosco SJO
Ave 7 and Calle 11,
San José. **Tel** 2258-1829.

**Mercado de
Artesanías
Nacionales**
Calle 11 and Ave 4,
San José.

Plaza de la Artesanía
Sarchí Sur, Sarchí.
Tel 2454-3430.

Indigenous Crafts

**Coco Loco Arts
& Crafts**
Chachagua, near La
Fortuna de San Carlos.
Tel 2468-0990.

Galería Dantica
Lighthouse Plaza,
Playa Herradura.
Tel 2740-1067.
San Gerardo de Dota.
Tel 2740-1067.

Galería Namú
Calles 5/7 and Ave 7,
San José.
Tel 2256-3412.
 galerianamu.com

Molas y Café
Atenas.
Tel 2466-5155.

Jewelry

Esmeraldas y Diseños
Sabana Norte, San José.
Tel 2231-4808.
 **esmeraldasydisenos.
com**

Garments

**Museo Comunitario
Boruca**
Boruca Village.
Tel 2514-0045.

Tienda Heliconia
Ave Central, Curridabat.
Tel 2253-1230.

Other Specialty
Stores

Cigar Shoppe
Calle 5 and Ave 3,
San José.
Tel 2257-5021.

Creaciones Santos
Calles 1/3 and Ave 3,
San Miguel de Escazú.
Tel 2296-1278.

Tobacco Shop
Centro Comercial
El Pueblo,
San José.
Tel 2223-0873.

Markets and
Malls

Mall San Pedro
Ave Central and
Circunvalación,
San José.
Tel 2283-7540.

Multiplaza
Autopista Prospero
Fernández,
Escazú.
Tel 2201-6025.

What to Buy

With a wide selection of quality items sold in shops and galleries throughout the country, there is no shortage of mementos to take home. Hand-crafted objects made from tropical hardwoods, such as bowls, boxes, and kitchen articles, as well as aromatic coffee beans and coffee products of various kinds, are must-buys. Ceramics are excellent, as is jewelry, particularly gold necklaces and pendants that replicate pre-Columbian designs. T-shirts with wildlife motifs, and cuddly sloths, curling snakes made of wood, and other such toys, are popular choices.

Forbidden Items

Objects made from various protected species are commonly sold at local markets. It is illegal to buy anything made from turtle shells, furs such as ocelot and jaguar skins, or feathers of quetzals and other endangered bird species. Conservation groups also discourage buying items made of coral, as well as framed butterflies.

Handicrafts

Costa Rica's skilled artisans are concentrated in Sarchí, famous for its miniature oxcarts painted in gaudy patterns and colors, and for homespun rocking chairs of wood and leather. Dozens of artisans' studios produce a dizzying variety of crafts, which find their way into stores throughout the country. Moravia, near San José, is another center of crafts, particularly leather goods.

Leather Goods
Cowboy boots, purses, and attaché cases exude quality and are relatively inexpensive. Those made of caiman and snake skins should be avoided for conservation reasons.

Wooden bowl and spoons

Painted wooden box

Carved box

Colorful wooden earrings

Hand-painted miniature oxcart

Wooden Items
Costa Rica's precious hardwoods yield a wealth of objects. They include statuettes, animal figurines, carved boxes, and notably, lathe-turned bowls, some thin enough to be transparent when held up to the light.

Hammocks
Hammocks made of colored hemp rope, in a variety of designs, are sold on the sea shores. Roomy two-person models are also available.

Jewelry
Delicate brooches, necklaces, and earrings in 14-carat gold, often in combination with corals and semi-precious stones, are popular. Street hawkers sell bright necklaces of shells, hardwoods, and seeds.

Brooch

Pearl earrings

Necklace in gold and semi-precious stone

Seed necklace

Indigenous Crafts

Items made by Indian tribes can be bought at quality craft stores and, preferably, in indigenous reserves where income goes directly to the artists. Traditional weavings, carved gourds, painted masks, and musical instruments are often imbued with spiritual symbols.

Carved Gourds
Decorated with wildlife motifs, carved gourds are lightweight and can be used as vases.

Painted mask

Ocher Pottery
Pottery adorned with traditional Chorotega motifs are produced in Guaitíl, using traditional firing methods. Pots, plates, and vases of varying shapes and sizes can be bought at roadside stalls and cooperatives throughout Guanacaste.

Boruca mask

"Devil" Masks
Made of balsa wood, these masks made by the Boruca tribe should be bought directly from the carver. Other indigenous wooden goods include wall hangings.

Coffee liqueur

Organic coffee

A regional variety of coffee

Chocolate-coated coffee beans

Coffee

Coffee products range from gourmet roasted whole beans to coffee liqueurs. Be sure to buy export-quality coffee, as coffees sold for the domestic market are often of inferior quality and, if sold pre-ground, adulterated with large amounts of sugar.

Souvenirs

All manner of trinkets, utensils, and miscellaneous artistic creations are for sale at gift stores nationwide, from candles to stained-glass pendants. Typically, they are emblazoned with images of wildlife or rural scenes. The store at San José's international airport has a good selection.

Bright brooch

Candle

Ceramic plate

Painted metal jug

Stained-glass item

ENTERTAINMENT IN COSTA RICA

Cultural activities and live entertainment in Costa Rica have traditionally been somewhat restrained by the standards of many other Latin American countries. Nonetheless, Ticos have a tremendous love of music and dance, and there has been a blossoming of entertainment venues. Nightlife, especially in San José, is excitingly diverse. Theater and classical concerts are an integral part of San José's social life, and even smaller cities usually have theater spaces and *glorietas* (bandstands) where live musicians perform. Music festivals are staged both indoors and outdoors, and country fairs called *ferias* are in full swing year-round. Every town has numerous discos, and karaoke bars are popular with lower-income Ticos. Entertainment in country towns revolves around *topes* (horsemanship shows) and *retornos* (rodeos) that spill onto the streets with traditional live music and dance.

Information

A calendar of major events is carried in Spanish and English on the website of the Instituto Costarricense de Turismo (Costa Rican Tourism Institute, or ICT; *see p296*). The website also has addresses of theaters, nightclubs and similar venues. *Tico Times* (*see p301*), which is available in many hotels, also provides listings of artistic events and entertainment, as do the "Tiempo Libre" and "Viva" sections of the *La Nación* daily newspaper. *San José Volando* and *GAM Cultural What's Going On* are free monthly publications that contain information about live concerts and other entertainment.

Costa Rican
Tourism Institute
logo

Theater

Costa Rica has a long tradition of producing great theater, and Josefinos are passionate theatergoers. San José has several small theaters, which offer everything from mainstream and experimental theater, to comedy and puppet shows, at affordable prices. Most productions are in Spanish and are typically restricted to Thursday–Sunday evenings. Mime performances are the main attraction at **Teatro Chaplin**. The country's oldest theater company, the English- language **Little Theatre Group**, performs at the **Teatro Laurence Olivier**, which doubles as a lively cultural center and has a jazz club and movie theater. The Teatro Eugene O'Neill, located inside the **Centro Cultural Costarricense-Norteamericano** (Costa Rican-North American Cultural Center), also hosts theater performances, plus monthly musical concerts on weekends.

Classical Music, Ballet, Dance, and Opera

Costa Rica's middle class are enthusiastic lovers of classical music. The nation's foremost venue for classical and ballet performances is San José's **Teatro Nacional** (*see pp114–15*). It was inaugurated to great national pride in 1897 with a performance of *El Fausto de Gournod* by the Paris Opera. The theater hosts the **Orquestra Sinfónia Nacional**, founded in

The opulent interior of the auditorium of Teatro Nacional

A lively traditional dance in progress in Pueblo Antiguo, San José

1970, which performs a series of concerts each year between April and December. It also holds performances by the **Compañía de Lírica Nacional** (National Lyric Opera Company), the country's only opera company, from June to August. The companies feature many of the world's best-known works in their repertoires. International orchestras and singers also perform in the Teatro Nacional. Evening performances at the theater are considered an occasion to dress up for. Prices in the *galería* (galleries) are generally below $5, depending on the particular performance in question.

Theater production in Costa Rica has a long tradition, boosted in the early 1900s when a number of South American dramatists settled here, and drama was introduced to the high school curriculum. The **Teatro Mélico Salazar** *(see p112)* stages drama, musicals, classical concerts, and occasional performances of traditional Costa Rican singing and dancing. The theater is also the principal venue of Costa Rica's **Compañía Nacional de Danza** (National Dance Company), a world-class organization founded in 1979, which has an extensive repertoire of contemporary and classical works.

It is advisable to book in advance, which you should do directly with the venue or event organizers.

Jazz

Jazz clubs have grown in number in recent years, and jazz trios play in several hotel lobbies and bars. The main venue is San José's **Jazz Café**, a red-brick structure with a classic bohemian ambience. Leading international performers such as Chucho Valdés and Irakere have played here. Jazz Café also has a venue in Escazú. San José's jazz buffs also frequent the Shakespeare Gallery in the **Sala Garbo**, which hosts live jazz on Monday evenings.

Traditional Music

Rather limited in form and style, the country's popular music is a more restricted version of the *marimba* cultures of Nicaragua and Guatemala. The *marimba* (xylophone), *quijongo* (single-string bow with gourd resonator), and guitar provide the backing for such traditional folk dances as the *punto guanacasteco*, the national dance *(see p287)*. Live *marimba* music is performed at *ferias*, a few tourist venues, and city plazas on weekends. A good place to experience traditional music and dance is **Pueblo Antiguo** *(see p129)*. Indigenous communities perform ritual dances accompanied by drums, rattles, and ceramic flutes.

The Teatro Mélico Salazar, one of San José's popular cultural venues

Dancing the night away at a beach resort nightclub

Nightclubs and Discos

San José and key tourist resorts have swanky dance clubs. Many of the best nightclubs are associated with leading hotels, and several larger beach resorts feature discos. Less sophisticated venues are everywhere, catering to the dance-crazy Ticos. The predominant music is Latin: *cumbia*, salsa and, especially, merengue, often interspersed with reggae and world-beat tunes.

In San José, the well-to-do can be found at the various bars and clubs along San Pedro's Avenida Central, and in San Rafael de Escazú. **Discoteque Planet Mall**, popular with teenagers, claims to be the largest disco in Central America. A more down-to-earth and always crowded option is **El Cuartel de la Boca del Monte**, with an earthy atmosphere, eclectic patrons, and live music by many of Costa Rica's leading bands. Several discos and bars can be found in the alleyways comprising **El Pueblo**, while the Los Yoses and San Pedro districts have many bars and clubs catering to students and well-off young Ticos. Calle de la Amargura (Street of Bitterness), leading to the university, is lined with student bars, and draws few foreigners. Bars in "Gringo Gulch," a red-light area of central San José, mostly cater to an older foreign clientele, including the city's large number of expatriate residents. Take care with whom you interact in this locality, and always use taxis at night.

Most of the clubs don't begin to liven up until midnight, and many don't close until dawn. Attire is usually quite casual, with jeans permitted; shorts are generally not allowed, except at beach resorts.

Casinos

Costa Rica has dozens of casinos, concentrated in the capital city. They are mostly associated with large, expensive hotels. Several casinos are clustered in the infamous Gringo Gulch. Some casinos are open 24 hours.

The most popular casino games are craps, *tute* (a version of poker), canasta, which resembles roulette, and *veinte un* (21), a variant of blackjack. Visitors should be aware that the odds are far more favorable to the house than they are in the US.

Dance Schools

Many visitors come to Costa Rica to learn to dance. Several reputable *academias de baile* (dance schools) offer residential courses where you can pick up some fancy foot skills in hip-swiveling *cumbia*, merengue, salsa, and whatever the latest Latin dance craze may be. Most classes are typically in Spanish. The well-known **Merecumbé** has several schools in San José and major highland cities.

Festivals

Costa Rica's annual calendar is full of festivals, large and small (see pp36–9). Many of them celebrate the country's diverse cultures, such as the Fiesta de los Diablitos (see p236) of the Borucas and Puerto Límon's extravagant Caribbean-style Carnaval (see p219). Costa Rica's best-known music festivals include the nationwide **Credomatic Music Festival**, which is held at two dozen venues throughout the country. Many of the towns in Catholic Costa Rica honor their

A Caribbean-style performance in a resort in Guanacaste

The Punto Guanacasteco

The national dance is the *punto guanacasteco*, a toe-and-heel dance performed in traditional regional costumes. The women wear white bodices and colorful frilly satin skirts. The men wear white shirts and pants, satin sashes, and cowboy hats. The slow, twirling *baile típico* (typical dance) features the tossing of hats and scarves, as males interrupt the proceedings in turn to shout rhyming verses aimed at winning over a love interest.

Dancers performing the
punto guanacasteco

patron saints on specific days of the year. Nationally, the most important religious festival is the Día del Virgen de los Angeles, which is celebrated in Cartago's Basílica de Nuestra Señora de los Angeles *(see pp148–9)* in August. Nicoya's Fiesta de la Yeguïta *(see p196)*, held in mid-December, is one of the nation's most colorful regional festivals.

Cinema

Most cities have cinemas, although those in smaller towns are often ramshackle. San José and other large cities have modern multiplex cinemas up to the standards of North America and Western Europe. **Cinepolis** and others show first-run Hollywood and international movies, which are usually subtitled in Spanish.

Dubbed films are advertised with the phrase *hablado en español*. International art-house movies are shown at **Sala Garbo**. Costa Rica has no major cinema industry of its own.

Peñas

San José's intellectuals enjoy *peñas* (circles of friends), bohemian get-togethers that evolved from Latin America's Leftist revolutionary movement of the 1970s. Poetry is recited and plaintiff *nueva trova* music is performed at *peñas*, also called *tertulias*. They are leading outlets for experimental music and literature by such avant-garde performers as Esteban Monge and Canto America. Typical venues are private homes and cafés. An active venue is **TeoréTica**, a hip art gallery that hosts literary readings, round-table discussions, and other cultural events.

DIRECTORY

Theater and Cultural Centers

Centro Cultural Costarricense-Norteamericano
San Pedro, San José.
Tel 2225-9433.
w centrocultural.cr

Little Theatre Group
Tel 8858-1446.
w littletheatregroup.org

Teatro Chaplin
Calles 11/13 and Avenida 12, San José.
Tel 2221-0812.
w teatrochaplin.com

Teatro Laurence Olivier
Calle 28 and Avenida 2, San José.
Tel 2222-1034.

Classical Music, Ballet, Dance, and Opera

Compañía de Lírica Nacional
Tel 2240-0333 (ext. 311).
w mcj.go.cr

Compañía Nacional de Danza
Tel 2222-2974.
w mcj.go.cr

Orquestra Sinfónia Nacional
Tel 2240-0333.
w osn.go.cr

Jazz

Jazz Café
Calle 7 and Avenida Central, San Pedro, San José.
Tel 2253-8933.

Plaza Itzkatzú, Autopista Prospero Fernández, Escazú.
Tel 2288-4740.
w jazzcafecostarica.com

Sala Garbo
Calle 28 and Avenida 2, San José.
Tel 2222-1034.
w salagarbocr.com

Nightclubs and Discos

Discoteque Planet Mall
Mall San Pedro, San José.
Tel 2280-4693.

El Cuartel de la Boca del Monte
Calles 21/23 and Avenida 1, San José.
Tel 2221-0327.

El Pueblo
Avenida Central, Barrio Tournón, San José.
Tel 2221-9434.

Dance Schools

Merecumbé
Tel 2224-3531.
w merecumbe.net

Festivals

Credomatic Music Festival
w eticket.cr

Cinema

Cinepolis
Autopista a Cartago, San José.
Tel 2518-0002.

Sala Garbo
See *Jazz*.

Peñas

TeoréTica
Calle 7 and Avenidas 9/11, San José.
Tel 2233-8775.
w teoretica.org

OUTDOOR ACTIVITIES AND SPECIALTY VACATIONS

The varied terrain, salubrious climate, and diversity of wilderness reserves in Costa Rica combine to afford a wealth of outdoor activities. Some of these, which have been spawned by the tourist boom of the past two decades, are unusual – canopy tours, for example, are a staple of the rain- and cloud forest reserves. Others are more conventional. Ample opportunities for hiking are provided by the trails that lace the superb national parks and reserves. Costa Rica is also well-geared fo biking and horseback riding. Both coasts offe fabulous surfing, and windsurfing is world class, with dedicated facilities at Lake Arenal and Bahía Salinas. Whitewater rafting is highly developed, while scuba divers and anglers are in for a treat. Wherever you are in the nation, the great outdoors is close at hand. A handy resource is *Costa Rica Outdoors*, a bimonthly publication available nationwide.

The range of activities offered at Selva Verde Lodge

Organized Tours

A plethora of tour operators in Costa Rica cater to visitors interested in particular activities. Companies offering a range of specialized tours include **Costa Rica Expeditions**, **Costa Rica Sun Tours**, and **Serendipity Adventures**. Operators dedicated to a specific activity are listed in the relevant subsection.

National Parks and Wildlife Reserves

Costa Rica has about 190 national parks, wildlife reserves, and related protected areas, with a combined area of almost 6,000 sq miles (15,500 sq km). Dozens of other privately owned reserves protect additional natural habitats. Protected areas continue to be created to link individual parks and reserves with the purpose of creating uninterrupted migratory corridors for wildlife. The national parks and reserves are organized into "conservation areas" administered by the **SINAC** (Sistema de Areas de Conservación/System of Conservation Areas), which is a division of MINAE (Ministerio de Ambiente y Energía/Ministry of Atmosphere and Energy).

La Amistad, covering an area of 749 sq miles (1,940 sq km), is the largest national park (*see p231*). This is also the most remote and inaccessible one, and hiking can be challenging. The most visited park is Parque Nacional Volcán Poás, which lies within a 2-hour drive of San José and has the most developed facilities (*see p144*). Also popular is Parque Nacional Manuel Antonio, which offers the advantage of easy access and an assortment of attractions, including beautiful beaches (*see pp172–3*). Parque Nacional Cahuita, on the Caribbean coast, features similar attractions (*see p222*).

Parque Nacional Chirripó (*see pp232–3*) and Parque Nacional Rincón de la Vieja (*see p186*) offer fabulous mountain hiking – Rincón has the added enticement of fumaroles and boiling mud pools. Guided boat tours make the rainforests and swamps of Parque Nacional Tortuguero accessible (*see p221*). A more challenging but no less rewarding destination is Parqu Nacional Corcovado, perhaps the nation's premier rainforest environment (*see p243*). Reserv Biológica Bosque Nuboso Monteverde is the top cloud forest reserve (*see p181*). A useful source of information on various reserves is **Amigos de los Parques Nacionales**.

Wildlife-Viewing

Viewing animals and birds in the wild is the prime attraction for the majority of visitors to Costa Rica. It's easily done, even without visiting protected reserves, as wildlife is literally

Boat tour in Parque Nacional Tortuguero

Bird-watchers in Parque Nacional Manuel Antonio

everywhere outside city limits. Morpho butterflies, toucans, monkeys, and coatis can be seen from your hotel porch, depending on location. However, most species are well disguised or reclusive, and spotting them often requires a combination of patience and planning. Hiring a naturalist guide is recommended – their trained eyes and knowledge of where and when to look for certain species will greatly increase your success rate. Guides can be hired through Costa Rica Expeditions, which also offers nature trips of its own. A particularly good way to view wildlife is to take a natural history cruise aboard a small ship, with daily excursions ashore. Leading companies include **National Geographic Expeditions**.

On a nature trip, dress in greens and browns to blend in with the surroundings. Silence is imperative. Bring a pair of binoculars. Laminated spotters' charts are available at book- and souvenir stores. Companies specializing in birding include **Horizontes**.

Hiking

For those who like to experience nature on foot, Costa Rica is a dream come true. Thousands of miles of trails traverse the countryside, offering opportunities to explore the most remote terrain. Many trails are well marked and easy to hike, while others provide a rugged challenge to even the most experienced hikers. **Librería Universal** and the **Instituto Geográfico**

Nacional sell detailed topographic maps.

The majority of trails are associated with the national parks and wildlife reserves, where facilities are usually restricted to the ranger stations and/or private lodges near the entrances. Many of the larger parks have only basic huts, sometimes a full day's hike from each other – hikers will need to be self-sufficient in terms of camping equipment and food. Always inquire about the distance to the next hut, and the difficulty of the hike. You will need to get permission to camp anywhere other than at designated campsites. For overnight hikes, always report to a ranger station at the beginning and end of your trip. Permits and local guides are essential for certain hikes, such as those across the remote Talamancas.

Look out for venomous snakes – never leave your tent or cabin door open (see p299). Hikers in Parque Nacional Corcovado and other lowland rainforest reserves may come across bands of aggressive wild

pigs called peccaries. If threatened, climb a tree and wait until the animals depart. Otherwise, the best bet is usually to stand still: most charges are bluffs.

Lightweight yet sturdy waterproof hiking shoes are essential, as is a water bottle and a backpack with room for a waterproof jacket with hood. Apart from sunscreen and insect repellent, other recommended items are a first aid kit, as well as a flashlight and spare batteries. Pack your gear in a plastic bag before placing it in your backpack to ensure that it remains dry. Clean up the campsite before leaving – only footprints should be left behind.

Canopy Tours

With its soaring trees and deep valleys, it is no surprise that Costa Rica has dozens of canopy tours to whisk you between treetops and across gorges (see pp28–9). Zipline tours provide an adrenalin-packed ride, but don't expect to see much wildlife. The **Original Canopy Tour** has four locations around the country.

Zipline canopy tour, Arenal Theme Park

Horseback riding on one of Costa Rica's many beaches

Horseback Riding

Costa Rica affords numerous opportunities for equestrian pursuits. Tour operators and hotels can make all the necessary arrangements for rides, which are usually on the small, mild-tempered local *criollo* horse.

Guanacaste province has several ranches specializing in horse riding. **Hacienda Lodge Guachipelín** *(see p257)* is an excellent location, as is the **Buena Vista Lodge** *(see p257)*. Another good place is **Club Hípico La Caraña**, near Escazú.

Cycling and Motorcycling

Touring the country by bicycle is an excellent way to meet local people and to enjoy the spectacular scenery. However, many roads are potholed and cycling in highland areas requires caution due to fog, blind bends, and speeding traffic. Several companies specialize in bicycle tours: **Backroads**, in North America, and **Coast to Coast Adventures**, in Costa Rica, are two reputable outfits. Most international airlines will let you bring your own bicycle as checked luggage, if properly packed.

Costa Rica's rugged terrain is particularly suited to mountain biking, and Ticos (Costa Ricans) are enthusiasts of the sport.

Adventure motorcycle touring has grown in popularity. **MotoDiscovery** offers organized tours.

Golf and Tennis

The country has six 18-hole courses, as well as four 9-hole ones. Additional courses are in the offing. In the Nicoya Peninsula, the leading greens are at the **Four Seasons Resort** *(see p256)* and the **Reserva Conchal Golf Club**. The best of the Central Highlands courses are at the **Cariari Country Club** and **Parque Valle del Sol**.

Many hotels and beach resorts have tennis courts available free of charge for guests to use. Non-guests are usually allowed to play on these courts for a fee.

Whitewater Rafting and Kayaking

Costa Rica's high rainfall and mountain terrain combine to provide ideal conditions for whitewater rafting *(see p156)*. The Reventazón and Pacuare Rivers of the Central Highlands are renowned, but every region has world-class whitewater. Tumbling from the country's highest mountain, Río Chirripó (Class III–IV) creates dozens of explosive rapids. It merges with Río General (Class III–IV), known for its challenging rapids. Río Corobicí (Class I–II) is fed by dam-released waters and flows between tree-lined banks in the heart of Guanacaste. It offers a float perfect for families, as wildlife is plentiful and easily seen. Río Savegre (Class III–V) flows out of the mountains of the Central Pacific. The steep upper section is a demanding thriller; the river slows lower down as it passes through African oil palm plantations.

The rafting industry is well regulated, and operators conform to international standards. Life jackets and helmets are mandatory. Trips cost between $70 and $100 per day, including transport, meals,

The serene Parque Valle del Sol golfing greens

Kayaking in Lake Angostura, near Turrialba

and equipment. Overnight trips involve camping or stays at remote riverside lodges. Numerous companies offer rafting trips, including **Ríos Tropicales**. Take sunscreen and suitable attire. A warm jacket for mountain runs is a good idea. Expect to get wet – pack a set of dry clothes and shoes.

Sea kayaks are an ideal means of exploring the mangrove systems of the coasts. One of the major rafting operators, Ríos Tropicales, also features trips on kayaks. Various other nature tour operators offer kayaking trips, and many resort hotels rent kayaks for exploring sheltered bays. With luck, dolphins may appear alongside. If you plan on kayaking alone, *The Rivers of Costa Rica: A Canoeing, Kayaking and Rafting Guide*, by Michael W. Mayfield and Rafael E. Gallo, is indispensable; it is available from San José's **7th Street Books.**

Surfing and Windsurfing

Thousands of visitors flock to Costa Rica each year to ride the waves that wash ashore along both the Pacific and Caribbean coastlines. Some of the best surfing beaches are in Northern Nicoya (*see p191*). Most airlines permit you to check a surfboard as luggage free of charge. However, there is no shortage of surf shops at key surf spots such as Tamarindo, Jacó, and Puerto Viejo de Talamanca. Playa Pavones (*see p244*) is another excellent location, but you will need to bring your own

equipment. Dedicated surf camps give their own meaning to the term "bed and board."

Bahía Salinas (*see p184*) and Laguna de Arenal (*see pp204–6*) are marvelous for wind-surfing, thanks to consistently high winds. Both have wind-surf centers.

Sportfishing

The challenge of landing a world-record catch draws hundreds of anglers to Costa Rica's waters every year. Most sportfishing is on a catch-and-release basis. The Pacific coast (*see p171*) is fabulous for deep-sea fish, such as sailfish, tuna, dorado, and swordfish. Marlin are the big prize: the fish run off Nicoya in November–March; the central and southern Pacific are best in August–December.

On the Caribbean side, anglers use light tackle in rivers, lakes, and lagoons to hook tarpon, snook, and garfish. Caño Negro, as well as the rivermouths of the San Juan and Colorado Rivers, feature some of the world's best tarpon fishing: the best time is December–March. Trout fishing is popular in mountain streams, particularly on the northern slopes of the Talamancas. Laguna de Arenal is renowned for massive rainbow bass; **Rain Goddess** offers fishing trips here (*see p206*). Permits required for freshwater

Sportfishing charter sign

Fishing yacht anchored at Bahía Drake

fishing are organized by the operators. Several sportfishing lodges cater exclusively to anglers. Boat charters offered from sportfishing centers, such as Flamingo, Quepos, Tamarindo, Golfito, and Zancudo, typically cost $250–400 for a half day and $350–650 for a full day. Fishing tackle is sold and rented at **La Casa del Pescador**. Excellent sources of angling information are **Club Amateur de Pesca** and local fishing expert Jerry Ruhlow's weekly column in the *Tico Times*.

Spiritual Retreats

A non-profit spiritual community off the beaten track, **Samasati Nature Retreat** offers a sweat lodge and classes in subjects like meditation, yoga, health and well-being, and tantra.

Surfing on the high waves off Playa Jaco

Scuba Diving in Costa Rica

The warm waters off Costa Rica provide splendid opportunities for divers. The country's prime site is Isla del Coco, which offers some of the world's finest scuba diving for seeing marine animals. Other dive spots include the Murciélagos Islands in Northern Nicoya; the coral reefs of Playa Manuel Antonio, Parque Nacional Ballena Marina, and Isla del Caño on the Pacific side; and Gandoca-Manzanillo and Cahuita on the Caribbean. Marine turtles and moray eels can be spotted everywhere. Other commonly seen large marine creatures include manta rays, grouper, tuna, jewfish, and several types of sharks and whales. However, visibility is less than high at most dive sites, especially during the rainy season when river runoff clouds the oceans.

Getting ready for a dive involves careful checking of all equipment, especially the breathing apparatus.

While underwater, it is wise to swim in a group so as to assist each other in times of need.

Starfish can be seen creeping slowly atop the reefs.

Tropical fish of varied hues and shapes inhabit the waters.

Corals, generally poorly developed in Costa Rica, are at their most colorful here.

Isla del Caño

This island boasts the largest coral formations in Costa Rica, attracting a rainbow of tropical fish. Also seen here are octopus, sea horses, and starfish. Dolphins cavort in near-shore waters. Diving trips are offered from Bahía Drake (see p242).

Several angelfish species, such as king, queen, and French angelfish, are found around Isla del Caño (see p236).

At Punta Gorda, off Playa Ocotal, scuba divers are sure to see a vast number of eagle rays flap past. Also seen are golden rays, as well as stone fish and sea horses.

Isla del Coco (see p245) is said to be a site of hidden gold, but its real treasure lies underwater, and includes huge schools of hammerhead sharks. Accessed by live-aboard boats, this is only for experienced divers.

Islas Murciélagos, the most favored dive site in the northwest, is renowned for white tip sharks, marlin, and other giant pelagics. Several outfitters in Playas del Coco (see p190) offer trips.

Swimming

Most large hotels, and many smaller ones, have swimming pools. Ocean water temperatures typically range between 25 and 30° C (77–87° F). However, extreme caution is required when swimming in the oceans: Costa Rica averages about 200 drownings a year due to riptides. These fast-moving water currents are typically associated with beaches with high volumes of incoming surf and where retreating water funnels into a narrow channel that can drag you out to sea. Many of the most popular beaches have riptides. If you get caught in one, do not struggle against the current or try to swim to shore: this will quickly exhaust you. Swim parallel to the shore to exit the current. Avoid swimming near river estuaries, where crocodiles may lurk, and in ocean waters off beaches where marine turtles nest, as sharks are often present.

Scuba Diving

Almost all the beach resorts near the prime dive sites have scuba operators. You can rent or buy gear here, and at **Mundo Aquático**, in San José. **El Ocotal Diving Safaris** and **Rich Coast Diving** are two respected dive operators based at Playa Ocotal and Playas del Coco, respectively *(see p190)*. Trips to

Divers about to go underwater off Costa Rica's Pacific coast

Isla del Coco, for experienced divers, are offered aboard the **Okeanos Aggressor**, which sails from Puntarenas on 8-, 9-, and 10-day voyages.

DIRECTORY

Tour Operators

Costa Rica Expeditions
Calle Central/2 and Ave 3, San José.
Tel 2257-0766.
W costaricaexpeditions.com

Costa Rica Sun Tours
Edificio Cerro Chato, La Uruca, San José.
Tel 2296-7757.
W crsuntours.com

Serendipity Adventures
Apartado 90-7150, Turrialba.
Tel 2558-1000.
W serendipityadventures.com

National Parks and Wildlife Reserves

Amigos de los Parques Nacionales
Tel 2263-4162.
W proparques.org

SINAC
Calle 25 and Ave 8/10, San José.
Tel 2248-2451.
W sinac.go.cr

Wildlife-Viewing

Horizontes
Tel 2222-7022.
W horizontes.com

National Geographic Expeditions
1145 17th Street NW, Washington, D.C. 20037, USA.
Tel 888-966-8687.
W nationalgeographicexpeditions.com

Hiking

Instituto Geográfico Nacional
Calles 9/11 and Ave 20, San José.
Tel 2523-2000 (ext. 2630).

Librería Universal
Calles Central/1 & Ave Central, San José.
Tel 2222-2222.
W universalcr.com

Canopy Tours

Original Canopy Tour
Tel 2291-4465.
W canopytour.com

Horseback Riding

Club Hípico La Caraña
Tel 2282-6754.
W lacarana.com

Cycling and Motorcycling

Backroads
801 Cedar St, Berkeley, CA 94710, USA.
Tel (510) 527-1555.
W backroads.com

Coast to Coast Adventures
P.O. Box 2135-1002, San José. **Tel** 2280-8054.
W ctocadventures.com

MotoDiscovery
685 Persimmon Hill, Bulverde, TX 78163, USA.
Tel (830) 438-7744.
W motodiscovery.com

Golf

Cariari Country Club
Tel 2293-3211.
W clubcariari.com

Parque Valle del Sol
Tel 2282-9222.
W vallesol.com

Reserva Conchal Golf Club
Tel 2654-3000.
W reservaconchal.com

Whitewater Rafting and Kayaking

Ríos Tropicales
Tel 2233-6455.
W riostropicales.com

7th Street Books
Calle 7 and Ave Central/1, San José. **Tel** 2256-8251.

Sportfishing

Club Amateur de Pesca
Tel 2232-3430.
W clubamateurpescacr.com

La Casa del Pescador
Calle 2 and Ave 16/18, San José. **Tel** 2222-1470.

Spiritual Retreats

Samasati Nature Retreat
Hone Creek.
Tel 2224-1870.
W samasati.com

Scuba Diving

El Ocotal Diving Safaris
Tel 2670-0321 (ext. 120).
W ocotaldiving.com

Mundo Aquático
109 yd (100 m) N of Mas X Menos, San Pedro, San José. **Tel** 2224-9729.
W mundoac@racsa.co.cr

Okeanos Aggressor
Tel 800-348-2628.
W aggressor.com

Rich Coast Diving
Tel 2670-0176.
W richcoastdiving.com

SURVIVAL GUIDE

PRACTICAL INFORMATION

It is possible to visit all but the most remote parts of Costa Rica with relative ease, either with a rented vehicle or by public transport. The country has a superb tourist infrastructure, especially in the realms of ecotourism and adventure travel. Rarely will visitors be far from tourist facilities. National tourist offices are found only in San José; in smaller towns and beach resorts, travel agencies and tour operators double as tourist information bureaus. On the whole, tour operators are extremely professional. However, many aspects of day-to-day life in Costa Rica are slow and often bureaucratic. Some patience and flexibility are required to help cope with the minor frustrations.

When to Go

Costa Rica is best visited in the dry season, which runs from December to April. However, there are regional variations (see p40) – the Caribbean and Southwest Pacific, for example, receive torrential rains year-round.

The wet season is also the hottest time of the year, and it can be torrid, especially in Guanacaste. Many dirt roads become impassable during this time. However, prices are lower than during the dry season, when many hotels are booked solid.

Visas and Passports

All visitors need a valid passport, a return or onward ticket, and adequate finances to support themselves for the duration of their stay. Some visitors need visas. Entry requirements are prone to change so check before travel. A tourist card will be issued on arrival; valid for 90 days, this can be extended at a *migración* (immigration) office in any major city.

If transiting via the USA, you must apply for the Electronic System for Travel Authorization (**ESTA**) before traveling.

Customs Information

Buying or exporting archaeological artifacts is illegal and subject to harsh penalties, so be sure to buy only certified reproductions. Items covered by the Convention on International Trade in Endangered Species (CITES) are also prohibited. Visit www.cites.org for more information.

The Chamber of Tourism in Santa Elena, Monteverde

Tourist Information

Brochures and maps are available free of charge at the **Instituto Costarricense de Turismo (ICT)** bureaus at the two international airports (see p302). Outside San José, visit tour agencies for information on the local area. Backpacker hostels, hotel tour desks, and websites are other useful sources of information.

Admission Prices and Opening Hours

Entry prices vary considerably, although most public museums and art galleries are free or charge only a minimal fee. Most national parks cost between $6 and $10. Private reserves and nature centers are typically more expensive, but they often include guided tours and/or activities.

Museum opening hours vary. Bear in mind that many museums close for lunch and on Mondays. National parks are typically open daily from 8am until 4pm.

For opening hours of shops and banks, see p278 and p300.

Language

The official language of Costa Rica is Spanish, which is spoken without the Castilian lisp. A basic knowledge of this language is an advantage, though virtually everybody working in the tourism and service industries speaks English. Traditional languages also exist, but most indigenous people speak Spanish.

Etiquette and Smoking

Courtesy is greatly valued in Costa Rica. It is normal to shake hands or kiss on one cheek when greeting. Use proper titles such as *señor, señora,* and *señorita. Quedar bien* (to appear well) is a form of behavior intended to leave a good impression, but be aware that it can also involve making false promises simply to please the listener. It is a good idea to ask more than one person for directions.

Costa Rica has enacted a law banning smoking in bars, restaurants, and other enclosed public spaces.

◄ Zipline canopy tour, Monteverde

Taxes and Tipping

Hotels and restaurants add a 13 percent sales tax, which is also applicable to most store purchases. In addition, restaurants add a 10 percent service charge to all bills.

It is the norm to tip hotel service staff; taxi drivers are optional *(see p306)*. Tour guides should be tipped depending on the quality of their service and presentation; $2 per person per day is the norm for group tours. Additional tips are usually given only for exceptional service. See also Where to Stay *(p251)* and Where to Eat and Drink *(p263)*.

Travelers with Special Needs

Some airports and the newer hotels and restaurants provide wheelchair ramps and adapted toilets. Few wildlife parks have accessible trails or toilets, although the situation is improving. **Shaka Beach Retreat** at Playa Santa Teresa, provides surfing lessons for wheelchair-bound visitors.

Traveling with Children

Costa Ricans are very fond of children, and most restaurants have high chairs and special kids' menus *(see p263)*. Hotels permit children under 16 to stay at no extra charge if they share a room with their parents. Many tour companies and eco-lodges provide special family programs, while most museums and private attractions offer free entry for children under the age of six, and discounts for those aged between six and 12. Car rental companies do not offer children's car seats, so bring your own. Baby foods, diapers, and all other necessities are widely available in local stores.

Parents should consult with their doctor about any recommended vaccinations. The **Hospital Nacional de Niños** in San José is the local children's hospital.

Gay and Lesbian Travelers

Costa Ricans are tolerant of homosexuality, although public displays of affection between members of the same sex may provoke strong reactions, especially in rural areas. San José has several gay nightclubs and gay-only hotels, as does Manuel Antonio, the most popular destination for gay travelers.

Traveling on a Budget

Costa Rica is popular with budget travelers, who can find affordable accommodations at *cabinas*, backpacker hostels, and surf camps. It is possible to eat well and inexpensively at *sodas* (food stalls) or by ordering *casados* (set menus). Bus travel is also cheap, and most tourist attractions offer discounts to students and seniors.

Time and Electricity

Costa Rica is 6 hours behind Greenwich Mean Time (GMT) and 1 hour behind New York's Eastern Standard Time (EST). The country has not adopted daylight saving time.

Electrical current is 100 volts, but many hotels in remote areas generate their own power, with a nonstandard voltage.

Responsible Tourism

There are positive attitudes to responsible tourism throughout Costa Rica, as shown by the many conservation schemes. Travelers can contribute to local welfare by buying crafts directly from artisans, hiring local guides, and patronizing community ecotourism projects. Consider volunteering with programs that help save endangered wildlife or contribute to the development of impoverished communities. **Costa Rica Expeditions**, for example, has a program that lets guests at Tortuga Lodge teach English to local children.

DIRECTORY

Visas and Passports

ESTA
W https://esta.cbp.dhs.gov

Tourist Information

Instituto Costarricense de Turismo (ICT)
E of Juan Pablo II Bridge, Autopista General Cañas, San José.
Tel 2299-5800.
W visitcostarica.com

Useful websites
W costaricaexpert.net
W ticotimes.com

Travelers with Special Needs

Shaka Beach Retreat
Tel 2640-1118.
W shakacostarica.com

Traveling with Children

Hospital Nacional de Niños
Paseo Colón, Calle 20, San José.
Tel 2222-0122.

Responsible Tourism

Costa Rica Expeditions
Tel 2257-0766.
W costaricaexpeditions.com

Tortuga Lodge, where guests can take part in an English-teaching program

Personal Security and Health

Generally regarded as a safe destination, Costa Rica has a stable democracy and a reputation for neutrality. This can lull visitors into a sense of security that may occasionally prove to be false. Tourists can be targets for theft, scams, and even violent crime, so it is wise to take a few basic safety precautions.

The country has a relatively advanced health system, and you will rarely be far from medical assistance in times of need. Keep an eye out for venomous snakes and other potentially harmful creatures that inhabit the wild. It is also wise to be aware of the country's natural hazards, including dangerous riptides and the sun's powerful tropical rays.

Tourist police patroling the beach at Tamarindo, on the Pacific coast

Police

Costa Rican police officers are professional, usually polite, and happy to help tourists. Their standard uniform is dark blue. The bicycle police, wearing white shirts and blue shorts, patrol major cities and tourist centers on bike, while *Tránsitos* (traffic police) patrol the highways, using radar guns to catch speeders.

Attempts by individual police officers to extract *mordidas* (bribes) are fairly rare. To make a complaint against an officer, note their name and badge number and report them to the **Organismo de Investigación Judicial (OIJ)**.

What to Be Aware Of

Keep photocopies of your passport and other important documents in the hotel safe, along with your valuables. Be aware of your surroundings at all times, especially on city streets. Avoid wearing jewelry in public and do not leave your belongings unattended. Be especially cautious of scams involving your rental car *(see p307)* and of anyone offering unsolicited assistance of any kind, especially if you have tire problems; a common distracting ploy involves would-be thieves deflating your tires, then offering to help. Women should avoid dark and isolated areas. Never hitchhike. If you are a victim of serious crime, contact the OIJ's **Victim Assistance Office**.

Pedestrians do not have the right of way in Costa Rica, and extreme care is required when crossing the road. Always look both ways, even on one-way streets, since buses are allowed to travel in both directions on many roads, and the direction of traffic may change at certain times of day. Be careful at junctions too, as many drivers ignore stop signs and even red lights. When walking, keep your eyes open for deep holes and uneven sidewalks. When driving, watch for live-stock and massive potholes, which are often indicated by a stick placed inside them.

In an Emergency

Costa Rica has a single number for **emergencies**: 911. If things go wrong, your first port of call should be your embassy; depending on the circumstances, they may be able to help.

Most major towns and tourist centers have a **Cruz Roja** (Red Cross) station with an ambulance service. This is supplemented by private ambulance services on 24-hour call. However, in remote areas, you may find it quicker to take a taxi to the nearest clinic or hospital.

Lost and Stolen Property

In the event of loss or theft of belongings, inform the police within 24 hours; you will need an official police report for insurance purposes. If your passport is lost or stolen, contact your embassy or consulate at once. Loss or theft of credit cards should be reported to the relevant company *(see p300)*.

Hospitals and Pharmacies

Costa Ricans are served by the state-run Instituto Nacional de Seguridad (INS) hospitals, which also provide an emergency service to tourists for a nominal fee *(see p307)*. Most public hospitals are well run, if overcrowded, but rural clinics are often poorly equipped. Private hospitals – such as San José's **Hospital Clínica Bíblica** and Escazú's **Hospital CIMA** – conform to North American and European standards. Hotels and embassies usually have a list of reliable doctors. Most tourist centers also have private dental clinics.

Farmacias or *boticas* (pharmacies), numerous in

Red Cross logo

Exterior of a *farmacia* (pharmacy) in San José

cities nationwide, sell an extensive range of drugs over the counter, including some that require a doctor's prescription in the US, Canada, and Europe. However, visitors with prediagnosed conditions are advised to bring their own medication.

Minor Hazards

The tropical sun can be fierce; always use sunscreen and a hat when outdoors. Drink plenty of fluids to guard against dehydration. Heat and high humidity may cause heatstroke – if you suffer from thirst, nausea, fever, and dizziness, consult a doctor. Wash and dry clothes often to prevent prickly heat and athlete's foot.

Cover up well and use lots of insect repellent to avoid diseases such as dengue fever, which is spread by mosquitoes. Symptoms include fever, headaches, and joint pains, usually lasting about 10 days, after which a month-long recovery is normal. Insect repellents and *espirales* (coils) can be bought locally. Minor insect bites can be treated with antihistamines, but if they become infected, you should seek the advice of a local doctor. If you get bitten by a venomous snake or a wild animal that may carry rabies do not panic, try not to move, and seek immediate medical attention.

Insect repellent and a mosquito coil for protection against bites

Shun tap water if possible, and follow basic precautions with food *(see p263)* to avoid diarrhea and parasitic infections such as giardiasis. If you are affected by diarrhea, drink lots of bottled water and see a doctor if the condition becomes chronic.

Travel and Health Insurance

Tour and travel agencies sell a wide range of insurance policies, covering baggage loss, theft, and trip cancellation. Ideally, however, travel insurance should also cover medical expenses, since public health care is not always adequate, and treatment in private hospitals and clinics can be expensive. You may need to pay for treatment while in Costa Rica and then make a claim on your insurance when you return home. Prior to departure, check whether your domestic health insurance policies cover you while abroad.

Vaccinations

No specific vaccinations are required to enter Costa Rica. Malaria can be found along the southern Caribbean coast, and antimalarial medication is therefore recommended for visitors to that area. It is also wise to be immunized against typhoid and hepatitis A and B, and to make sure that your polio and tetanus vaccinations are up to date.

DIRECTORY

Emergency Numbers

Cruz Roja
Tel 128 or 119.

Emergencies
Tel 911.

Organismo de Investigación Judicial (OIJ)
Tel 2295-3312.

Police
Tel 127 or 2222-1365.

Victim Assistance Office
Tel 2295-3643.

Hospitals

Hospital CIMA
Tel 2208-1000.

Hospital Clínica Bíblica
Tel 2522-1000.

Embassies

Canada
Oficentro Ejecutivo La Sabana, Edificio 5, Sabana Sur, San José.
Tel 2242-4400.

UK
Centro Colón, Paseo Colón, Calles 38/40, San José. Tel 2258-2025.
W ukin.costarica@fco.gov.uk

USA
Boulevard a Pavas, San José.
Tel 2519-2000.
W sanjose.usembassy.gov

Natural Disasters

In the event of an earthquake, move away from tall structures. Do not use elevators. If you are indoors, the safest place is usually in a doorway. Keep a flashlight and shoes near your bed at night.

Obey all instructions at volcanic parks, such as Poás, Arenal, and Turrialba, which became active in 2009 after being dormant for a long time. Arenal is especially volatile, and visits to the immediate area – notably Tabacón *(see p202)* – are always risky. Never hike in restricted zones.

Beware of riptides, which are strong currents that can drag swimmers out to sea *(see p290)*. Flash floods are common during heavy rainfall, when waterfalls and rivers must be avoided.

Banking and Currency

The Costa Rican currency is the colón, but US dollars are also widely accepted. Only larger banks are able to exchange other foreign currencies; however, most tourist hotels will change money at rates similar to those offered by the banks. Large hotels, restaurants, and shops usually take major credit cards, whereas traveler's checks are rarely accepted. It is wise to have small-denomination dollar notes, since stores rarely take $50 and $100 bills, due to the prevalence of counterfeit bills in circulation.

DIRECTORY

Banks

Banco de Costa Rica
Calles 4/6 and Ave 2, San José.
Tel 2284-6600.

Banco Nacional
Calles 2/4 and Ave 1, San José.
Tel 2212-2000.

Credit & Debit Cards

MasterCard
Tel 0800-011-0184 (lost cards).
w mastercard.com

Visa
Tel 0800-011-0030 (lost cards).
w visa.com

Traveler's Checks

Barclays Bank
w barclays.com

Thomas Cook
w thomascook.co.uk

Banks, ATMs, and Exchange Bureaus

The largest banks are the **Banco de Costa Rica** and **Banco Nacional**, both with branches countrywide. Most banks are open on weekdays from 8am to 4pm, but avoid visiting them on a Friday, which is payday for many Costa Ricans. In rural areas, you may have to wait in line for a considerable time to transact any business.

Many of the bigger banks provide *cajeros automáticos* (ATMs), which accept major bank and credit cards to withdraw cash. Be aware of your surroundings when using an ATM, and avoid counting your money in public. The country's two international

airports and the major border crossings *(see p311)* have *casas de cambio* (foreign exchange bureaus), but you will receive a better rate of exchange at banks and hotels. Any other establishment offering to change your currency is doing so illegally. Many tourists are swindled by unofficial money-changers on the street; be sure to steer clear of these touts.

Credit and Debit Cards

The most widely accepted credit cards are **VISA**, **MasterCard**, and, to a lesser extent, American Express and Diners Card. A VISA card (and sometimes a MasterCard) allows you to

obtain cash advances at banks. Many hotels will also offer cash advances on your credit card.

Traveler's Checks

Buy traveler's checks at your local bank at home or via the websites of **Thomas Cook** and **Barclays Bank**. These checks are generally more secure than credit cards, and in the event of loss or theft, you can claim a refund. Traveler's checks can be exchanged for cash at banks for a commission; however, few places accept them as currency.

Currency

The Costa Rican currency is the colón (¢), which is often called *peso*. Money is sometimes colloquially referred to as *plata* or *pista*, and cash as *efectivo*. Always carry some coins and small-denomination bills for tips and minor purchases in small establishments.

1,000 colones

2,000 colones

5,000 colones

10,000 colones

Bank Notes and Coins

Bank notes come in denominations of 1,000, 2,000, 5,000, 10,000, 20,000, and 50,000 colones and display famous historical figures on the front and Costa Rican ecosystems on the rear.

Costa Rican coins come in denominations of 5, 10, 25, 50, 100, and 500 colones. Coins minted a while ago are in silver; the newer ones are golden in color. Loose change is sometimes called *menudo*.

50 colones

100 colones

500 colones

Media and Communications

Telecommunications in Costa Rica are highly developed. Ticos are avid users of cell phones, despite reception being erratic in many areas. The postal service, however, is slow and unreliable. As well as several international channels, Costa Rica has 12 local TV channels and more than 100 radio stations. There are three major Spanish newspapers and a few English-language publications.

An Internet café and photocopying center in Cahuita

International and Local Telephone Calls

There are public telephones on main streets and plazas in every Costa Rican town. In remote villages, they are often found at a *pulpería* (grocery store), where the owner may place the call and charge by the minute. Most public phones require a *tarjeta telefónica* (phonecard), available from supermarkets, stores, and banks. Kolbi phonecards are sold in denominations from 100 colones to $20 and can be used with any phone.

Making calls from your hotel room is expensive, but you can save money by calling the operator at companies such as **AT&T**, **Worldcom**, and **Sprint** and charging the call to your credit card. A cheaper alternative is to use a call center. Many Internet cafés offer free Skype.

Dialing Codes

- Costa Rica's country code is 506.
- Costa Rican telephone numbers have eight digits; there are no area codes.
- Dial 113 for information. International operators speak English.

Cell Phones

North American cell phones usually work within Costa Rica, but European phones do not. Cell phones are useful when traveling in remote areas, but coverage may be patchy.

Prepaid Sim cards can be bought at the Kolbi booth in the baggage claim area of San José's Juan Santamaría International airport.

Internet and Email

Usually, large hotels have business centers, and budget hotels have Wi-Fi or broadband plug-in modems in a communal area. Internet cafés are found in every town and in many small villages too. Service can be slow and erratic.

Postal Services

Most towns and villages have *oficinas de correos* (post offices), which are usually open 8am–4pm Monday to Friday. The mail service in Costa Rica is slow, inefficient, and subject to theft, so send any important documents and valuable items via an international courier service such as **DHL**. Major hotels allow you to drop off postcards and letters at the front desk.

Costa Rican Addresses

Although most towns are organized into *avenidas* and *calles* (streets), few buildings have numbers, and people rarely know their own street address. Mail deliveries are usually made to *apartados* (post office boxes).

Newspapers and Magazines

Costa Rica's three big Spanish-language daily newspapers – *La Nación*, *La Prensa*, and *La República* – are sold at streetside stalls, hotel gift stores, and a few newsagents in major cities. *The Tico Times* is an English-language weekly covering news and events.

Television and Radio

Most hotels, with the exception of wilderness lodges and budget *cabinas*, offer in-room TVs. Upscale establishments often have a cable or satellite service, with stations such as CNN and MTV, some key European channels, and Costa Rican stations. Large business hotels also offer pay-per-view films.

The country has more than 120 radio stations, which broadcast mainly in Spanish. Super Radio (102.3 FM) has music and news in English.

DIRECTORY

International Telephone Calls

AT&T
Tel 0800-011-4114.

Sprint
Tel 163 or 0800-013-0123.

Worldcom
Tel 0800-014-4444.

Postal Services

DHL
Calles 30/32 and Paseo Colón, San José. **Tel** 2209-6000.

Newspapers and Magazines

The Tico Times
[w] ticotimes.net

TRAVEL INFORMATION

Most visitors to Costa Rica arrive at San José's Juan Santamaría International Airport, near Alajuela. An ever-larger number of international flights land at Daniel Oduber International Airport, 7 miles (11 km) west of Liberia, which is the airport of choice of most major US carriers. The country is also served by several bus companies, and some visitors travel from North America by car. Cruise ships berth on both the Pacific and Caribbean coasts, bringing passengers on day excursions. Costa Rica's domestic transportation system includes small planes serving regional airstrips and buses of varying quality. Rental vehicles are a practical alternative to public transport and grant maximum freedom. Most places in the country are within a day's drive of San José. However, the highway system is dilapidated in parts, and driving can be a challenge in certain areas, especially during the wet season. Costa Rica's train service is limited to commuter trains between San José and Heredia.

The terminal at San José's Juan Santamaría International Airport

Arriving by Air

Leading US airlines, such as **American Airlines**, **Frontier**, **Delta**, **JetBlue**, **Spirit Airlines**, **United**, and **US Airways**, offer scheduled direct flights to Costa Rica. **Grupo Taca**, the regional airline of Central America, has scheduled flights from several cities in the US. Services are either direct or routed via gateways such as Dallas or Miami; others make one or more stops en route in El Salvador, Mexico City, or Managua, in Nicaragua. Both **Air Canada** and Grupo Taca offer a service from Canada.

From Europe, **Air France** and **Iberia** operate direct scheduled flights, while **British Airways** and other carriers connect via Miami. **Condor** has charters from Germany. There are no direct flights from Australia or New Zealand; however, visitors from these countries can catch a connecting flight from Los Angeles.

Tickets and Fares

Flights to Costa Rica often sell out, especially during the dry season, so book well in advance; the earlier you buy, the lower the fare. It is worth comparing the airlines' fares against those available at travel websites such as **Travelocity**, **Expedia**, and **Orbitz**. Round-trip tickets tend to cost less than one-way fares, and traveling midweek is usually cheaper than at the weekend. Charter flights offer a better deal than scheduled flights, although more restrictions apply. If you are after a beach holiday, an inclusive flight-and-hotel package with a charter airline or tour operator will likely work out cheaper than independent travel.

On Arrival

Present your tourist card and customs form (both issued by your airline; see p296). The baggage-claim area at Juan Santamaría has an ATM and a foreign exchange bureau that offers poor rates. An official tourist information bureau and a number of car-rental agencies are located immediately beyond the Customs Hall. Daniel Oduber Airport has similar facilities.

Getting to San José

There are usually taxis outside Customs at Juan Santamaría International. First, pick up a ticket from the dispatcher, being sure to double-check the fixed price to your chosen destination; then, confirm the rate with your driver before departure, as many use crafty ruses to charge more. **Taxi Aeropuerto**, which operates the orange airport taxis, takes reservations. Some hotels provide a shuttle service, either free or for a fee. Budget travelers can use the **Tuasa** public buses which link the airport to San José and Alajuela.

If driving to San José, try to recover from jetlag before renting a car. There have been instances of rental cars being hijacked on the main highway, so be vigilant.

Departure Tax

All travelers flying out of Costa Rica must pay a departure tax of $28. You can pay this in advance, upon arrival, at the check-in hall, or at banks and tour agencies at any time during your stay.

Arriving by Land

There are three border crossings for vehicles: at Peñas Blancas (between Costa Rica and Nicaragua), and at Paso Canoas and Sixaola (both between Costa Rica and Panama). Pedestrians can also cross to/from Nicaragua at the town of Los Chiles. Visas are not necessary to enter either Nicaragua or Panama, as temporary tourist visas are issued at the border. Transit permits and insurance can be arranged through **Sanborn's**. Note that rental cars may not be taken across borders.

Many visitors travel to and from Costa Rica by bus. Companies such as **Transnica** and **Ticabus**, both with terminals in San José, provide bus services between various Central American countries. Another option is to cross the border on foot and catch onward buses on the other side. Keep a close eye on your personal belongings on bus trips.

Visitors driving between the US and Costa Rica should allow at least two weeks for the 2,300-mile (3,700-km) road journey.

Enjoying a waterfall tour on the Reventazón River

Arriving by Sea

Several cruise ships include Puerto Caldera (on the Pacific) and Puerto Limón (Caribbean) on their itineraries, and allow passengers to disembark for day-long excursions.

Organized Tours

Companies such as **Costa Rica Connection** and **Costa Rica Experts**, in North America, and **Journey Latin America**, in the UK, offer a wide range of special-interest vacations, as well as customized tour arrangements. Nature-oriented trips geared toward bird-watching and other wildlife-viewing are especially popular. Other special-interest vacations include bicycling, whitewater rafting, kayaking, sportfishing, surfing, and scuba diving (see pp288–93). **National Geographic Expeditions'** nature-themed cruise-tours offer a unique way of exploring several hard-to-reach destinations.

DIRECTORY

Arriving by Air

Air Canada
Tel 1-888-247-2262.
w aircanada.com

Air France
Tel (33) 9 69 39 02 15.
w airfrance.com

American Airlines
Tel 1-800-433-7300.
w aa.com

British Airways
Tel 0844 493 0787.
w british-airways.co.uk

Condor
Tel (49) 0180-5-707 202.
w condor.com

Delta
Tel 800-321-1212.
w delta.com

Frontier
Tel 1-800-432-1359.
w frontierairlines.com

Grupo Taca
Tel 1-800-400-8222.
w taca.com

Iberia
Tel (34) 902-400-500.
w iberia.com

JetBlue
Tel 800-539-2583.
w jetblue.com

Spirit Airlines
Tel 801-401-2200.
w spiritair.com

United
Tel 1-800-864-8331.
w united.com

US Airways
Tel 1-800-428-4322.
w usairways.com

Tickets and Fares

Expedia
w expedia.com

Orbitz
w orbitz.com

Travelocity
w travelocity.com

Getting to San Jose

Taxi Aeropuerto
Tel 2222-6865.
w taxiaeropuerto.com

Tuasa
Ave 2 and Calles 12/14,
San José. Tel 2222-5325.

Arriving by Land

Sanborn's
Tel 1-800-222-0158.
w sanbornsinsurance.com

Ticabus
Tel 2248-9636.
w ticabus.com

Transnica
Tel 2223-4242.
w transnica.com

Organized Tours

Costa Rica Connection
P.O. Box 15832, San Luis Obispo, CA 93401.
Tel 1-800-345-7422.
w crconnect.com

Costa Rica Experts
Tel 1-800-827-9046.
w costaricaexperts.com

Journey Latin America
Tel 020 8747 8315.
w journeylatinamerica.co.uk

National Geographic Expeditions
Tel 1-888-966-8687.
w nationalgeographicexpeditions.com

Getting Around Costa Rica

Despite Costa Rica's compact size, traveling overland can take quite a long time due to the varying conditions of the road network. On the plus side, buses are inexpensive and can be combined with local jeep-taxi services to reach the more isolated spots. Air travel is especially convenient for people on a tight schedule and those who wish to visit remote regions or several attractions that are spaced far apart. Reaching Isla Tortuga and some sights in Golfo Dulce and the Osa Peninsula involves the use of a ferry or boat service. Hitchhiking is not common or safe in Costa Rica. For more on driving, see pp306–307.

Green Travel

Consider ways to reduce your impact on the environment when making travel arrangements. If possible, rent a hybrid vehicle. When exploring national parks and wetlands by boat, choose tour companies and private guides that use canoes or non-polluting four-stroke, not two-stroke, engines. Consider flying with **Nature Air**, which claims to be the world's first carbon-neutral airline and offsets emissions from every flight with a contribution to rainforest protection. Finally, travel with local guides and businesses as much as possible to ensure that your money stays within local communities.

Domestic Flights

Scheduled domestic flights from San José's Juan Santamaría International Airport are offered by **Sansa**. The company links the capital with 16 domestic airstrips, using 22- and 35-passenger Cessnas. Sansa's published itineraries change frequently and are not 100 percent reliable. A slightly superior service is offered by Nature Air, which flies to the same destinations from Tobias Bolaños Airport, located about 1.2 miles (2 km) west of Parque Sabana in San José. Nature Air offers children's discounts.

Note that the baggage allowance is 30 lb (14 kg) for Sansa and 15–40 lb (7–18 kg) for Nature Air, depending on fare

A twin-engine airplane flying over Quepos, on the Pacific coast

class. This is considerably less than for international flights, so be sure to plan your baggage accordingly.

Airplane tickets can be purchased through travel agents and tour operators, or directly from the airlines. Reservations should be made as far in advance as possible, especially for travel during peak times, such as Christmas, Easter, and the dry season (Dec–Apr). The timetables vary between wet and dry seasons (see pp36–7).

Private companies offer an on-demand charter service to airstrips nationwide using 4- to 8-seater aircraft. You need to charter the entire aircraft, including the return journey, if no additional passengers sign up.

Local Buses and Terminals

More than a dozen private companies offer a bus service linking San José to towns and villages nationwide. Services between large cities are usually aboard comfortable air-conditioned vehicles with reclining seats. Shorter trips between smaller towns and villages are typically on older, more basic second-class buses. The ICT (see p297) publishes a bus schedule.

For intercity travel, *directo* buses offer a fast and often nonstop service, while the *corriente*, or normal, service is slower, with more stops en route. The fares are rarely more than $10. Advance reservations are recommended for intercity travel, especially on Fridays and Saturdays, when demand peaks. If you can, avoid traveling at the weekend. Arrive at the bus station well ahead of your departure time to secure a good seat. Travel with as little baggage as possible, and guard your belongings at all times against theft. Rural buses can be waved down at *paradas* (bus stops) along their routes.

In most towns, the bus terminal is close to the main plaza. Some towns have more than one; for example, there are two large bus terminals in San José, with additional bus stations all around downtown. Buses to the Caribbean leave from Gran Terminal Caribe, and those to most other parts of the country from a series of bus stops concentrated in an area called "Coca Cola", which is located west of downtown. The Coca Cola terminal has a reputation for pickpockets and muggings, so be on your guard in this area.

A shuttle bus run by Interbus

colectivo (pickup truck) heading for Puerto Jiménez

DIRECTORY

Green Travel

Nature Air
Tel 2299-6000.
w natureair.com

Domestic Flights

Sansa
Tel 2229-4100.
w flysansa.com

Tourist Buses and Organized Tours

Grayline
Tel 2220-2126.
w graylinecostarica.com

Interbus
Tel 2283-5573.
w interbusonline.com

Commuter Trains

Tuasa
Tel 2222-5325.

Tourist Buses and Organized Tours

A direct shuttle service linking the most popular tourist destinations is offered by **Interbus** and **Grayline**; both also have shuttles between San José and Juan Santamaría Airport. Interbus offers door-to-door pickup and dropoff, while Grayline has discounts for children and seniors.

Sightseeing bus tours give useful overviews of Costa Rica or specific regions; some focus on nature-viewing and other activities. Leading operators include Grayline and Costa Rica Expeditions (see p307).

Taxis and Colectivos

Taxis can be found around the central plazas in most towns. In San José, you can also call one of several taxi companies (see p309). Licensed taxis are red (though airport taxis are orange), with a white triangle on the front door showing the license number. For journeys under 8 miles (12 km), drivers are required to use their *marias* (meters), but many will make an excuse not to do so in order to be able to charge more. The rates for longer journeys are negotiable. Never take an unlicensed private taxi – several tourists have been robbed by the drivers or their accomplices. Many taxis lack functioning seat belts. Make sure yours works before setting off.

Jeep-taxis serve many communities that are difficult to reach due to mountainous or unpaved roads. The most remote communities and tourist destinations are also served by *colectivos*, usually open-bed pickup trucks with seats and awnings. They follow fixed routes and can be flagged down anywhere along the route. *Colectivos* normally charge a flat fee, regardless of distance.

For more information on taxis, see p308.

Commuter Trains

Operated by **Tuasa**, *trenes interurbanos* (commuter trains) link downtown San José to Heredia, with seven stops along the 6-mile (10-km) route. The fare for the 30-minute journey is 355 colones ($0.70). A train also links San José with Cartago, with five stops en route. It costs 555 colones ($1.10).

Boats and Ferries

Car and passenger ferries link Puntarenas with Naranjo and Paquera, in Nicoya. There is also a water-taxi service between Puntarenas and Paquera, Jacó and Montezuma, and Sierpe and Bahía Drake, along the Tortuguero Canal, and in Golfo Dulce. Visitors can also go on boat trips on Costa Rica's many rivers, canals, and swamps.

Passengers waiting to board a boat at Isla Tortuga

Traveling by Car

Driving is the best way of exploring Costa Rica, as a car grants relatively easy access to some of the country's most remarkable scenery. Roads between towns are usually paved, but you still need to watch out for potholes. Minor roads are often dirt and gravel, turning into muddy quagmires during the wet season. A four-wheel drive vehicle is essential for exploring the countryside. Conditions are often hazardous, so take precautions. Do not drive at night, and carry a road atlas published by a reputable company rather than one bought locally. The use of seat belts is compulsory, but few Costa Ricans wear them, and laws are rarely enforced. If you're traveling with young children, bring a child seat, as car rental agencies do not supply them.

A busy street in San José

Roads and Tolls

Only 20 percent of Costa Rica's 18,650 miles (30,000 km) of highway are paved, with the Central Highlands taking up a large chunk of the total. The percentage of unpaved roads increases as you travel away from San José. Three major highways, linking San José to Cartago, San Ramón, and Orotina via the new Autopista del Sol, are toll expressways.

It is difficult to find accurate maps, but the National Geographic Adventure Map and the detailed Costa Rica Nature Atlas are recommended.

Costa Ricans drive on the right-hand side of the road, and the speed limits are 50 mph (80 km/h) on major highways, and 37 mph (60 km/h) on secondary roads. *Tránsitos* (traffic police) patrol the highways in blue cars and on motorcycles, using radar guns to catch speeders. They are not allowed to collect money, though occasionally a corrupt official may try to extract a bribe *(see p298)*. Fines should be paid at a bank or at the car rental agency.

Directions and Signs

Major highways are well signposted. Although most towns also have street signs, the majority of Costa Ricans continue to refer to well-known landmarks when giving directions.

Road signs use international symbols. *Alto* means "stop," *ceda* means "yield," and *mantenga su derecha* means "keep right." *Túmulo* indicates a road bump ahead, while *derrumbe* denotes a landslide or falling rocks.

Road Hazards

Drive slowly to avoid bending a wheel on a pothole. Watch for people and animals in the road, especially outside towns, where few roads have sidewalks. During the wet season, mountain roads are often foggy and subject to landslides, while lowland roads are prone to flooding.

Beware drivers running stop signs, overtaking when there is barely enough room to do so, or driving too close to the vehicle in front. Costa Ricans often use their left-turn signal to indicate to drivers behind that it is safe to overtake. Be careful, though: the vehicle may actually be turning left.

In the event of an accident, call **Tránsitos**. Do not leave you vehicle, and do not let the other party move theirs. If possible, obtain the *cédulas* (identification) and license number of the other driver. If anyone is injured, call the Cruz Roja *(see p299)*. Rental cars have a red triangle; place this in the road a safe distance from your accident site, or make a small pile of stones and branches to warn other drivers. If you own the vehicle, report the accident to the **Instituto Nacional de Seguridad (INS)**, which handles all insurance claims.

Parking

Car break-ins are common throughout Costa Rica. Never leave any items in a parked vehicle, especially at beach locations, where signs warn of the severity of the threat of theft from parked cars. Avoid parking on the street overnight; instead use one of the many inexpensive parking lots with security guards.

Gas Stations

Unleaded gas, or *gasolina*, is sold as either super or regular; the latter is lower-octane and less expensive. Diesel is cheaper still. *Gasolineras* (gas stations) are plentiful in towns, but much scarcer in rural areas, especially

A road sign indicating the route and the distance to several destinations

Nicoya. It is wise to refill whenever the tank drops to half-full. In remote areas, gasoline is usually available at *pulperías* (grocery stores), where it may cost twice as much as at gas stations.

Gas stations are typically open from 6am to midnight, but some operate round the clock. They are not self-service, and most will accept credit cards.

Breakdown Services

In the event of a breakdown, call your car rental agency, which will send a repairman. All reputable agencies have a 24-hour service for such emergencies. Major cities, plus *gasolineras* on major highways, have tow-truck services. Elsewhere, you may need to find a local farmer and tractor to haul you out of a troublesome situation, such as being stuck in mud.

Car and Motorcycle Rental

Most car rental agencies ask that drivers be at least 25 years old, but some will rent to people aged over 21. You will need a valid driver's license and a credit card for paying deposit and settling your bill. If you wish to stay for more than three months, you will need a domestic driver's license.

International car rental firms such as **Alamo**, **Budget**, and **Hertz** have local franchises at the international airports. San José and a few leading tourist centers also offer some local agencies. Prices are generally lower during the wet season, and unlimited-mileage options tend to work out the cheapest.

When pre-booking, always get a written confirmation. Liability insurance to cover damages to other vehicles or persons is mandatory. Check if it's included in the quote; if so, get it confirmed in writing. It is also wise to purchase additional coverage for the vehicle, though some rental agencies may accept your domestic auto

A four-wheel drive vehicle on a dirt road near Ojochal, southern Costa Rica

insurance. Check with your insurance or credit card company whether your policy covers travel in Costa Rica.

Before signing the contract, ensure that the vehicle is in good condition and keep a note of any scratches or other faults. You may be asked to sign a blank credit card slip, which is torn up when the car is returned intact. When returning the car, bring a trusted friend, if possible: unscrupulous agency employees may tamper with the vehicle if you leave it unattended while settling your bill. Check the final bill for any questionable charges, which you may dispute.

Stop sign

A four-wheel drive (4WD) vehicle is vital for rural areas, where extra traction is required. Companies such as **U-Save** have a wide variety of 4WD vehicles, while Costa Rica's Temptations *(see p293)* offers pre-planned self-drive tours. All-terrain vehicles (ATVs), scooters and bicycles can be rented at many beach resorts. **Costa Rica Motorcycle Tours & Rental** rents motorcycles and arranges tours for people aged 25 or older. The wearing of a helmet is mandatory.

Off-Road Driving

A 4WD vehicle is essential for exploring Costa Rica beyond the main cities. A manual-shift vehicle is preferable to an automatic for handling the steep, rock-strewn tracks that lead to many national parks and

ecolodges. Keep your speed down on corrugated and loose-gravel roads, where it is easy to lose traction.

Some rivers require fording, especially in western Nicoya and the Osa Peninsula. Use caution in the wet season, when rivers can be too deep or fast-flowing to ford. Ask the locals about current conditions. Edge slowly into the river, as rushing forward can flood and stall the engine. If necessary, wade the river in advance to ascertain the best route across. In wet season, it's easy to get stuck in mud.

Getting Around San José

Most places of interest in Costa Rica's capital are centrally located, and within walking distance of one another and of many hotels and restaurants. The best way to explore central San José is on foot, though you will need to rely on some form of transport to reach the suburbs and outlying areas. The city's public transportation network is crowded, but an efficient taxi system eases the burden of traveling around by bus. It is not advisable to drive around San José, especially during the morning and afternoon rush hours, when the roads become extremely congested.

Traffic on a busy thoroughfare in downtown San José

Buses

Running from 5am to 10pm, buses in San José are cheap but tend to be overcrowded. There is no central terminal for city buses, and routes are identified not by number but by destination, shown above the front window. Free route maps are available from the ICT office at Juan Santamaría International Airport.

An important bus route is Sabana-Cementerio, which links the city center to Parque Sabana *(see p128)*, running eastbound along Avenida 10 and westbound along Avenida 3. Public buses to the airport depart from Avenida 2, Calles 12/14. Buses to San José's suburbs fill up fast, and you should board at the original departure point.

Pay your fare (125–250 colones) by dropping the money into the electronic counter upon boarding. Do not stand by the counter, which also records passengers; if it registers you twice, you will have to pay twice. Watch out for pickpockets when traveling by bus. It is a good idea to wear your money belt inside your clothes.

Walking

The most practical way to explore the heart of San José is by walking, since being on foot permits you to enjoy the city at close quarters. The city center is laid out in an easy-to-understand grid pattern that makes for convenient strolling. However, the sidewalks are narrow and crowded, and pedestrians are often forced to step into the street. Take great care, as downtown streets are thronged with traffic. Do not assume that vehicles will stop at pedestrian crossings or give way to pedestrians on the road when traffic lights turn to green. Be especially careful of buses, which often drive onto the sidewalks when turning corners. There are usually cafés close

Paseo de los Estudiantes, one of San José's few pedestrianized streets

at hand, allowing you to escape the heat and noise. Be prepared for late-afternoon showers, especially during the rainy season, when you will certainly need an umbrella. These can be bought at roadside stalls.

Beware of pickpockets, especially in crowded places. Avoid wearing jewelry and carry your valuables in a money belt. Hold your camera in front of you, with the strap over your neck rather than on your shoulder. Keep to busy, well-lit areas at night, when you should avoid the streets northwest of the Mercado Central *(see p112)* and southwest of Parque Central *(see p110)*, as well as Parque Nacional *(see pp122–3)* and Parque Morazán *(see p120)*.

Taxis

Taxis are numerous, but they can be in short supply during rush hour and heavy rains. They can be hailed on the street or summoned by phone or via your hotel concierge. The main taxi rank in San José is around Parque Central. Licensed taxis are red; an illuminated sign on the roof indicates that the taxi is available. Most taxis take four passengers.

You can pay in colones or dollars. Fares begin at 530 colones and rise by 380 colones for every kilometer. Taxis are good value by US and European standards – rarely does a fare within the city center cost more than $5. Taxis are required by law to use their *marias* (meters) for journeys of less than 8 miles (12 km). Many drivers decline to do so, hoping to be able to charge you extra. Taxi drivers do not expect tips, but a 10 percent gratuity is appreciated.

Many private drivers offer an unlicensed taxi service. They usually charge more than licensed taxis and have a reputation for being unsafe. Never take an unlicensed taxi, however trustworthy you believe the driver to be.

TG 106 502010 NICOYA

Sign on a local taxi

Red taxis near San José's Catedral Metropolitana

Driving

Even if you are used to driving in cities, exploring San José by car can be a nerve-racking experience and one that is best avoided. *Josefinos* are aggressive drivers and often display a marked lack of consideration for other road users. Many drivers will proceed through red lights if no traffic is coming the other way, especially at night, when extreme care is needed. The speed limit on urban streets is 18 mph (30 km/h).

Route 39, also known as the Circunvalación, runs around the west, south, and east of the city. Avenida Central leads east to the University of Costa Rica and the busy suburb of San Pedro (see p125). To the west, Paseo Colón links the city center to Parque Sabana and the Autopista General Cañas, which leads to the airport and Alajuela. Another freeway, the Autopista

Prospero Fernández, runs west from Parque Sabana to the town of Escazú (see p129), where it becomes the Autopista del Sol, leading to the Pacific lowlands. Traffic normally flows in both directions along Paseo Colón, except 7–9am Monday to Friday, when it is one-way eastbound, and 8am–5pm on Sundays, when it is closed to traffic altogether.

The one-way system and grid pattern in the city center help lubricate traffic flow, but congestion can persist throughout the day. During rush hour, Avenidas 8 and 9 are usually the best routes to follow when traveling westbound; Avenida 10 is recommended for those who are heading east.

Non-commercial vehicles are banned from the city between 6am and 7pm Monday to Friday under a *pico y placa* ("rush hour and license plate") scheme. The specific days are assigned according to the last digit of each vehicle's license plate, and the numbers rotate every six months. Tourist rental cars are not exempt.

There are many parking lots in San José's city center and you should have no trouble finding one. At most, you need to pay an attendant to watch over your car. They

Cautionary sign for seat belts

may require you to leave your ignition keys. Be sure to never leave anything inside the car, even in secure, guarded parking lots.

Road Names and Addresses

Within the city center, even-numbered *avenidas* lie north of Avenida Central, while odd-numbered ones are to the south; even-numbered *calles* are west of Calle Central, and odd-numbered ones are to the east as far as the Circunvalación. Avenida Central is pedestrianized between Calle 6 and Calle 7, as are Calle 2 between Avenidas 2 and 3, and Calle 17 (Bulevar Ricardo Jiménez) between Avenidas 1 and 8. Street signs went up in much of the city in 2012. Traffic lights, which are normally suspended over the center of junctions, are often difficult to see.

Avenida 2 is one of San José's main thoroughfares

General Index

Acknowledgments

Dorling Kindersley would like to thank the following people whose contributions and assistance have made the preparation of this book possible:

Main Contributor

Christopher P. Baker was born and raised in Yorkshire, England, and received his B.A. with Honours (1976) in Geography from the University of London. He holds two Masters' degrees – in Latin American Studies and in Education. He has made his living as a full-time professional travel writer/photographer/tour leader since 1983.

Baker's numerous books include guides to California, Colombia, Cuba, Dominican Republic, Jamaica, and Puerto Rico, and an award-winning literary book, *Mi Moto Fidel: Motorcycling Through Castro's Cuba*. He has been published in more than 150 newspapers, magazines, and journals worldwide. He has won many awards, including the prestigious Lowell Thomas Award "Travel Journalist of the Year."

Baker has appeared on many radio and TV shows, lectures aboard cruise ships, and has addressed prominent entities such as the National Geographic Society, the National Press Club, and the World Affairs Council. He also leads tours of Costa Rica, Cuba, and Colombia for MotoDiscovery and for National Geographic Expeditions as a National Geographic Resident Expert.

Fact Checkers

Christopher P. Baker, Ana Voiculescu

Proofreader

Sonia Malik

Indexers

Hilary Bird, Jyoti Dhar

Dorling Kindersley, London

Publisher: Douglas Amrine.
Publishing Manager: Jane Ewart
Senior Editor: Christine Stroyan
Senior Cartographic Editor: Casper Morris
Senior DTP Designer: Jason Little

Revisions Team

Brigitte Arora, Sheeba Bhatnagar, Uma Bhattacharya, Tessa Bindloss, Nadia Bonomally, Louise Cleghorn, Hannah Dolan, Conrad Van Dyk, Anna Freiberger, Vinod Harish, Mohammad Hassan, Huw Hennessy, Skye Hernandez, Shobhna Iyer, Claire Jones, Jasneet Kaur, Juliet Kenny, Sumita Khatwani, Vincent Kurien, Maite Lantaron, Jude Ledger/Pure Content, Lynda Lohr, Carly Madden, Alison McGill, Sonal Modha, K C Nash, Harry Pariser, Animesh Pathak, Susie Peachey, Helen Peters, Rada Radojicic, Marisa Renzullo, Ellen Root, Simon Ryder, Sands Publishing Solutions, Azeem Siddiqui, Susana Smith, Priyansha Tuli, Dora Whitaker.

DK Picture Library

Hayley Smith, Romaine Werblow

Production Controller

Wendy Penn

Additional Special Photography

Christopher P. Baker, Alan Briere, Jonathan Buckley, Martin Camm, Geoff Dann, Greg & Yvonne Dean, Phillip Dowell, Hanne & Jens Erik-esen, Neil Fletcher, Frank Greenaway, Josef Hlasek, Johnny Jensen, Colin Keates, Dave King, Mike Linley, Ray Moller, David Murray, Stephen Oliver, Brian Pitkin, Alex Robinson, Rough Guides/Greg Roden, Clive Streeter, Harry Taylor, Tropical Birding/Nick Athanas, Mathew Ward, Laura Wickenden, Peter Wilson, Jerry Young.

Special Assistance

Many thanks for the invaluable help of the following individuals and establishments: Adolfo Rodríguez Herrera; Mrs. Dora Sequeira, Alejandra Jimenez Solis, and Andrea Bolaños Waters, Museo del Oro Precolombino; Dr. Luis Diego Gómez, Organización para Estudios Tropicales at La Selva; Mauricio P. Aymerich, Small Distinctive Hotels; Michael Snarskis.

Photography Permissions

Dorling Kindersley would like to thank the following for their assistance and kind permission to photograph at their establishments: Café Britt; Centro Costarricense de Ciencias y Cultura, San José; Costa Rica Expeditions; Fábrica de Carretas Joaquín Chaverrí, Sarchí; Museo del Oro Precolombino, San José; Museo Nacional, San José; Teatro Nacional, San José; Zoo Ave Wildlife Conservation Park; and all other cathedrals, churches, museums, hotels, restaurants, shops, galleries, national and state parks, and other sights too numerous to thank individually.

Picture Credits

Key – a-above, b-below/bottom, c-center, f-far, l-left, r-right, t-top.

The publishers would like to thank the following individuals, companies, and picture libraries for their kind permission to reproduce their photographs:

AKG Images: 44crb; **Alamy Images**: 20b; Arco Images 75c, /C.Steimer 87br; Arco Images GmbH; Stephen Bay 12b; Sabena Jane Blackbird 18;

Maxime Bessieres 302cl; blinckwinkel/Hartl 83clb; blinckwinkel/Layer 95bl, /Schmidbauer 81cra; BonkersAboutPictures 301cl; Rick & Nora Bowers 99tr; Jordi Camí 134; Caro/Kruppa 98tr; Howard Cheek 71clb; Loetscher Chlaus 71br; Sylvia Cordaiy Photo Library Ltd/Richard Wareham 186bc; Jan A. Csernoch 10cl, 294-295; Lee Dalton 76br, 79cra; Danita Delimont/Kevin Schafer 24bl, 57bc, 80tl, / Keith and Rebecca Snell 24br, 64br; O. Digoit 72bl; FLPA/NULL 81clb; Frans Lanting Studio 69c, 69br, 76–7c, 81tl; Chris Fredriksson 309tl; Bob Gibbons 25cr; Michelle Gilders 65cr; Eirik Grønningsæter 76bc; Göran Gustafson 64bl; Paul Harrison 24tb; Hemis/Franck Guiziou 58tr, 296cra, 298cl, 299tl; imageBROKER 192-193, 252bl; ImageSync Ltd 24crb; Jon Arnold Images Ltd 13br; Ronald Karpilo 259br; M. Krofel Wildlife 82tl; Michael J. Kronmal 79tl; Kuttig – Animals 70clb; Yadid Levy 307tr; Lonely Planet Images/Christer Fredriksson 223bl; LOOK Die Bildagentur der Fotografen GmbH/ Knorad Wothe 96br; Oyvind Martinse 99tl; Neil McAllister 147tc; McPHOTO/SCO/blickwinkel 70br; Michael Patrick O'Neill 75bc; Papilio/Robert Pickett 93clb; Stuart Pearce 71tl; Photoshot Holdings Ltd 223cra; Anthony Pierce 84cla, 84br; Prisma Bildagentur AG/Newman Mark 76clb; Robert Harding Picture Library Ltd/Pearl Bucknall 231br; Stephen Frink Collection/Masa Ushioda 75tl, / James D Watt 91tl; Martin Strmiska 53b; Dave and Sigrun Tollerton 167cra; Jeff Veevers 10br; Visual&Written SL/VWPICS/Kike Calvo 75br; WaterFrame 74cr, 74bc, 238-239; WILDLIFE GmbH 25cb; WorldFoto 64cla; **AM Costa Rica Link**: 36cl, 283tr; **John Anderson**: 22t, 123br, 124tr, 171cb, 184tr; **Ardea**: M. Watson 55tr; **Axiom, London**: Ian Cumming 39bc, 219br.

Banco Central de Costa Rica: 300cl, 300c, 300clb, 300cb, 300bl, 300br.

Café Britt: 32br; **Casa Corcovado Jungle Lodge:** 261tl; **Hotel Casa Turire:** 254tl, 270tr; **Chirripó Cloudbridge Reserve**: Bill Green 231tl; **Chris Baker Compositions**: Christopher P. Baker 33bc, 33bcr, 48bc, 61tl, 61bl, 86bl, 94crb, 98cl, 98c, 111tl, 117cb, 123tl, 124bl, 124crb, 125tl, 129cl, 139cla, 146cr, 146bc, 151cr, 151clb, 151bc, 158cl, 159tl, 168tl, 185cl, 191cra, 207bc, 213br, 215b, 220clb, 229cr, 237br, 283c(a), 283c(b), 283c(c), 285t; **Corbis**: 45tr, 46br, 91cra; Theo Allofs 79clb; Tony Arruza 38b, 171cl; Bettman 45cb, 46crb, 47clb, 48tr, 48cb, 49clb, 189bc; Gary Braasch 26cl, 26clb, 29br, 60bc, 161b, 222tl; Tom Brakefield 67tl, 67cr, 68cla; Christie's Images 196bl; Ralph A. Clevenger 211cb, 211bl, 245cra; W. Perry Conway 69bc; Michael and Patricia Fogden 70cr, 78, 79br, 87tl, 93br, 99c, 100tc, 167cb, 167bl, 179br, 181tc, 183c, 183bc, 211cr, 218tl; D. Robert & Lorri Franz 81br; Stephen Frink 188tr, 210bc;

Gallo Images/Martin Harvey 77bc; Bill Gentile 49bl; Derek Hall/Frank Lane Picture 241tc; Gray Hardel 292c; Jan Butchofsky-Houser 19b, 187ca; Dave G. Houser 33cla, 199b; JAI / John Coletti 106; Johnér Images/Lars-Olof Johansson 64clb; Wolfgang Kaehler 57tr, 245br; Kit Kittle 287tc; Bob Krist 59tr; Frans Lanting 66, 67crb, 80cra; Joe McDonald 87cra; Mary Ann McDonald 68bc; Michael Maslan Historic Photograph 47bl; Stephanie Maze 21br; moodboard 100c; Amos Nachoum 25cra, 85clb, 245crb, 292bl, 292bc; David A. Northcott 93tl; Sergio Pitamitz 89dc; Radius Images 97br; Jose Fuste Raga 309b; Carmen Redondo 195cl; Robert Harding World Imagery/ Marco Simoni 65crb; Martin Rogers 22bl, 32cra, 105bl, 175b, 217cr; Roger Tidman 99tc, 99cl; Jeffrey L. Rotman 104br, 292br; Kevin Schafer 26clb, 27br, 30tr, 31tl, 57c, 58bl, 67br, 72cr, 93cra, 177t, 195br, 211clb, 212tl, 232cla, 233cra, 245cla; Science Faction/Norbert Wu 167cla; Paul A. Souders 84clb, 208tl; Specialist Stock / Masa Ushioda 84cr; Brian A. Vikander 145tr; Visuals Unlimited/Thomas Marent 86cr; Jim Zuckerman 62; **Corbis Sygma**: C. Rouvieres 195cla, 195bl; **Corcovado Adventures Tent Camp**: 249tl; **Costa Rica Expeditions**: 54br, 297bl, 303tr; **Costa Rica Photo Album**: © Rodrigo Fernandez and Millard Farmer 4cr, 20tl, 21tr, 21c, 23tr, 23br, 37tl, 39tl, 105tl, 156cla, 201tl, 203tl, 204br, 205cr, 207clb, 207bl, 207br, 279br, 289br, 290tl, 290br, 291br.

Dantica Lodge and Gallery: 150t; **Dreamstime. com**: 2tamsalu 102-103; Alexstork 160; Greg Amptman 221br; William Berry 2-3, 14tc; Jan Csernoch 14bl; Max Herman 191cl; Hugoht 11br; Kjersti Joergensen 246-247; J.c. Martinez 15bc; Mclein 91bl; Mtilghma 198.

El Sano Banano Hotel: 250tc, 263tl, 286tl.

Rodrigo Fernandez: 38tc, 148br, 264cla, 265tl, 282c, 282cb, 282crb(a), 282crb(b), 283cb, 283crb, 283bl, 283bc, 283br, 286br, 300bc; **FLPA**: Claus Meyer 82cra; Minden Pictures/Gerry Ellis **77**br, / Konrad Wothe 96bc, /Marcel van Kammen 98tl, / Mark Moffett 211br, /Michael & Patricia Fogden 92clb, 96cla, 96cb, /Piotr Naskrecki 50–51; Jurgen & Christine Sohns 101tr; **Florblanca Resort:** 251t, 255br; **Forest Light**: Alan Watson 150t; **Four Seasons**: 150cla, 248cl.

Getty Images: AFP/Daniel Garcia 99cr, / Mayela Lopez 54cl, /Yuri Cortez 101tl; DEA/G. DAGLI ORTI 97tc; Digital Vision/Tom Brakefield 68br; Carlo Farneti Foster 83tl; Gallo Images/ Danita Delimont 80crb; The Image Bank/Marco Simoni 94cla; Minden Pictures/Michael & Patricia Fogden 63b; National Geographic/Brian J. Skerry 74cla, 74br, /Roy Toft 73bl, 97cb; Oxford Scientific/ Michael Leach 82br; Oxford Scientific/

Mary Plage 83cra; Photodisc/Tom Brakefield 101cr, /Paul E Tessier 95tl; Purestock 100cl; Riser/ Kevin Schafer 65bl; Stone/Stuart Westmorland 94bl; Visuals Unlimited, Inc./Thomas Marent 73tr; Ginger: 273tr; **Philip Greenspun**: 37br.; **Greentique Hotels of Costa Rica:** Santa Juana Mountain Tour 169tr.

Hilton Worldwide: Double Tree Resort 256tr.

Iguana Lodge/Perla de Osa: 277br; **Interbuses Uno De Costa Rica SA:** 304br.

Restaurante Jauja: 272bl.

Kalu: 266bl.

Lonely Planet Images: Chris Barton 32clb; Tom Boyden 188cla; Charlotte Hindle 306br; Luke Hunter 188br, 227b, 240bl.

Finca Maresia: 260bl; **Mary Evans Picture Library:** 46tc; Explore/Courau 42; **Masterfile:** 278cla, 280br. **Jean Mercier:** 27cb, 144cr, 144b, 212bl; **Museo de Cultura Indígenas:** 5c, 34tr, 34–5c, 35tc, 35c, 35clb, 35bl, 35br, 36br, 209clb, 225bc, 225br, 236bc, 282bc, 283tc, 283cra; **Museo del Oro Precolombino:** 116ca, 117tl, 117bl, 280cla, 282br; Alejandro Astorga 35cra.

Nature Air: 304c; **Naturepl.com:** Edwin Giesbers 77tc; Mary McDonald 92cra; Pete Oxford 75bl; Shattil & Rozinski 77c; Lynn M. Stone 60cl.; **NHPA/Photoshot:** Tony Crocetta 89cra; Melvin Grey 101tc; Adrian Hepworth 88–9t; James Carmichael JR 92cla; John Shaw 80br.

Orosi Lodge: 269tr.

Park Café: 262br; **Photolibrary:** Age fotostock/ Eric Baccega 69bl, /Georgie Holland 85cr; All Canada Photos/Wayne Lynch 90ca; Animals Animals/Lynn Stone 76cla; Bios/Jean-Claude Carton 88bl, /Olivier Digoit 87cl, /Sylvain

Cordier 77bl; Michael Boyny 52; Franck & Christine Dziubak 97bc; Thierry Montford 69tc; Oxford Scientific (OSF) 92br, 96cr, /David B Fleetham 74–75, /Michael Fogden 70cla, /Roy Toft 24c, / Konrad Wothe 96–7, 97bl; Peter Arnold Images/Gerard Lacz 68crb, /Heinz Plenge 68–9; WaterFrame – Underwater Images/ Masa Ushioda 90bl; **Photoshot:** Haroldo Palo 82 clb; **Sergio Pucci:** 24cb, 25cl, 25bl, 25bc.

Rancho Armadillo: 257br; **Rancho Margot:** 258tl; **Robert Harding Picture Library:** Robert Harding Productions 140bc; **Reuters:** Juan Carlos Ulate 33cra.

Seasons by Shlomy: 274bl; **Sky Photos:** 27crb, 28cl, 29tl, 29cr, 104clb, 178tr, 178cl, 178clb, 203br; **Small Distinctive Hotels:** 24cr, 248bc, 291tl; **Stashu's Con Fusion:** 276tl; **SuperStock:** Biosphoto 15tc, Heeb Christian / Prisma 118-119, Hemis.fr 11tl, imagebroker.net 142-143, 226, Alvaro Leiva / age fotostock 174, 214.

Tabacón Grand Spa Thermal Resort: Ave del Paraíso 275tl; **Taj Mahal Restaurant:** 267tl; **Ticowind:** 206tr.

Unicorn Multimedia, Inc.: 197br, 232br, 233tl, 233bc.

Hotel Villa Caletas: 271br.

Xandari Resort & Spa: 249cr, 253tc, 268bc.

Front endpaper: Left - **Alamy Images:** Jordi Camí bl; **Corbis:** JAI / John Coletti bc; **Dreamstime.com:** Alexstork cl; **SuperStock:** Alvaro Leiva / age fotostock tl; Right - **Dreamstime.com:** Mtilghma tc; **SuperStock:** imagebroker.net bl,/ age fotostock / Alvaro Leiva cra.

Jacket Images: Front: **Alamy Images:** imageBROKER / Stefan Huwiler c; Spine: **Alamy Images:** imageBROKER / Stefan Huwiler t.

All other images © Dorling Kindersley. For more information see **www.dkimages.com**

Phrase Book

Costa Rican Spanish is essentially the same as the Castilian spoken in Spain, although there are some differences in vocabulary and pronunciation. The most noticeable is the pronunciation of the soft "c" and the letter "z" as "s" rather than "th." Costa Ricans tend to be formal, and often use *usted* (rather than *tú* for "you," even if they know the person well. Common courtesies of respect are expected. Always say *buenos dias* or *buenas tardes* when boarding a taxi, and address taxi drivers and waiters as *señor*. Many colloquialisms exist, such as *¡upe!*, which is used to announce your presence outside someone's home when the door is open. *Buena suerte* ("good luck") is often used to wish someone well on parting.

The most common term throughout the country is *pura vida* ("pure life"), used as a common reply to questions about your wellbeing and as an expression that everything is great. *Tuanis*, popular with the young, is another phrase meaning things are positive. If you hear a Costa Rican referring to *chepe*, he or she is speaking about San José. If you wish to decline goods from street vendors, a polite shake of the head and a *muchas gracias* will usually suffice. Adding *muy amable* ("very kind") will help to take the edge off the refusal.

In an Emergency

Help!	¡Socorro!	soh-**koh**-roh
Stop!	¡Pare!	**pah**-reh
Call a doctor!	¡Llame a un médico!	yah-meh ah oon **meh**-dee-koh
Fire!	¡Fuego!	foo-**eh**-goh
Could you help me?	¿Me podría ayudar?	meh poh-**dree**-yah ah-yoo-**dahr**
policeman	policía	poh-lee-**see**-ah

Communication Essentials

Yes	Sí	see
No	No	noh
Please	Por favor	pohr fah-**vohr**
Thank you	Gracias	**grah**-see-ahs
Excuse me	Perdone	pehr-**doh**-neh
Hello	Hola	oh-**lah**
Good morning	Buenos días	**bweh**-nohs dee-ahs
Good afternoon	Buenas tardes	**bweh**-nahs **tahr**-dehs
Good night	Buenas noches	**bweh**-nahs **noh**-chehs
Bye (casual)	Chao	**cha**-oh
Goodbye	Adiós	ah-dee-**ohs**
See you later	Hasta luego	ah-stah loo-**weh**-goh
Morning	La mañana	lah mah-**nyah**-nah
Afternoon	La tarde	lah **tahr**-deh
Night	La noche	lah noh-cheh
Yesterday	Ayer	ah-**yehr**
Today	Hoy	oy
Tomorrow	Mañana	mah-**nyah**-nah
Here	Aquí	ah-**kee**
There	Allá	ah-**yah**
What?	¿Qué?	keh
When?	¿Cuándo?	**kwahn**-doh
Why?	¿Por qué?	pohr-keh
Where?	¿Dónde?	**dohn**-deh
How are you?	¿Cómo está usted?	**koh**-moh ehs-tah oos-**tehd**
Very well, thank you	Muy bien, gracias	mwee **bee**-ehn **grah**-see-ahs
Pleased to meet you	Mucho gusto	moo-choh **goo**-stoh
I'm sorry	Lo siento	loh see-**ehn**-toh

Useful Phrases

That's fine	Está bien	ehs-**tah** bee-ehn
Great/fantastic!	¡Qué bien!	keh **bee**-ehn
Where does this road go?	¿Adónde va esta calle?	ah-**dohn**-deh bah ehs-tah **kah**-yeh
Do you speak English?	¿Habla inglés?	**ah**-blah een-**glehs**
I don't understand	No comprendo	noh kohm-**prehn**-doh
I want	Quiero	kee-**yehr**-oh

Useful Words

big	grande	**grahn**-deh
small	pequeño/a	peh-**keh**-nyoh/nyah
hot	caliente	kah-lee-**ehn**-teh
cold	frío/a	**free**-oh/ah
good	bueno/a	**bweh**-noh/nah
bad	malo/a	**mah**-loh/lah
open	abierto/a	ah-bee-**ehr**-toh/tah
closed	cerrado/a	sehr-**rah**-doh/dah
left	izquierda	ees-key-**ehr**-dah
right	derecha	deh-**reh**-chah
near	cerca	**sehr**-kah
far	lejos	**leh**-hohs
up	arriba	ah-**ree**-bah
down	abajo	ah-**bah**-hoh
early	temprano	tehm-**prah**-noh
late	tarde	**tahr**-deh
now/very soon	ahora/ahorita	ah-**ohr**-ah/ah-ohr-**ee**-tah
more	más	mahs
less	menos	**meh**-nohs
very	muy	mwee
a little	(un) poco	oon poh-**koh**
opposite	frente a	**frehn**-teh-ah
below/above	abajo/arriba	ah-**bah**-hoh/ah-**ree**-bah
entrance	entrada	ehn-**trah**-dah
exit	salida	sah-**lee**-dah
stairs	escaleras	ehs-kah-**leh**-rahs
elevator	el ascensor	ehl ah-sehn-**sohr**
toilets	baños/servicios sanitarios	bah-nyohs/sehr-**vee**-see-yohs sah-nee-**tah**-ree-ohs
women's	de damas	deh **dah**-mahs
men's	de caballeros	deh kah-bah-**yeh**-rohs
sanitary napkins	toallas sanitarias	toh-**ah**-yahs sah-nee-**tah**-ree-yahs
tampons	tampones	tahm-**poh**-nehs
condoms	condones	kohn-**doh**-nehs
toilet paper	papel higiénico	pah-**pehl** hee-**hyen**-ee-koh
(non-)smoking area	área de (no) fumar	**ah**-ree-ah deh (noh) foo-**mahr**
camera	la cámara	lah kah-mah-rah
(a roll of) film	(un rollo de) película	(oon roh-yoh deh) peh-**lee**-koo-lah
batteries	las pilas	lahs **pee**-lahs
passport	pasaporte	pah-sah-**pohr**-teh
visa	visa	**vee**-sah

Post Offices and Banks

post office	oficina de correos	oh-fee-**see**-nah deh kohr-**reh**-ohs
stamps	estampillas	ehs-tahm-**pee**-yahs
postcard	una postal	**oo**-nah pohs-**tahl**
postbox	apartado	ah-pahr-**tah**-doh
cashier	cajero	kah-**heh**-roh
ATM	cajero automático	kah-heh-roh ahw-toh-**mah**-tee-koh
bank	banco	**bahn**-koh
What is the dollar rate?	¿A cómo está el dolar?	ah koh-moh ehs-**tah** ehl doh-**lahr**

Shopping

How much does this cost?	¿Cuánto cuesta esto?	kwahn tohkwehs-tah ehs-toh
Do you have?	¿Tienen?	tee-yeh-nehn
Do you take credit cards/	¿Aceptan tarjetas de	ahk-sehp-tahn tahr-heh-tahs

traveler's checks?	crédito/cheques de viajero?	deh kreh-dee-toh/cheh-kehs deh vee-ah-heh-roh
discount	un descuento	oon dehs-koo-ehn-toh
expensive	caro	kahr-oh
cheap	barato	bah-rah-toh
clothes	la ropa	lah roh-pah
size, clothes	talla	tah-yah
size, shoes	número	noo-mehr-oh
bakery	panadería	pah-nah-deh-ree-ah
bookstore	librería	lee-breh-ree-ah
grocer's	pulpería	pool-peh-ree-ah
market	mercado	mehr-kah-doh
shoe store	la zapatería	lah sah-pah-teh-ree-ah
supermarket	el supermercado	ehl soo-pehr-mehr-kah-doh
travel agency	la agencia de viajes	lah ah-hehn-see-ah deh vee-ah-hehs

Sightseeing

bay	bahía	bah-ee-ah
beach	playa	plah-yah
building	edificio	eh-dee-fee-see-oh
cathedral	catedral	kah-teh-drahl
church	iglesia	ee-gleh-see-ah
farm	finca	feehn-kah
forest	bosque/selva	bohs-keh/sehl-bah
garden	jardín	hahr-deen
lake	lago	lah-goh
mangrove	manglar	mahn-glahr
mountain peak	cerro	seh-roh
mountain range	cordillera	kohr-dee-yeh-rah
museum	museo	moo-seh-oh
neighborhood	barrio	bah-ree-oh
port	puerto	poo-her-toh
ranger station	puesto de guardia	poo-ehs-toh deh goo-ahr-dee-ah
river	río	ree-oh
trail	sendero	sehn-deh-roh
theater	teatro	teh-ah-troh
tourist information office	oficina de turismo	oh-fee-see-nah deh too-rees-moh
viewpoint	mirador	mee-rah-dohr
ticket	el boleto/la entrada	ehl boh-leh-toh lah ehn-trah-dah
guide (person)	el/la guía	ehl/lah gee-ah
guide (book)	la guía	lah gee-ah
guided tour	una visita guiada	oo-nah vee-see-tah gee-ah-dah
map	el mapa	ehl mah-pah

Health

I feel ill	Me siento mal	meh seh-ehn-toh mahl
We need a doctor	Necesitamos un médico	neh-seh-see-tah-mohs oon meh-dee-koh
drug store	farmacia	fahr-mah-see-ah
medicine	medicina	meh-dee-see-nah
ambulance	ambulancia	ahm-boo-lahn-see-ah
mosquito coils	espirales	ehs-pee-rah-lehs

Transportation

When does the... leave?	¿A qué hora sale el...?	ah keh oh-rah sah-leh ehl
Is there a bus to...?	¿Hay un bus a...?	eye oon boohs ah...
bus station	la estación de autobuses	lah ehs-tah-see-ohn deh aw-toh-boo-sehs
ticket office	la boletería	lah boh-leh-teh-ree-ah
airport	aeropuerto	ah-ehr-oh-poo-ehr-toh
customs	la aduana	lah ah-doo-ah-nah
taxi stand/rank	la parada de taxis	lah pah-rah-dah deh tahk-sees
car rental	rent a car	rehn-tah-car
motorcycle	la moto(cicleta)	lah moh-toh(see-kleh-tah)
bicycle	la bicicleta	lah bee-see-kleh-tah
4WD	doble tracción	doh-bleh trahk-siohn

water-taxi	una panga/un bote	oo-nah pahn-gah/oon boh-teh
aerial tram	teleférico	teh-leh-feh-ree-koh
insurance	los seguros	lohs seh-goo-rohs
gas station	gasolinera	gah-soh-leen-ehr-ah
garage	taller de mecánica	tah-yehr deh meh-kahn-ee-kah
I have a flat tire	Se me ponchó la llanta	seh meh pohn-shoh lah yahn-tah

Staying in a Hotel

I have a reservation	Tengo una reservación	tehn-goh oo-nah reh-sehr-vah-see-ohn
Do you have a vacant room?	¿Tienen una habitación libre?	tee-eh-nehn oo-nah ah-bee-tah-see-ohnlee-breh
double room	habitación doble	ah-bee-tah-see-ohn doh-bleh
single room	habitación sencilla	ah-bee-tah-see-ohn sehn-see-yah
room with a bath	habitación con baño	ah-bee-tah-see-ohn kohn bah-nyoh
shower	la ducha	lah doo-chah
The ... is not working	No funciona el/la...	noh foon-see-oh-nah ehl/lah
Where is the dining-room/bar?	¿Dónde está el restaurante/el bar?	dohn-deh ehs-tah ehl rehs-toh-rahn-teh/ehl bahr
hot/cold water	agua caliente/fría	ah-goo-ah kah-lee-ehn-teh/free-ah
soap	el jabón	ehl hah-bohn
towel	la toalla	lah toh-ah-yah
key	la llave	lah yah-veh

Eating Out

Have you got a table for ...?	¿Tienen mesa para ...?	tee-eh-nehn meh-sah pah-rah
I want to reserve a table	Quiero reservar una mesa	kee-eh-roh reh-sehr-vahr oo-nah meh-sah
The bill, please	La cuenta, por favor	lah kwehn-tah pohr fah-vohr
I am a vegetarian	Soy vegetariano/a	soy veh-heh-tah-ree-ah-no/na
waiter/waitress	mesero/a	meh-seh-roh/rah
menu	la carta	lah kahr-tah
fixed-price menu	menú del día	meh-noo dehl dee-ah
wine list	la carta de vinos	lah kahr-tah deh vee-nohs
glass	un vaso	oon vah-soh
bottle	una botella	oo-nah boh-teh-yah
knife	un cuchillo	oon koo-chee-yoh
fork	un tenedor	oon teh-neh-dohr
spoon	una cuchara	oo-nah koo-chah-rah
breakfast	el desayuno	ehl deh-sah-yoo-noh
lunch	almuerzo	ahl-moo-ehr-soh
dinner	la cena	lah seh-nah
main course	el plato fuerte	ehl plah-toh foo-ehr-teh
starters of the day	las entradas el plato del día	lahs ehn-trah- das dish ehl plat-toh dehl dee-ah
rare	término rojo	tehr-mee-noh roh-hoh
medium	término medio	tehr-mee-noh meh-dee-oh
well done	bien cocido	bee-ehn koh-see-doh
chair	la silla	lah see-yah
napkin	la servilleta	lah sehr-vee-yeh-tah
Is service included?	¿El servicio está incluido?	ehl sehr-vee-see-oh ehs-tah een-kloo-ee-doh
ashtray	cenicero	seh-nee-seh-roh
cigarettes	los cigarros	lohs see-gah-rohs
food stall	una soda	oo-nah soh-dah
neighborhood bar	una cantina/un bar	oo-nah kahn-tee-nah/oon bahr

Menu Decoder *(see also pp264–5)*

el aceite	ah-see-eh-teh	*oil*
las aceitunas	ah-seh-toon-ahs	*olives*
el agua mineral	ah-gwa mee-neh-rahl	*mineral water*
el arroz	ahr-rohs	*rice*
el azúcar	ah-soo-kahr	*sugar*
una bebida	beh-bee-dah	*drink*
boca	boh-kah	*a type of snack*
el café	kah-**feh**	*coffee*
la carne	kahr-neh	*meat*
el cerdo	sehr-doh	*pork*
la cerveza	sehr-**veh**-sah	*beer*
el chocolate	choh-koh-**lah**-teh	*chocolate*
la ensalada	ehn-sah-lah-dah	*salad*
la fruta	froo-tah	*fruit*
el helado	eh-lah-doh	*ice cream*
el huevo	oo-eh-voh	*egg*
el jugo	ehl hoo-goh	*juice*
la leche	leh-cheh	*milk*
la mantequilla	mahn-teh-kee-yah	*butter*
la manzana	mahn-sah-nah	*apple*
los mariscos	mah-rees-kohs	*seafood*
el pan	pahn	*bread*
las papas	pah-pahs	*potatoes*
las papas a la francesa	pah-pahs ah lah frahn-seh-sah	*French fries*
las papas fritas	pah-pahs free-tahs	*potato chips*
el pastel	pahs-tehl	*cake*
el pescado	pehs-kah-doh	*fish*
picante	pee-kahn-teh	*spicy*
la pimienta	pee-mee-yehn-tah	*pepper*
el pollo	poh-yoh	*chicken*
el postre	pohs-treh	*dessert*
el queso	keh-soh	*cheese*
el refresco	reh-frehs-koh	*soft drink/soda*
la sal	sahl	*salt*
la sopa	soh-pah	*soup*
el sánguche	sahn-goo-she	*sandwich*
el té negro	teh neh-groh	*tea*
la torta	tohr-tah	*burger*
las tostadas	tohs-tah-dahs	*toast*
el vino blanco	vee-noh blahn-koh	*white wine*
el vino tinto	vee-noh teen-toh	*red wine*

Culture and Society

campesino	cahm-peh-see-noh	*peasant*
canton	cahn-tohn	*county*
carreta	cah-reh-tah	*oxcart*
cumbia	coom-bee-ah	*Columbian music*
Josefino	hoh-seh-fee-noh	*resident of San José*
marimba	mah-reem-bah	*kind of xylophone*
merengue	meh-rehn-geh	*fast-paced Dominican music*
sabanero	sah-bah-neh-roh	*cowboy*
salsa	sahl-sah	*Cuban dance music*
Tico/ costarricense	tee-coh/cohs-tah-ree-sehn-seh	*Costa Rican*

Numbers

0	cero	**seh**-*roh*
1	uno	**oo**-*noh*
2	dos	*dohs*
3	tres	*trehs*
4	cuatro	**kwa**-*troh*
5	cinco	**seen**-*koh*
6	seis	*says*
7	siete	**see**-*eh-teh*
8	ocho	**oh**-*choh*
9	nueve	**nweh**-*veh*
10	diez	*dee-***ehs**
11	once	**ohn**-*seh*
12	doce	**doh**-*seh*
13	trece	**treh**-*seh*
14	catorce	*kah-***tohr***-seh*
15	quince	**keen**-*seh*
16	dieciséis	*dee-eh-see-***seh-ees**
17	diecisiete	*dee-eh-see-see-***eh**-*teh*
18	dieciocho	*dee-eh-see-***oh**-*choh*
19	diecinueve	*dee-eh-see-***nweh**-*veh*
20	veinte	**veh**-*een-teh*
30	treinta	**treh**-*een-tah*
40	cuarenta	*kwah-***rehn**-*tah*
50	cincuenta	*seen-***kwehn**-*tah*
60	sesenta	*seh-***sehn**-*tah*
70	setenta	*seh-***tehn**-*tah*
80	ochenta	*oh-***chehn**-*tah*
90	noventa	*noh-***vehn**-*tah*
100	cien	*see-***ehn**
500	quinientos	*khee-nee-***ehn**-*tohs*
1,000	mil	*meel*
1,001	mil uno	**meel** *oo-noh*
5,000	cinco mil	**seen**-*koh meel*

Time

one minute	un minuto	*oon* mee-**noo**-toh
one hour	una hora	**oo**-nah **oh**-rah
Monday	lunes	**loo**-nehs
Tuesday	martes	**mahr**-tehs
Wednesday	miércoles	mee-**ehr**-koh-lehs
Thursday	jueves	hoo-**weh**-vehs
Friday	viernes	vee-**ehr**-nehs
Saturday	sábado	**sah**-bah-doh
Sunday	domingo	doh-**meen**-goh
January	enero	eh-**neh**-roh
February	febrero	feh-**breh**-roh
March	marzo	**mahr**-soh
April	abril	ah-**breel**
May	mayo	**mah**-yoh
June	junio	**hoo**-nee-oh
July	julio	**hoo**-lee-oh
August	agosto	ah-**gohs**-toh
September	setiembre	seh-tee-**ehm**-breh
October	octubre	ohk-**too**-breh
November	noviembre	noh-vee-**ehm**-breh
December	diciembre	dee-see-**ehm**-breh

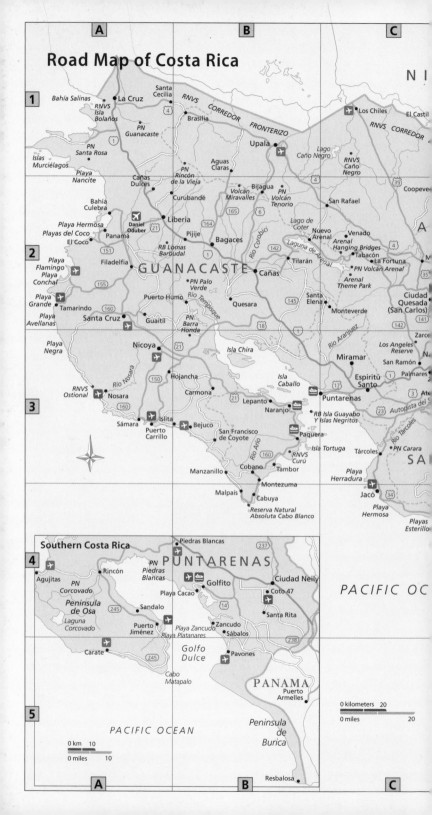